RECOMMENDED

Bed & Breakfasts™
NEW ENGLAND

Praise for previous editions:

"A beautifully designed and nicely written guide . . . a welcome addition to the tiny minority of regional lodging books that represent a personal visit by the author combined with no fee by the lodging place for inclusion in the book."

—*The Boston Globe*

"*Recommended B&Bs New England* . . . is the latest in a fine series of guides to the nation's best B&Bs."

—*Honeymoon* magazine

"If you like accommodations with character, this is the right bed and breakfast guide for you . . . charmingly written."

—*Independent Publisher*

HELP US KEEP THIS GUIDE
UP TO DATE

Every effort has been made by the author and editors to make this guide as accurate and useful as possible. However, many things can change after a guide is published—establishments close, phone numbers change, facilities come under new management, etc.

We would love to hear from you concerning your experiences with this guide and how you feel it could be made better and be kept up to date. While we may not be able to respond to all comments and suggestions, we'll take them to heart, and we'll also make certain to share them with the author. Please send your comments and suggestions to the following address:

The Globe Pequot Press
Reader Response/Editorial Department
P.O. Box 480
Guilford, CT 06437

Or you may e-mail us at:
editorial@GlobePequot.com

Thanks for your input, and happy travels!

INSIDERS' GUIDE®

RECOMMENDED BED & BREAKFASTS™ SERIES

RECOMMENDED
Bed & Breakfasts™
NEW ENGLAND

FOURTH EDITION

Eleanor Berman

INSIDERS' GUIDE®

GUILFORD, CONNECTICUT
AN IMPRINT OF THE GLOBE PEQUOT PRESS

INSIDERS' GUIDE®

Copyright © 1998, 2000, 2002, 2006 by Eleanor Berman

Text design by Nancy Freeborn
Interior illustrations by Mauro Magellan and Olive Metcalf

ISSN: 1539-3534
ISBN-13: 978-0-7627-3026-1
ISBN-10: 0-7627-3026-9

Manufactured in the United States of America
Fourth Edition/First Printing

The prices and rates listed in this guidebook were confirmed at press time. We recommend, however, that you call establishments before traveling to obtain current information.

Contents

Introduction

Propped up in a canopy bed, with the fireplace glowing across the room and a snowy hillside in view through a whole wall of windows, I am ready to move to Vermont. When I settle in on the coast, with the ocean in view, my mind is changed—I want to live in Maine.

All of New England is tempting when you stay in its prize accommodations: the small, personal bed-and-breakfast inns found throughout the region. Without a public dining room to bring in outsiders, intimate bed-and-breakfast inns give the feeling of a stay with friends. Even if the building is historic, it is someone's home and is on a personal, livable scale that often inspires wishful thoughts of "I wish I could live this way." More than one innkeeper has been bitten by the bug while staying at an inn.

This book is a collection of nearly 200 of the best bed-and-breakfast inns in the six New England states. I inspected many inns before I made these selections, hoping to include a range of properties. These run the gamut from ultimate luxury, with antique furnishings and romantic Jacuzzis for two, to simple farmhouses where families are welcome to stay and help with the chores. Most are small, but they vary in size from two to eighteen guest rooms. What all have in common is a warm and caring resident innkeeper, most often the owner.

You'll quickly see that I am partial to inns with quiet locations and scenic views; to me, seeing a mountain or an ocean or rolling hills from my window is part of the romance of a journey to New England. A few choice properties have artistic owners who have created unusual decor and wonderful gardens that will surely inspire ideas to bring back home. Several inns have swimming pools, tennis courts, or both, making for a vacation getaway. A few properties offer more than breakfast, usually dinner by advance request on weekends. Since these meals are small affairs for inn guests only, the evening feels like a private dinner party at home rather than dining in a restaurant.

Each entry gives basic information about facilities and rates. The rates quoted are per room per night, based on double occupancy. Most inns have minimum stays of two or three nights on weekends in busy seasons, and just about every New England inn is more expensive during the fall foliage season, so that information is not listed for each individual property. Check with the inns that interest you for details.

Check also on policies concerning children. While many innkeepers love families and go out of their way to make them feel at home, inns intended for quiet, romantic getaways aren't usually the best choices for young children. Some inns discourage children because they just aren't set up to accommodate extra guests in their bedrooms. Unless an entry tells you explicitly that children are welcome, it's best to call and ask about guidelines when you are traveling with kids younger than age sixteen.

I've added Web site addresses—in many instances, an excellent way to see pictures of the inns. Some of the Web addresses indicate a site that lists many inns, and rather than give an extended address, I've simply indicated the sites, such as www.bbonline. If you look under the state headings on these sites, you will be able to find individual inns easily.

If you are a smoker, ask about the inn's policies in advance. While an occasional inn may have a small area designated for smoking, in most cases it is limited to outdoor porches and lawns.

I want to stress that every inn in this book has been personally visited by me or an associate whose judgment I trust, and that no one paid to be in this book. (Before you rely on any guidebook to inns, find out whether the copy is essentially a paid ad. It will make a difference in the objectivity and reliability of the information.)

When I began this book, I thought I would omit descriptions of owners, since they do change. But I quickly changed my mind. You can't separate these inns from their innkeepers. What sets bed-and-breakfast inns apart from other lodgings is that they are so much a reflection of their owners, and meeting these interesting people is part of the pleasure of staying in their inns. Many inngoers become fast friends with their hosts, keep in touch during the year, and look forward to regular visits.

When owners do change over time, the personality of the inn will change, so if you visit one of these inns and find new owners, please write to me in care of The Globe Pequot Press (P.O. Box 480, Guilford, CT 06437) to tell me about your stay. I'd also welcome letters about other properties that you think should be visited for possible inclusion in future editions of this book.

I hope this book will lead you to many happy inn excursions—and to added appreciation for New England's many wonderful settings.

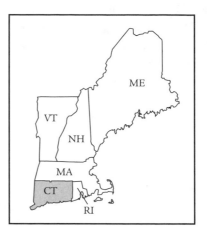

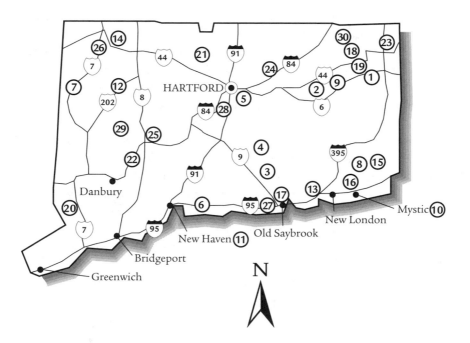

CONNECTICUT

Numbers on map refer to towns numbered below.

1. Brooklyn, Friendship Valley Inn *2*
2. Coventry, Bird-in-Hand *3*
3. Deep River, Riverwind *4*
4. East Haddam, Bishopsgate Inn *6*
5. Glastonbury, Butternut Farm *7*
6. Guilford, The B&B at Bartlett Farm *9*
7. Kent, The Inn at Kent Falls *10*, Starbuck Inn *11*
8. Ledyard, Stonecroft *12*
9. Mansfield Center, The Fitch House Bed and Breakfast *14*
10. Mystic, House of 1833 *16*
11. New Haven, Swan Cove *17*, Three Chimneys Inn *19*
12. New Preston, Apple Blossom Country Inn *20*
13. Niantic, The Inn at Harbor Hill Marina *21*
14. Norfolk, Manor House *23*, Mountain View Inn *24*
15. North Stonington, Antiques and Accommodations *26*
16. Old Mystic, Old Mystic Inn *27*, Red Brook Inn *28*
17. Old Saybrook, Deacon Timothy Pratt Bed & Breakfast *29*
18. Pomfret, Cobbscroft *31*
19. Pomfret Center, Feather Hill Bed & Breakfast *32*
20. Ridgefield, West Lane Inn *34*
21. Simsbury, The Linden House *35*, Merrywood Bed & Breakfast *36*
22. Southbury, The Cornucopia at Oldfield *38*
23. Thompson, Lord Thompson Manor *39*
24. Tolland, Tolland Inn *41*
25. Waterbury, House on the Hill *42*
26. West Cornwall, Hilltop Haven *44*
27. Westbrook, Captain Stannard House *45*, Talcott House *47*, Welcome Inn *48*
28. Wethersfield, Chester Bulkley House *49*
29. Woodbury, Hummingbird Hill *50*
30. Woodstock, Elias Child House *51*

FRIENDSHIP VALLEY INN

60 Pomfret Road (Route 169)
P.O. Box 845
Brooklyn 06234
(860) 779–9696
Fax: (860) 779–9844

■ The front of the house dates from 1795, the back from 1740. The flag out front is a replica of a rare 1795 version with fifteen stars and fifteen stripes. There's no doubt that this home on the National Register of Historic Places embodies history, and owner Beverly Yates savors every bit of it. When she was a teacher and counselor in Houston, Texas, Beverly and her architect husband, Rusty, were smitten on trips to New England, where history buff Beverly was fascinated with the heritage. Deciding this was where they wanted to be, Rusty found a position in Boston, and in 1995 Beverly launched a new career as innkeeper.

The house they found is in the historic district of Brooklyn, one of Connecticut's most charming and least-spoiled hamlets. Beverly tells you proudly that they are only the sixth family to live here; she has named guest rooms to honor the earlier residents and posted a brief biographical sketch to describe each one.

The rooms are spare, immaculate, and filled with antiques. The Wendel Room, saluting the previous owner, has an antique twin bedroom suite from France. The Tyler Room is done with a walnut Victorian bed, a fireplace, and nice touches such as a handmade quilt and lace pillows. For romance, there is the Prince Suite, once a blacksmith shop, a light and airy room with white walls, a beamed cathedral ceiling, a mahogany carved four-poster rice bed, a whirlpool bath, and a private entrance.

Families or friends traveling together can choose the two-room Benson/Kingsley Suite, with both a queen-size four-poster and a double bed.

Those searching for a TV will find it hidden in an old wooden cabinet in the living room, a pleasant room with a fireplace.

WEB SITE: friendshipvalleyinn.com

INNKEEPERS: Beverly and Charles (Rusty) Yates

ROOMS: 3 rooms, 2 suites; 1 with whirlpool; 3 with fireplace; all with private bath, clock, radio

ON THE GROUNDS: 12 wooded acres, flagstone patio with wrought iron furniture, flowers

RATES: $140–$170, including full breakfast and afternoon tea

CREDIT CARDS ACCEPTED: Master-Card, Visa, American Express

OPEN: Year-round

HOW TO GET THERE: From Interstate 395 take exit 91 and follow Route 6 west to Route 169 north. The inn is ¼ mile farther on the east side of the road.

Guests also tend to gravitate to the library, where you'll find a handsome Oriental rug on the old wide floorboards and a wing chair with a throw that invites settling in front of a fire with one of the many books on the shelves. Also on display are Beverly's collections of enamel boxes, nutcrackers, and miniature English cottages.

Breakfast is served on fine china at a big table in front of the dining-room fireplace or on the sunporch overlooking the lawn; when the weather is right, it may be moved to the terrace garden bordered by a picket fence. The menu offers juice, fruit, a variety of breads, and main courses that might be quiche, eggs, or pancakes with bacon or sausage. Early risers find coffee and tea awaiting them in the library.

Reveling in the history that surrounds her, Beverly will gladly tell you how the inn got its name or about the hidden basement entrance that was part of the Underground Railroad, and she will show you the mantel in the dining room that was removed from a nearby home owned by Moses Cleveland, who went on to become the founder of Cleveland, Ohio. She also gives directions to local landmarks such as the Nathan Hale Homestead or the Prudence Crandall Museum. This hostess' sincere enthusiasm for her home and its surroundings is contagious, adding extra pleasure to a visit.

What's Nearby: Brooklyn is home to a historic green as well as the New England Center of Contemporary Arts, which displays work by living artists. Nearby towns offer a variety of diversions—antiquing in Putnam, hiking at Pomfret Farms, and a remarkable mansion and gardens, Roseland Cottage, waiting to be toured in Woodstock.

BIRD-IN-HAND

2011 Main Street
Coventry 06238
(860) 742-0032

The original house dates from 1731; the "new" addition was in 1748. Innkeeper Susan Crandall is following a tradition of hospitality that goes back to 1800, when this colonial home became the Bird-In-Hand Tavern, a place for rest and refreshment. She has carefully retained the look and spirit of the past.

Many of the original features of the house remain, including wide floorboards and working fireplaces. The stone open-hearth fireplace is part of the old wood-paneled keeping room.

The downstairs parlor has handsome period furnishings and woodwork around the fireplace. What was the ladies' parlor is now the dining room, also with a fireplace.

Guest rooms are furnished with many lovely antiques. Each has its own colonial color scheme, and most have a working fireplace. The Anna White Room is named for the wife of the original owner of the house. It has a bird theme and features a down comforter and a filmy net canopy. There's a whirlpool tub in the bathroom.

The Mary Rose Room is in blue and white with a four-poster bed. A secret closet in this room was believed to have hidden slaves riding to freedom on the Underground Railroad. The Dunham Room has a queen bed and is decorated with country quilts and a teddy bear collection.

The Cottage, once a chicken coop, has taken on new life as a separate apartment with a kitchen and its own great room with a fireplace and a TV/VCR.

Susan fulfilled a lifelong dream when she became an innkeeper. For now, she is also continuing with her occupation in advertising sales, so she sometimes serves a continental breakfast on weekdays. She looks forward to weekends, when she has time for a full home-cooked meal with special dishes such as French toast or frittatas, served in an authentic old New England setting.

What's Nearby: Coventry is known for its Caprilands Herb Farm, a rustic eighteenth-century farmhouse surrounded by thirty herb gardens; tours, lunches, and teas are offered. It is also the birthplace of Connecticut's state hero, Nathan Hale, whose family home, circa 1776, is open to the public. There is a town lake with a beach area as well as two local golf courses and some prime antiquing. The University of Connecticut at Storrs is a short drive away.

WEB SITE: www.thebirdinhand.com

INNKEEPER: Susan Crandall

ROOMS: 4 rooms, all with private bath, robes; 1 with TV/VCR; 3 with working fireplace; 1 with whirlpool bath

ON THE GROUNDS: Enclosed porch, lawn with perennial flower beds and herb garden

RATES: $100–$160, including continental breakfast on weekdays, full breakfast on weekends

CREDIT CARDS ACCEPTED: Master-Card, Visa, American Express

OPEN: Year-round

HOW TO GET THERE: From Interstate 84 eastbound take exit 59, and follow Interstate 384 to the end; it runs into Route 44 into Coventry. Turn right onto Route 31 south (Main Street). Bird-in-Hand is 3½ miles on the right.

From I–84 westbound take exit 67, and turn left onto Route 31 south toward Coventry to Route 44; turn left onto Route 44 to rejoin Route 31 south (Main Street), and follow directions above.

RIVERWIND

209 Main Street
Deep River 06417
(860) 526–2014

■ One of the attractions of a bed-and-breakfast inn is its uniqueness, reflecting the tastes and personalities of the owners. So those who know the old Riverwind will find a new look since Elaine and Leo Klevens took over, less whimsical than the long-

established inn, but no less pleasing. The house has many places to mingle, including a big living room with a fireplace, a beamed keeping room with a 12-foot open stone hearth, and a study with yet another fireplace. All are furnished with comfortable country antiques.

The nine bedrooms are all different, each with its own appeal. The beds range from country pine and carved oak to iron and brass. Smithfield Room has a cheerful red, white, and blue American theme inspired by the quilt that graced a high maple rope bed. Quilt is named for the Star of Bethlehem quilts that grace the two full four-poster beds. For romance, Champagne & Roses offers a four-poster bed, a Japanese steeping tub (as well as a shower), a private deck in the treetops, and a gas fireplace for winter warmth. The Moonlit Suite, under the eaves on the third floor, is the place for complete privacy, plus a wood-burning fireplace, a two-person Jacuzzi, a TV, and a refrigerator. It comes with a Mission-style, queen-size bed, plus a double sleigh bed in an alcove in case you want to bring the family.

The inn serves a big country breakfast, and afterward, you can have a seat in a rocker on the big front porch, chat with your fellow guests, and watch the world go by.

What's Nearby: You can enjoy a riverboat cruise on the Connecticut River or come to this river town in summer for a unique annual fife-and-drum festival; a Fife and Drum Museum is open anytime. Take a drive to nearby Essex for a ride into the countryside aboard the vintage cars of the Valley Railroad, a visit to the Connecticut River Museum, and a browse through a host of tempting shops. Chester is the place to shop for handicrafts. Gillette Castle State Park in Hadlyme offers river views, picnic grounds, and an intriguing mansion for touring. The Goodspeed Opera House is nearby in East Haddam (see page 7), and Cantfield Wood Preserve is less than a mile from the inn, with more than 200 acres of hiking trails.

WEB SITE: www.riverwindinn.com

INNKEEPERS: Elaine and Leo Klevens

ROOMS: 9 rooms, 1 suite, all with private bath, clock, radio, robes, air-conditioning, Wi-Fi

ON THE GROUNDS: Patio

RATES: $120–$225, including full breakfast

CREDIT CARDS ACCEPTED: Master-Card, Visa, American Express

OPEN: Year-round

HOW TO GET THERE: Take Interstate 91 or Interstate 95 to Route 9. Take exit 4 off Route 9, and then turn left onto Route 154. Riverwind is 1½ miles farther on the right.

BISHOPSGATE INN

Goodspeed Landing
P.O. Box 290
East Haddam 06423
(860) 873–1677

■ Having the Goodspeed Opera House within walking distance is a decided bonus, but this vintage colonial, circa 1818, has ample charms of its own. The wood-block prints of Minnesota scenes are clues that the innkeepers, the Kagel family, are from Minneapolis, where both Colins, father and son, worked in banking. They have kept the warmth and Early American aura of the popular inn they took over, while adding their own touches, including a lot of artwork throughout the inn.

The original old wide floorboards, dark beams, and ample fireplaces of the house remain. The downstairs sitting room has wood paneling, a leather sofa, and armchairs in front of the big, brick fireplace and lots of books and games for guests.

The upstairs landing is another sitting area offering still more books and a big, comfortable reading chair. A child's rocker, here occupied by a bunny, is one of many children's chairs that Jane Kagel has collected and placed around the house. Colin's father was master of the hunt, accounting for the fox motif and horse paintings throughout the house.

The bedrooms presently have printed paper or solid painted walls, lace-trimmed curtains, and beds with brass, four-poster, and iron headboards, feather mattresses, and lots of pillows. All the rooms have interesting antiques and green plants to brighten them up. Lisa Kagel made the quilts in every room, while Jane is responsible for the needlepoint. Each room is equipped with a marble game that the family discovered in Wales.

WEB SITE: www.bishopsgate.com

INNKEEPERS: The Kagel family: Colin, Jane, Colin Jr., and Lisa

ROOMS: 5 rooms, 1 suite, all with private bath and robes; 4 with working fireplace; suite has sauna and outside deck

ON THE GROUNDS: Lawn with sitting areas

RATES: $115–$185, including full breakfast

CREDIT CARDS ACCEPTED: MasterCard, Visa

OPEN: Year-round

HOW TO GET THERE: Take Interstate 95 to exit 69, Route 9, and proceed west to exit 7, East Haddam. Take a left at the first blinking light and then a right at the first traffic light, and follow Route 82 over the bridge 1½ blocks to Bishopsgate; the driveway is on the left.

The Directors Suite is located in a 1970 addition to the house. Done in gray and white, it has a cathedral ceiling with beams, a private deck, and a bathroom with double sinks and a sauna.

The Kagels take pride in their breakfasts, served at a long trestle table in front of a fireplace. Each morning brings new treats such as crustless spinach quiche, strawberry cream-cheese croissants, and the house specialty, baked breakfast Genesis, a puffy egg, milk, cheese, and bread confection.

What's Nearby: The big attraction in East Haddam is the Goodspeed Opera House, a Victorian jewel box that is renowned for its revivals of vintage musicals. Bishopsgate is perfectly situated for all the lures of the Connecticut River Valley, including cruises on the river, a steam train ride through the countryside, tours of Gillette Castle, and shopping and dining in the lovely riverside town of Essex.

BUTTERNUT FARM

1654 Main Street
Glastonbury 06033
(860) 633–7197
Fax: (860) 659–1758

▧ Driving down the Main Street of Glastonbury, lined with fine colonial homes, there's no clue as to what is waiting when you turn into the driveway of Butternut Farm. You'll be facing the barn that is home to animals as winning as the illustrations from a children's storybook—a herd of prize dairy goats, a clutch of one hundred bantam chickens, flocks of fancy pigeons, geese, pheasants, and ducks. If the day is fine, many of them will likely be out to greet you.

The animals are the "children" of innkeeper Don Reid, whose other passion is the beautiful home he shares with three Abyssinian cats and scores of exquisite antiques—a combination that has earned write-ups all over the country.

The house was built by one Jonathan Hale in two stages, beginning in 1720. Reid moved in more than forty years ago. While he pursued careers first in banking and then in teaching, he brought the home back to its original condition, exposing the eight wide fireplaces, ceiling beams, and cornice detailing; polishing the broad pumpkin pine floors; and painstakingly removing the paint that hid the fine paneling gracing many of the rooms.

WEB SITE: www.butternutfarm
bandb.com

INNKEEPER: Don Reid

ROOMS: 2 rooms and 1 suite in the main house, 1 barn apartment, all with private bath, air-conditioning, phone, clock, radio, sherry, chocolates, TV

ON THE GROUNDS: 2 acres with patio, flower and herb gardens, barn with prize animals

RATES: $90–$110, including a full breakfast

CREDIT CARDS ACCEPTED: American Express

OPEN: Year-round

HOW TO GET THERE: From Interstate 91 take exit 25, Route 3, to Route 2 east. In Glastonbury, take exit 8, turn right onto Hebron Avenue for ½ mile to Glastonbury Center. Turn left onto Main Street, and go south for 1‰ miles to the farm. Turn left onto Whapley Road and enter the barnyard driveway. From Interstate 84 exit at Route 2 east and follow the directions above.

Having provided the proper setting, he proceeded to furnish it with the finest eighteenth-century antiques. For nearly thirty years he has been welcoming guests to share his gracious home.

There's a sitting room with a particularly striking William and Mary tiger maple highboy. A second parlor in a recent addition to the house showcases marbled trim on the fireplace and a corner cabinet displaying late-nineteenth-century Chinese porcelain. My favorite room is the dining room, with its deep red walls, round table, early-eighteenth-century banister-back chairs, and real candles in the candelabra.

The less formal den is furnished with a comfortable sofa and with a TV and VCR, a library of videos, and shelves of books.

Breakfast is served at 8:30 A.M. in the original kitchen or in a charming breakfast room with blue and white checked curtains at the windows. The menu always features fresh eggs from the barn and homemade jams.

The period bedrooms are in colonial colors such as mustard and blue and are furnished with rag rugs and antique beds, including one with a canopy and another with a cherry pencil-post bed. There is nothing old-fashioned about the amenities, such as phone, TV, and even hair dryers. An apartment in the barn comes with a kitchen and its own terrace.

Ask soft-spoken Don Reid about his animals and he lights up. He'll happily point out the Rhode Island Red, leghorn, and Japanese bantam chickens; the Silkies with fluffy heads; the exotic India fantail white pigeons; and the Swiss alpine goats. Reid labels himself "a gentleman farmer going through his second childhood." His guests are apt to call him a charming host with exceptional taste and contagious enthusiasm.

What's Nearby: Glastonbury, a quiet town of fine homes and a classic green, is home to a branch of the Connecticut Audubon Society, which administers a forty-eight-acre park and trail system. It borders on Wethersfield, which offers myriad attractions (see page 50).

THE B&B AT BARTLETT FARM

564 Great Hill Road
Guilford 06437
(203) 457–1657
Fax: (203) 457–1628

■ Way out in the country, this old-fashioned white farmhouse with the big wraparound porch has been in the Bartlett family since 1784. The present occupants, Sam and Diana, occupy one wing of the house with their young twins, plus two golden retrievers and three cats. The rest of the house is for guests who want to enjoy a true taste of country living.

WEB SITE: www.thebartlettfarm.com

INNKEEPER: Diana Bartlett

ROOMS: 3 rooms, all with private bath, air-conditioning, TV, clock

ON THE GROUNDS: 200 acres of lawn and farmland, goats, sheep, chickens, bison, donkey, deer

RATES: $105–$115, including full breakfast

CREDIT CARDS ACCEPTED: MasterCard, Visa

OPEN: Year-round

HOW TO GET THERE: Take Interstate 95 to exit 58. Southbound, take a right at the end of exit; northbound, take a left at the end of the exit to Route 77 north. Follow Route 77 for about 5 miles. After passing the light at the intersection of Routes 77 and 80, take the fourth left onto Hemlock Avenue. At the end of Hemlock, bear right to Great Hill Road. The farm is ¾ mile ahead on the left. The driveway is after the house, before the red barn. Take a left into the driveway and a left again to park behind the house.

The farm remains active year-round. Haying and Christmas trees provide most of the income, but something is happening every season, with maple syruping in late winter, baby animals in spring, vegetables growing for a small garden market in warm weather, and the pumpkin harvest in fall. There are goats to milk and eggs to gather for those willing to get up early to help.

An unusual menagerie of animals at the farm includes fallow deer, a buffalo and donkey, pigs, cattle, and sheep that were originally acquired as a petting zoo for families arriving to buy a Christmas tree. Kids of all ages enjoy offering apples to the donkey or the deer.

The updated farmhouse is informally and pleasantly furnished. A print sofa and easy chair surround the brick fireplace in the living room, where guests gather to chat or watch TV. A hearty farm breakfast of pancakes, eggs, home fries, sausage or bacon, and biscuits or muffins is served from 8:30 to 9:30 A.M. at the long harvest table on weekends, with a continental menu on weekdays. Many of the foods, including the eggs, are farm fresh.

Guest rooms are country comfortable with quilts on the beds. They have modern amenities such as private baths, TVs, and queen-size beds. The cozy Winter Bedroom, with a four-poster, at one time was occupied by Sam's grandparents. Aunt Bertha's Room, named for Gramps's sister, has a nice view of the garden and pasture. The Guest Room, where the grandkids used to sleep when they came to visit, now has one twin and one queen-size bed, a good choice for families.

Bartlett Farm is a rare chance to enjoy observing life on a real farm in the country. Bring the kids.

What's Nearby: Guilford is a lovely old colonial town with a classic New England green surrounded by fine homes and shops. In mid-July, the Guilford Handcraft Center fills the green with an annual three-day exposition of the best work of New England craftsmen. Three important historic homes are open for touring, including the 1639 Henry Whitfield House, one of the oldest stone houses in the country, and the Hyland House, a saltbox circa 1600. The 1735 Thomas Griswold House is pretty enough to have adorned a postage stamp. Nearby is Stony Creek, the departure point for cruises around Connecticut's Thimble Islands. Hammonasset State Beach, the largest in the state, is about ten minutes north along the shore in Madison.

THE INN AT KENT FALLS

107 Kent-Cornwall Road
Kent 06757
(860) 927–3197
Fax: (860) 927–3239

■ This classy inn, opened in 2003, is a great addition to the area. Owner Ira Goldspiel worked in merchandising and marketing at Armani and Gap before he decided on a country life, and he brought great style with him when he chose this handsome colonial home dating from 1741. The decor, clean and contemporary, nicely accents the original features of the house, such as beams, wooden floors, and five fireplaces.

The living room is furnished almost all in white, with one soft paisley sofa as an accent. A dark wood corner cabinet goes well with the room's dark beams. The burnished floors are bare. The dining room has eight chairs set around a big, square, dark wooden table, and a wall of windows look out at the grounds. The generous continental breakfast may include crepes or French toast and goodies from a local

WEB SITE: www.theinnatkentfalls.com

INNKEEPER: Ira Goldspiel

ROOMS: 4 rooms, 2 suites, all with private bath, air-conditioning, TV, CD player, phone, Internet access; some suites with fireplace (nonworking)

ON THE GROUNDS: 2½-acre property, outdoor pool

RATES: Rooms $155–$245, suites $295–$325, including continental breakfast

CREDIT CARDS ACCEPTED: MasterCard, Visa, American Express

OPEN: Year-round

HOW TO GET THERE: The inn is on Route 7, 2 miles north of Kent, between the town and Kent Falls State Park.

baker. The den is a comfortable room where guests can gather to watch TV or listen to the stereo on comfortable puffy couches, and the wicker-furnished screened porch surrounded by tall trees is delightfully cool on a sunny day.

Bedrooms are also contemporary in feel, done in subdued color schemes. All have a feature I really appreciate: good reading lights. The Lakes Room is one of the nicest, with a four-poster king-size bed, a 6-foot claw-foot tub plus a shower in the bath, and fireplaces in both bedroom and bath. The Meadow Room offers big dormer windows and an antique brass bed, while the Falls Suite provides an adjoining small library to curl up with a book, plus a claw-foot soaking tub and a rainfall shower.

One of the best features of this inn is the lovely free-form outdoor pool, surrounded by a flagstone terrace. It's a perfect retreat whether you relax for the day or refresh after a day of sightseeing.

Want more pampering? The obliging innkeeper can arrange for a massage in your room or in the pool house.

What's Nearby: Kent is a shopper's mecca, filled with antiques shops and art and crafts galleries. Beautiful natural surroundings lure hikers and canoeists. Kent Falls State Park is a fine place for a picnic, and the Sloane-Stanley Museum holds an outstanding collection of Early American tools assembled by artist Eric Sloane, whose reconstructed studio is on the grounds.

STARBUCK INN

88 North Main Street
Kent 06757
(860) 927–1788
Fax: (860) 927–1688

This pleasant center-hall colonial is on the main road, but set back by a deep front lawn. Since Peter and Betsy Starbuck arrived in 2003, the inn has been renovated and upgraded top to bottom. All the rooms now have queen- or

WEB SITE: www.starbuckinn.com

INNKEEPERS: Betsy and Peter Starbuck

ROOMS: 5 rooms, all with private bath, air-conditioning, robes, TV, phone, dataport

ON THE GROUNDS: Front lawn, 2 acres of lawn at the rear

RATES: $110–$200, including full breakfast, afternoon tea

CREDIT CARDS ACCEPTED: Master-Card, Visa, American Express

OPEN: Year-round

HOW TO GET THERE: The inn is on Route 7, just north of the shops in Kent.

king-size beds, custom-built armoires, pillow-top mattresses, fine linens, and down comforters. Stylish fabric headboards, dust ruffles, chairs, and window treatments are carefully coordinated.

Guests gather in the airy living room, where comfortable chairs and a sofa are gathered around the fireplace. Afternoon tea is served here at 4:00 P.M., a proper English tea with homemade sandwiches, pâtés, and desserts.

Breakfast is at your convenience from 8:00 to 9:30 each morning and includes fresh ingredients from the inn's gardens and organic eggs from a local farmer. Some favorite recipes include baked egg, cheese, and sausage scramble, and another baked dish combining eggs, milk, cream cheese, and chopped sausage. Everyone raves about the special Starbuck home fries.

After breakfast you can take a chair on the back lawn and enjoy the expansive vistas.

The Starbuck Inn offers a special plus: Once you arrive, you never need a car. All of Kent's appealing shops and restaurants are a stroll away. In fact, if you are traveling from New York City, you don't need a car at all. The Bonanza bus from the city stops just down the road.

What's Nearby: See What's Nearby on page 11.

STONECROFT

515 Pumpkin Hill Road
Ledyard 06335
(860) 572–0771; (800) 772–0774
Fax: (860) 572–9161

■ This creamy yellow 1807 Georgian colonial represents many people's fantasy of the perfect country house, surrounded by six and a half acres of lawn, old stone walls, and woodland, with all the character of the old retained and enhanced by stylish new decor.

The front entry to the main house is a charming introduction to what lies ahead, with a cheerful mural featuring hot-air balloons ascending the staircase. The Great Room lives up to its name, with a big, inviting floral sofa placed in front of a 9-foot-wide Rumford fireplace. Like much of the house, the furnishings here are French country in style, and the deep yellow walls make the room sunny year-round.

The Snuggery, the original borning room, or nursery, of the house, is now a small library, and the Red Room is another quiet spot for reading. Old wooden floors throughout are graced with handsome rugs.

Choosing a favorite guest room here is a happy dilemma. Joan's nomination is the Buttery on the main floor, the oldest room (circa 1740), still with its original beams, doors, and hardware. It also has its own terrace.

WEB SITE: www.stonecroft.com

INNKEEPER: Joan Egy

ROOMS: 4 rooms in the main house (3 with fireplace); 4 rooms and 2 suites in the air-conditioned Grange with fireplace and two-person whirlpool bath; all with private bath and robes

ON THE GROUNDS: Patio, lawn, gardens, croquet, darts game in the barn; nature preserve with trails adjacent

RATES: $150–$270 in the main house, $195–$300 in the Grange, including full breakfast daily, wine and cheese on Saturday, and afternoon tea in winter; dinner available by reservation

CREDIT CARDS ACCEPTED: MasterCard, Visa, American Express, Discover

OPEN: Year-round

HOW TO GET THERE: Take Interstate 95 to exit 89, Allyn Street, and proceed north for 3½ miles.

But the Stonecroft Room upstairs is hard to resist, with a working fireplace and a wraparound mural showing the inn and grounds as they might have looked in 1820. Guests are challenged to find the resident ghost—and to spot a bit of artistic license, the Beatles, tucked into the picture. The room is furnished with a beautiful reproduction handmade tiger maple pencil-post bed and a chest-on-frame to match.

In 1998 the post-and-beam barn on the property was renovated to become the Grange, with four luxury guest rooms, two suites, and a highly praised dining room available to guests for dinner by reservation. Though the Grange dining room makes this a full-service inn rather than a bed-and-breakfast, the main house is removed from this activity, and the ambience remains small and personal. The inn seems to me too special to remove from the book.

Those who want a more luxurious stay may well appreciate the new rooms. They are a mix of English and French country styles. The Briar Rose Room has a painted French canopy bed, while Orlando's Room features a walnut sleigh bed. The upstairs suites are sumptuous, right down to the lavish baths with double sinks, bidets, towel warmers, and walk-in showers plus whirlpool baths.

The Grange dining room is decorated in the style of an English country manor, complete with fireplace. French doors open to a stone terrace for outdoor dining when weather permits. Elegant breakfasts here feature dishes such as pear-almond waffles with maple crème or smoked salmon omelettes with whole-wheat biscuits.

The grounds of the house are exceptional, especially the many old stone walls. The sense of being away from it all is made stronger by the Nature Conservancy land that surrounds the property. An equestrian center down the road offers rides in the conservancy grounds, a wonderful way to appreciate this very special rural setting.

What's Nearby: Ledyard, a quiet country town, is the unlikely home of the Foxwoods Casino, one of the most successful casinos in the United States. The lavish $193 million Mashantucket Pequot Museum includes a 22,000-square-foot replica of an early Pequot village, complete with rushing water and sound effects, as well as life-size dioramas, artifacts, art, and interactive media depicting the history of the Mashantucket Pequot Tribal Nation. For those looking for other kinds of entertainment, Mystic is just a few miles away.

THE FITCH HOUSE BED AND BREAKFAST

563 Storrs Road/Route 195
P.O. Box 163
Mansfield Center 06250-0163
Phone/Fax: (860) 456–0922

Col. Edwin Fitch, one of Connecticut's early builder-architects, designed and built this beautiful columned Greek Revival mansion in 1836 to impress his future father-in-law, and he definitely achieved his goal. The handsome home also helped launch Fitch's career as an architect. It is now listed on the National Register of Historic Places. Kay Holt grew up in this house, which has been in her family for more than seventy years, and she and her husband, Tony, are proud stewards of its architectural and historical heritage.

The house is furnished in keeping with its period, with fine antiques found in every room. Guests gather in a spacious living room with polished floors, fine rugs, and wing chairs invitingly placed in front of the fireplace. Other inviting rooms include the Empire-style music room/library and a sunny solarium, built in 1910, with walls of windows looking out on the lawn and perennial gardens. The long-established gardens were begun about the same time as the solarium.

The views add to the pleasure when an elegant breakfast on fine china is served in the solarium each morning from 7:30 to 9:00. Guests begin with a first course of fresh fruit and a freshly baked fruit bread (strawberry bread is one favorite) accompanied by assorted teas and coffee brewed in a French-press pot. Entrees such as shirred eggs, the "world's best oatmeal," and a French rolled omelette are among the house specialties. After breakfast, the hospitable hosts make sure that snacks and beverages are available at all times.

The attractive guest rooms upstairs are named for earlier inhabitants of the house. The Fitch Room is where Edwin Fitch and his wife lived from 1836 to 1848. This sunny room overlooking the garden boasts a queen size four-poster bed and Winslow Homer prints of the American Civil War on the walls.

WEB SITE: www.fitchhouse.com

INNKEEPERS: Kay and Tony Holt

ROOMS: 3 rooms, all with air-conditioning, cable TV, wireless Internet access, alarm clock, hair dryer, iron and ironing board; 2 with private bath; 1 with working fireplace

ON THE GROUNDS: 40 acres with extensive lawns, stone walls, mature trees, and formal gardens; walking trails through the woods

RATES: $110–$125, including full breakfast

CREDIT CARDS ACCEPTED: MasterCard, Visa

OPEN: Year-round

HOW TO GET THERE: Coming from Hartford and points west, take Interstate 84 east to exit 68 (UConn exit), then Route 195 south for 11 miles. The Fitch House (number 563) is on Route 195 on the right, just before (north of) the junction of Route 89 in Mansfield Center. From Boston and points east, take I–84 west, exit 72, to Route 89 south (toward Mansfield). Continue for about 15-plus miles on Route 89, which ends at the junction of Route 195; turn right onto Route 195 north. The Fitch House is the second building on the left, not counting the church. No signs are visible from the road except the number of the house.

The Adams Room, distinguished for the pale blue reproduction French wallpaper, circa 1795, is named after Fitch's wife, Alice Adams, who was the inspiration for the building of the house. It is furnished with a double four-poster bed and one twin bed. The young girls whose portraits hang on the wall are the innkeeper and her sister.

The Golding Room, named for the second owner of the home, a wealthy local silk manufacturer, is especially appealing for its queen-size bed with a ruffled canopy and the working fireplace. The prints on the wall are by Currier and Ives.

The inn offers nightly turndown service for guests.

As longtime residents, the Holts are very familiar with the "Quiet Corner," this lovely part of Connecticut, and can steer you to golf, tennis, hiking, shopping, antiquing, museums, and some very fine dining, as well as some local secrets, such as the fabulous ice cream made at the nearby University of Connecticut.

Be sure to ask about their many special holiday and theme weekends, especially the Dining with the President circa 1870 Gourmet Weekend held in the summer. Offered in conjunction with the Roseland Cottage Museum in Woodstock, it offers the chance to enjoy a gourmet dinner with a Ulysses S. Grant look-a-like and to learn to cook Victorian desserts and tea-time treats. Other specials include a Victorian Christmas Weekend worthy of Charles Dickens featuring a dinner that ends with flaming plum pudding, a 1950s Drive-In Movie night, and two Walking Weekends each October.

What's Nearby: The University of Connecticut and Eastern Connecticut State University are each less than 4 miles from the inn, offering museums, concerts, summer theater, and famous UConn basketball. The inn is part of the "Quiet Corner" of northeastern Connecticut, where much parkland has been set aside, offering prime hiking. See What's Nearby for Coventry, Pomfret, Thompson, Tolland, and Woodstock, on pages 4, 32, 41, 42, and 53 respectively, for other "Quiet Corner" attractions.

HOUSE OF 1833

72 North Stonington Road
Mystic 06355
(860) 536–6325; (800) 367–1833

Built in 1833 by a local banker, this Greek Revival mansion, a national landmark, has been beautifully restored and is imposing on the outside, inviting within.

Two formal parlors greet guests. The first centers around the Belgian white marble fireplace, with a gold striped settee on one side, a wing chair opposite. Ornate lamps with tall figurines are accent pieces. The second room boasts a black marble fireplace and a handsome nineteenth-century crystal chandelier. Potted palms and ferns and orchids from the owner's private collection add greenery and warmth to the rooms.

Beyond is the dining room, also in period decor, where guests can choose a table for two or a group table for the sumptuous breakfast that is served each morning.

Each of the five romantic guest rooms is spacious, with comfortable seating areas and a fireplace, and handsome antique furnishings. It's difficult to choose a favorite. The Oak Room, done in deep mauve with a striking black floral wall and Chinese red accents, boasts a Victorian queen-size bed with a tall carved headboard and a turn-of-the-twentieth-century settee. The adjacent private bath has a lovely Arts and Crafts vanity with period tiles, a brass sink, and an oversize tub for two.

WEB SITE: www.houseof1833.com

INNKEEPERS: Robert Bankel and Evan Nickles

ROOMS: 5 rooms, all with private bath, wood-burning fireplace, clock, fresh flowers; 2 with whirlpool bath

ON THE GROUNDS: 3 acres with swimming pool, tennis court; complimentary bicycles

RATES: $99–$249, including full breakfast and afternoon refreshments

CREDIT CARDS ACCEPTED: MasterCard, Visa

OPEN: Year-round

HOW TO GET THERE: Take Interstate 95 to exit 90, go north on Route 27 to the Old Mystic General Store, bear right at the stop sign, and continue approximately ½ mile; inn is on the right.

The Peach Room, the former library, has elaborate moldings and built-in bookcases, a hand-carved Chinese canopy bed, and a private porch. The cheerful Ivy Room has four big windows with views of the grounds, while the Veranda Room features a nineteenth-century French bronze and tole king-size bed and its own private porch. The Cupola Room is a lovers' favorite, with an Empire canopy bed swathed in purple and mauve fabric and a two-person whirlpool. This room also has private access to the fourth-floor cupola, a look-out furnished with period rocking chairs.

The three-acre grounds offer two welcome amenities, a good-size swimming pool and a tennis court. Not far from the inn, the River Road follows a winding path close to the Mystic River, where you can spy seafaring ships, sea captains' homes, and a host of migratory birds. Follow the path to the end, and you'll be in the heart of the Mystic village Historic District.

What's Nearby: Mystic Seaport, a re-creation of a nineteenth-century maritime village complete with tall ships for boarding, is the Northeast's major maritime attraction. Mystic Marinelife Aquarium is an equally popular attraction, and the quaint town of Mystic has shopping galore as well as the chance to board the windjammer *Mystic Whaler* for a trip out to sea. Two casinos are within driving distance of Mystic—Mohegan Sun in Uncasville, and Foxwoods in Ledyard. Foxwoods has an additional attraction, the lavish Mashantucket Pequot Museum. For more about the museum, see What's Nearby on page 14.

SWAN COVE

115 Sea Street
New Haven 06519
(203) 776–3240
Fax: (203) 776–8649

■ Enter this seemingly modest 1890 Victorian in the city's City Point Historic District, and you

WEB SITE: www.swancove.com

INNKEEPER: Raquel Seacord

ROOMS: 1 room, 3 suites, all with private bath, air-conditioning, TV; suites have sitting room, kitchen, dining area, work desk with modem, ironing board, hair dryer

ON THE GROUNDS: On a city block, small garden between buildings

RATES: $99–$325 (highest rates on weekends), including continental breakfast

CREDIT CARDS ACCEPTED: MasterCard, Visa, American Express

OPEN: Year-round

HOW TO GET THERE: Take Interstate 95 to exit 44 (marked "Kimberly Ave/10") in the city of New Haven. Turn right at the bottom of the exit ramp onto Kimberly Avenue. Go past McDonald's and turn right at the first light onto E. T. Grasso Boulevard (Route 10). Go straight ahead and continue toward the water. After an underpass, E. T. Grasso Boulevard becomes Sea Street, entering the residential area of Oyster Point. Look for number 115, turn at the corner, and go past the inn to the second house. Turn right into the driveway to park.

are in for a surprise. Artistic hostess Raquel Seacord has turned each floor of the home into unique and spacious suites featuring the antiques and fabrics she and her husband have collected in travels around the world.

When I stepped into what I thought was the attractive inn living room, I learned it was just part of the first-floor suite, complete with brick wall, woodstove, beams, books and plants, a dining area, and a bedroom with an antique armoire, one of many handsome antiques.

Downstairs, the Solarium Suite has no feel of a basement. Instead you are in a wonderful space with old stone walls, brick arches, a Mexican tile floor, a fireplace, lots of windows at ground level, an indoor garden, and a 6-foot glass-roofed solarium. The colorful textiles are from Central America, Mexico, and Turkey, and there is a handsome English desk among many antiques.

The third-floor Treetops Suite is a complete change of mood, done in neutral plaids and checks with equestrian accents. The living room features a cathedral ceiling with a large peaked window. And then there is the Safari Queen Suite, with dark walls and big bay window, beamed ceiling, and a woodstove in the fireplace and subtle safari prints in the bedroom and bath.

Raquel also sometimes offers rooms on the second floor, her own quarters. After more than a decade of innkeeping, she tired of inviting guests into her rooms for breakfast, and in 2005 renovated the house next door, where the main floor now offers four tables for two in the expansive open kitchen and adjoining sitting room. Each table is covered with cloth and napkins in a charming Provençal print fabric; chairs are a mix of antiques, wood and upholstered. She serves a continental breakfast with her trademark fruit parfaits. Versatile Raquel, who recently studied cooking in France, hopes to begin putting her knowledge to work serving a full breakfast emphasizing healthy foods and also to begin giving cooking lessons here on healthy cooking a la Provence.

Upstairs is one more bedroom, the Loft Room, done with her usual flair, with Mexican tile and a bathroom with a walk-in shower done in hand-tumbled natural stone from Italy. It's another unusual touch in an inn like no other.

What's Nearby: New Haven is a magnet for theater fans who love its Long Wharf Theater and the Yale Repertory Theater; Wooster Street is a legend among pizza lovers. Free tours are available for Yale's beautiful Gothic campus, which includes a notable art museum, the impressive Yale Center for British Art, and the Yale Collection of Musical Instruments. Other museums worth exploring are the Peabody Museum of Natural History, with a famous dinosaur room, and the New Haven Colony Historical Society, whose displays include Eli Whitney's cotton gin, which was manufactured here.

THREE CHIMNEYS INN

1201 Chapel Street
New Haven 06511
(203) 789–1201; (800) 443–1554
Fax: (203) 776–7363

■ Bed-and-breakfast lovers bound for New Haven have an excellent choice, the Three Chimneys Inn, an exuberant Victorian circa 1870. And the location could not be better—Chapel Street is one of the city's prime areas for trendy shops and dining, and the inn is within walking distance of the Yale campus with its myriad attractions.

Set behind a wrought iron fence with a small formal garden in front, the inn welcomes guests with its gingerbread trim, flowerpots lining the front steps, and, on the porch, hanging baskets spilling over with bright flowers or seasonal decorations. Step inside to a parlor with an 11-foot ceiling, hand-carved woodwork, and twin fireplaces, where overstuffed chairs and sofas invite you to settle in for conversation, watching TV, or enjoying an evening cordial. There's a masculine feel to this room, with golf and tennis memorabilia over the mantel.

The library is where afternoon refreshments are served. This room is a comfortable place for reading or quiet relaxing in front of the fire.

The Morning Room, the sunny gold breakfast area, has its own set of twin fireplaces. Guests are greeted with greenery and flowers, soft music, and a selection of morning papers. Chef Michael Marra offers an "entree of the day," which might be buttermilk banana pancakes, a garden omelette, or a raspberry-strawberry blintz,

WEB SITE: www.threechimneysinn.com

INNKEEPER: Jane M. Peterson

ROOMS: 11 rooms, all with private bath, air-conditioning, TV, VCR, phone, clock, radio, wireless high-speed Internet connection; 7 with freestanding electric fireplace

ON THE GROUNDS: Veranda, seasonal gardens, on-site parking

RATES: $216, including full breakfast and afternoon refreshments

CREDIT CARDS ACCEPTED: MasterCard, Visa, American Express, Discover

OPEN: Year-round, except December 24–26

HOW TO GET THERE: From Interstate 95 take downtown New Haven exit 47, and proceed to the end of the connector, North Frontage Road, at the corner of York Street. Turn right onto York, and then left at the third traffic light onto Chapel Street. The inn is 1½ blocks farther on the right.

accompanied by breakfast meats plus home-baked scones and muffins.

Up the grand oak staircase, the rooms are spacious and well appointed. Rooms have big, comfortable four-poster beds; reproduction Georgian and Federal period furnishings; and dramatic color schemes using deep shades such as dark green and terra-cotta red. Additional sofa beds make them ideal for families. In all the rooms, Oriental-style rugs cover the hardwood floors, beds have color-coordinated comforters, and there are full-size desks and attractive sidepieces such as upholstered chaise longues and armoires hiding the TV/VCR. The renovation also provided such conveniences as air-conditioning, dual-line phones, and wireless Internet connections.

The inn lost a bit of its personal feel when management opted to go after meetings by offering two conference rooms downstairs. But a manager is always on hand to see that guests are well cared for. The Three Chimneys remains an inn-lover's oasis in New Haven.

What's Nearby: See What's Nearby on page 19.

APPLE BLOSSOM COUNTRY INN

137 Litchfield Turnpike
(Route 202)
P.O. Box 2370
New Preston 06777
(860) 868–9954
Fax: (860) 868–3619

■ Though the attractions are many, bed-and-breakfast inns are scarce in this choice section of the Litchfield Hills. So it was good news for travelers when this homey 1842 country home 3 miles from Lake Waramaug began inviting overnight guests.

WEB SITE: www.appleblossominn.com

INNKEEPER: Susan Hogan and Doris Reimer

ROOMS: 3 rooms, all with air-conditioning; 1 with private bath and fireplace

ON THE GROUNDS: Screened porch, 1 acre of lawns with stone walls, gardens

RATES: $100–$150, including continental breakfast

CREDIT CARDS ACCEPTED: MasterCard, Visa, American Express

OPEN: Year-round

HOW TO GET THERE: From Route 7 take Route 202 east. Continue past the junction of Route 47 and Route 202; the inn is 1½ miles from that intersection on the right-hand side

You feel at home at once in the comfortable living room centered on the white wooden fireplace, with polished wood floors, country print upholstery, a rocker, and airy white curtains at the windows.

The choicest of the three upstairs rooms has beams, a king-size bed, and a working fireplace. A handsome embroidered white bedspread brightens the queen bed in the second room, and there's a cheerful print on the full bed in the smallest room.

A generous continental breakfast always features muffins fresh from the oven, yogurt, cereal, and seasonal fresh fruits. On warm days, you can take your coffee to the screened porch or out on the back lawn, surrounded by perennial gardens and old stone walls.

What's Nearby: The inn is 2 miles from the hamlet of New Preston, home to tempting shops and restaurants and the gateway to Lake Waramaug, a scenic lake ringed with hills and offering a state park with picnic areas and a sandy beach. White Memorial Foundation, with miles of hiking trails and a nature museum, is 3 miles east on Route 202. The picture-book colonial towns of Litchfield and Washington are each less than 10 miles from the inn.

THE INN AT HARBOR HILL MARINA

60 Grand Street
Niantic 06357
(860) 739–0331
Fax: (860) 691–3078

Perched high on a hill directly above the boat-filled marina on the picturesque harbor of the Niantic River, the inn has a view that positively dazzles. Porches, lawns, and patios are perfectly placed to take in the scene.

The white clapboard inn building looks new but is actually a century old. In the early 1900s it was a boardinghouse known as the Bayview. After a ten-year complete renovation it was better than new, and the Labries arrived as innkeepers in 2002.

Taking over the inn was a dream come true for the couple, Connecticut residents who already knew and loved the area. Sue is an avid gardener, accounting for the lovely plantings around the inn. Dave likes planning, meaning that guests will find wonderful written materials

suggesting itineraries to help them make the most of their stay. Name a good restaurant or attraction in the area, and chances are there are written directions to help you find your way. They seem to enjoy pampering guests. Come back in the afternoon, and you'll find a refrigerator stocked with complimentary water, soda, beer, and wine and fresh baked goodies to snack on. On the mantel in the sitting area is a pineapple, the award they received in 2005 from the local tourism agency, Mystic Coast and Country, for their hospitality and service.

WEB SITE: www.innharborhill.com

INNKEEPERS: Sue and Dave Labrie

ROOMS: 9 rooms, all with private bath, water views, air-conditioning, TV, hair dryer, clock; some with fireplace; two with private deck

ON THE GROUNDS: Large patio directly on the water overlooking a boat-filled marina, gazebo, ample seating, grill

RATES: $125–$225, including continental breakfast weekdays, full breakfast weekends

CREDIT CARDS ACCEPTED: MasterCard, Visa, American Express

OPEN: Year-round

HOW TO GET THERE: Take Interstate 95 to exit 74. Turn right onto Route 161 south and follow to the end. Turn left onto Main Street (also known as Route 156). Continue for 1 block and turn left onto Smith Avenue. Take your first right onto Grand Street. The driveway is on the left.

One big downstairs room serves both as a small sitting area and breakfast room. Guests can choose the long table for eight or tables for two to enjoy the buffet of tasty breads, muffins, fresh fruit, and granola served every day. On weekends a hot dish such as French toast or a strada is added.

Eight guest rooms on the second and third floors are named for Long Island Sound lighthouses; all face the water. They are simply and comfortably furnished, with white walls set off by dark wood trim, varying color schemes, and, as you would expect, wide windows to take in the view. Several have a fireplace. Choicest and most spacious are corner rooms such as Mystic Seaport or Little Gull Island, each offering both a fireplace and a private balcony.

The largest room, the Race Rock Suite,

is to the side on the main floor, with a private entrance and porch. It is fitted with a refrigerator, microwave, and wet bar.

The inn is within walking distance of the Niantic's small town Main Street, with shops and a few restaurants. The inn will loan you a kayak to paddle the river, and you can bask on local beaches. Your hosts may even take you out for a ride on their boat, the *Innstyle*.

There is also much to see in neighboring towns along the Connecticut shore, but be forewarned: Once you take a seat in the shaded gazebo on the lawn to gaze out to sea, you may not want to leave.

What's Nearby: Niantic is a small river town close to Connecticut's Long Island Sound shoreline. It is within an easy drive of Mystic Seaport, summer concerts at Harkness Memorial Park in Waterford, the beaches of New London, and the museums of Old Lyme.

MANOR HOUSE

69 Maple Avenue
Norfolk 06058
(860) 542–5690; (866) 542–5690

Manor is not an exaggeration. This is a perfectly elegant gabled 1898 Victorian Tudor on five acres, with baronial fireplaces, cherry paneling, gracefully carved arches, elaborate moldings, and twenty Tiffany stained-glass windows. The house was built for Charles Spofford, the architect of London's subway system and the son of Ainsworth Spofford, head of the Library of Congress under Abraham Lincoln.

The living room is grand in size, with cherry paneling and beams, and a 6-foot fireplace decorated with a bas-relief above the mantel of a horse-drawn chariot and driver. But comfortable sofas and easy chairs pulled up around the fire are inviting, perfect places to settle in with a book. There's also a delightful enclosed porch.

Guests gather in a dining room featuring Tiffany windows, an Italian tile fireplace, and a crystal chandelier. An appropriately elaborate breakfast offers juices, fruit, muffins, and a changing menu of banana stuffed French toast, blueberry pancakes, Belgian waffles, or eggs to order.

The rooms up beyond the grand cherry-paneled staircase vary in size, but all have their own appeal and a variety of prize antiques. The largest is the 30-by-18-foot Spofford Room, with windows on three sides, a wood-burning fireplace, a king-size

WEB SITE: www.manorhouse-norfolk.com

INNKEEPERS: Michael Dinsmore and L. Keith Mullins

ROOMS: 8 rooms, 1 suite, all with private bath, clock, radio, robes; some with whirlpool bath, balcony; 2 with wood-burning fireplace; 2 with gas fireplace

ON THE GROUNDS: Spacious lawns, patio, gazebo

RATES: $190–$255, including full breakfast

CREDIT CARDS ACCEPTED: MasterCard, Visa, American Express, Discover

OPEN: Year-round

HOW TO GET THERE: Maple Avenue is off Route 44 directly across from the village green. Watch for the sign, turn in, and proceed about 400 yards; the inn is on the left.

canopy bed, and a private balcony. The Lincoln Room, one of the smaller quarters, has a fireplace, a fine view of the grounds, and a carved antique bed. The Country French Room offers an antique French bed and a big bathroom with cedar walls and ceiling, a shower with a skylight, and a soaking tub big enough for two; the English Room includes a whirlpool bath; and the Morgan Room has a deck as well as a whirlpool tub for two.

The obliging innkeepers will help you make the most of this scenic area, arranging kayaking or canoeing excursions and guiding you to the best local shopping spots. They will also add to the romance of this special inn by arranging for in-room massages or preparing a picnic basket and supplying bikes for an excursion for two.

What's Nearby: This lovely New England town is home to two state parks with scenic hiking and cross-country skiing, concerts at the Yale Summer Music School, and lovely perennial display gardens at Hillside Garden. Hayrides and sleigh rides are available at Loon Meadow Farm. Auto racing at Lime Rock is a short drive away.

MOUNTAIN VIEW INN

67 Litchfield Road
Norfolk 06058
(860) 542–6991
Fax: (860) 542–5111

If Victoriana is your love, you'll love this inn. Dean and Jean Marie Johnson are also fans, and since 2004, when they took over this splendid home built in the 1870s, they have filled it with carved love seats and fancy chairs, fainting couches, lacy curtains, and other favorite furnishings of the period, right down to the Victorian pump organ in the parlor. Deep red is the predominant color, on the living room walls, up the stairs,

WEB SITE: www.mvinn.com

INNKEEPERS: Dean and Jean Marie Johnson

ROOMS: 7 rooms, all with private bath, air-conditioning

ON THE GROUNDS: 3 acres of lawn and woodland

RATES: $110–$225, including buffet breakfast

CREDIT CARDS ACCEPTED: MasterCard, Visa, American Express, Discover

OPEN: Year-round

HOW TO GET THERE: Take Route 44 to the Norfolk Village Green. The inn is ¼ mile past the green driving south on Route 272, on the left.

and on many of the couches and chairs. Below the railing on the stairway is the embossed gold paper known as anaglypta, another authentic Victorian touch. Dean's paintings of a giant red rose complement the decor in many rooms.

This is a rambling home covering some 6,000 square feet, with four fireplaces on the first floor. Past the entry is a bar where a plate of fresh-baked cookies awaits and sherry is served before and after dinner.

Beyond is the dining room, a change of pace with dark wood wainscoting and a 1920s Arts and Crafts feel. The long dining table seats twelve, and breakfast is buffet style, with dishes such as quiche, bread pudding, apple bread, cereals, and fruit. A game table to the side will suit those who prefer a table for two. At the end of the room is a leather sofa and the only TV for guests.

The seven guest rooms are along the rambling halls upstairs. All are decorated in period decor. I'm partial to Room 2, with red and white floral striped wallpaper, an antique four-poster hung with netting pulled back at the sides, a red and gold spread and pillows, a fainting couch, and an interesting red enameled chest. Room 6 has a similar bed and a softer blue and ivory color scheme. Room 3, done with a jacquard-pattern damask bed cover, offers a spacious sitting area with a red settee and two chairs in a big floral print. Room 4, another room with a four-poster net canopy, has an enclosed porch with a day bed.

Dean is an interesting host, a former college art professor with a passion for historic art preservation and nineteenth-century culture. Jean Marie continues with her outside career as an organizational consultant, but she shares her husband's fondness for the inn and for Victoriana. With her sister-in-law and partner, Jill Bumbera, who doubles as inn manager, Jean Marie has added to the Victorian feel of the inn with a vintage clothing shop, the Gilded Peacock, occupying the sun porch and overflowing into the entry.

What's Nearby: See What's Nearby on page 24.

ANTIQUES AND ACCOMMODATIONS

32 Main Street
North Stonington 06359
(860) 535–1736; (800) 554–7829
Fax: (860) 535–2613

■ Even the lightning rods on the roof are antiques in this beautiful yellow clapboard Victorian, which once graced the cover of *Country Inns* magazine. Inspired by many years of traveling in Britain, owners Ann and Tom Gray, former antiques dealers, have indulged their love for things English with formal Georgian decor featuring fine examples of eighteenth- and nineteenth-century antiques in every room. The setting they chose is a small quiet village, about a ten-minute drive from Mystic, Rhode Island beaches, or the Foxwoods Casino.

A handmade needlepoint rug shows off well on the polished hardwood floor of the small parlor, which has long printed draperies, a camelback sofa, wing chairs, and the Grays' collection of English and American tea caddies displayed around the room.

The dining room has striking wallpaper in pale yellow with a formal floral print, as well as a gleaming brass chandelier, a fine gilt mirror with a painted floral inset, nineteenth-century paintings, and two rare George III sconces on the walls. Gleaming silver and crystal are displayed on the sideboard, a corner hutch, an elegant small side table, and the formal table with Chippendale chairs, where a four-course breakfast is served each morning by candlelight with classical music playing in the background.

The starter might be a pear compote with raspberry liqueur or fresh-picked berries. Main dishes could be salmon omelette, crab soufflé, asparagus topped with poached eggs and hollandaise, or banana waffles. On warm days, the meal can be moved out to the stone patio in the garden; the flowers and herbs planted here are used for cooking and garnishing.

WEB SITE: www.antiquesandaccommodations.com

INNKEEPERS: Ann and Tom Gray

ROOMS: 3 rooms, all with private bath, air-conditioning, TV; 1 with fireplace

ON THE GROUNDS: Porch, gardens

RATES: $99–$189, including full breakfast

CREDIT CARDS ACCEPTED: MasterCard, Visa

OPEN: Year-round

HOW TO GET THERE: From Interstate 95 going north, take exit 92 to Route 2 west. Go about 2¼ miles past shops to the sign for North Stonington, and turn right to reach the inn, at the corner on the right.

The bedrooms have soft floral papers with matching fabrics for curtains, skirted tables, dust ruffles, and pillows that add accents to the white candlewick bedspreads. Antique four-poster queen-size beds with embroidered canopies add a romantic touch. Jeni's Room on the first floor has a working fireplace, as well as hand-hooked rugs, a crystal chandelier, and interesting still lifes and etchings on the walls. Two rooms upstairs include the largest room in the house, the Susan Room, the only one not named for a family member. Susan was the first bride to honeymoon at the inn.

Like many antiques lovers, the Grays just can't stop collecting, so they will happily sell almost any of the pieces you admire in the inn in order to make room for their new finds.

What's Nearby: Mystic Seaport, Foxwoods Casino, and the ocean beaches of Watch Hill, Rhode Island, are all a short drive from the tiny village of North Stonington. Authentic colonial fireplace cooking can be sampled at Randall's Ordinary, a nearby restaurant.

OLD MYSTIC INN

52 Main Street
P.O. Box 733
Old Mystic 06372
(860) 572–9422
Fax: (860) 572–9954

■ This cozy red colonial house, circa 1784, was perhaps best known as the Old Mystic Book Shop, renowned for its antique books and maps. The sign still shows a bespectacled gent reading a book. It was this literary heritage that prompted the previous innkeepers to name the guest rooms after New England authors and to equip each room with samples of works by the appropriate writer. So you can relax in your canopy bed and bone up on Hawthorne, Melville, Dickinson, or Thoreau while you are here.

The keeping room in the inn is country cozy, with low ceilings, stenciling, wing-back chairs, a fireplace, and braided rugs on the original old wide floorboards. The dining room is especially cheery, with a bay window, white lace curtains, and fresh flowers on four tables set with white linen and floral print napkins.

Guests assemble from 8:30 to 9:30 A.M. for a gourmet breakfast prepared by owner Michael Cardillo, who is a graduate of the Culinary Institute of America. Among his specialties are banana-stuffed French toast, Belgian waffles, and scrambled eggs with fine herbs served in puff pastry with sauce mornay and oven-roasted potatoes. The changing entrees are accompanied by juice, homemade pastries and

WEB SITE: www.oldmysticinn.com

INNKEEPER: Michael S. Cardillo Jr.

ROOMS: 8 rooms, all with private bath and air-conditioning; 2 with whirlpool bath; 6 with working fireplace

ON THE GROUNDS: Lawn with hammock, gazebo, picnic tables, gardens

RATES: $125–$185, including full breakfast, afternoon refreshments, and wine and cheese on Saturday evening

CREDIT CARDS ACCEPTED: MasterCard, Visa, American Express

OPEN: Year-round

HOW TO GET THERE: Take Interstate 95 to exit 90, and follow Route 27 north 1½ miles to a stop sign. Bear to the right; the inn is across from the Old Mystic Country Store.

muffins, and breakfast meats. In the summer, breakfast is often served on the side porch.

Bedrooms are simple and fresh, decorated with hand stenciling, folk art, and comforters. The carriage house has larger guest rooms, some with cathedral ceilings, three with fireplaces, and two with a whirlpool bath. But the feel is still country colonial. The Frost Room, for example, has sunny prints in yellow and blue, sunflower stenciling, and a canopy bed.

Behind the inn is a lovely lawn with perennial gardens, a gazebo, a hammock for lazing, and plenty of room for a game of croquet or bocce.

What's Nearby: Old Mystic is near Mystic; see What's Nearby on page 17.

RED BROOK INN

P.O. Box 237
Old Mystic 06372
(860) 572–0346

Ruth Keyes will tell you she never felt at home in California. With a house filled with the Early American antiques she loves, she longed to live where they belonged. When her youngest child left for college, Ruth came to New England and in 1980 bought the kind of home she had dreamed about, the Crary Homestead, circa 1770, complete with a big open-hearth fireplace.

In 1984, Ruth moved the Halley Tavern to the site. She did all the painting and stenciling herself, using the same original colors she found inside cupboards or beneath layers of paint on the woodwork.

WEB SITE: www.redbrookinn.com

INNKEEPER: Ruth Keyes

ROOMS: 2 rooms with private bath and fireplace; 1 with whirlpool bath

ON THE GROUNDS: Patio, woods, walking trails

RATES: $95–$189, including full breakfast and afternoon refreshments

CREDIT CARDS ACCEPTED: None

OPEN: Year-round

HOW TO GET THERE: From Interstate 95, take exit 89, Allyn Street, and head north 1½ miles to the traffic light at Gold-star Highway. Turn right (east), and proceed slowly to the next corner. The driveway is at that corner. Turn left into the drive and turn right toward the red house.

All the rooms are furnished with authentic colonial furniture and antiques and early lighting devices. Bedrooms have canopy or four-poster beds, old blanket chests, and stenciled walls. There are quilts on the beds and down comforters. Both bedrooms have working fireplaces to take care of winter chills.

The parlor is furnished with a Federal style sofa, a cherry cabinet, an Oriental carpet on the old wide floorboards, and wrought iron candle stands.

Guests gather for breakfast in the keeping room. Fresh fruit, blueberry or pumpkin pancakes, and sausage may be on a typical menu. In the afternoon, Ruth serves tea with cookies or lemon cake, or hot cider and doughnuts.

The big kettles and iron tools in the fireplace are for more than show. Ruth learned how to cook over the coals out of necessity when the house was without electricity for ten days in 1985, thanks to Hurricane Gloria. She boiled coffee over the hearth, baked bread in the beehive oven, cooked pancakes on the griddle, and somehow provided both breakfast and dinner for her delighted guests. Now her fireplace cooking is something of a local legend.

DEACON TIMOTHY PRATT BED & BREAKFAST

325 Main Street
Old Saybrook 06475
(860) 395–1129; (800) 640–1195
Fax: (860) 395–1229

This is a dream colonial, built in 1746 by Timothy Pratt, a carpenter and a deacon in the meetinghouse across the street. Turned into a private school in the 1790s, it was beautifully restored in the 1990s and furnished to fit its period, with guest rooms designed for luxury and romance. The house still boasts many of its original hand-hewn beams, wide-board floors, wainscoting, and a beehive oven.

The elegant parlor is all in blue and white, with a camelback sofa and wing chair grouped around one of the home's eight fireplaces. The floors are polished to a sheen, and tall windows bring in the sunlight. In the afternoon, tea or hot chocolate, freshly baked cookies, and port wine are served.

The formal dining room is also lovely, with soft green walls, a fireplace, and the original wainscoting and corner cupboard, painted white. On weekends, a three-course breakfast is served by candlelight on fine china. Bacon and egg custard, popovers, cinnamon swirl French toast, and peach cobbler are among the favorite dishes. On weekdays a continental breakfast is served, with fresh fruits and baked treats such as orange-cranberry foccacia bread.

You cannot go wrong with any guest room here. All have canopy or four-poster beds, fireplaces, and whirlpools in the bath. I liked the first-floor Library Room, with a love seat beside the fireplace and shelves with collectibles and books, and the Gambrel Room upstairs, for its beams and cathedral ceiling. While I'd rather be in the main house, the rooms in the adjacent James Gallery and Soda Fountain building are equally attractive, and I'd certainly be happy in the English Cottage room, with its dramatic red walls, chaise longue, and cathedral ceiling with a skylight.

The Gallery building, which dates from 1790, has an interesting past and is listed on the National Register of Historic Places. It was originally part of the Humphrey Pratt Inn, where the Marquis de Lafayette stayed in 1824. Humphrey was Deacon Pratt's brother. From 1911 to 1967 it was run by Anna L. James, the

WEB SITE: www.pratthouse.net

INNKEEPERS: Shelley Nobile and Jimmy Driscoll (owners); Pat McGregor (innkeeper)

ROOMS: 4 rooms and 1 suite in main inn, 3 rooms in adjacent building, all with private bath, air-conditioning, fireplace, whirlpool (except suite), TV, phone, modem line, clock, radio, stereo/CD player, hair dryer, iron; high-speed wireless in main house

ON THE GROUNDS: Located on a city block, large yard, garden and fountain with seating

RATES: $110–$200, including continental breakfast weekdays, full breakfast weekends

CREDIT CARDS ACCEPTED: MasterCard, Visa, American Express

OPEN: Year-round

HOW TO GET THERE: Take Interstate 95 to exit 67, and bear right at the exit ramp to Route 154 west. At the third light, turn left onto Main Street (Route 154 continued). The inn is 9/10 mile ahead on the right.

first licensed African American woman pharmacist in Connecticut. It has returned to its earlier incarnation as part of an inn and also includes a gift shop and an original 1896 soda foundation serving old-fashioned ice-cream favorites.

The inn has a pleasant lawn out back, shaded by a 200-year-old maple, with gardens, a fountain, and a hammock for two. The Timothy Pratt House is part of the town's Historic Walking Tour, taking in many eighteenth-century colonial and nineteenth-century Federal homes. You can also walk to some of the shops on Old Saybrook's main street, and you're ½ mile from a beautiful cove, lined with majestic old sea captains' homes and scenic vistas, a good spot for kayaking or canoeing. The beaches and lighthouses of Long Island Sound are about a mile away, a pleasant long walk or a short bike ride. The inn will gladly supply you with beach passes and bikes.

What's Nearby: Old Saybrook is the town where the Connecticut River meets Long Island Sound, and it has a beautiful harbor and waterfront, including restaurants with water views. The Deacon Timothy Pratt House is part of a long and very attractive Main Street lined with shops and historic homes. The town's historic house museum, the General William Hart House, is right across the street from the inn. It is also a short drive to interesting art museums in Old Lyme, a one-time artists' colony, and to Connecticut River towns such as Essex, lined with sea captains' homes and home to the Connecticut River Museum and the vintage train rides of the Valley Railroad. For more about towns along the river, see What's Nearby on pages 5 and 7.

COBBSCROFT

349 Pomfret Street
Pomfret 06250
(860) 928–5560
Fax: (860) 928–3608

▨ Tucked almost out of sight into the tall shrubbery, this delightful home, circa 1830, is filled with the personality and good taste of the artist-owners, Tom and Janet McCobb. Tom is well known in the area for his watercolors, which can be seen in the studio and shop behind the house. As for Janet, her talents run the gamut, from sponge-painting the walls to creating the theorem paintings and mirrors that adorn them.

Janet is responsible for the raspberry pink walls in the comfortable, long, low-ceilinged living room. The decor is a mix of traditional and antique furniture. The mantel is lined with decoys and a menagerie of small metal animals, and the walls are chockablock with paintings. Some of the oils are Dutch, gathered when Tom's family

WEB SITE: www.cobbscroft.com

INNKEEPERS: Tom and Janet McCobb

ROOMS: 3 rooms, all with private bath, phone, clock, radio, robes, air-conditioning; 1 suite with gas fireplace

ON THE GROUNDS: Gardens, gift shop, studio where painting workshops are held

RATES: $85–$110, including full breakfast

CREDIT CARDS ACCEPTED: MasterCard, Visa, American Express, Discover

OPEN: Year-round

HOW TO GET THERE: Take Interstate 95 to Interstate 395 north, get off at exit 93 (Route 101), and then go 1/10 mile west to Route 169 north. Continue 2 miles on Route 169 to the inn, on the right just before the school crossing lights.

lived in the Dutch Indies. This inviting room is where everyone gathers to listen to some of the extensive collection of CDs or to watch TV.

The dining room is more formal, with sunny yellow walls and a handsome Queen Anne table, where blue and white plates, deep blue goblets, and ornate silver are set on blue linen. Burnished silver service pieces glow on the sideboard. Breakfast usually consists of juice, fruits, bacon, eggs or pancakes, and tempting baked goods ranging from pastries to cobblers.

Up the narrow stairs are bedrooms with painted headboards and chests—Janet's handiwork. One room is decorated with pink and white check and ticking fabrics, while another has floral prints. All are distinctive, and one of the bathrooms has a bathtub circa 1893.

Out the side door, an arbor is the gateway to a lawn with lush flower beds and bigger metal sculptures resembling the miniatures on the mantel. Beyond are the open fields and hills that make this unspoiled "Quiet Corner" of Connecticut a favorite of nature lovers. And in back is the clapboard cottage where you can buy one of Tom's paintings or some of Janet's handiwork, along with the other artistic cards and gifts she has assembled in her little shop. The McCobbs offer painting workshops here periodically, and you may well be inspired to sign up!

What's Nearby: Handsome Pomfret, home to three prep schools, has lots of open spaces for scenic drives and hiking at the Bafflin Sanctuary. Choice antiquing can be found in town and in nearby Putnam, art awaits at the New England Center of Contemporary Arts in Brooklyn, and house and garden tours are offered at Roseland Cottage, operated by the Society for the Preservation of New England Antiquities.

FEATHER HILL BED & BREAKFAST

151 Mashamoquet Road
Pomfret Center 06259
(860) 963–0511; (866) 963–0522
Fax: (860) 928–0671

■ Though it was built in 1936, this center hall colonial looks brand new, and for good reason. Angela and Fred Spring completely remodeled the house and doubled its size before opening for business in July 2004. In addition to the formal living and dining rooms, the inviting home now includes the Pavilion Room, a sunny wicker-furnished family room with sliding glass doors; bright new bedrooms, and a 20-by 40-foot swimming pool between the house and the Feather Nest Cottage, a guest cottage also recently redone.

The name comes from the many birds that are attracted to the wooded nine-acre property, easy to spot at the many feeders on the lawn. Waking to the songs of the birds is one of the inn's pleasures.

Guest room names are also avian inspired. They are simply and pleasantly furnished, each with its own decor. Downy Nest is a corner room done in blue, Golden Crane's Nest has an antique brass and black bed, and a dark green and red color scheme carried out in the print comforter and plaid bed skirt. Robin's Nest, with a four-poster bed, soft floral coverlet, and pink curtains and bed skirt, is one of two accommodations with a Jacuzzi. The other is Dove's Nest, a two-room suite with a mahogany four-poster with a creamy satin bedspread, and a little sitting room with a love seat and wicker chairs.

The cottage, which sleeps four, is a private retreat with its own comfortable living room with a fireplace, dining area, full kitchen, and a handsome white pineapple-post queen-size bed in the bedroom.

WEB SITE: www.featherhillbedand breakfast.com

INNKEEPERS: Angela and Fred Spring

ROOMS: 3 rooms, 1 suite, and 1 private 3-room cottage, all with private bath, air-conditioning, TV, radio, phone, hair dryer, robes, clock, dataport, iron and ironing board, VCR, CD player; 2 rooms with whirlpool bath; cottage with full kitchen

ON THE GROUNDS: Swimming pool, patio, 9 acres of woodland, walking trail

RATES: Rooms $100–$148, suite $175, cottage $200, including full breakfast

CREDIT CARDS ACCEPTED: MasterCard, Visa, American Express

OPEN: Year-round

HOW TO GET THERE: Take Interstate 395 to exit 93, and drive 4½ miles east on Route 101. The inn is just past Route 44, the next building after a bank.

Breakfast, served at a big round table in the airy dining room, begins with an inn trademark, a warm fruit compote, followed by main courses that may include stuffed French toast, omelettes, or another house specialty, waffles served with fruits of the season.

Afterward, depending on the weather, you can head for the pool, watch the birds from one of the two inn decks, or settle in front of the fireplace in the living room. The Airline Trail crossing the property is part of a 30-mile state park along an old railroad bed, open for hiking, biking, and cross-country skiing. The entrance to Mashamoquet Brook State Park, with hiking trails, lake swimming, and picnic grounds, is just ⁷⁄₁₀ mile down, across the road.

What's Nearby: See What's Nearby on page 32.

WEST LANE INN

22 West Lane
Ridgefield 06877
(203) 438–7323
Fax: (203) 438–7325

For those who want the charm of an inn and the privacy and amenities of a hotel, the West Lane Inn fills the bill. Like many of the fine homes that line Ridgefield's gracious lanes, this three-story, white clapboard beauty with dark shutters was built in the 1840s, when the town was a favored summer retreat for wealthy New Yorkers. The rounded bay window on the second floor is echoed in the lines of the columned and railed front porch, adding to the distinctive appearance of the house. In summer, the porch is hung with an array of flowering plants.

The refurbishment that turned the home into an inn in 1978 carefully retained the original rich oak paneling and ornate railed stairway, the first things you see as you enter the lobby and sitting-room area. In winter, a blazing fire warms the scene.

The furnishings are a mix of colonial and modern, chosen mainly for comfort. The cheerful breakfast room has yellow print wallpaper, fresh white curtains, hanging plants at the windows, and fresh flowers on the round tables for two or four. Guests are served a continental breakfast of juice, fruit, cereals, breads, and homemade muffins or coffee cake. A full menu is available at extra charge.

The oversize upstairs bedrooms offer either one or two queen-size beds, restful color schemes, wall-to-wall carpeting, and conveniences such as individual climate control, TV/VCR, iron, and telephone. Each has a sitting area with wing chairs, and two have working fireplaces. The well-appointed bathrooms have heated towel racks, hair dryers, and full-length mirrors; some even have bidets.

Rooms in the cottage building on the grounds are smaller, but they have kitchens and private decks overlooking the lawns.

What's Nearby: Ridgefield offers choice antiquing nearby and two major sights in town: the restored Keeler Tavern, still bearing the cannonball that struck during the Revolutionary War, and the Aldrich Museum, a showcase for cutting-edge contemporary art, with a sculpture garden out back. Nearby is the home of American Impressionist artist J. Alden Weir, a National Historic Site. The town's other claim to fame is gourmet dining. One of the culinary stars is Stonehenge on Route 7; another, Bernard's, is right next door to the West Lane, so you need only stroll across the lawn to find a wonderful dinner. The innkeepers will gladly help with reservations.

WEB SITE: www.westlaneinn.com

INNKEEPERS: Maureen Mayer and Deborah Prieger

ROOMS: 18 rooms, all with private bath, air-conditioning, phone, radio, TV/VCR, hair dryer, iron, free wireless DSL; 2 with fireplace. Some rooms are in a newer cottage on the grounds and have efficiency units.

ON THE GROUNDS: Broad lawn with majestic maples and flowering shrubs

RATES: Rooms $145–$215, suites $180–$275, including continental breakfast; full breakfast menu available at extra charge

CREDIT CARDS ACCEPTED: MasterCard, Visa, American Express, Discover

OPEN: Year-round

HOW TO GET THERE: From Interstate 684 or Route 7 from the Merritt Parkway, take Route 35 into Ridgefield. The inn is on Route 35 at the south end of town.

THE LINDEN HOUSE

288/290 Hopmeadow Street
(Route 10)
Simsbury 06089
(860) 408–1321
Fax: (860) 408–9072

This classic Victorian house was built in 1860, but it might as well be new. The innkeepers, Julia and Myles McCabe, were ready for a change from their careers with the New York City Board of Education, and they loved the looks of this house each time they drove by. But it was in such disrepair, they had to gut the interior completely. After many months of work, it opened to guests in October 1998, better than new, with floors gleaming and many modern conveniences, such as central air-conditioning, which the Victorians would no doubt have appreciated.

WEB SITE: www.lindenhousebb.com

INNKEEPERS: Julia and Myles McCabe

ROOMS: 6 rooms, all with private bath, TV, clock, radio, robes, chocolates; 1 room with whirlpool bath; 4 rooms with fireplace

ON THE GROUNDS: Wraparound porch, patio, gazebo, 2½ acres with mountain views

RATES: $130–$150, including full breakfast

CREDIT CARDS ACCEPTED: MasterCard, Visa

OPEN: Year-round, except Christmas and New Year's Day

HOW TO GET THERE: From Interstate 91 take exit 36 to Route 178 west; continue for about 6 miles, and then turn right onto Route 185 west for about 2½ miles to Route 10/Route 202. Turn left, and the inn is ¼ mile farther on the left.

Every effort was made to preserve features such as the original mantels, some of the doorknobs and hardware, and the stairs at the guest entrance that wind up three flights to a Victorian turret. The baths have restored pedestal sinks and claw-foot tubs.

The guest rooms are good size with high ceilings, nice floral papers, and varying color schemes and furnishings. Some have views of the mountains behind the inn. I'd recommend the first-floor room with a big fireplace, an Oriental rug, a four-poster bed, and a whirlpool bath in the bathroom.

The living/dining room is quite spacious, with an open feeling and furnishings that are more colonial than Victorian. Breakfast includes hot dishes such as quiche or pancakes.

The inn is on Route 10, a busy road, but convenient for the area's many attractions. The congenial Irish-born hosts will make you feel right at home.

What's Nearby: Three centuries of local history have been collected at the Simsbury Historical Society, including the first copper coins struck in America and a one-room schoolhouse. Off Route 185 is Talcott Mountain State Park, with a four-state vista from the top of its 165-foot Heublein Tower. Drive north on Route 10 to the International Skating Center of Connecticut, where you can take a spin on the ice or watch the action—Olympic competitors can often be seen practicing there. A short drive south on Route 10 brings you to Avon and the Farmington Valley Arts Center, where you can visit artists' studios and shop at a collective gallery. Tubing and canoeing are popular pastimes on the nearby Farmington River.

MERRYWOOD BED & BREAKFAST

100 Hartford Road (Route 185)
Simsbury 06070
(860) 651–1785, (866) 637–7993
Fax: (860) 651–8273

■ Just off a main road, yet secluded and private, this antiques-filled home is spacious, gracious, and filled with interesting collections, furniture, and fine rugs.

A former executive with Pratt and Whitney, Michael Marti has traveled all over the world, and the walls are adorned with some of the treasures he has gathered, such as masks from Venice, Japan, Saudi Arabia, and Africa. Mike is also a self-described "auction hound" whose unusual finds make for intriguing displays, such as a collection of children's royal garments from India, including dozens of pairs of shoes. The antique rugs draped on furniture around the house are both from travels and auctions, he says. Gerlinde collects textiles and has been in the antiques business, so there are many exceptional pieces throughout their home.

There are many places to feel at home here. Besides a comfortable, well-furnished living room with a fireplace, the inn has a cozy library with books and a puzzle table where guests can gather. Tea can be served in the library in the afternoon, sherry in the evening. I'm partial to the glass-walled garden room filled with plants and furnished with wicker, where the view of the expansive lawn surrounded by tall trees is pleasant even on a winter day.

The ornate dining-room furniture is Jacobean style from the late 1600s, some originals, some reproductions. Guests are given an extensive menu each evening and can choose what they want for breakfast the next day and when—anytime between 6:00 and 10:00 A.M. Merrywood specialties include French Toast Bananas Foster, Eggs Hussarde, and poached eggs on toast with a Marchand sauce (mushrooms, ham, shallots, garlic, and wine), served with tomato and a hollandaise

WEB SITE: www.merrywoodinn.com

INNKEEPERS: Michael and Gerlinde Marti

ROOMS: 2 rooms, 1 suite, all with private bath, TV, VCR, phone, clock radio, mini-bar, air-conditioning, robes, slippers

ON THE GROUNDS: 5 very private acres rimmed with trees, with extensive lawns, patio, fountain, small pond

RATES: Rooms $165, suite $195, including full breakfast; passes to Simsbury Health Club

CREDIT CARDS ACCEPTED: All

OPEN: Year-round, except last two weeks of September

HOW TO GET THERE: From Interstate 91, take exit 35B to Route 218 west, and continue for 4⁸⁄₁₀ miles to Route 185 west. Turn right, and follow Route 185 for 3⁷⁄₁₀ miles to the Merrywood driveway on your right; watch for the stone-pillared entry with sign.

topping. Breakfast is served by candlelight on antique English porcelain with turn-of-the-twentieth-century cut stemware.

Rooms are named for their furnishings. The Empire Room, which features American furniture from the Empire period, 1800–1840, looks out on a terrace and woods. The Victorian Room has a love seat and chair circa 1860 to 1890 and a queen-size bed with a lace canopy that is actually a 20-foot Quaker lace tablecloth. Shelves in this room show off collections of cut glass, cloisonné, and fans. The large living room of the Continental Suite offers French and Italian settees and a nineteenth-century Dutch marquetry secretary. The bedroom under the eaves is cozy, and the kitchenette is equipped with a minifridge, sink, and microwave. There's a small sauna in the bathroom.

Occasionally the Martis book guests for their own serene Oriental suite, where the oversize bathroom provides a steam shower and whirlpool bath. If it is available, grab it!

What's Nearby: See What's Nearby on page 36.

THE CORNUCOPIA AT OLDFIELD

782 Main Street North
Southbury 06488
(203) 267–6707; (888) 760–7947
Fax: (203) 267–6703

■ Southbury's first bed-and-breakfast is a beauty. Listed on the National Register of Historic Places, the Georgian Federal home has been a community landmark since it was built by John Moseley in 1818. It looks better than ever since the Edelsons arrived. They have respected the history of the house while making it a warm haven for guests. Even the formal front parlor is an inviting place to read or have a quiet chat.

As in years past, the keeping room with its big warming fireplace is the heart of the house. White walls with colonial red wooden accents make for a perfect period setting, and the big-print sofa and leather wing chairs invite relaxing in front of the fire. The room offers a TV, VCR, and CD player and an ample supply of movies, as well as board games.

The formal dining room, with its handsome brass chandelier, long floral drapes, carved mantel, and traditional furnishings, is a fine setting for a special breakfast.

WEB SITE: www.cornucopiabb.com

INNKEEPERS: Christine and Ed Edelson

ROOMS: 4 rooms, all with private bath, fireplace, air-conditioning, CD/radio alarm clock, wireless Internet access; 1 with whirlpool tub; 2 with private deck

ON THE GROUNDS: Swimming pool, herb and perennial gardens, water garden with goldfish pond, gazebo, hammock

RATES: $150–$250, including full breakfast

CREDIT CARDS ACCEPTED: MasterCard, Visa, American Express, Discover

OPEN: Year-round

HOW TO GET THERE: Take Interstate 84 to exit 15, Southbury, and proceed north on Route 6 just past the Route 67 intersection to Buck's Hill Road. Turn right on Buck's Hill; the inn is the first driveway on the right.

It isn't easy choosing a favorite room here. I might opt for the Admiral Aston Room, a spacious room done in smart black and white, with a king-size pencil-post bed. It offers a fireplace, whirlpool bath, and my favorite spot, a deck with views of the lovely grounds.

The John Moseley Room, the former master bedroom, has a soft blue color scheme and a king bed that can become two twins. The Selena Aston Room, with a restful pastel palette and a white iron bed, has French doors opening to a private balcony with views of the gardens and stream.

The guest pantry on the second floor is a hospitable touch, with complimentary soft drinks, coffee, tea, hot and cold water, a microwave, and snacks as a courtesy to guests.

The large backyard is a special treat. There's a secluded pool, a gazebo, gardens, a double hammock, and lots of room for lawn games.

What's Nearby: The southern gateway to the Litchfield Hills, Southbury has a busy modern shopping center as well as its own historic district. Kettletown, 5 miles to the south, is a park with hiking, fishing, swimming, and nature trails. Southbury adjoins Woodbury, Connecticut's antiquing capital, and is an easy, scenic drive to the colonial beauty of towns such as Litchfield and Washington, recreation at Lake Waramaug, and fun at Quassy Amusement Park.

LORD THOMPSON MANOR

Route 200, P.O. Box 428
Thompson 06277
(860) 923–3886
Fax: (860) 923–9310

◼ It's no surprise to learn that this romantic inn, once featured in *Victoria* magazine, has been chosen by lots of couples

WEB SITE: www.lordthompsonmanor.com

INNKEEPERS: Jackie and Andrew Silverston

ROOMS: 2 rooms and 4 suites, all with clock, radio, robes; suites have private bath and fireplace

ON THE GROUNDS: 42 acres, patio, walking trails

RATES: $165–$205, including full breakfast

CREDIT CARDS ACCEPTED: MasterCard, Visa, American Express, Discover

OPEN: Year-round

HOW TO GET THERE: From Interstate 395 take exit 99, turn onto Route 200 east, and go about ¼ mile to the second left driveway.

for their weddings. Many book the entire inn for weekend reunions with friends and family.

The thirty-room mansion at the end of a ½-mile-long wooded driveway was built in 1917 as a summer home for a wealthy Providence mercantilist, John Gladding. During the Great Depression, it was acquired by the Marian Fathers, who still maintain a residence across the road. In 1989, Jackie and Andrew Silverston bought the inn and brought it back to its former glory.

A circular drive leads up to the creamy stucco building, with tall green shutters at the windows and a pair of columns guarding the door. The entry wallpaper is a handsome dark paisley, and the stairs leading up have a wonderful banister of wood and wrought iron.

Past the entry is a 20-by-30-foot drawing room with 10-foot ceilings, parquet floors, Oriental rugs, rich paneling of African gum wood, and a marble fireplace. A beige velvet sofa faces the fireplace, flanked by green leather wing chairs. Glass doors next to the mantel open to shelves filled with interesting books on design and architecture, including one on the famous Olmsted brothers, who designed the landscaping of the grounds.

Several smaller rooms extend from both sides of the drawing room, including a billiards room, sunroom, and dining room, enough space so that a small meeting need not disturb inn guests. The pleasant breakfast room is decorated with deep purple grape vines. Fruit- and berry-patterned dishes and wine-colored glasses on the tables carry out the theme. Breakfast consists of freshly squeezed juice and freshly ground coffee, fresh fruit, homemade bread or scones, and a daily specialty that may be Finnish pancakes with country ham or waffles and sausage.

The upstairs rooms all have equestrian names, but they vary greatly. The choicest accommodations are the suites, particularly Thoroughbred Suite I, the former master bedroom, an enormous room with a hunt motif (complete with boots and saddle), a carved four-poster bed, dark green walls, and paisley fabrics a la Ralph Lauren.

The Morgan Suite is more feminine, done in pale peach with cream trimming. All the suites are large and have private baths, fireplaces, and queen-size beds.

The other rooms are much smaller and share baths. They are pleasantly albeit simply done, with wicker sidepieces and sheer white curtains.

Not all of the Olmsted landscaping remains, but the forty-two-acre grounds are still lovely, with a path around the rim to savor the scene.

What's Nearby: Thompson is one of the prettiest of Connecticut's "Quiet Corner" villages, with a green surrounded by vintage colonial homes. The refurbished White Horse Inn on the green has been serving travelers since 1814. Nearby you'll find antiquing in Putnam, hiking in Pomfret, and sightseeing in Brooklyn and Woodstock.

TOLLAND INN

63 Tolland Green
Tolland 06084
(860) 872–0800; (877) 465–0800
Fax: (860) 870–7958

The sleek four-poster bed in your room, the graceful benches, the tin lighting fixtures over the bed, the beautiful cherry trestle table in the dining room—all were crafted by Stephen Beeching, a talented artisan as well as a gracious innkeeper.

The Tolland Inn, which is opposite the venerable town green, dates from the late 1700s. It was built as a private residence but expanded one hundred years ago to become an inn. Since Susan Beeching had grown up in an innkeeping family on Nantucket and Stephen's mother was a longtime tourism official in Connecticut, running an inn seemed a natural occupation. They bought the home in 1985 and, after two years of hard work renovating and restoring, opened for business with a nice combination of historic ambience and modern comforts. Susan continues her career in teaching while Stephen does the innkeeping and, when time allows, woodworking to order. Ask to see the photo album of his creative work.

Downstairs, the inn offers a formal parlor, the dining room, and—the room I liked best of all—a two-level sunporch with a Rumford fireplace and a platform rocker for

WEB SITE: www.tollandinn.com

INNKEEPERS: Stephen and Susan Beeching

ROOMS: 5 rooms and 3 suites, all with private bath, phone, air-conditioning, TV, VCR, wireless broadband access; some with hot tub, fireplace

ON THE GROUNDS: Wraparound porch with rockers, garden

RATES: Rooms $95–$130; suites $120–$202, including full breakfast

CREDIT CARDS ACCEPTED: All major cards

OPEN: Year-round

HOW TO GET THERE: From Interstate 84 take exit 68, and follow Route 195 north into Tolland. The inn is on the left, opposite the green, just past the intersection with Route 74.

contemplating the flames. Stephen is responsible for the raised paneling and coffered ceiling in this sunny room, where breakfast often is served. Scones and Belgian waffles are among the house specialties.

Quarters on the main floor include a charming room with a queen-size canopy bed and a special room with a fireplace, a hot tub for two, TV/VCR, microwave, and refrigerator. This room offers complete privacy, even its own entrance.

Suites upstairs include two with gas fireplaces and hot tubs for two. I thoroughly enjoyed my stay in an upstairs suite decorated with Nantucket island posters. There is a sitting area with lots of books for borrowing, a working fireplace, and a bay window with garden views. Even the most modest rooms have nice appointments such as hooked rugs and claw-foot tubs in the bath. And all have examples of the innkeeper's talent, proof that fine handcraftsmanship is still alive and well in New England.

What's Nearby: Located between Hartford (18 miles) and Sturbridge, Massachusetts (25 miles), Tolland is a typical eighteenth-century New England village with a village green surrounded by period homes, town offices, and churches. Three historic homes are open for touring, including the Old Tolland County Jail Museum and 1893 Wardens Home. The Tolland County Courthouse houses a genealogical library. The many activities at the UConn campus are nearby, as is Coventry, home to the well-known Caprilands Herb Farm and the Nathan Hale Homestead.

HOUSE ON THE HILL

92 Woodlawn Terrace
Waterbury 06710
(203) 757–9901

House is an understatement. This is a mansion, a twenty-room Victorian built in 1888 for one of Waterbury's leading industrialists. The second owner was the city's mayor and the third is Marianne Vandenburgh, who moved here in 1980 and has been hosting a warm bed-and-breakfast since 1986.

Marianne hasn't tried to fill the house with fancy Victoriana. She has kept the furnishings simple in order to highlight the outstanding architectural features of the building, such as the beautiful winding stairway and the wooden beadwork over the doors on the second floor. The feel throughout is comfortable rather than fussy, and personal, with lots of books and collectibles around the house. I especially liked the col-

WEB SITE: www.houseonthehill.biz

INNKEEPER: Marianne Vandenburgh

ROOMS: 4 suites, all with private bath, air-conditioning, TV, clock radio, hair dryer, refrigerator; 3 with microwave ovens, phone with dataport, electric teakettle

ON THE GROUNDS: 1½ acres of lawn, beautiful gardens

RATES: $110–$175, including full breakfast

CREDIT CARDS ACCEPTED: MasterCard, Visa, American Express, Discover

OPEN: Year-round

HOW TO GET THERE: Take Interstate 84 to exit 21 and go right on Meadow Street (it turns into Willow Street). Turn right on Pine Street, continue just past Woodlawn Terrace, and turn into the driveway, which is the first left.

lection of eggshells in a variety of wooden holders on the living room mantle and the stained-glass fire screen. A sofa and chairs at a round coffee table make for easy conversation. The second living room is a library, lined with glass-fronted bookcases, an ideal place to settle in with your own book. On a nice day, however, everyone heads for the big side porch, where dark green wicker and wooden Adirondack chairs are placed to give a perfect view of the beautiful garden. There's a hammock in case you crave a little snooze.

In the dining room, two wicker love seats and two chairs are set at the round table. Most of the rooms have built-ins, and this one is no exception, with a china closet in one corner, a big breakfront along one wall, and a fireplace on another. The ceiling is covered with a whimsical wallpaper decorated with giant gold leaves.

Marianne is a caterer and food columnist as well as an innkeeper, and her breakfasts are legendary, with many ingredients from her own garden. I sampled her famous "green eggs," scrambled eggs flavored with fresh-picked lemon and garlic chive, parsley, and basil, served with bacon and delicious bread from the local artisan bakery. The meal started with fresh juice, sliced melon, and blackberries from the local farmers' market.

All the guest quarters are spacious suites, with many built-in drawers. The queen-size beds are made up with designer sheets, and there are good reading lights and conveniences such as refrigerators and electric kettles. In winter, the bedding changes to cozy flannel. The furniture is a mix, pleasant but with no attempt to be magazine-perfect.

I especially liked the Westover Suite, with a printed headboard and comforter, a coordinated checked bed skirt, an armchair, a couple of wicker chairs, and its own porch. This is a room for those who like soaking in the tub, as it is the only room without a shower. The Garden Suite is a two-bedroom suite, ideal for families or two couples traveling together.

On the third floor, one part of the house is the Turret Suite, and another wing is the Old Maid's Suite, the former maids' quarters under the eaves, equipped with a sink, toaster, espresso maker, and a refrigerator. The bed has an especially cheerful blue and white star quilt.

Be sure to ask your hostess what to see in the area. Marianne loves Waterbury, and she'll guide you to all the best places in town.

What's Nearby: In the 1860s, Waterbury was known as the Brass Capital of the World and was a pioneer in America's clock and watch industry. While those original factories may be gone, they produced great wealth and equally great generosity. The community's industrialists have been responsible for buildings by some of America's top architects past and present, as well as two excellent attractions. The Mattatuck Museum features art by illustrious painters who have worked in Connecticut, including early artists such as John Trumbull and Frederic Church, and later masters including Yves Tanguy, Alexander Calder, and Arshile Gorky. One fascinating exhibit is a room displaying some 10,000 buttons, a donation of the Waterbury Companies, successor to a company that has been making buttons in Waterbury since 1812. The Timexpo Museum, a history of timepieces, is maintained by Timex, the successor to the Waterbury Clock Company.

Downtown, don't miss the restored showplace Palace Theater and the Connecticut Store, a unique emporium featuring everything made in Connecticut, from wiffle balls to furniture.

HILLTOP HAVEN

175 Dibble Hill Road
West Cornwall 06796
(860) 672–6871

■ Talk about being on top of the world! The road curves up and up and up until you reach this fabulous spot with tri-state vistas of the Berkshire foothills and the Taconic and Catskill Mountains. The view is for all seasons, equally spectacular from the wraparound flagstone veranda or the library, a soaring room with a vaulted ceiling, fieldstone walls, and windows on three sides.

The house has been in the Van Dorn family since the 1930s. Everett Archer Van Dorn summered here with his parents as a child. In 1988, he rearranged the house to establish an intimate bed-and-breakfast inn. Since there are only two bedrooms and the innkeeper lives in a separate suite with a private entrance, guests have the feeling of a private hideaway in the clouds.

This is not your ordinary inn; it is infused with the personality of the owner. Rooms are filled to the brim with family mementos, books, and collectibles. The stone library has a 5-foot-wide fireplace, three antique chandeliers, a pair of Victorian love seats, and a 6-foot-wide Tudor Revival oak table with matching sideboard and serving table, all inlaid with fine marquetry. The Victorian reading room has its own 4-foot fireplace, a Renaissance Revival lady's desk, a 7-foot Empire sofa, and a mix of Chinese and Victorian accessories. The Mandarin Sunset Reading Room is done with Chinese bookcases, a Tientsin Chinese rug, and a European tiled woodstove. There are lots of books, but you may have trouble concentrating on reading since floor-to-ceiling glass on two walls takes in the views over the valley. Antique stained-glass doors open to a hallway to the paneled guest rooms. They are named for the style of their beds—the Sleigh Room and the Brass Room.

WEB SITE: www.hilltopbb.com
INNKEEPER: Everett Van Dorn
ROOMS: 2 rooms, both with private bath, views, air-conditioning, phone
ON THE GROUNDS: 63 hilltop acres, flag-stone terrace with views of three states
RATES: $145, including full breakfast
CREDIT CARDS ACCEPTED: None
OPEN: Year-round
HOW TO GET THERE: Directions with reservations

Everett and his associate, Victoria Marks, serve a late-morning breakfast at 9:00 or 10:00 A.M. in the library or on the terrace. House specialties such as Grand Marnier French toast or quiche are presented on family vintage Staffordshire china with fine silver and crystal. In the evening, Everett offers sherry. It's a touch of gracious living in a rustic retreat like no other.

What's Nearby: West Cornwall is a picturesque village best known for the covered bridge leading into town across the Housatonic River; the river is a favorite with canoeists and anglers. There are several interesting little shops and a couple of good restaurants in town. Mohawk Mountain Ski Area is 3½ miles from the inn, and there is excellent hiking nearby on the Appalachian Trail and at Macedonia State Park and the 700-acre Northeast Audubon Center. Choice antiquing awaits nearby in the beautiful towns of the Litchfield Hills.

CAPTAIN STANNARD HOUSE

138 South Main Street
Westbrook 06498
(860) 399–4634
Fax: (860) 399–0072

▇ Named for the sea captain who built this fine clapboard home with a cupola in the mid-1880s, the Captain Stannard is an informal and relaxing place to be. There is a comfortable feeling of space in the public areas. The Great Room has a big billiards table with a Victorian lighting fixture above, plus a game table for chess or cards and a cozy library corner. Guests have a choice of two smaller lounges with TV, and a desk is set up with a phone and Internet access.

The large bright dining room, big enough to hold a grand piano in the corner, has tables for two, four, or six. You can choose to sit by the fireplace or at the window with views of the grounds while you enjoy some of the house specialties, such as cheese baked strada or pineapple upside-down French toast with ham. The owners' collection of heirloom teacups is on display.

Two guest rooms are upstairs in the house, with six more in the attached barn. All have a mix of country furnishings, each one different. Seven have queen-size beds; the eighth offers twins. All are stocked with complimentary beverages and snacks.

Since the Brewster family arrived from Manhattan in 2004, they've done a lot with the outside as well as the interior of the inn. There's a brand new deck with rockers across the back of the house facing the lawn, the gardens have never looked better, there are umbrella tables and chairs beside a wishing pond, and the lawn has been opened up to be perfect grounds for croquet or bocce.

Guests also enjoy the fact that the beach is only a block away, and the innkeepers have passes, towels, and beach chairs available.

WEB SITE: www.stannardhouse.com

INNKEEPERS: Mary, Jim, and Kathryn Brewster

ROOMS: 8 rooms, all with private bath, clock radio, air-conditioning

ON THE GROUNDS: Back deck, double yard with a small pond and gardens

RATES: $125–$199, including full breakfast and afternoon snacks

CREDIT CARDS ACCEPTED: MasterCard, Visa

OPEN: Year-round

HOW TO GET THERE: Take Interstate 95 to exit 65, go south on Route 153 for ⁹⁄₁₀ mile, and then turn west on Route 1 and left on South Main Street.

What's Nearby: Westbrook, a village on the Connecticut shoreline, has its own town beach and is within a short drive to Hammonasset Beach State Park. It is a major boating center with six marinas, including Pilot's Point, the second largest in New England, accommodating 1,500 boats. Surrounding towns have choice antiquing, and large outlet shopping malls are located in Westbrook (Interstate 95, exit 64) and neighboring Clinton (I–95, exit 63). The many attractions of Essex and the Connecticut River Valley are also nearby (see page 5).

TALCOTT HOUSE

161 Seaside Avenue
Westbrook 06498
(860) 399–5020

■ Bright and breezy, this is a dream of a shingled beach house right across the road from Long Island Sound, with peerless water views. The look is simple but elegant, with high ceilings and a dramatic great room measuring 50 by 25 feet with fireplaces at either end. The room is painted a deep coral shade, with white accents and columns marking off the living and dining spaces. The look is clean and fresh, with floors polished to a shine and no frills or curtains to detract from the windows that run the length of the room.

A comfortable seating area groups sofas and chairs in front of one fireplace, and a grand piano and a TV can provide entertainment. The room is decorated with antiques and finds from the innkeeper's global travels.

One downstairs guest room has its own patio. Upstairs, every room has windows facing the water. They are comfortable and nicely appointed, but once again without frills. Windows have blinds that come down at night but don't take away from the daytime views.

Room 2 has a large bathroom and panoramic views. I liked Room 3, with a four-poster bed and a rocker facing the picture window. In fact, I liked almost everything about this inn, one of the few places in Connecticut where you can be directly on the water.

What's Nearby: See What's Nearby on page 46.

WEB SITE: www.talcotthouse.com

INNKEEPER: Lucy Bingham

ROOMS: 4 rooms, all with private bath, ocean view

ON THE GROUNDS: Patio facing Long Island Sound, with a small beach directly across the street

RATES: $175–$225, including continental breakfast

CREDIT CARDS ACCEPTED: MasterCard, Visa, American Express

OPEN: April through September

HOW TO GET THERE: Take Interstate 95 to exit 65, follow Route 153 south to the town green, turn right on Route 1, proceed for 9/10 mile, and turn left onto Seaside Avenue. The inn is the last house on the right.

WELCOME INN

433 Essex Road (Route 153)
Westbrook 06498
(860) 399–2500
Fax: (860) 399–1840

This snug Victorian farmhouse, built in 1895, was once part of a strawberry farm and still has a cozy country feel. Owner Helen Spence has created a pleasant, relaxed atmosphere.

Guests gather in the bright bay-windowed common room to enjoy the many magazines and games or sip a glass of sherry in front of the fireplace. When they settle in front of the TV set or use the VCR, popcorn is often an added attraction. Lace curtains at the windows, classic New England Hitchcock furniture, built-in pine hutches, and a china cabinet displaying pottery and family antiques make the dining room a perfect setting for the country breakfast served from 9:00 to 10:00 A.M. Fruit from local farms and homemade baked goods are on the menu. On warm days, breakfast is often served on the outside deck. Complimentary soft drinks and snacks are always available in the common room.

WEB SITE: www.welcomeinnbandb.com

INNKEEPER: Helen P. Spence

ROOMS: 4 guest rooms (1 can be combined with an additional room to become a suite), all with TV, phone, air-conditioning, clock radio; 3 with private bath

ON THE GROUNDS: Deck, garden, lawn for badminton or volleyball

RATES: $99–$165, including full breakfast weekends, continental breakfast weekdays; refreshments; and beach passes

CREDIT CARDS ACCEPTED: MasterCard, Visa, American Express

OPEN: Year-round

HOW TO GET THERE: Take Interstate 95 to exit 65 and proceed a short distance north on Route 153, or take Route 9 to exit 3 and drive south on Route 153.

Bedrooms are small but nicely done, a mix of Victorian and country, with flowery wallpapers, and lacy curtains, pine pieces, or a four-poster bed. Room 3 is the largest, furnished with two beds, a rocker, and a wicker settee. It can become a suite combined with the adjacent bedroom, an ideal setup for two couples or a family. You'll find a split of wine and candles waiting in your room.

In summer, the inn supplies free beach passes so you can take advantage of Westbrook's location by the sea.

What's Nearby: See What's Nearby on page 46.

CHESTER BULKLEY HOUSE

184 Main Street
Wethersfield 06109
(860) 563–4236
Fax: (860) 257–8266

■ This handsome white-brick Greek Revival home dating from 1830 puts you in the historic district of Old Wethersfield, a gem of a community, settled in 1634 and with more than 150 homes built before 1850.

Inside are wide pine floors, hand carved woodwork, and lots of period antiques. The parlor welcomes with a love seat and two armchairs facing the fireplace. On the floor is a floral Oriental carpet in tones of pink, gold, and beige. Tea is served here each afternoon on a lowboy set with a lovely china teapot and matching cups.

The dining room also has a fine Oriental rug and a fireplace that glows warmly on chilly mornings. Guests are seated at a large mahogany table for eight or a smaller table in front of two side windows. On one wall is a claw-foot mahogany buffet; opposite is a nice grandfather clock.

WEB SITE: www.chesterbulkleyhouse.com

INNKEEPER: Tom Aufiero

ROOMS: 5 rooms, all with phone, clock radio, robes; 3 with private bath; 2 with shared bath

ON THE GROUNDS: Patio

RATES: $95–$125, including full breakfast and afternoon tea.

CREDIT CARDS ACCEPTED: MasterCard, Visa, American Express, Discover

OPEN: Year-round

HOW TO GET THERE: Take Interstate 91 to exit 26. At the stop sign at the end of the ramp, turn right from the south or left from the north. Turn left again on Main Street. The inn is the fourth house on the left.

Breakfast, served from 7:00 to 10:00 A.M. at guests' convenience, usually consists of juice, fruits, fresh baked muffins, and a hot dish. Among the inn specialties are Finnish pancakes topped with sliced bananas, strawberries, and blueberry sauce and cornflake-dipped French toast.

Each guest room has its own ambience. One is furnished with a French dark mahogany queen-size bed and has a soft mauve color scheme; another is done in blues and has a matching double bed and dresser with an interesting inlaid pattern. The largest bedroom, decorated in beige and light green, offers a handsome king-size pineapple post bed.

Bathrobes are provided for guests who occupy one of the two front rooms sharing a bath. One is done in pink and blue Laura Ashley prints and has an iron double bed, while the other is decorated with beige and burgundy print wallpaper and provides two mahogany sleigh beds. A comfortable upstairs common room beckons with a TV, books, and magazines.

The inn is just across the street from the town's most famous historic homes and within a stroll of the Wethersfield Cove, an inlet off the Connecticut River and a beautiful walk at sunset.

What's Nearby: Wethersfield is one of the oldest towns in Connecticut; the Webb-Deane-Stevens Museum offers the chance to tour three prize eighteenth-century homes. More history is found at the Wethersfield Historical Society Museum and archives; at the society's Hurbut-Dunham House, a Georgian circa 1790; and at the Cove Warehouse, which exhibits local maritime history. Wethersfield also borders Hartford and its major attractions, including the Mark Twain House, the oldest statehouse in America, and the Wadsworth Atheneum, one of New England's finest art museums.

HUMMINGBIRD HILL

891 Main Street South
Woodbury 06798
(203) 263–3733

■ "I want people to take off their shoes, put their feet up, and feel at home," says innkeeper Sharon Simmons. With a hostess like Sharon to welcome you, and dozens of antiques shops just down the road, an enjoyable stay is all but guaranteed at Hummingbird Hill.

The red clapboard house on the hill and its barn-style garage look as if they've been here forever, but the home was actually built in 1953. The homey living room has comfortable seating and a piano. It is painted an airy white with soft blue accenting the fireplace. Just outside is a heated porch overlooking the gardens, delightful most of the year.

The leafy hills behind the house are in view through the bay window of the attractive dining room, done

E-MAIL: hummingbird@wave-length.net

INNKEEPER: Sharon Simmons

ROOMS: 2 rooms with shared bath, each with robes, phone, clock radio

ON THE GROUNDS: Porch, patio, 1¼-acre grounds, perennial gardens

RATES: $90–$120, including continental breakfast

CREDIT CARDS ACCEPTED: MasterCard, Visa

OPEN: Year-round

HOW TO GET THERE: From Interstate 84 take exit 15 to Southbury, drive north on Route 6 into Woodbury, turn right onto Scuppor Road, and right again into the driveway. The inn is 3³⁄₁₀ miles from exit 15.

with red and white hunt print wallpaper. Fresh fruit from local farms and homemade pastries start the day right.

One of the two bedrooms has pastel striped wallpaper, a white iron king-size bed, and soft pouf curtains. The second room offers twin beds, green and white curtains and spreads, and wallpaper in a coordinated floral print. Robes are provided for using the shared bath.

Sharon turned her family home into a bed-and-breakfast when she was widowed in 1998, and she genuinely enjoys having company, gladly sharing tips about local shops, restaurants, and scenic drives. It is her warmth that makes a stay in this modest home so special.

What's Nearby: Woodbury is known as the antiques capital of Connecticut, with dozens of shops lining the main street, Route 6. If you can tear yourself away from the shops, you'll find a prize garden at the Glebe House Museum, walking trails at the Flanders Nature Center, and tennis or skiing at the Woodbury Ski and Racquet Club. All of the charming villages of the Litchfield Hills are within an easy drive.

ELIAS CHILD HOUSE

60 Perrin Road
Woodstock 06281
(860) 974–9836; (877) 974–9836
Fax: (860) 974–1541

■ What a pretty picture this country charmer makes: horses in the pasture, and a dark clapboard farmhouse, circa 1714, rimmed by a low stone wall. Inside you'll find the original floors, paneling and wainscoting, twelve-over-twelve windows, and nine fireplaces. The two walk-in cooking hearths and a beehive oven are not just for show. MaryBeth often does open-hearth cooking demonstrations, and she bakes the inn's delicious bread in that oven.

The living room is cozy, with a brick fireplace rimmed with soft green wood, a homey ruffled sofa, wing chairs, a TV, and lots of books and family photos.

Walk farther to find the inn's real delight, the Keeping Room, a great room with beams and the huge open hearth where guests are invited to participate in the cooking demonstrations held in cooler weather. A sofa, rockers, a wooden love seat, and a high-back "settle" provide plenty of comfortable seating. Books and magazines are piled on a unique coffee table, fashioned from an old three-seater outhouse seat. There's a churn where the hostess makes her own whipped cream, and an ice box where a colonial menu is posted. When I visited, it listed "cheese bread, ham, ginger yams with apples, lavender cake with whipped cream."

Outside is a screened porch with old wooden walls and a beamed high ceiling. Wicker seating, a chaise, and a rocker invite you to have a seat and enjoy the peaceful views of the pasture and Duke and Big Red, the two inn horses. And there's a good-size pool in view as well, quite a welcome sight on a warm summer day.

The dining room has its own open hearth. One big breakfast table seating eight and a smaller oval seating four are set with MaryBeth's great-grandmother's china. The expansive menu includes juice, fruit dishes such as peaches and blueberries in Amaretto sauce, French vanilla yogurt, omelettes, specialties such as cheese and egg casserole with sausage or caramelized French toast, and home-baked treats such as date, raisin, and apple bread or cherry cobbler. The choices offered are posted at night so you can leave your order for the next morning.

Upstairs, past the spinning wheel in the hallway, guest rooms are simply furnished country style, with lots of antiques and family mementos. In summer, rooms are graced with flowers from the garden. Each has a fireplace and a history.

The largest is Suite Aimee, named for the family's youngest daughter, Amy, with a filmy canopy bed and embroidered quilt and a small bed that belonged to MaryBeth's grandmother, Mabel. There are pictures of Mabel over the bed and on the vanity table. The crib in the passageway and the crazy quilt behind it are more family heirlooms. Both the bedroom and sitting room have fireplaces. The hearth is made of ballast brick that was carried for weight in empty sailing vessels to the colonies.

Polly's Room, with a pretty blue quilt on the bed and a fireplace framed with cranberry red wood, was named for Polly Denning, who married Elias Child in 1791 and lived in this house. Caroline's room, named for Elias's sister, has a three-quarter bed as well as a queen-size bed, both with winter coverlets from the 1800s.

WEB SITE: www.eliaschildhouse.com

INNKEEPER: MaryBeth Gorke-Felice and Tony Felice

ROOMS: 4 rooms, all with private bath, fireplace, air-conditioning, clock radio

ON THE GROUNDS: 47 acres, swimming pool, hammock, and chairs on grounds, walking trails in nearby forest

RATES: $100–$135, including full breakfast

CREDIT CARDS ACCEPTED: MasterCard, Visa, American Express, Discover

OPEN: Year-round

HOW TO GET THERE: Take Route 169 to South Woodstock, turn west on Route 171, and proceed 2½ miles to West Woodstock. Make a left onto Perrin Road; Elias Child House is ahead on the left.

Way out in the country, this inn is a true getaway. Have a dip in the pool, follow a walking trail in the forest nearby, or just sit back on the lawn and enjoy the peace and quiet, rare commodities in today's busy world.

What's Nearby: Woodstock is a charming hilltop town of old stone walls, towering shade trees, and historic houses, the earliest dating from 1686, others spanning three centuries. The sightseeing attraction in town is Roseland Cottage, a salmon pink Gothic-style home built in 1864 for a wealthy New York newspaper publisher who installed the best of everything, right down to a private bowling alley. The house, gardens, and barns are maintained by the Society for the Preservation of New England Antiquities. The Woodstock Fair, held on Labor Day weekend, has been a tradition for some 150 years. There's apple picking in fall and many beautiful drives. Route 169 through the center of town has been declared a National Scenic Highway. This is also choice antiquing country, especially in nearby Putnam. Historic Old Sturbridge Village, in Massachusetts, is about a twenty-minute drive away.

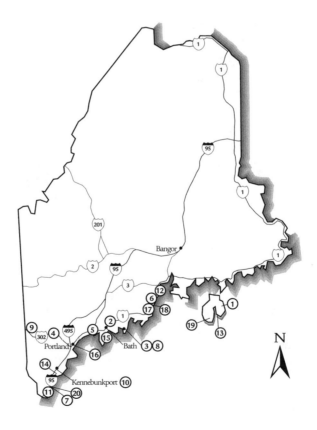

MAINE

Numbers on map refer to towns numbered below.

1. Bar Harbor, Atlantean Inn 56, Manor House Inn 57, The Ridgeway Inn 59
2. Bath, The Inn at Bath 60
3. Boothbay Harbor, Anchor Watch 61
4. Bridgton, The Noble House 63
5. Brunswick, Brunswick Bed and Breakfast 64
6. Camden, Nathaniel Hosmer Inn 66, Norumbega 67, Swan House 69
7. Cape Neddick, Cape Neddick House 70
8. East Boothbay, Five Gables Inn 71
9. Fryeburg, Admiral Peary House 73
10. Kennebunkport, Captain Fairfield Inn 74, Captain Lord Mansion 75, The Captain's Garden House 77, Inn at Harbor Head 78
11. Kittery, Portsmouth Harbor Inn and Spa 79
12. Lincolnville, Inn at Sunrise Point 80
13. Northeast Harbor, Maison Suisse 82
14. Ogunquit, Hartwell House 84, Trellis House 85
15. Phippsburg, Popham Beach Bed & Breakfast 86
16. Portland, Pomegranate Inn 87
17. Rockland, Captain Lindsey House Inn 89
18. Rockport, Rockport Harbor House 91
19. Southwest Harbor, Kingsleigh Inn 1904 92
20. York Harbor, Edwards' Harborside Inn 93

ATLANTEAN INN

11 Atlantic Avenue
Bar Harbor 04609
(207) 288–5703; (800) 722–6671
Fax: (207) 288–8092

■ Among the many lovely "cottages"
built in Bar Harbor in the early 1900s, this
one stands out, perhaps because it was built by a prominent Bar Harbor architect,
Frederick Savage, as his own home. In 2004, when Heidi Burnham and Gary Rich
decided to trade their engineering careers and life in a Boston suburb for a more sat-
isfying lifestyle, this was the house they fell in love with, and they've done it full justice.

The spacious living room manages to be both formal and welcoming. Gold patterned wallpaper and a gold sofa lit by the brass chandelier give the room a soft
glow, and green top swags on the tall windows add a dramatic touch. It holds one of
the inn's eight fireplaces.

Another fireplace is found in the dining
room, where guests are seated at several
small tables. Breakfast is a treat, a fresh fruit
dish followed by creations such as apple
Clafouti, asparagus and sun-dried tomato
goat cheese quiche, or raspberry-stuffed
baked French toast. Light refreshments are
served in the afternoon, and the butler's
pantry is stocked with snacks around the
clock.

The bedrooms have been done with
care, wall coverings carefully coordinated
with accent pillows and comforters. The
Wingwood Chamber on the first floor is a
favorite, with its own private entrance and
porch. It boasts a queen canopy bed, a fireplace, and a whirlpool for two in the bath.

Upstairs, Edgemere is a prime room,
with floral wallpapers and filmy white curtains, a spacious sitting area, a king-size
four-poster, and a fireplace. Baymeath has
two brass double beds and a blue color

WEB SITE: www.atlanteaninn.com

INNKEEPERS: Heidi Burnham and
Gary Rich

ROOMS: 6 rooms, 2 suites, all with
private bath and air-conditioning; 5
with fireplace; 4 with whirlpool, TV,
clock radio, iron, Wi-Fi

ON THE GROUNDS: ½ acre of lawn
and garden

RATES: Rooms $100–$150, suites
$140–$260, including full breakfast
and afternoon refreshments

CREDIT CARDS ACCEPTED: Master-
Card, Visa, American Express

OPEN: Year-round (except two suites
closed October 31 to May 31)

HOW TO GET THERE: Follow Route 3
south from Ellsworth all the way to
downtown Bar Harbor (15 miles),
and then take a left at the stop sign
onto Mt. Desert Street. Turn right
onto Main Street, then take the second left, Atlantic Avenue. The inn is
on the right.

scheme, while Talleyrand has a queen four-poster and attractive crewel-style print wallpaper and accents. Both also boast fireplaces.

On the third floor are two two-bedroom suites, tucked under cozy eaves, each with a whirlpool tub. Reef Point has an oversize bath with a two-person whirlpool beside the window with a skylight overhead,

The inn has lovely grounds and a garden with a pond and fountain. The location gives you the best of both worlds, on a quiet street just a short stroll from the center of town.

The innkeepers are not the only ones happy about their move to Maine. Their suburban pets are also thriving. Bessie, a cocker spaniel, and Ditto, fondly described as "a mutt," have established themselves as official greeters, while Petey, the cat, is more private, happily ruling the roost in the basement and the owners' quarters.

What's Nearby: Just a few minutes from Bar Harbor is Acadia National Park, one of the most beautiful spots in New England and a microcosm of the best of Maine—rockbound coastline, lakes and ponds, and Cadillac Mountain, the highest point on the eastern seaboard. The town of Bar Harbor is loaded with shops and scenic views of Frenchman's Bay.

MANOR HOUSE INN

106 West Street
Bar Harbor 04609
(207) 288–3759; (800) 437–0088
Fax: (207) 288–2974

■ There are some inns that manage to create a feeling of warmth and welcome as soon as you walk in the door. Manor House Inn is one of them. Built as a twenty-two-room, three-story mansion in 1887 and listed on the National Register of Historic Places, it has the grand spaces of the Victorian era and many authentic period pieces, but the soft and pretty decor makes you feel immediately comfortable and at home. As a bonus, it has one of the best locations in Bar Harbor, away from traffic but a short stroll from town.

An inspired choice of wallpapers helps create the inn's special ambience. The entrance foyer has colorful flowers on a light background that picks up the creamy white wood of the Victorian fireplace and the railing of the graceful staircase. The living-room paper is burgundy with lighter flowers, this time contrasting nicely with an ornate, mirrored white fireplace. The upholstered pieces are comfortable, a grand piano stands in the corner, and there's not a bit of distracting clutter.

WEB SITE: www.barharbormanorhouse.com

INNKEEPER: Stacey and Ken Smith

ROOMS: 9 rooms in the main house, 3 accommodations in the Chauffeur's Cottage, 4 rooms/suites in Acadia Cottage, and 2 individual cottages; all with private bath, clock, radio; some with fireplace

ON THE GROUNDS: Porch, patio, gazebo

RATES: $80–$250, including full breakfast and afternoon tea

CREDIT CARDS ACCEPTED: MasterCard, Visa, American Express, Discover

OPEN: Mid-April through late October

HOW TO GET THERE: Take Route 3 east onto Mount Desert Island and into Bar Harbor. Turn left onto West Street, which is the first cross street as you enter town, and the inn is a few blocks farther, on the right.

The deep red coordinates in color with a geometric pattern in the adjoining dining room. Beyond is the butler's pantry, where coffee, tea, and cookies are available all day and where the innkeepers lay out a lavish breakfast buffet each morning. Cranberry bread, muffins, cereals, juice, and fresh fruit are standards; the hot dish on the day I visited was French toast with a choice of homemade apple cider sauce or Maine maple syrup, and sausage. Breakfast can be enjoyed at the social dining-room table for eight or taken into the living room, where you can mingle or not as you please. On request, a tray can be brought to your room instead.

Rooms in the inn differ greatly in size and are labeled with numbers rather than names. The largest is Room 5, facing the front on the second floor, an enormous space with a tall carved and inlaid Victorian headboard, a fireplace, a marble-top dresser, two wicker chairs around a table, and a chaise in an alcove, thoughtfully set next to a good reading light. Here, as in all the rooms, the floral wallpaper has carefully coordinated borders, the rug has been chosen to complement the quilt, and the bed is piled with pillows.

Down the hall the rooms grow progressively smaller, but no less attractive. Room 4 has a fireplace, and Room 2 has a private sitting room across the hall. The inn sends out a floor plan so you can see exactly what you are getting. The third-floor rooms have cozy spaces created by the eaves and gables of the house. The front room is a sitting room with TV available to all guests.

On the grounds are two garden cottages and the original Chauffeur's Cottage, a romantic outpost where rooms have private entrances, cathedral ceilings, stained glass, and fireplaces. Suite A is the top choice, with a skylight over the bed, a love seat in front of the Franklin fireplace in the living room, and a totally private deck in the trees.

Acadia Cottage, a replica of a New England farmhouse, was added in 2000 at the back end of the property. An ideal romantic hideaway, the rooms and suites offer fireplaces and whirlpool tubs, as well as telephones and TV sets.

The wide, wicker-filled front porch of the main house is a good place to watch the world go by. And when you want to join the action, downtown Bar Harbor is five minutes away, so you never have to worry about where to "pahk your cah"! Both Stacey and Ken grew up in Bar Harbor, so they can steer you to all the best places.

What's Nearby: See What's Nearby on page 57.

THE RIDGEWAY INN

11 High Street
Bar Harbor 04609
(207) 288–9682; (800) 360–5226

Travelers who like the intimacy of a small inn will enjoy this 1884 Victorian home on a tree-lined street near town. The trim house with peaked roof and railed porch was totally refurbished in 1994, retaining nice features such as the bay window in the living room, now adorned with lace curtains, and the ornate mantels over the fireplaces in the living and dining rooms. Furnishings are country with Victorian accents and a few nice antiques, such as the working pump organ in the entry hall.

The living room has polished hardwood floors, a sectional couch, and Victorian-style chairs. The cheerful dining room has a definite country look. The buffet breakfast set out each morning offers home-baked breads, scones, cereals, and one hot dish such as pancakes, eggs, or quiche. Breakfast may be moved to the porch on pleasant summer days.

Afternoon refreshments are also served outside when the weather is fine. Otherwise, you can enjoy afternoon treats in front of the fire in the living room.

Guest rooms are named for classic old Bar Harbor cottages. Schooner Head has a wine and ivory color scheme, a nautical theme, and a small private deck. Rose Briar is romantic Victorian, featuring an iron bed, a wicker rocker, and a claw-foot tub in the bath. I've always liked the coziness of eaves, so I appreciate the Stanwood Room tucked

WEB SITE: www.theridgewayinn.com

INNKEEPERS: Jennifer and Andre Lozano

ROOMS: 3 rooms, 2 suites, all with private bath, clock, radio, air-conditioning

ON THE GROUNDS: Front porch

RATES: Rooms $45–$120, suites $70–$160, including buffet breakfast, afternoon refreshments

CREDIT CARDS ACCEPTED: Master-Card, Visa

OPEN: Year-round

HOW TO GET THERE: Take Interstate 95 north to Augusta. Follow Routes 1/3 to Ellsworth. From Ellsworth continue on Route 3 for 18 miles. Turn left at the stop sign to Mt. Desert Street (still Route 3), and make the third left onto High Street.

away on the third floor and done with a fresh blue and white color scheme. Greenway Court, the honeymoon suite, has a king-size bed, a sitting area furnished in wicker, and a bathroom with a two-person whirlpool bath, pedestal sink, and separate shower.

The inn's location is a big plus, on a quiet residential street but within easy walking distance of Bar Harbor's many shops and restaurants.

What's Nearby: See What's Nearby on page 57.

THE INN AT BATH

969 Washington Street
Bath 04530
(207) 443–4294; (800) 423–0964
Fax: (207) 443–4295

This 1810 Greek Revival home was built during Bath's heyday as a shipbuilding mecca. The parlors, dining room, and many guest rooms are properly elegant, but since innkeeper Elizabeth Knowlton took over in 2005, they have acquired a lot of fresh color, with new coats of paint and paintings on the wall.

The double parlor welcomes with a dark marble fireplace, pale walls, a rose-colored print sofa and crewel-covered wing chair, a lively patterned rug, and red and blue striped swags at the window.

The dining room, my favorite room in the house, has bold red walls with white trim and lots of plants at the windows. There's a grand chandelier over the table and a shell cabinet at the side showing off Elizabeth's grandmother's Deruta china collection. Guests are seated at the long, polished mahogany table for a full breakfast that begins with fresh fruit, homemade granola, and organic yogurt, followed by a hot entree. Among the appetizing selections are lemon-blueberry or orange–poppy seed pancakes, waffles with caramelized apples, a leek and chard frittata, and a green chile and cheese egg puff.

Two very nice guest rooms on the first floor have beamed ceilings, wide

WEB SITE: www.innatbath.com

INNKEEPER: Elizabeth Knowlton

ROOMS: 8 rooms, all with private bath, air-conditioning, TV, VCR, clock radio, and telephone; 2 with wood-burning fireplace; 2 with whirlpool bath; 3 with private entrance

ON THE GROUNDS: Porches, gardens, terrace

RATES: $125–$185, including full breakfast

CREDIT CARDS ACCEPTED: MasterCard, Visa, American Express, Discover

OPEN: Year-round

HOW TO GET THERE: Going northbound on Interstate 95, take exit 44 (formerly exit 6A), South Portland, onto Interstate 295 north. Continue to exit 28, Brunswick, and follow Route 1 north. Continue for about 11 miles to Bath, and follow the HISTORIC BATH exit sign. Drive underneath this sign and downhill 2 short blocks to a red light. Turn left at the light (the Kennebec River is now on your right) and travel north on Washington Street for ½ mile. The inn is a white clapboard house on the right. Parking is in the back. Turn right just beyond the inn sign onto North Street and make an immediate right into the parking area.

pine floorboards, and private entrances. They include the Garden Room, which is fully wheelchair accessible, and the East Room, with a wood-burning fireplace, a king-size bed that can become twins, and a sofa/daybed. These two rooms can be combined to form a suite, as can other rooms at the inn.

Upstairs are attractive rooms furnished with antiques, some with fireplaces.

A ground-level addition to the house has more modern amenities. Two rooms called the Fo'c'sle and the Captain's Cabin have been specially designed, each with low ceilings, beams, and a brick wall with a fireplace that can be seen from the bed or from the two-person, heated whirlpool bath, features not even dreamed of in those old shipbuilding days.

A very nice recent addition to the house is a stone terrace at the back and a lovely garden of annuals and perennials. The garden is one of Elizabeth's passions, so you can expect it to be better every year.

What's Nearby: The inn is in the picturesque historic district of Bath, a block from the Kennebec River and a short walk from shops and dining. The Maine Maritime Museum in Bath is a major attraction, and the Chocolate Church for the Arts presents a variety of evening entertainment throughout the year. Nearby towns such as Wiscasset are happy hunting grounds for antiquers, and neighboring Brunswick offers the attractive campus and museums of Bowdoin College (see page 66). Also close by are rugged Reid State Park and Popham Beach, one of the most beautiful beaches in Maine.

ANCHOR WATCH

9 Eames Road
Boothbay Harbor 04538
(207) 633–7565; 633–5319

■ The Burnt Island light flashes a welcome to this small sea captain's home with the best location in Boothbay Harbor, up the hill and

WEB SITE: www.anchorwatch.com

INNKEEPERS: Diane Campbell and Kathy Reed

ROOMS: 5 rooms, all with private bath, clock, radio; 4 with deck or porch and dazzling view; 1 with fireplace

ON THE GROUNDS: Lawn with benches and chairs, waterside patio, pier for fishing

RATES: $149–$164, including full breakfast

CREDIT CARDS ACCEPTED: Master-Card, Visa

OPEN: March through December

HOW TO GET THERE: From Route 1 take Route 27 south to Boothbay Harbor, follow Commercial Street to its dead end, and just before the end, turn left onto Eames Road.

away from the busy town but still within walking distance of everything. You can sit on the deck or the lawn, watch the lobster boats hauling their traps, or admire the sunset, safely above the crowds.

The reason for all the people in the town below is that Boothbay Harbor is the boating center of the central Maine coast, with many cruise boats tied up at the piers. One of the most popular outings is the daily trip to Monhegan Island on the *Balmy Days II*, captained by Bill Campbell, the son of innkeeper Diane Campbell. Diane, a former English teacher, first took in guests mostly as an accommodation for occasional passengers who needed a place to stay, but as she grew more enamored with innkeeping, she expanded a dormer and added private baths and decks. The improvements keep coming; for example, a deck with a view of the water for the Nereid Room. Now her daughter, Kathy, is helping with the innkeeping.

Each fresh, pretty room is named for a Monhegan ferryboat of the past and has dazzling ocean views. The furnishings are simple and comfortable, and all rooms offer stenciling, old trunks, quilts, and other country accessories. The Balmy Days on the first floor has a private water-view porch, a private entrance, and a TV.

May Archer on the second floor is especially appealing, with pink walls with a rose border, pink and white print curtains, and two wing chairs in a bay window looking out to sea. This room also has its own deck. The Gov. Douglas Room on the third floor has an expanded deck and a dormer wall covered by a painting of the same lighthouse you see out the window.

The small downstairs parlor provides a fireplace for cooler days. The long, narrow breakfast room is sunny year-round, with tables set along a wall of windows facing the sea. Diane did the wall stenciling to match the blue and white print valance. Her hearty breakfasts might mean main dishes of egg-and-cheese pie, apple crepes, or blueberry blintzes with raspberry sauce, served with muffins, fruit, and juice.

Landscaping on the property has added a path to the shore, a patio by the water, and a private pier. If all those views make you want to get out to sea, you'll get a bonus—guests receive a discount on tickets for the harbor tour on the boat *Novelty*.

What's Nearby: Lively Boothbay Harbor is the boating capital of midcoastal Maine, with lots of ways to go out to sea—including a not-to-be-missed day trip to rugged and beautiful Monhegan Island. Downtown will tempt you with shops and galleries and lots of dining places on the water.

THE NOBLE HOUSE

81 Highland Road
Bridgton 04009
(207) 647–3733; (888) 237–4880
Fax: (207) 647–3733

This big 1903 Queen Anne house with the interesting peaked roof has a prime location, on a hill across the road from sparkling Highland Lake. Guests have direct access to the lake from the inn's private beach, making this a special summer haven.

The house was originally built as a summer escape, but it has evolved into a year-round inn with a pleasant informal ambience. The Whelchels have kept the casual feel while upgrading the decor since they arrived in 2003.

The rooms are spacious, with a fireplace, books, and both a grand piano and an antique organ in the parlor and another fireplace in the formal dining room. Guests like to gather in the casual den, where there is a TV, VCR, complimentary soft drinks, and the "bottomless" cookie jar.

A buffet breakfast is served in the sunny breakfast room, with house specialties such as apple-stuffed Noble House crepes or Florentine pie with Parmesan and savory ham. On warm days, breakfast may move to the porch or, when there is a chill in the air, to the dining room in front of the fireplace.

Guest rooms ramble up and down stairs. Each is different; take your pick of four-poster, iron, brass, pine, or maple headboards. The Honeymoon Suite and the Library Suite on the second floor are special, each with a turret-style window as well as a porch. The Honeymoon Suite has a filmy canopy bed and a whirlpool tub. The Garden Room on the main floor has its own whirlpool tub and offers French doors leading to a patio. Several accommodations are suitable for families. The Staples Suite, also opening to the patio, is especially family-friendly. It has a bunk nook complete with bedtime storybooks, and lawn games are available just outside the door.

Computer-minded guests will be glad to know that the inn offers a guest desktop

WEB SITE: www.noblehousebb.com

INNKEEPERS: Rick and Julie Whelchel

ROOMS: 9 rooms, 3 suites, all with private bath, air-conditioning, clock, hair dryer, high-speed wireless Internet access; some with whirlpool and porch or patio. Some suites also offer TV, DVD, VCR, and CD players, and robes.

ON THE GROUNDS: 4 hillside acres, Adirondack chairs, veranda, picnic table, gas grill

RATES: Rooms $99–$160, suites $120–$207, including full breakfast, use of canoe

CREDIT CARDS ACCEPTED: MasterCard, Visa

OPEN: Year-round

HOW TO GET THERE: From Interstate 95 take exit 48 (formerly exit 8) in Portland, and drive west on Route 302 about an hour to Bridgton. Turn left at the traffic lights, follow Main Street through town, and turn right on Highland Road at the park. The inn is ¼ mile farther on the right.

computer and cable modem outlets for laptops, as well as high-speed wireless access through the inn.

What's Nearby: Bridgton is a small town in the Lakes Region of western Maine, with Long Lake and big Sebago Lake nearby. Golf and tennis are available at the Bridgton Highlands Country Club, and antiques and crafts shops in town are a short walk from the inn. In winter, skiing at Shawnee Peak at Pleasant Mountain is 5 miles away. The many outlet stores and White Mountain scenery in North Conway, New Hampshire, is a half-hour drive. This is a great area for backcountry drives through tiny villages; the innkeepers will gladly offer suggestions.

BRUNSWICK BED AND BREAKFAST

165 Park Row
Brunswick 04011
(207) 729–4914; (800) 299–4914
(outside Maine, for reservations only)

■ Quilts old and new brighten the walls all around this hospitable inn overlooking the town green, nicely situated within walking distance of both town shops and the Bowdoin College campus.

The living room, painted a pleasing yellow and warmed with a fireplace, is filled with light from floor-to-ceiling triple-hung windows. A pair of navy blue sofas and a couple of rockers are sociably placed around a big coffee table piled with books and magazines. The breakfast room offers five tables set for two or four and its own fireplace for chilly days. In summer a farmers' market brightens the Brunswick scene; in winter ice skaters are in motion on the

WEB SITE: www.brunswickbnb.com

INNKEEPERS: Mercie and Steve Normand

ROOMS: 14 rooms (8 in main house, 6 in carriage house), garden cottage; all with private bath, air-conditioning, wireless Internet access, clock, radio, telephone, robes; carriage house rooms, suites, and cottage have TV

ON THE GROUNDS: Picket fence, small yard, wide front porch, rear deck, gardens

RATES: $120–$230, including full breakfast

CREDIT CARDS ACCEPTED: Master-Card, Visa, American Express

OPEN: Year-round, except January

HOW TO GET THERE: From Interstate 95 take exit 28, Brunswick, following Pleasant Street into town. Turn right onto Maine Street, left onto Fitch Place (right before railroad tracks), and then left onto Park Row, a small street that curves to parallel Maine.

artificial pond. In warm weather, everyone tends to congregate on the front porch to continue watching the action.

Breakfasts are usually served from 8:00 to 9:00 A.M. A meal might include Maine blueberry cornmeal pancakes with bacon, or baked eggs with raspberry streusel coffee cake. Fresh fruit, homemade granola, yogurt, and cereals are always available.

The inn was expanded in 2004 with the renovation of the carriage house at the rear of the property. It adds six bright and airy guest rooms with lots of interesting angles and spaces, plus two new sitting rooms for guests, a kitchenette, and a meeting room.

The rooms in both buildings are carefully color coordinated, decorated with a blend of antiques, original artwork, and Maine-made furniture. Room 7, a suite tucked beneath the dormers on the third floor in the original inn, has cozy angled ceilings, a king-size iron bed, a skylight, a claw-foot tub plus a shower in the bath, and a spacious sitting area with a sleeper sofa and a TV. Room 14 in the carriage house is another interesting space, with lofty ceilings and a skylight.

One of the most delightful spaces at the inn is the cottage nestled in the gardens. It has a private deck, a cathedral ceiling, a queen-size bed, a living-dining area and a kitchen, and a spiral stair to a sleeping loft with two twin beds.

The Normands became innkeepers almost by accident. Mercie decided to come along in 1990 when her husband, Steve, was looking for in-town space for his architectural practice. When they were shown this pretty old house in the historic district, they were smitten. The house had nicely divided living space for the family, and with teenage children who were old enough to help out, they reasoned they could turn it into a bed-and-breakfast and still continue their careers. The children are grown now, and Mercie is a full-time innkeeper. She is also an avid quilter, thrilled to have large walls to fill with the quilts she loves—and guests are invariably delighted with the colorful results.

What's Nearby: Brunswick offers strolls along the handsome campus of Bowdoin College and past many historic homes. There are several interesting museums on campus, and in summer Bowdoin is host to the Maine State Music Theater. Many other events are held at Brunswick's Thomas Point Beach, including the annual Maine Festival, featuring state performing artists and artisans. Just a few miles to the north in Bath, the Maine Maritime Museum celebrates the state's seafaring heritage; to the south in Freeport, L. L. Bean and outlet bargains beckon.

NATHANIEL HOSMER INN

4 Pleasant Street
Camden 04843
(207) 236–4012; (800) 423–4012

■ With a little bit of Williamsburg and a little bit of Shaker influence, this small charmer, circa 1810, has an authentic Early American aura plus the best location in Camden—on a quiet residential block just a short stroll from all the action in the harbor.

The inn was once two houses, as you can see from the double doors in front, and it boasts many rooms and an amazing seventy-two doors and fifty-two windows. The pine armoire in the front sitting room is among many interesting antiques and reproductions throughout the house, and there are lovely hand-colored etchings of New England scenes on the walls. Open-hearth fireplaces, wing and Windsor chairs, candle stands, and original wide floorboards add to the colonial feel.

I was particularly taken with the dining room, which has wide-board floors, its own fireplace, and a handcrafted tin chandelier over the table lending a soft glow to breakfasts. A bountiful breakfast includes juice, fruits, pastries, yogurt, and granola, along with a daily hot dish such as crème brûlée French toast, Greek frittatas, or Aussie omelettes made with mushrooms, cheddar, and shrimp.

The bedrooms vary in size, but all have a colonial look, with wood-framed windows

WEB SITE: www.nathanielhosmerinn .com

INNKEEPERS: Deborah and Glenn Eichel

ROOMS: 7 rooms, all with private bath, clock; 5 with air-conditioning

ON THE GROUNDS: Patio, gardens

RATES: $95–$175, including full breakfast

CREDIT CARDS ACCEPTED: Master-Card, Visa

OPEN: Year-round

HOW TO GET THERE: Coming from the south, take Route 1 into Camden; 1 short block past the flashing red light, turn right onto Wood Street, continue for 1 block, and then turn right onto Pleasant Street. The inn is on the left.

with simple white curtains and handsome quilts on the beds, and all are light and bright. They offer a choice of twin, queen-size, and king-size beds. The Captain Jesse Room on the first floor is appealing, with an old poster queen-size canopy bed, an antique rocker, and four sunny windows. Elizabeth's Classroom on the second floor was once the schoolroom where Miss Elizabeth Hosmer taught Camden children. Her bookshelves now hold books for your reading pleasure.

The inn, which is on the National Register of Historic Places, is filled with stories from the past. The Eichels enjoy having guests who share their appreciation for the history of the house.

What's Nearby: The mountains meet the sea in Camden, making for a magnificent harbor setting. You can board a picturesque windjammer in the harbor, browse in dozens of shops in town, or head for Camden Hills State Park, where hiking is exceptional. In winter, the Camden Snow Bowl on Ragged Mountain offers skiing with an ocean view. Art lovers should take the short drive to Rockland for the Farnsworth Museum.

NORUMBEGA

61 High Street
Camden 04843
(207) 236–4646; (800) 363–4646
Fax: (207) 236 0824

■ They say this is the most photographed building on the coast of Maine, and it is easy to see why. Norumbega is a storybook castle by the sea, an 1886 Victorian complete with a peaked three-story round turret, seven fireplaces, and enough balconies and terraces with ocean views to please any princess.

The massive fieldstone-and-shingle home with slate roof, listed on the National Register of Historic Places, was a private residence until 1984, when it was restored as a luxury bed-and-breakfast.

The golden oak and mahogany woodwork downstairs is phenomenal, from rich paneling to floors inlaid with intricate geometric designs. The elegantly furnished living room has an ornate fireplace (one of four on the main floor), period furnishings, and windows looking out to sea. The furnishings give the feeling of a grand English country house.

Breakfast is served either in the front dining room or the conservatory. The dining room, originally a sitting room, has tables spaced around a baby grand piano that is topped with an oversize vase holding seasonal arrangements. Breakfast includes

WEB SITE: www.norumbegainn.com

INNKEEPER: Joann Reuillard

ROOMS: 11 rooms, 2 suites, all with private bath, king-size beds, phone with dataport, clock, robes; some with TV; 1 suite with whirlpool bath

ON THE GROUNDS: 4 acres; patio with ocean view; landscaped lawns with two gazebos, cutting garden, croquet court

RATES: Rooms $99–$340, suites $250–$475, including full breakfast, pantry privileges, and hors d'oeuvres at evening cocktail hour; dinner available for inn guests

CREDIT CARDS ACCEPTED: MasterCard, Visa, American Express, Discover

OPEN: Year-round

HOW TO GET THERE: The inn is on Route 1 about 1½ miles north of Camden, near the top of the hill on the right.

fresh fruits, home-baked breads and muffins, a variety of egg dishes, and breakfast meats. Dinner is also available here on request for inn guests.

The bedrooms, appropriately named for English castles and palaces, are spacious and airy, with striped or floral wallpapers, and all have king-size beds. Many have private terraces, but all have access to the balconies that border each floor.

Each room boasts its own special attractions. Warwick has both a fireplace and a prime water view from a bay window. In the bath are a modern shower as well as an old-fashioned claw-foot tub. The Library Suite houses the original library of the house, including an upper balcony of fine mahogany. The Arundel Room on the garden level is decorated in burnt sienna tones and has brick and stone archways. The king-size bed is a four-poster, and features include a TV, a large Jacuzzi, and a private deck overlooking the gardens.

Though they look out at the Camden hills rather than the sea, I'm especially fond of the rooms in the round turret of the house, such as Sandringham, the former master bedroom, with a bay window and fireplace, and Windsor, decorated in a light blue, and with a four-poster bed set in the turret.

But if money were no object, I would immediately settle into the Penthouse Suite, tucked away up a spiral staircase nestled under the eaves and nicely done in soft green florals. The suite provides four-way panoramic views from a private deck as well as the spacious living room. The bathroom offers an oversize tub and a marble shower, and the living room is equipped with a fireplace, a TV, and a minifridge stocked with soda and water. There's also a foldout couch, but who would want company in this romantic hideaway?

What's Nearby: See What's Nearby on page 67.

SWAN HOUSE

49 Mountain Street
Camden 04843
(207) 236–8275; (800) 207–8275

■ This intimate Victorian, circa 1870, has a good location, nicely situated at the foot of Mount Battie, away from busy Route 1 but within an easy walk downhill to Camden's shops and harbor. The rooms are furnished with nice antiques and interesting small touches, such as a coffee table made from a deer sleigh in the formal parlor. The cozy library offers a needlepoint Monopoly game board under glass on top of a hand-crafted Amish table.

Lyn and Ken Kohl bought the inn in 1993—a natural transition, they say, since she was in the hospitality business with Hyatt and he dealt with customer service. They think of the little things that make guests happy, like having one breakfast table set aside in a living-room alcove for those who don't wish to socialize in the morning.

WEB SITE: www.swanhouse.com

INNKEEPERS: Lyn and Ken Kohl

ROOMS: 5 rooms, 1 suite, all with private bath, phone, clock, radio, free wireless broadband Internet access

ON THE GROUNDS: Gazebo, hiking trail to Mount Battie

RATES: $110–$175, including full breakfast and afternoon refreshments

CREDIT CARDS ACCEPTED: MasterCard, Visa, but cash preferred

OPEN: Year-round

HOW TO GET THERE: From Route 1 continue through the town of Camden, and turn left past the town at the junction with Route 52, Mountain Street. The inn is 3½ blocks up the hill on the right.

Incidentally, the name of the inn comes from the family named Swan, who built the house. Guest rooms named for various swans, like Leda, Whistler, and the Swan Lake Loft, are simply a pleasant bit of whimsy by the innkeepers.

The day starts at the inn with breakfast in a delightful glass-enclosed sun-porch that stretches across the front of the house. Juice, homemade granola, fresh fruit, home-baked muffins and coffee cakes, and a hot dish such as sour cream blueberry pancakes with bacon or sausage compose the usual menu.

The room decor is country, with a few Victorian accents. There are two guest rooms in the main house, but the choicest lodgings are the four in the Cygnet Annex, a converted carriage house behind the inn. All of these are fantasy hideaways, each with a private entrance, but I give the prize to the Trumpeter Room, an aerie with a four-poster bed, a skylight, vaulted ceiling, and a private deck looking out into the woods.

The shady gazebo on the grounds is the perfect place to relax after a day of sight-seeing.

What's Nearby: See What's Nearby on page 67.

CAPE NEDDICK HOUSE

200 Route 1, P.O. Box 70
Cape Neddick 03902
(207) 363–2500
Fax: (207) 363–4499

This is an inn with a secret. The Victorian farmhouse looks inviting enough, with a flower-festooned porch and front gardens, but you must come inside, away from busy Route 1, to discover the hidden treasure. At the rear of the house is a deck overlooking ten quiet, totally private, wooded acres and a growing collection of gardens.

The Goodwin family has lived in this house since it was built in 1885. One of the buildings on the property, now a shop, used to be the Cape Neddick Post Office, oper-ated by the Goodwins for seventy-five years.

The eighth generation, Dianne and John, opened the house as a bed-and-breakfast in 1983, and Dianne's friendliness and exten-sive knowledge of the area is another rea-son why Cape Neddick House is a special place to stay. I had been to York several times before, but Dianne gave me a widened perspective and led me to inland pleas-ures I had overlooked, such as the wonderful view from the top of Mt. Agamenticus.

The feeling of this inn is simple, cheerful country at its best, whether you settle by the fire in the living room, gather by the woodstove in the kitchen, or head for that great deck out back. Bedrooms are named for New England states. Vermont is done in country oak, Connecticut has a songbird theme, while spacious Maine is deco-rated with garden wallpaper in watercolor hues and offers two double beds. The

WEB SITE: www.capeneddickhouse .com

INNKEEPER: Dianne Goodwin

ROOMS: 4 rooms, 1 suite, all with private bath and air-conditioning; suite with fireplace

ON THE GROUNDS: Deck overlooking 10 acres of lawn, gardens, and woodland

RATES: $85–$175, including full breakfast

CREDIT CARDS ACCEPTED: None

OPEN: Year-round

HOW TO GET THERE: Take Interstate 95 northbound to exit 7 (formerly exit 4), York-Ogunquit (last exit before toll), and turn left at the light to Route 1 north. The inn is 3½ miles ahead on the left.

Massachusetts–Rhode Island Suite is the place for special occasions, with a tall Victorian headboard and a working fireplace. I'm partial to New Hampshire because it overlooks the woodlands in back.

Breakfast in the congenial dining room means treats such as fresh fruit garnished with just-picked flowers and herbs, cinnamon popovers with wild raspberry jam, blueberry cheese tortes, and strawberry scones. A bouquet from the garden always graces the table in season.

Dianne shares some of her recipes in woodstove cooking classes where she teaches how to make soups and dishes like feta and spinach stuffed bread and her own "rocky coast candy." She also gladly shares seeds from her gardens, where the plantings include old-fashioned blooms like cosmos and cleome, Oriental lilies, and special areas, such as a butterfly garden.

Inspired by the arrival of her first grandchild, Dianne's grandmother's garden is a delight, with stepping stones, hand- and footprints, and blueberries for picking, meant for grown-ups and little ones to share.

What's Nearby: Cape Neddick is part of York (see page 95). The location of the inn makes it convenient for hiking or horseback riding at Mt. Agamenticus, and Cape Neddick Beach is a great area for beachcombing. Route 1 will take you to nearby pleasures such as the Rachel Carson Wildlife Sanctuary, the Kittery outlets, craft and antiques shopping, and the majestic beauty of the Marginal Way in neighboring Ogunquit.

FIVE GABLES INN

107 Murray Hill Road
P.O. Box 335
East Boothbay 04544
(207) 633–4551; (800) 451–5048

■ This rambling, gabled hotel on a quiet cove of Linekin Bay is the last remaining nineteenth-century seaside hotel in the Boothbays. Formerly known as the Forest House, it was nicely restored with a mix of nostalgia and modern amenities in 1989 and took on new life as the Five Gables Inn. Tranquillity, prime water views, and a delicious breakfast are among its many lures.

The look is sophisticated country. A big common room still has its original wood floors, now adorned with Oriental rugs. A sitting area with wing chairs and shelves of books and games is near the fireplace, while other comfortable chairs are placed at the window to take in the view. A long sideboard serves as a divider for the front section of the room, where tables for six or eight are set for breakfast.

Innkeeper Mike Kennedy, a trained chef, sets out a generous buffet of fresh fruit;

WEB SITE: www.fivegablesinn.com

INNKEEPERS: Mike and De Kennedy

ROOMS: 16 rooms, all with private bath, phone, clock, radio; 5 with fireplace; 15 with water view

ON THE GROUNDS: Large wraparound porch, garden

RATES: $140–$210, including full breakfast and afternoon tea

CREDIT CARDS ACCEPTED: Master-Card, Visa

OPEN: Mid-May through October

HOW TO GET THERE: Take Route 1 to Route 27 and continue to Route 96 through East Boothbay. Turn right at the yellow light on Murray Hill Road. The inn is ½ mile farther on the right.

homemade granola; assorted breads and muffins; hot main dishes such as frittata, quiche, blueberry-stuffed French toast, or pancakes; as well as one hot side dish such as roasted potatoes or blueberry crisp. On summer days it can be enjoyed on the wide wraparound porch looking out at the cove.

Mike was a chef, contractor, and occasional actor in Atlanta before moving north. De Kennedy, who left the corporate world, has enjoyed the chance to use her talent for decorating. Her hand-crocheted afghans lend a personal touch to many rooms. Rooms are immaculate, done with sheer white swag curtains at the windows and accessories such as patchwork quilts, straw hats over the bed, and mirrors in old picture frames. Two are furnished with Shaker-style pencil-post beds, and all but one offer views of the bay.

The rooms vary in size from quite small to spacious. Room 14, the largest room, is under the cozy eaves on the third floor, with armchairs flanking the fireplace and a king-size brass-and-iron bed. I stayed in Room 6, a cheerful, smaller, second-floor room done in blue prints with a red wing chair and a handsome pine chest. All the rooms provide a comfortable sitting area with a reading lamp, an amenity I always appreciate.

There's much to do in this area, and Boothbay Harbor is only 3½ miles away, but this is a spot where you will be tempted to just relax. The hammock on the porch is a delicious place to laze, the yard has seating in a lovely garden, and a gazebo beckons at the water's edge.

Anyone who is thinking of changing careers ought to have a talk with the Kennedys, who did so in style. When they decided to take a midlife break, they signed on as crew members on a 51-foot yacht in French Polynesia for two months, and then spent six months backpacking through Southeast Asia before settling on a new lifestyle as keepers of an inn by the sea.

What's Nearby: Only a few miles from the bustle of Boothbay Harbor, East Boothbay is a quiet boater's haven, ideal for bicycling. The bay and a public dock are across the way from the inn; excellent dining is just down the road.

ADMIRAL PEARY HOUSE

9 Elm Street
Fryeburg 04037
(207) 935–3365; (800) 237–8080

■ That's *the* Admiral Peary, famed for his North Pole explorations, and he really lived here for several years when he was town surveyor before he set out on his adventures. Now the house is a gracious oasis, just minutes away from the bustle and shops of North Conway, New Hampshire.

This is a large home, filled with nooks and crannies, but life revolves around the big country kitchen/sitting room with its woodstove, barn-board walls, and beamed ceiling. A sitting area with a comfortable sofa flanks a massive brick fireplace and an armoire hiding a TV set. A pool table is nearby.

Guests are seated at several small tables with Windsor chairs for breakfast , which might include fresh fruit, muffins, breads, and main courses such as ginger pancakes with pear sauce or a frittata of mushrooms and prosciutto.

Outside is a big screened porch with cheerful wicker furnishings.

The front of the house, which dates from 1865, has a sitting room with a marble fireplace, a formal dining room, and a greenhouse alcove.

The guest rooms upstairs are nicely done with pretty quilts on the beds and comfortable seating. The Jo, named for Peary's wife, Josephine, is cozy, with a slanted roof and nooks and crannies. The Henson, honoring Peary's exploring companion, Matthew Henson, is a sunny room facing southwest; the Pathfinder has splendid garden views; and the North Pole, the most spacious guest room, has western vistas of Stark Mountain. The secluded Admiral's Quarters at the front of the house is a more formal room with a tall four-poster bed. Inuit, a minisuite reached via a private staircase, offers a gas-fired stove for chilly evenings.

WEB SITE: www.admiralpeary house.com

INNKEEPERS: Hilary Jones and David Schlottmann

ROOMS: 7 rooms, all with private bath, clock radio or CD player, Wi-Fi

ON THE GROUNDS: 7 acres, lawn garden, screened porch

RATES: $95–$169, including full breakfast

CREDIT CARDS ACCEPTED: Master Card, Visa, American Express, Discover

OPEN: Year-round

HOW TO GET THERE: From Route 302 take the street directly across from the post office and proceed to number 9, a sprawling white house on the right.

The most interesting history belongs to the Snow Baby, which is named for Peary's Daughter, Marie, who was born in the Arctic. The innkeepers think that this room, with its handsome archway, may well have been young Robert Peary's room on his return from Bowdoin College.

What's Nearby: Fryeburg, the oldest town in the White Mountains, is also the home of one of New England's oldest and most famous country fairs each October. This quaint and peaceful town is just 6 miles from the action and outlet stores of North Conway, New Hampshire, and convenient to downhill skiing. In summer you can hike in the mountains or go canoeing and swimming in the Saco River.

CAPTAIN FAIRFIELD INN

8 Pleasant Street
P.O. Box 3089
Kennebunkport 04046
(207) 967–4454; (800) 322–1928
Fax: (207) 967–8537

■ Capt. James Fairfield was one of the wealthy nineteenth-century sea captains whose fine homes now grace the shady streets of Kennebunkport. His 1813 mansion, listed on the National Register of Historic Places, has become a warm inn where today's guests feel right at home. Step into the pretty parlor, which is decorated with soft blue wainscoting and trim and pleated floral treatments at each window. A camelback sofa and wing chairs invite you to relax in front of the fireplace, admire the handsome mahogany highboy in the corner, chat with other guests, or look through one of the books stacked on the coffee table. You are welcome to take a book to the garden and relax under the big elm trees.

Breakfast is served in the sunny dining room, where antique Persian rugs adorn the polished hardwood floors and original art work adorns the walls. Full breakfasts are served beginning at 8:30 A.M. They include such memorable dishes as an Omelet Fairfield with sausage, spinach, sautéed mushrooms, and cheese, or johnnycakes with

WEB SITE: www.captainfairfield.com

INNKEEPERS: Leigh and Rob Blood

ROOMS: 9 rooms, all with private bath, telephone, alarm/CD player, TV/DVD, wireless Internet, hair dryer, garden view, air-conditioning; many with fireplace

ON THE GROUNDS: Lawn seating, gardens, patio

RATES: $110–$325, including full breakfast and afternoon refreshments

CREDIT CARDS ACCEPTED: Master-Card, Visa, American Express, Discover

OPEN: Year-round

HOW TO GET THERE: From Interstate 95 take exit 25 (formerly exit 3), Route 35 south, and proceed about 5½ miles to the intersection with Route 9. Turn left on Route 9, go over the bridge into Dock Square, and then take a right after the monument onto Ocean Avenue. Continue 5 blocks, then turn left onto Green Street. The inn is 1 block farther, at the corner of Green and Pleasant Streets.

wild Maine blueberries. The butler's pantry has fixings for coffee or tea all day and a refrigerator for guests.

All the rooms have sitting areas and generous-size baths. Two favorites are the front corner rooms, Sweet Liberty and Captain Fairfield, both with a fireplace and a view of the town green. The library room on the ground floor is quite special, with a lace canopy bed, a fireplace, a whirlpool tub for two, and a private porch. Brig McDonough, a fireplace room upstairs, has a tall carved four-poster and a handsome carved antique armoire.

If you are curious about the original Captain Fairfield, the innkeepers will be happy to tell you of his colorful life and the unusual saga of his portrait. The Bloods are enthusiastic about their home and will be happy to steer you to all the best in Kennebunkport; the center of the village is a quick and easy stroll from the inn.

What's Nearby: A favorite posh summer resort for the wealthy since the late 1880s, Kennebunkport offers both fine beaches and prime examples of Maine's rocky shoreline. The village is packed with shops and excellent dining places.

CAPTAIN LORD MANSION

Pleasant and Green Streets
P.O. Box 800
Kennebunkport 04046
(207) 967–3141; (800) 522–3141
Fax: (207) 967–3172

Kennebunkport shows its maritime history with many wonderful sea captains' mansions, but none to match this graceful three-story yellow beauty with the cupola on top, built in 1812 by the owner of the ships many of those captains sailed. Grand in scale and lavishly furnished, the Captain Lord Mansion has everything going for it—history, romance, and luxury. One of the few inns to be awarded four diamonds from AAA, it has been featured in countless magazine spreads.

The feel is formal but never stuffy, thanks to the relaxed personalities of married innkeepers Bev Davis and Rick Litchfield, onetime ad executives, who rescued and restored the house in 1978 and seem to make it better every year. In the past few

WEB SITE: www.captainlord.com

INNKEEPERS: Rick Litchfield and Bev Davis

ROOMS: 15 rooms, 1 suite, all with private bath, gas fireplace, air-conditioning, phone, clock, radio, CD player, hair dryer; many with double whirlpool; beach towels and chairs available in summer

ON THE GROUNDS: Lawns, memory garden

RATES: $149–$499, including full breakfast and afternoon refreshments

CREDIT CARDS ACCEPTED: Master-Card, Visa, Discover

OPEN: Year-round

HOW TO GET THERE: From Interstate 95, the Maine Turnpike, take exit 25 (formerly exit 3), Kennebunk, turn left onto Route 35 south, and continue 5½ miles to Route 9 east. Turn left, go over the bridge, take the first right onto Ocean Avenue, and then the fifth left, Green Street (3⁄10 mile), off Ocean. The mansion is in the second block on the left.

years alone, they have invested more than a half million dollars in redecorating and upgrades. All the rooms now have fireplaces and air-conditioning. The bathrooms all have heated marble floors; many have double whirlpool baths or steam showers or jet showers, and antique pedestal vanities.

Classical music is often playing in the background as you enter the "gathering room," measuring 26 by 20 feet and boasting a beamed ceiling, wainscoting, fine Oriental rugs on the pumpkin pine floors, three elaborately draped bay windows, and an oversize fireplace that was the home's original 1812 cooking fireplace. As in the rest of the house, the style is Federal, with camel-back sofas and tall wing chairs. At one end of the room, beneath a sparkling chandelier, is a dining table and Chippendale chairs that belonged to the original Lord family.

The guest rooms are so spectacular that choosing a favorite is almost impossible. The ultimate is the Ship Merchant Suite on the first floor, with fireplaces both in the bedroom and one of the two extravagant baths. The first bath is equipped with a ten-jet hydro-massage waterfall shower; the second has two sinks and a whirlpool tub for two in front of the fireplace.

Every room has a large seating area. Custom-made draperies, dust ruffles, and throw pillows have been carefully coordinated by Bev with the wall coverings and upholstery fabrics. No two are alike. Merchant has a bright red and white striped bunting border design at the ceiling and cream walls. Like many of the rooms, the windows have sheer white curtains topped with swags, in this case cherry red to match the carpet. Mary Lord, a striking room with a filmy canopy over the bed, has a sophisticated beige and black color scheme and leopard accents.

Two breakfast sittings are offered at harvest tables in the kitchen, with Rick presiding to share history and anecdotes with guests. On the menu are fresh fruit, cereal, yogurt, and entrees ranging from Belgian waffles and blueberry pancakes to asparagus soufflés and egg-and-cheese frittatas. Breads vary daily, and whether the menu offers sticky buns, zucchini bread, or apple muffins, you can be sure that they will be delicious.

Bev's memory garden outside, planted with more than 1,000 tulips, has paving stones carved with the names of guests who have been to the inn ten times or more. The list grows every year.

What's Nearby: See What's Nearby on page 75.

THE CAPTAIN'S GARDEN HOUSE

Green and Main Streets
P.O. Box 800
Kennebunkport 04046
(800) 967–7748

■ The owners of the much-lauded Captain Lord Mansion (see page 75) have opened a serene, more intimate bed-and-breakfast near their original inn. This Federal-style 1807 home is small, with only four guest rooms, and is less palatial than the mansion, but it does not lack for luxury in the guest rooms. The bedrooms have been decorated with Bev Davis's flair and carefully coordinated color schemes. Lois and Susan have fishnet canopy beds, Daniel and Nathaniel are furnished with tall four-posters, and all have cozy gas fireplaces.

WEB SITE: www.captainsgarden house.com

INNKEEPERS: Rick Litchfield and Bev Davis

ROOMS: 4 rooms, all with private bath, phone, CD player, air-conditioning, gas fireplace; 1 with double whirlpool tub

ON THE GROUNDS: Screened porch, gardens

RATES: $125–$299, including full breakfast, free use of bikes, beach chairs, and towels

CREDIT CARDS ACCEPTED: All major cards

OPEN: Year-round

I'm a bit partial to Lois for its white arched window frames and brick accents. Nathaniel, on the first floor, has cheerful yellow wallpaper, an antique wardrobe, and a double Jacuzzi/tub shower in the marble bath. Everyone finds down comforters and pillows, and complimentary water and soft drinks in the room.

For breakfast guests are seated in Windsor chairs around a long table in front of the open hearth fireplace. Like guests at the Captain Lord, they are treated to an elaborate three-course breakfast, prepared by their own chef. Afterward, free bikes or beach towels and chairs are available, but the favorite retreats for many are the swing

HOW TO GET THERE: From Interstate 95, the Maine Turnpike, take exit 25 (formerly exit 3), Kennebunk. Turn left onto Route 35 south and continue 5½ miles to Route 9 east. Turn left, go over the bridge, take the first right onto Ocean Avenue, and then the fifth left, Green Street (⁷⁄₁₀ mile). The inn is in the second block on the left, beyond the Captain Lord Mansion at the corner of Green and Main Streets.

or the chaise on the porch or an Adirondack chair on the lawn, peaceful spots to sit back and enjoy the tranquillity of a special small inn.

What's Nearby: See What's Nearby on page 75.

INN AT HARBOR HEAD

41 Pier Road
Kennebunkport 04046
(207) 967–5564
Fax: (207) 967–1294

■ This shingled, hundred-plus-year-old cottage by the sea has a dream location on the water. I could sit for hours on the back lawn watching the boats go by and gazing at the pine-covered islands in the distance. The sloping lawn leads to a dock, where you can dangle your feet in the water.

The house itself is charming, with water views from many rooms. Eve and Dick Roesler, owners since February 1998, have added their own distinctive touches to the decor.

WEB SITE: www.harborhead.com

INNKEEPERS: Eve and Dick Roesler

ROOMS: 2 rooms, 2 suites, all with private bath, air-conditioning and ceiling fan, clock, radio, CD player, robes, beach passes and towels; some with whirlpool bath, balcony, fireplace

ON THE GROUNDS: Deck and lawn seating with water views, gardens, private dock

RATES: Rooms $160–$260, suites $245–$325, including full breakfast and afternoon refreshments

The main sitting room is formal, with long draperies lit by the glow of a crystal chandelier. The library is more intimate, with gold walls hung with paintings, a fireplace, and a picture window facing the ocean. The dining room has been redone in Oriental style, furnished with a large mahogany table and chairs and with accents of fresh flowers and bonsai. Eve prepares an elegant breakfast, including dishes such as poached pears with raspberry sauce, crabmeat quiche, or wild Maine blueberry buttermilk pancakes.

My top choice among the guest rooms is

CREDIT CARDS ACCEPTED: MasterCard, Visa

OPEN: May through October

HOW TO GET THERE: Take Interstate 95 north to exit 25 (formerly exit 3), Kennebunk, and turn left onto Route 35 east, following the signs to Kennebunkport. Route 9 intersects with Route 35 at Kennebunkport. Follow Route 9 east about 2 miles from Kennebunkport to Cape Porpoise. Leave Route 9 where it turns sharply left; go straight ahead on Pier Road ¼ mile past the Wayfarer Restaurant to the inn, on the right.

the Summer Suite, done in floral chintz and wicker. It has a private balcony to enjoy the view. The bathroom has a cathedral ceiling with skylight, a whirlpool bath, and a bidet. French doors in the Garden Room lead to a deck facing the harbor.

The inn is secluded, away from the bustle of town, but just down the road is Cape Porpoise, and the chance to watch the lobster boats and working fishing fleet come in. It's Maine just the way you hoped it would be.

What's Nearby: See What's Nearby on page 75.

PORTSMOUTH HARBOR INN AND SPA

6 Water Street
Kittery 03904
(207) 439–4040
Fax: (207) 438–9286

The address is Maine, but as the name suggests, this three-story brick Victorian built in 1880 is on the banks of the Piscataqua River, just a stroll across the Memorial Bridge from the many attractions of Portsmouth, New Hampshire. You can sit in a rocker on the porch and watch the sun set over the steeples of Portsmouth.

The Bowditches, born and bred New Englanders, have lived in Maine since 1981. Since they took over the inn in May 2004, they have added a touch of elegance indoors and done an extensive makeover of the gardens, adding a restful shade garden complete with seating and fountain behind the inn and spa.

A major addition is the full-service day spa in the attached converted barn.

WEB SITE: www.innatportsmouth.com

INNKEEPERS: Nathaniel Bowditch and Lynn Spann Bowditch

ROOMS: 5 rooms, all with private bath, TV/VCR, wireless Internet, phone, ceiling fan, air-conditioning in season

ON THE GROUNDS: Porch with rockers, gardens, full-service day spa

RATES: $110–$216, including full breakfast

CREDIT CARDS ACCEPTED: MasterCard, Visa

OPEN: Year-round

Among the wide range of offerings are facials, manicures, pedicures, and massages, including massages for couples.

The inn sitting room is decorated with fine eighteenth- and early-nineteenth-century antiques and a Steinway upright piano that guests are welcome to play. The inn also serves as gallery space for original artwork of local artists who are members of the Kittery Art Association.

Breakfast changes with the season. Among the favorite dishes are the Portsmouth Harbor Inn Pear Crumble; the end-of-summer Harvest Strata made with fresh tomatoes, pesto, and prosciutto; and the blueberry-pecan French toast.

HOW TO GET THERE: From Interstate 95 driving north, take exit 7. Go right at the end of the ramp onto Market Street Extension. Drive ⁹⁄₁₀ of a mile into Portsmouth, take a left onto Bow Street, and follow to its end (the second stop sign). Turn left onto State Street and the Memorial Bridge (Route 1) into Maine. Immediately after the bridge, make a sharp left onto Water Street. The inn is the first building on the right.

Rooms are named for gundalows, the working boats that once plied the Piscataqua. Four of the five bedrooms have water views, and all are done with pleasant country antiques. I like Dido, a second-floor corner room with windows on three sides, and the two third-floor rooms, Royal George and Alice, with skylights and claw-foot tubs in the baths.

From the inn you can stroll across the bridge into Portsmouth with its many excellent restaurants, or just walk across the street to Warren's Lobster House, a local seafood landmark.

What's Nearby: Besides the attractions of Portsmouth (see page 186), the inn is near the dozens of outlet stores along Route 1 in Kittery and is a good home base for exploring the beaches and towns of the lower coast of Maine. The innkeepers can help with driving maps and suggestions.

INN AT SUNRISE POINT

Fire Road 9
Lincolnville
Mailing address:
P.O. Box 1344
Camden 04833
(207) 236–7716; (800) 435–6278
Fax: (207) 236–0820

▨ Tranquillity, water views, a private beach, and wood-burning fireplaces in every room—these are among the amenities you'll find in the renovated turn-of-the-twentieth-century main house or the adjoining guest cottages that make up the Inn at Sunrise

Point. The inn is away from the crowds, way down an unpaved road at the water's edge in Lincolnville, but it is just 4 miles away from the center of Camden.

There is an airy California look to the decor. The living room has a wall of windows, ship models on the mantel, a blue and white color scheme, and wicker pieces. The adjoining paneled library with a stone fireplace is a bit cozier. Besides books, there are videos that can be borrowed for the VCR in your room.

My favorite room by far is the round glass-walled and domed conservatory where breakfast is served from 8:30 to 9:30 A.M. to the tune of classical music. Along with the usual breakfast treats, pancakes, blueberry muffins, and such, this inn has a delicious specialty, homemade Irish soda bread. Innkeeper Stephen Tallon is Irish, and he has had so many requests for his soda bread recipe that it has been posted on the inn's Web site. Stephen and Deanna lived in many parts of the world and enjoyed successful careers in publishing before coming to this spot that they describe as "heaven on earth." In addition to a new life as innkeepers, they became parents for the first time in the fall of 2005, welcoming daughter Ava Patricia.

Rooms at the inn are named for Maine writers and artists and feature their work. All have the same light pine furniture. The rooms in the main house are not large but have a pleasant, open feeling, with cathedral ceilings and cool, light blue, yellow, or rose color schemes. The TV set is hidden in an armoire. Fireplaces are nicely tiled, and you'll likely find fresh flowers when you check in. The bathrooms are well equipped and have oversize tubs. Every room has its own temperature controls—and its own ocean view.

Cottage rooms are more spacious and offer still more comforts, including minifridge, wet bar, whirlpool bath for two, and private deck. All the cottages have ocean-view decks, but if you want to be closest to the water, FitzHugh Lane is just 10 feet from the edge of a cliff above the beach, and Winslow Homer is a close rival. The Levitin cottage, once the private quarters of the inn's first owner, is now available to guests who want a living room, full kitchen, and a peerless panorama.

WEB SITE: www.sunrisepoint.com

INNKEEPERS: Deanna and Stephen Tallon

ROOMS: 3 rooms in main house, 4 guest cottages, 1 suite, 1 loft suite, all with private bath, TV/VCR, fireplace, phone with dataport, clock, radio, CD player, robes; cottages have double whirlpool bath, wet bar, minifridge, private deck; suite has kitchen

ON THE GROUNDS: 4 private acres on ocean beach

RATES: Rooms $225–$330, cottages and suites $250–$405, including full breakfast and late-afternoon appetizers

CREDIT CARDS ACCEPTED: MasterCard, Visa, American Express

OPEN: May through October

HOW TO GET THERE: The inn is 4 miles north of Camden off Route 1. Turn right at the Fire Road 9 sign (FR 9), and drive down to the water.

All of it is simple and fresh, keyed to beach living—and the main attraction for many is that totally private beach waiting at the end of the long lawn. It is small and a bit stony, but listening to the lapping of the waves is a guaranteed tranquilizer.

What's Nearby: Lincolnville is just north of Camden Hills State Park, with its superb hiking and ocean views, and only a few miles from Camden shops and dining. The Lobster Pound Restaurant at Lincolnville Beach is a classic.

MAISON SUISSE

Main Street, P.O. Box 1090
Northeast Harbor 04662
Phone/Fax: (207) 276–5223;
(800) 624–7668

▪ If I were to imagine a fairy-tale cottage, this might well be it—a landmark built in the late nineteenth century by a noted local architect, Fred Savage, with all the eccentric charm and whimsy of the classic shingle-style architecture of that period. It is in an unlikely but very convenient location, smack in the center of the poshest village on Mount Desert Island, tucked behind a rustic and quite wonderful rock garden of heather, cranberry bushes, and woody plants. The garden is the legacy of a former owner from Switzerland, who is also responsible for the inn's name.

Inside, the look is clean and uncluttered. The rooms are spacious, with highly polished floors, attractive scatter rugs, and a few nice antiques. Two living rooms share back-to-back fireplaces. One focuses on a bay window filled with geraniums and offers lots of books and comfortable wing chairs and sofas to enjoy them. An alcove with a guest refrigerator has a glass wall looking into the trees, bookshelves on either side, and a low carved bench with a cushion in front of the window. The second sitting room is lined with more books in wooden cases that contrast with the white walls.

The guest rooms seem to wander all over the house, up and down stairs. Many rooms have private sitting areas or decks, and a number have an extra bed for kids, who are welcome. Owners Beth and David White, who mark their twentieth anniversary at the inn in 2007, report that a lot of guests have come on their honeymoons, then returned a few years later with their families. The couple met while attending Brown University and were living in Providence when they vacationed in Northeast Harbor, were struck by the beauty, and said to themselves, "Some people actually live here full time and vacation in the city!" They've never regretted the move.

The summery bedrooms seem just right for this breezy harbor resort town, with pastel colors, ruffled white curtains, flowery fabrics, wicker pieces, and lots of windows. One of my favorites is a corner room with a floral queen-size canopy bed, eaves, and its own porch. One two-bedroom suite has a canopy, a bay window, and a fireplace. Another has a canopy bed and French doors to the porch from one room, and a second bedroom with a double cannonball antique bed. Typical of the unpredictable nature of the house is a first-floor room with hand-silk-screened wallpaper where you walk two steps up to reach the room, two steps down to the bath.

The most recent development at the inn is the renovation of the adjacent Peregrine Lodge building, reaching through a landscaped path through a wooded area. The decor is similar, but the rooms are slightly larger, all with king-size beds, and have special individual features such as harbor or mountain views, fireplaces, balconies, or terraces.

WEB SITE: www.maisonsuisse.com

INNKEEPERS: Beth and David White

ROOMS: 6 rooms, 4 suites in main house; 5 rooms, 1 suite in Peregrine Lodge; all with private bath, clock, radio; TV on request; some with porch or terrace or fireplace

ON THE GROUNDS: Patio

RATES: Rooms $165–$235, suites $245–$400, including breakfast at the cafe-bakery across the street

CREDIT CARDS ACCEPTED: Master-Card, Visa

OPEN: May through October

HOW TO GET THERE: Take Route 3 from Ellsworth across the bridge onto Mount Desert Island, follow Route 102/198 to the Somesville intersection, and turn left toward Northeast Harbor, remaining on Route 198 to Main Street. Maison Suisse is on the left; a gravel lane on the left side of the inn leads to the parking lot.

This is one inn where you need not worry about what time to come down for breakfast. Guests walk across the street anytime between 7:00 and 11:00 A.M. to a local cafe and bakery, the Colonel's, where they can order anything and everything on the menu—on the house.

As they look toward their twentieth year at the inn, Beth and Dave are still full of plans—maybe clear the woods to make room for a wedding tent or put in a croquet lawn, more balconies, more antiques, or possibly convert the sunroom into a breakfast room. One thing you can be sure will not change is the warm hospitality found at this special inn.

What's Nearby: Northeast Harbor is the most upscale community on Mount Desert Island, with quality shops lining Main Street, fine dining, and a beautiful harbor. It is adjacent to all the beauty, hiking, biking, and water activities of Acadia National Park; a walking trail down the street from the inn connects to Acadia's trails.

HARTWELL HOUSE

312 Shore Road, P.O. Box 1937
Ogunquit 03907
(207) 646–7210; (800) 235–8883

■ The British flag out front is the clue: This is not your usual Ogunquit inn. Right on Shore Road, within easy walking distance of beach and shops, this is an elegant oasis filled with English antiques.

The handsome formal parlor has wide floorboards and a carved mantel facing a high-back settee and overstuffed easy chairs. It leads out to the spacious back lawn and gardens with a lily pond.

The dining room seats eight at Windsor chairs around a polished maple trestle table, lit by a crystal chandelier. The furniture includes sixteenth-century Welsh cupboards and a hutch.

Afternoon tea and an occasional breakfast are served in the wicker-filled, glass-enclosed porch at the front of the house, a room that is always bright thanks to a long wall of tall, arched windows.

Nine rooms in the main house are large and airy; the choicest rooms face the back lawn. Four rooms have French doors leading to balconies overlooking the gardens. Two garden apartments have private entrances and a full kitchenette.

Among my favorites are the York Room, furnished with a queen canopy bed in wine and taupe and a Queen Anne settee and chairs, and the Polly Reed Room, decorated in French red and yellow provincials and coordinating plaids. The spacious Polly Reed bathroom has a sink set into an antique chest and a two-person whirlpool.

Three suites and four rooms in a second building across the road are more contemporary in feel, with lots of pine pieces. All have French doors leading to a balcony or terrace. The suites are equipped with a microwave, sink, and refrigerator.

WEB SITE: www.hartwellhouseinn.com

INNKEEPERS: Jim and Trisha Hartwell (owners), Paul and Gail Koehler (resident innkeepers)

ROOMS: 11 rooms, 3 suites, 2 garden apartments, all with private bath, air-conditioning, phone

ON THE GROUNDS: 2 acres of lawns and gardens, patio

RATES: Rooms $120–$225, suites $175–$245, including full breakfast, afternoon tea

CREDIT CARDS ACCEPTED: MasterCard, Visa, American Express, Discover

OPEN: Year-round

HOW TO GET THERE: From the south take Interstate 95 to exit 7 (formerly exit 4) in Maine, and follow Route 1 north for 7 miles until you see the Ogunquit Playhouse. Turn right onto Bourne Lane, and then right again onto Shore Road. The main inn is ahead on the right.

What's Nearby: The name Ogunquit means "beautiful place by the sea," and you'll see why when you walk along the famous Marginal Way overlooking the ocean. A longtime artists' colony for its picturesque site, Ogunquit boasts Maine's best beaches as well as a host of art galleries and shops. Take in a performance at the Ogunquit Playhouse, one of the pioneer summer stock theaters in the United States, and have at least one dinner at the Ogunquit Lobster Pound on Route 1, the kind of no-frills, great seafood place that Maine is all about.

TRELLIS HOUSE

2 Beachmere Place, P.O. Box 2229
Ogunquit 03907
(207) 646–7909; (800) 681–7909

■ *Ogunquit* is an American Indian word for "beautiful place by the sea," an apt description. The Marginal Way, a walkway on the cliffs beside the water, is one of the great shoreline strolls. Add some of the best, most accessible beaches in Maine, and it's no wonder that things get crowded in summer.

The Trellis House is one of the few inns where you can be within walking distance of all the action and still be away from traffic. On a quiet lane just off Shore Road, it was built as a typical New England summer cottage in 1907, and it has been restored and redecorated with an eclectic mix of the comfortable and the antique. Pat and Jerry Houlihan took over the inn in 1993 after running small businesses, attracted by the fact that they would be the entire staff. They enjoy being in charge and interacting with their guests.

Walk in past the wraparound screened porch and you'll find classical music playing in the little formal parlor. Pale upholstered armchairs await in front of the fireplace, and the room is filled with handsome furnishings such as an Oriental rug, an antique clock, and a corner cabinet full of china collectibles.

WEB SITE: www.trellishouse.com

INNKEEPERS: Pat and Jerry Houlihan

ROOMS: 8 rooms, 3 in main house, 4 in carriage house, 1 cottage, all with private bath, air-conditioning, clock, hair dryer, refrigerator, iron and ironing board; some with fireplace

ON THE GROUNDS: Wraparound screened porch, gardens

RATES: $95–$180 including full breakfast

CREDIT CARDS ACCEPTED: MasterCard, Visa

OPEN: April through November

HOW TO GET THERE: From Route 1, turn east onto Shore Road, and watch for a left turn to Beachmere Place.

The dining room has attractive upholstered captain's chairs around the table, a mix of antique chests, and another whatnot cabinet. Breakfast, served from 8:30 to 10:00 A.M., consists of juice, homemade muffins, and the hot entree of the day. One of the house specialties is ginger pancakes.

Upstairs rooms, each different, include a two-room suite and a room with an alcove with very special ocean views. The adjacent carriage house offers spacious rooms with fireplaces and private decks overlooking the gardens, and the Barbary Cottage is a private hideaway for romantics.

One of my favorite parts of this inn is the wicker-furnished porch on the main house—such a cool and pleasant retreat at the end of the day.

What's Nearby: See What's Nearby on page 85.

POPHAM BEACH BED & BREAKFAST

4 Riverview Avenue
Phippsburg 04562
(207) 389–2409
Fax: (207) 389–2379

The white frame Coast Guard station with its red roof and distinct tower has stood on this site at Popham Beach since 1883. Originally it was a U.S. Lifesaving Station, constructed to protect the lives of mariners threatened by tide, wind, fog, or rough seas. The U.S. Coast Guard took over in 1935, continuing rescue missions until 1971, when the station was decommissioned.

It remained a familiar but neglected landmark until Peggy and Helge Johannessen came across the building by accident one day in 1991 and were smitten. The couple have been restoring the house room by room ever since and eventually moved in. They have created this a unique and charming beachside bed-and-breakfast stop, full of authentic character. You can even go up in the old tower for the view.

Peggy has furnished the house with country flair, retaining the white walls and wooden ceilings but brightening the place with antiques, plants, wreaths, and fresh flowers. Many of the unusual antiques come from Norway, Sweden, Belgium, and Scotland, where the couple has lived.

She has painted the entry floor in a cheerful salmon and white checkerboard pattern. It opens to the dining room, where a long table is surrounded with an artful mix of country chairs. A bountiful breakfast is served here at 8:30 A.M. each day, with fresh fruits and a changing array of hot dishes such as frittatas or French toast, with breakfast meats and a selection of breads.

The living-room furniture is a mix of country and antiques; the walls are adorned with ship models and old paintings. A big cabinet and chest of drawers were moved down from the old men's bunkroom. The windows look directly out at the water. The library, with two wooden walls lined with bookshelves, is now a bedroom with two wicker chairs at the bay window to savor the view. The big bunkroom has been redone in nautical blue and white, a nice contrast with the wooden ceiling. The views from its windows needed no improvement. The Captain's Quarters offers pine furniture and a summery floral bedspread as well as a sofa bed.

The beauty of Popham Beach and the surrounding area was featured in the Kevin Costner movie *Message in a Bottle*. The inn as viewed from the water was among the opening scenes of the movie, and another scene was filmed on the south deck.

What's Nearby: Popham Beach and its expanse of sand at the mouth of the Kennebec River overlooking the Atlantic are somewhat of a secret, seldom crowded, and the people of nearby Bath hope it stays that way. You can beachcomb, watch for ospreys and cormorants, and in spring gaze at sixty or seventy seals sleeping on a nearby island. The Phippsburg peninsula south of Bath is also historic, the birthplace of the area's shipbuilding legacy with the *Virginia*, a thirty-ton ship, built in 1607. There are tiny villages to explore, and you can go back to Civil War days by climbing through Fort Popham, built in 1865. You can also drive into Bath to admire the fine homes in the historic district and visit the Maine Maritime Museum. Wiscasset, several miles north of Bath, is antiquing territory.

WEB SITE: www.pophambeach
bandb.com

INNKEEPERS: Peggy and Helge Johannessen

ROOMS: 4 rooms, 1 suite, all with private bath, clock, radio

ON THE GROUNDS: Popham Beach is directly in front of the Inn.

RATES: $175–$215, Including full breakfast

CREDIT CARDS ACCEPTED: Master-Card, Visa

OPEN: Year-round

HOW TO GET THERE: Follow signs for Route 209 south from Bath. After Junction 217, look for the Popham Beach sign, and follow the signs for the bed-and-breakfast, making a left and following Route 209 to Fort Popham. Turn right just before Spinneys, and follow Beach Road for ¼ mile. The inn is on the left.

POMEGRANATE INN

49 Neal Street
Portland 04102
(207) 772–1006; (800) 356–0408

■ There's a fresh surprise in every room of this sophisticated, stylish inn, an

WEB SITE: www.pomegranateinn
.com

INNKEEPER: Isabel Smiles

ROOMS: 8 rooms, 1 suite, all with private bath, air-conditioning, TV, phone, clock, radio; some with fireplace

ON THE GROUNDS: Terrace

RATES: $95–$265, including full breakfast and afternoon refreshments

CREDIT CARDS ACCEPTED: MasterCard, Visa, American Express

OPEN: Year-round

HOW TO GET THERE: Coming from the south on Interstate 95, take exit 44 (formerly exit 6A) to Interstate 295. Get off at exit 4, cross the viaduct, and go right immediately to the Danforth Street ramp. Take the first left to Vaughn Street, proceed 5 blocks to Carroll Street, turn right, and go 1 more block. The inn is at the corner of Carroll and Neal.

1884 Italianate colonial revival house on the National Register of Historic Places, located in the fashionable Western Promenade neighborhood only minutes away from downtown Portland.

An interior designer and partner in an antiques business before her 1988 move from Greenwich, Connecticut, Isabel Smiles brought panache to Portland, along with her extensive personal antiques and modern art collections. She found an inspired local artist, Heidi Gerquest, to festoon the guestroom walls with bright original art, from Matisse-like blue flowers in bottles to a lemon yellow world of white doves and green leaves to a fanciful multicolored garden of flora that extends from the walls to the headboard. American, English, and Chinese antiques and Oriental rugs somehow seem just right amid this whimsy. Gerquest's touch also enlivens pieces of furniture such as a wooden sofa frame in shades of mustard and yellow.

Even a traditional room with a four-poster canopy bed has original touches, a bold rose and maroon color scheme, an antique hand-painted chest, a folk painting, and a lively swirl border. Equally pleasing rooms in the adjoining carriage house have an added asset—working tile fireplaces. Smiles's unerring eye is responsible for a delightful setting in the long sitting and dining room as well, combining unlikely elements such as marble columns, Greek statuary, Hudson River school paintings, and whimsical painted pieces into a harmonious whole. My favorite small touches are the oversize ceramic flowers set in pots in the window at the end of the room.

Playful faux touches are everywhere, from the swags painted over the windows to the marbling on cornices and tubs in the bathrooms. The black-and-white tiles in the entry and much of the other faux painting was done by Isabel's talented daughter, Amy Russack.

Breakfast is served in the attractive living and dining room on colorful pottery at a long table with a painted swirl design. Whether the main dish is creamy quiche or currant pancakes, a full and hearty meal is assured.

When Isabel moved here, she was attracted by the lively cultural community in Portland, and she enjoys steering guests to the local theaters, the fine art museum designed by architect I. M. Pei, and the scores of shops in the Old Port section of town. At the end of the day, depending on the weather, you can return to a cold drink on a terrace draped in wisteria and honeysuckle or sip tea or wine in the sitting room while you decide which of Portland's many fine restaurants to choose for dinner.

What's Nearby: Portland, Maine's major city, is by the sea, with cruises from the wharves and the state's most photographed landmark, the Portland Head Lighthouse in nearby Cape Elizabeth. It is also a city filled with pleasures, from intriguing shops in the Old Port neighborhood to great art in the I. M. Pei–designed Portland Art Museum to the best dining north of Boston. The 1785 Wadsworth-Longfellow House and the Victorian Mansion will please history and American literature buffs.

CAPTAIN LINDSEY HOUSE INN

5 Lindsey Street
Rockland 04841
(207) 596–7950; (800) 523–2145
Fax: (207) 596–2758

■ Like most of the town of Rockland, the Captain Lindsey House has a plain facade that gives few hints to the pleasures that await. This small, stylish, and comfortable inn opened in 1994, a sign of the revival taking place all over town. Rockland still has the look of a no-frills working fishermen's town, but exciting things are happening here. The inn's owners, Ken and Ellen Barnes, took on a challenge with this 1832 building originally built by sea captain George Lindsey as his home. It had most recently been headquarters for the Camden Rockland Water Company. The company would never recognize it now.

Come inside the inn, past the wood-paneled check-in area, to find an elegant parlor with dark green walls, an oversize sofa and chairs in deep red and green plaid, a big white fireplace, and a fine Oriental rug. The glass-top coffee table holds antique leather-bound books, including a history of Rockland from 1888 to 1930. All over the room are Oriental accents—brass candlesticks, a red wooden ox, figurines, chests, and lamps. A wooden guardian angel watches over things in one corner. Another sitting area has chairs with lion arms and a lovely round wooden table with more Orientalia, a carved wooden basket, and a wooden bowl holding apples. Beyond is a narrow library stocked with rare and current books and magazines and furnished with a crewel upholstered love seat and chairs.

WEB SITE: www.lindseyhouse.com

INNKEEPERS: Ken and Ellen Barnes, Susan Barnes (owners)

ROOMS: 7 rooms, 2 suites, all with private bath, air-conditioning, TV, phone, clock, radio, hair dryer, magnifying mirror, robes, high-speed wireless Internet access

ON THE GROUNDS: Outdoor terrace

RATES: $85–$190, including buffet breakfast and afternoon tea. Sometimes packages are available combining two days at the inn with a three- or six-day cruise on the tall ship *Stephen Taber*; if you're interested, be sure to ask about them.

CREDIT CARDS ACCEPTED: MasterCard, Visa, American Express, Discover

OPEN: Year-round

HOW TO GET THERE: Rockland is in mid-coastal Maine, about 8 miles south of Camden. From Interstate 95 take Route 1 east; it will become Main Street in Rockland. Once you turn onto Main Street, Lindsey Street is about 7 blocks farther, on the left; get parking instructions from the inn staff.

The eclectic antiques in these rooms are what you might expect in the home of a nineteenth-century sea captain who has sailed to the Orient. Ken and Ellen are, in fact, captains themselves, at the helm of the schooner *Stephen Taber,* a windjammer that they restored some years ago and have been sailing along Maine's mid-coast since 1978.

Upstairs guest rooms are spacious, a good mix of old and new, with striped wallpapers, custom bedspreads, comfortable chairs, good reading lights, and TV sets behind the doors of the armoires. Every room has an antique desk, no two alike, and a variety of accent pieces such as French chairs and Oriental lamps. Bathrooms are modern and well appointed.

In the morning, guests come down to an informal oak-paneled breakfast room and take a seat at one of the trestle tables with built-in benches. The help-yourself spread includes fresh squeezed juice, fruits, yogurt, homemade granola, and a variety of baked goods.

Rockland has two major tourist draws, the windjammer fleet, moored not far from the inn, and the excellent Farnsworth Museum, best known for its gallery of Maine paintings by the Wyeth family. An adjacent old church has been converted to hold the Wyeth collection, and several fine galleries are nearby.

After admiring the art, you can go home to tea in the inn parlor, and then for dinner choose between walking next door for inexpensive fare at the Waterworks Pub or driving to one of the gourmet restaurants that have recently appeared in Rockland. The resident innkeeper will be ready with suggestions.

What's Nearby: A working seafaring town, Rockland is home to a major portion of Maine's windjammer fleet, a lure for both sailors and photographers. The Farnsworth Museum is a gem, especially for those who admire the works of N. C., Andrew, and Jamie Wyeth, and the museum has drawn several attractive art galleries to town. For worldlier pleasures, Camden is just a few miles up the coast.

ROCKPORT HARBOR HOUSE

11 Mechanic Street
Rockport 04856
(207) 236–8058

■ Rockport is exactly what many people imagine a perfect Maine village to be—small, noncommercial, with picturesque hilly lanes of cottages and a busy harbor where lobster boats and sleek sailing sloops are equally at home. The fishing and shipbuilding heritage dates from the early 1770s, and the entire village has been declared a historic district. The Rockport Harbor House does the town full justice, perched up the hill from the harbor, with dazzling views from the decks and out the big rounded windows that fill the house with light.

The house is built on levels that follow the hillside. From the front hall you step down into the airy living room, a gorgeous space with a cathedral ceiling, a skylight, and light, highly polished floors. It is tastefully furnished in what host Lynne Twentyman calls "minimalist modern," with a white cushioned sectional sofa, two French side chairs, and an Oriental rug. Down a few more steps, the solarium is all glass, a room that is bright on even the gloomiest day. Bedrooms down the hall are occasionally used for overflow guests.

INNKEEPERS: Lynne Twentyman and Jessica Ward

ROOMS: 2 rooms, each with private bath, clock, radio, skylights, harbor view; 1 with whirlpool bath, woodstove

ON THE GROUNDS: Pier with 30-foot sloop available for charter

RATES: $100–$185, including full breakfast; house is often rented by the week ($875–$1,200)

OPEN: Memorial Day to Labor Day

CREDIT CARDS ACCEPTED: None

HOW TO GET THERE: Call for directions.

The showstopper bedrooms are upstairs. I can't imagine anything more romantic than the master bedroom, which offers an iron-and-brass king-size bed, a woodstove, a whirlpool bath and oversize shower in the bathroom, and a private round deck looking down on the harbor. The second bedroom also has skylights, and clouds are painted on the slanted walls on either side of the door, artwork done by Lynne's daughter Jessica Ward long ago and nostalgically maintained by her mother.

Lynne, a script supervisor for movies and an instructor in the film department at New York University, has been coming to Rockport since she was three, and she built this fabulous house for herself and her family in 1988. It was daughter Jessica who came up with the idea of inviting bed-and-breakfast guests, with proceeds to help toward college expenses. They invited a friend, a chef at one of New York's noted breakfast spots, Sarabeth's Kitchen, to come up and teach them how to prepare proper breakfasts. Their rich dishes reflect their mastery of those lessons.

While the menu has been tamed, Lynne still bakes fresh bread and scones or muffins every morning, and she serves them with juice, fruit salad, and a variety of hot dishes, egg frittata and potatoes being one of the favorites. The kitchen has an open counter so that Lynne can talk to guests as she works. Getting to know nice people keeps innkeeping interesting, she says, and it isn't unusual for everyone to spend two or three hours conversing over the breakfast table. When weather permits, breakfast is served on the terrace—with harbor views for dessert.

It isn't surprising to find that picture-perfect Rockport has attracted artists. The Center for Maine Contemporary Art is just around the corner from the inn in a renovated old livery stable cum firehouse. The town is also the home of the Maine Photographic Workshops, a highly respected photography school whose galleries provide interesting browsing. Rockport will no doubt inspire you to pursue some photography of your own.

What's Nearby: The comings and goings of lobster boats and pleasure cruises make tiny Rockport harbor a fascinating place to be, constant inspiration for students at the prestigious Maine Photographic Workshops. The Center for Maine Contemporary Art shows work by area painters and artisans. The shops and scenery of Camden are only a five-minute drive up the coast.

KINGSLEIGH INN 1904

373 Main Street, P.O. Box 1426
Southwest Harbor 04679
(207) 244–5302
Fax: (207) 244–7691

▨ Picturesque Southwest Harbor is a fishing and boatbuilding community on the quiet side of Mount Desert Island, favored by those who love the beauty of Acadia National Park but want to get away from the crowds. Right on the edge of the little village is this small, cozy inn, with a flower-filled wraparound veranda overlooking a harbor where sailboats share the scene with the active fishing and lobstering fleet.

Dana and Greg Moos left careers in commercial real estate in the Washington, D.C., area to escape the "rat race" and took over in this peaceful spot in 2004. They brought a fresh look and feel to the inn, with warm colors, a mix of contemporary and traditional furnishings, and fine art.

WEB SITE: www.kingsleighinn.com

INNKEEPERS: Dana and Greg Moos

ROOMS: 7 rooms, 1 suite, all with private bath, clock, ceiling fan, robes, slippers; some with air-conditioning, harbor view; 2 with private deck; 1 with fireplace

ON THE GROUNDS: Wraparound porch overlooking the harbor, gardens

RATES: Rooms $110–$165, suite $175–$260, including full breakfast

CREDIT CARDS ACCEPTED: Master-Card, Visa

OPEN: Year-round

HOW TO GET THERE: From Ellsworth take Route 3 toward Bar Harbor. After crossing onto the island, bear to the right and follow Route 102 to Southwest Harbor, where it is called Main Street. The inn is on the left just past the center of the village.

Guests enter through the kitchen, which doubles as the reception area. They are welcome to sit at the counter stool and watch chef Dana preparing breakfast and baking the daily afternoon treats, giving a homey feeling to the inn.

The former parlor has a wood-burning fireplace with a mantel large enough to hold fresh flowers and a glowing candle. A less formal sitting room by the flower-filled porch has a beverage buffet where guests can help themselves to tea, cocoa, or espresso. Homemade baked goods are provided daily along with in-room homemade chocolates and port wine.

Guest rooms are decorated in country decor with Laura Ashley and Waverly fabrics. Two rooms with private decks are popular, but the real dazzler is the third-floor Turret Suite. It offers a living room with TV, a bedroom with a king-size rice-carved plantation bed, a fireplace, and panoramic harbor views from the turret, where two wing chairs and a telescope on a tripod invite you to gaze at the boats or the stars.

What's Nearby: Southwest Harbor has a cluster of interesting small shops, several excellent restaurants, and galleries just down the block from the inn, on Main Street. On cloudy days the Mount Desert Oceanarium and the Wendell Gilley Museum help pass the time. Don't miss the ten-minute ride to Thurston's in Bass Harbor for unbeatable Maine lobster. Acadia National Park is nearby for hiking, biking, and canoeing, and it's an easy drive to Bar Harbor shops and dining.

EDWARDS' HARBORSIDE INN

Stage Neck Road
P.O. Box 866
York Harbor 03911
(207) 363–3037

There's water, water everywhere around this comfortable old-fashioned inn, perfectly positioned at the spot where the harbor meets the ocean. Three sides of the turn-of-the-twentieth-century house face the water, and there's nothing nicer than taking a seat in one of the Adirondack chairs on the lawn and looking out at the sailboats or the sunset. Beyond the lawn is a small sandy beach. The inn has its own long dock where you can get a close-up look at local lobstermen unloading the day's catch. If you sign on for a fishing or lobstering excursion, they may pick you up right here.

Jay Edwards is a third-generation innkeeper. The mood he sets is homey, informal, and relaxing. Year-round, the sunroom is where guests gather to admire the ocean and harbor view, to enjoy breakfast, and to relax with wine and cheese in the afternoon. It is furnished with wicker and floral table covers. I stopped by on a gray, rainy day, and there was welcoming coffee and a still-spectacular view.

In the colder months, one spacious sitting room from a suite becomes the inn parlor, furnished with sofas, chairs, and patterned rugs. A fireplace, TV, board games, books, and a decanter of sherry on the sideboard make this a warm retreat when choppy winds blow.

WEB SITE: http://edwardsharbor side.com

INNKEEPER: Jay Edwards

ROOMS: 7 rooms, 3 suites, all with TV, phone, clock, radio, private bath; suites have whirlpool bath

ON THE GROUNDS: Beach, pier

RATES: $80–$140 for rooms with private bath, $50–$120 for rooms with shared bath, $160–$210 for suites, including continental breakfast and afternoon refreshments

CREDIT CARDS ACCEPTED: Master-Card, Visa

OPEN: Year-round

HOW TO GET THERE: Take Interstate 95 to York, exit 7 (formerly exit 4). Follow the signs to York Harbor, turn right onto Route 1, and then left on to Route 1A (for 1½ miles). Turn right onto Stage Neck Road; the inn is on the right, on the water.

The ten rooms come in assorted sizes and shapes and are pleasantly furnished. All have floral wallpaper, valances atop the windows (where they won't block the view or the breeze), color-coordinated quilts and dust ruffles, and a sitting area. The York Suite has water on three sides, floral wallpaper, a four-poster queen-size bed, upholstered rockers for taking in the view, and a big bathroom. A spa in the entry overlooks the harbor.

York is an interesting town with much to explore—providing you can tear yourself away from those tempting chairs on the lawn.

What's Nearby: York is a town with several personalities. York Harbor is the boating haven; York Beach is a favorite family area, with an amusement park and food stands as well as beach; Cape Neddick is the place for scenery—follow Nubble Road to reach the lighthouse that is one of Maine's most photographed landmarks. And then there is York Village, the oldest surviving English settlement in Maine, dating from 1624. Historic York maintains six eighteenth-century properties and also offers colonial crafts demonstrations in summer. Outlet malls in Kittery are fifteen minutes to the south.

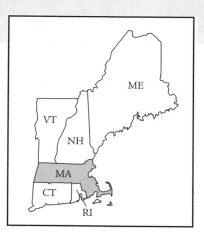

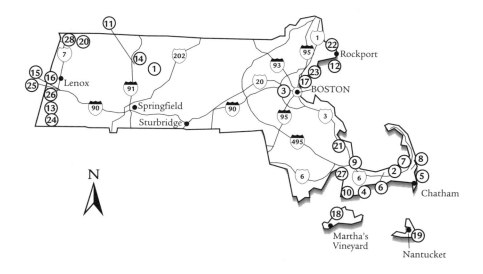

ME

VT

NH

MA

CT

RI

28 20
7
11
14
202
1
95 22 Rockport
93
23 12
15
16 Lenox
20
25
91
3 17 BOSTON
26
90
3
13
Springfield
90
95
3
24
Sturbridge
495
21

N

9
6
27 6 2 7 8
10 4 6 5
Chatham

18
Martha's
Vineyard

19
Nantucket

MASSACHUSETTS

Numbers on map refer to towns numbered below.

1. Amherst, Allen House *98*
2. Brewster, Captain Freeman Inn *99*
3. Cambridge, Mary Prentiss Inn *100*
4. Centerville, Fernbrook Inn *102*
5. Chatham, Captain's House Inn of Chatham *103*, Moses Nickerson House *105*
6. Dennis, Isaiah Hall Bed and Breakfast Inn *107*
7. Eastham, Whalewalk Inn *108*
8. East Orleans, Nauset House Inn *110*
9. East Sandwich, Wingscorton Farm Inn *111*
10. Falmouth, Inn on the Sound *113*, Mostly Hall *114*
11. Florence, The Knoll *115*
12. Gloucester, Harborview Inn *116*
13. Great Barrington, Dragonsfield *118*
14. Greenfield, Brandt House *119*
15. Lee, Applegate *121*
16. Lenox, Birchwood Inn *122*, Brook Farm Inn *124*, Cliffwood Inn *125*, Garden Gables Inn *126*, Rookwood Inn *128*, Walker House *129*
17. Marblehead, Harbor Light Inn *131*, Seagull Inn *132*
18. Martha's Vineyard, Thorncroft Inn *133*
19. Nantucket, Cliff Lodge *135*
20. North Adams, Blackinton Manor *136*, The Porches *138*
21. Plymouth, 1782 Whitfield House *140*
22. Rockport, Captain's House *141*, Eden Pines *142*, Old Farm Inn *143*, Seacrest Manor *144*
23. Salem, Amelia Payson House *146*
24. Sheffield, Berkshire 1802 House *147*
25. South Lee, Federal House Inn *148*, Historic Merrell Inn *149*
26. Stockbridge, Blue Willow *151*, Stockbridge Country Inn *152*
27. West Falmouth, Inn at West Falmouth *153*
28. Williamstown, Field Farm Guest House *154*, River Bend Farm *156*

ALLEN HOUSE

599 Main Street
Amherst 01002
(413) 253–5000

■ You can't miss this Victorian beauty, a prize 1886 Queen Anne "stick-style" home. The gaily painted gingerbread exterior, lavished with hanging plants and bordered by flowering shrubs, is replete with ornate carving and peaked gables, intricately carved Austrian verge board, Oriental Chippendale, and multiple relief shingles.

The interior has been restored with equal historic precision down to the last detail to reflect the aesthetic movement of the Victorian era, which emphasized art in interior decor. The house is filled with Eastlake-style furniture, period art, and reproduction wall coverings by Charles Eastlake and William Morris. The rush matting is original to the house, along with the hand-carved fireplace mantels.

The formal dining room is the setting for elaborate breakfasts that may feature stuffed French toast, eggs Benedict, Swedish pancakes, quiche, or Southwestern-style eggs.

Upstairs bedrooms vary in size from the back maids' rooms to front bedrooms large enough to accommodate three guests. All are furnished with Victoriana.

This painstaking restoration won the 1991 Historic Preservation Award from the Amherst Historical Commission for innkeepers Alan and Ann Zieminski. Those who want to appreciate this special decor should be sure that their lodgings are in the Allen House, not in the Amherst Inn where overflow guests are sometimes placed.

What's Nearby: A classic New England college town, Amherst offers three quite different campuses for touring—traditional Amherst College, the modern University of Massachusetts, and rustic Hampshire Col-

WEB SITE: www.allenhouse.com

INNKEEPERS: Alan and Ann Zieminski

ROOMS: 7 rooms, all with private bath, central air-conditioning

ON THE GROUNDS: 3 acres, veranda, gardens

RATES: $75–$175, including full breakfast and afternoon refreshments

CREDIT CARDS ACCEPTED: Master-Card, Visa, American Express

OPEN: Year-round

HOW TO GET THERE: From Massachusetts Turnpike and points south, take Interstate 91 north to exit 19, make a right onto Route 9 in Northampton, and go east past the Coolidge Bridge and Hadley into Amherst, where Route 9 is called College Street. Turn left onto South Whitney Street and right onto Main Street. Allen House is the second house from the corner past South Whitney. From the north take I–91 south to exit 20, turn left at the first light, go 1 mile, turn left at the light onto Route 9 east, and follow the previous directions from that point.

lege. The Pioneer Valley is known for its many crafts artisans, and nearby Northampton, the home of Smith College, has dozens of crafts galleries as well as distinctive dining. Area sightseeing includes Amherst's Mead Gallery and the Emily Dickinson Homestead, the Smith College Museum of Art, and a dozen house museums in Old Deerfield.

CAPTAIN FREEMAN INN

15 Breakwater Road
Brewster 02631
(508) 896–7481; (800) 843–4664
Fax: (508) 896 5618

■ This pretty peaked Victorian house with gingerbread-trim columns and a wraparound porch was built in 1860 for an aristocratic shipmaster, Capt. William Freeman. No doubt the captain would be pleased to know that a picture of his ship, the *King fisher,* hangs in the entry hall—and he would surely approve of the award-winning 1992 restoration that brought the house back to its early glory, also recorded in photos. The restoration won a place for the home on the National Register of Historic Places.

The high ceilings, ornate plaster moldings, herringbone floors, marble fireplace, and tall windows of the Victorian era lend grace to the formal living room, which is furnished in period decor. A fireplace also warms the dining room, which opens to a screened porch overlooking the pool.

Breakfast is served at tables for two or four. Expect a lavish morning menu, with freshly squeezed juice, fruit choices, and imaginative treats such as eggs Brewster, a variation of eggs Benedict using cranberry chutney and Italian ham.

In the afternoon, the inn's famous homemade cookies are offered along with beverages. In summer, guests like to sip the freshly made iced tea and lemonade while

WEB SITE: www.captainfreemaninn.com

INNKEEPERS: Donna and Pete Amadeo

ROOMS: 6 rooms, all with private bath; 6 luxury suites with whirlpool bath, fireplace, TV/VCR, refrigerator, phone, air-conditioning

ON THE GROUNDS: More than 1 acre of lawn, wraparound porch, patio, swimming pool, lawn games, bicycles free for guests' use

RATES: $145–$225, including full breakfast and afternoon refreshments

CREDIT CARDS ACCEPTED: MasterCard, Visa, American Express

OPEN: Year-round

HOW TO GET THERE: From the Mid-Cape Highway (Route 6), take exit 10, Route 124, toward Brewster. At Route 6A, turn right and then make an immediate left onto Breakwater Road, just before the First Parish Church. The inn is the first driveway on the left.

seated in rockers on the shady porch; in cooler months, they move into the parlor for tea or hot chocolate. The inn recently added a wine and beer bar on weekend evenings, a nice option.

Up the graceful center staircase are rooms furnished with canopy beds, wicker accents, and Victorian dressers and mirrors. The suites are lavish, with every kind of amenity—from embroidered canopies and fireplaces to whirlpool baths and VCRs. If you opt for a honeymoon, anniversary, or special occasion package, you also get a chilled bottle of champagne and two in-room massages by a professional masseuse.

Just off the main highway, but removed from the traffic, the inn's spacious grounds offer a pool and space for croquet or badminton. Brewster is blessed with some of Cape Cod's best restaurants, from the informal Brewster Fish House to the four-star Chillingsworth, all convenient to the inn.

Since the Amadeos arrived in 2003, they have added a popular event in winter, a series of cooking-school weekends featuring local experts.

What's Nearby: Brewster is convenient for all the pleasures of Cape Cod—beach, summer theater, museums, shops, golf, tennis, historic sites, fishing, whale watching, and sailing. The Cape Cod Rail Trail is nearby for bicycling. The New England Fire and History Museum and the Cape Cod Museum of Natural History are havens on rainy days.

MARY PRENTISS INN

6 Prentiss Street
Cambridge 02140
(617) 661–2929
Fax: (617) 661–5989

The year was 1843, and nearby Massachu-setts Avenue was a dirt road where sheep and cattle roamed when William Saunders built this columned Greek Revival residence as a country house for his newlywed son, William Augustus, and daughter-in-law, Mary Prentiss. The house had to be fine to be worthy of Mary, whose prominent family was among the founders of Cambridge in the 1600s (you can see their markers in the Historic Old Burying Ground off Harvard Square). Restored and converted to an inn, the house is now a historic landmark with vintage charm. And while the avenue now whizzes with cars, this block remains quiet, a prime residential neighborhood only about a ten-minute walk from Harvard Square.

Charlotte Forsythe, an artist and designer, was the ideal person to undertake the restoration. She added a new wing that looks like a miniature of the old, connecting it with a second-floor bridge, and she indulged her passion for antiques and her eye for the unusual.

You can see some of the happy results as soon as you come into the entry hall, filled with generous floral bouquets and boasting a bird's-eye-maple antique chest, an ornate gilt mirror, and a carved Victorian sofa tucked beneath the lovely original curved stairway. The breakfast and sitting room off the hall has high ceilings, formal printed drapes, a polished brass chandelier, and handsome Oriental rugs. The white wooden mantel over the fireplace and the corner whatnot shelves are adorned with an artfully placed collection of china cups and saucers. Several tables and chairs are ready for diners, and a wing chair with a good reading lamp invites guests to settle in after breakfast.

When the weather is warm, French doors are open to a spacious wooden deck filled with flowering plants and greenery. Here you can sit at an umbrella table to eat breakfast. A typical menu may begin with fresh fruit and yogurt and include such goodies as quiche and potatoes and fresh raisin scones.

Each bedroom has its own unique furnishings—painted and four-poster headboards, antique chests and armoires, skirted tables, fine fabrics, and unusual accessories.

Room 14 has a spacious sitting room, a handsome paisley quilt, and striking painted bedsteads. The bathroom is done with attractive dark floral wallpaper. Like several of the baths, it has a wide whimsical border done by Charlotte herself, with pieces of crockery, tiny watch faces, miniature dolls, and other ephemera embedded in the plaster.

Suite 9 is the designer's own favorite, done with a queen-size four-poster bed, yellow chintz print quilt and bed skirt, lace curtains, a Victorian love seat, and an antique chair. The suite also features a fireplace and a wet bar.

WEB SITE: www.maryprentissinn.com

INNKEEPER: Tangi Pina

ROOMS: 14 rooms and 6 suites, all with private bath, air-conditioning, TV, clock radio, phone, modem hookup, wireless Internet; some with fireplace, wet bar, microwave, whirlpool bath

ON THE GROUNDS: 1,000-foot plant-filled outside deck; limited number of free parking spaces for guests, by reservation

RATES: Rooms $109–$189, suites $139–$259, including full breakfast and afternoon tea

CREDIT CARDS ACCEPTED: MasterCard, Visa, American Express

OPEN: Year-round

HOW TO GET THERE: From the Massachusetts Turnpike take the Cambridge/Allston exit to Cambridge and Storrow Drive West. Exit at Harvard Square, continue over the Charles River bridge onto JFK Street, passing through Harvard Square to Massachusetts Avenue North. Prentiss Street is a right turn off Massachusetts Avenue approximately ½ mile from the square; the inn is a few doors in on the right.

The third-floor rooms are appealing, with dormer ceilings and beams. Room 17 has a skylight. Even the smallest room is cozy and inviting.

All this charm comes with modern comforts—air-conditioning, room phones, and remote-control cable TV. For those who plan to stay a while, some rooms are also equipped with a wet bar and microwave oven.

What's Nearby: Lively Harvard Square beckons with street entertainers, Harvard campus tours and museums, dozens of restaurants, and bookstores galore. Both the MIT campus and Boston are just a short subway ride away.

FERNBROOK INN

481 Main Street
Centerville 02632
(508) 775–4999

■ Many Cape Cod inns can boast of an interesting history, but few can equal the pedigree or guest list of this century-old, gabled Queen Anne Victorian. It was built in 1881 by hotelier Howard Marston of Boston's venerable Parker House. He commissioned the most renowned landscape architect of the day, Frederick Law Olmsted, to design the grounds, which include many exotic trees and a heart-shaped sunken Sweetheart Garden planted with pink and red roses among lily ponds.

In the 1930s, the house was purchased by Dr. Herbert Kalmus, a co-inventor of the Technicolor process, who hosted a long list of Hollywood greats, among them Walt Disney, Cecil B. DeMille, and Gloria Swanson. After Kalmus left the property to the Catholic Church, it was used as a summer residence for ten years by Cardinal Francis Spellman, who entertained many famous guests, including Presidents Kennedy and Nixon.

The celebrity guest list continued to grow, with names such as Bill Murray, Alec Baldwin, and others who have stayed here while visiting the Kennedy compound in neighboring Hyannis. Both Caroline and Kara Kennedy were married in Our Lady of Victory Catholic Church not far from the inn.

The house was refurbished completely in 1986 and then spruced up considerably when Mary Anne English took over the inn in the late 1990s. Her most recent project is the lap pool nestled in the sunken garden. She also renovated the ballroom, which now boasts floor-to-ceiling windows and a surround-sound music system, making it popular for functions.

Each room has an impressive canopy or four-poster bed and special features. The

WEB SITE: www.fernbrookinn.com

INNKEEPER: Mary Anne English

ROOMS: 6 rooms, 1 garden cottage, all with private bath, TV, radio; 2 with working fireplace; some with refrigerator

ON THE GROUNDS: Frederick Law Olmsted–designed sunken garden and rare plantings, 50-foot lap pool

RATES: $125–$175, including full breakfast

CREDIT CARDS ACCEPTED: None

OPEN: Year-round

HOW TO GET THERE: From the Mid-Cape Highway (Route 6), take exit 5, continue straight past the stop sign, and then take the first right onto Old Stage Road. At the next stop sign, turn left (still Old Stage Road) and continue past one set of lights. At the next stop sign, Old Stage becomes Main Street. Continue straight, and the inn is a few houses ahead on the left.

Cardinal Room on the first floor offers pyramid ceilings, a stained-glass window, a tile-faced fireplace, and a private entrance. The antiques-filled sitting room alcove of the Yellow Suite is in the round turret of the house. The Peach Room has a full view of the Sweetheart Garden, as does the Green Suite with its four full-length windows.

The wood-paneled Garden Cottage at the end of a pebbled path is delightful, furnished in wicker, and features its own porch.

The public rooms are formal turn-of-the-twentieth-century Victorian in style. Breakfast is served at 9:00 A.M. in a dining room whose built-in cabinets are filled with fine china and silver. The menu includes fresh orange juice, fruits, eggs to order, and choices such as pancakes and homemade breads.

Though the inn retains only one of its original eighteen acres, guests can still admire the rare Japanese trees and flower beds planned by Olmsted and stroll in his rose garden, one of the many reasons that this inn is unique.

What's Nearby: Centerville is a quiet outpost of bustling Hyannis, where you can shop, take in a show at the Cape Cod Melody Tent, visit the John F. Kennedy Hyannis Museum, board the Cape Cod Scenic Railroad, or sail out to sea on a harbor or whale-watching cruise or on a boat to Nantucket or Martha's Vineyard. Craigville Beach offers swimming in Nantucket Sound. The Centerville Historical Society, a fourteen-room mansion, saves a rainy day.

CAPTAIN'S HOUSE INN OF CHATHAM

369–377 Old Harbor Road
Chatham 02633
(508) 945–0127; (800) 315–0728
Fax: (508) 945–0866

■ "Wake up in 1839" invites the brochure, and indeed the Captain's House is a gracious return to the past, an authentic sea captain's home built in 1839 with Williamsburg decor that makes it one of the most elegant inns on Cape Cod.

Dave McMaster had already enjoyed two successful careers, as a commander in the U.S. Navy and then founder of a California computer company, when he and his English wife, Jan, spent their first overnight in an American bed-and-breakfast inn. "We really liked it," Jan says. "You have this beautiful house and you get to show it off and meet all kinds of interesting people. We said, 'We can do that.'" That was how the couple (who were already owners of a country pub and restaurant in Dorchester-on-Thames, just south of Oxford, England) decided it was time for a lifestyle change.

A two-year search for the perfect inn followed. They were attracted to the village feel of Chatham, which Jan says reminds her of England, and to the history and elegance of the inn. In 1993 they took over. Dave is in charge of marketing, finance, and maintenance while Jan supervises the kitchen and takes care of the guests.

They have kept the traditional decor and antiques that first attracted them, including Williamsburg-style wallpapers and fabrics, camelback sofas, Chippendale-style chairs, Oriental or braided rugs, and canopy beds in every room. The interesting antique beds are Jan's special passion, most of them acquired from a special dealer she found in Seekonk, Massachusetts.

The Greek Revival main house, a classic white clapboard with green shutters, was built by Capt. Hiram Harding, a wealthy packet skipper, and many of the guest rooms are named after the ships he sailed. Two rooms and two suites are in the main house, while others are found in the attached carriage house and in a cottage that was moved onto the property. The newest luxury accommodations are in the former stable. One of Jan's favorite rooms is Wild Pigeon, upstairs in the carriage house, which

WEB SITE: www.captainshouseinn.com

INNKEEPERS: David and Janet McMaster

ROOMS: 12 rooms, 4 suites, all with private bath, air-conditioning, TV/VCR, phone, clock, radio, robes, fireplace; some with whirlpool bath

ON THE GROUNDS: 2 acres of grounds with patio, heated outdoor pool, croquet, bikes for guests' use

RATES: Rooms $185–$350, suites $250–$425, including full breakfast and afternoon tea

CREDIT CARDS ACCEPTED: MasterCard, Visa, American Express, Discover

OPEN: Year-round

HOW TO GET THERE: From the Mid-Cape Highway (Route 6), take exit 11, Chatham. Turn left onto Route 137 past two stoplights to a T-junction, Route 28. Turn left and travel about 2 miles to the Chatham rotary, and then follow the rotary around to the left to Old Harbor Road heading toward Orleans. The inn is on the left about ½ mile ahead.

has a high ceiling with exposed beams, a dramatic four-poster bed, a nautical decorating scheme, a fireplace, and a small balcony.

Beyond the formal living room is the bright, airy sunroom where breakfast is served at tables for two or four set with linen tablecloths, fine china, and silver. A typical morning menu may include cantaloupe with raspberry sauce, a country vegetable omelette with sautéed potatoes, and cheese-herb bread. Among guests' favorite choices are the lemon-yogurt pancakes with cranberry syrup.

Jan's background shows in the proper English tea served each afternoon, which features scones with jam and cream and treats such as Irish Cream liqueur cake and chocolate shortbread. If hunger pangs strike after dinner, complimentary snacks are available in the kitchen each evening, along with coffee, tea, and hot chocolate. And decanters of port and sherry await in the library.

You can work all this off in the fitness center, with a few laps in the pool, or a round of croquet on the lawn. The inn will loan you tennis racquets and balls to use on local courts and provide towels, beach chairs, umbrellas, and coolers if you are headed for the beach. In fact, there's little they won't do at this gracious inn to insure that you have a wonderful stay.

What's Nearby: With Nantucket Sound on one side and the Atlantic Ocean on the other, Chatham attracts both fishing enthusiasts and beach lovers. Don't miss the panoramic view from Chatham Light. The upscale town is filled with shops and fine dining, and the Old Atwood House Museum, a 1752 sea captain's home, records the town's history.

MOSES NICKERSON HOUSE

364 Old Harbor Road
Chatham 02633
(508) 945–5859; (800) 628–6972
Fax. (508) 945 7087

◾ If you want proof of the romance of country inns, just ask Linda and George Watts. Linda had just traded her corporate insurance career in Pennsylvania for the role of innkeeper in 1995 when George, an accountant from Canada, came looking for a room. Love blossomed, and a year and a half later, the two were married at the inn, where they are now happily enjoying joint stewardship.

They couldn't ask for a better setting. Named for the whaling captain who built this rambling Greek Revival home in 1839, the inn retains its original wide pumpkin-pine floors, many fireplaces, and the old-fashioned elegance of an earlier time.

The English parlor welcomes with rose-patterned wallpaper, and vintage cranberry glass on the white wooden fireplace mantel picks up the color. Among the handsome furnishings are a needlepoint Aubusson rug on the floor and a tall antique lady's secretary desk holding a guest book. A brass-and-glass oval coffee table in front of the sofa offers books on New England.

Breakfast is served on a sunny, glass-enclosed terrace furnished in wrought iron. After a beginning of juice and a fresh fruit plate comes a main course that changes daily, with offerings such as quiche, waffles, blueberry pancakes, bacon-and-egg pie, or a house specialty, fruit pizza.

The largest of the guest quarters is Room 1, measuring a generous 30 by 24 feet. Located on the first floor, it offers a fireplace and French doors opening to the front veranda. The room is filled with unique pieces, including a hand-painted four-poster bed, a painted antique armoire, and a velvet settee.

Room 2 signals its mood with a heart on the door. It has flower stencils, a quilt on the wall, a pretty white coverlet on a four-poster pine bed, and a matching mirrored armoire.

The mood changes once again in Room 3, done in an airy blue and white color scheme, with wicker furnishings and a seashore theme, with sandpipers painted on the door and bird carvings and bottles on ledges over the windows. The stenciling and hand-hooked rug in Room 4 will please lovers of country. Romantics may favor Room 5, tucked at the top of a narrow staircase, with a Sheraton canopy bed and a big bay window overlooking the gardens.

Upstairs, Room 6 has its own outside entrance and lots of windows, while Room 7 has a fireplace and a masculine feel lent by dark Ralph Lauren paisley fabrics.

Chatham is a particularly picturesque Cape Cod town, filled with shops and good restaurants and with an active fishing fleet. The inn puts you within walking distance of tennis and golf courses and unspoiled beaches.

WEB SITE: www.mosesnickersonhouse.com

INNKEEPERS: George and Linda Watts

ROOMS: 7 rooms, all with private bath, phone, TV, air-conditioning, clock, radio

ON THE GROUNDS: Shaded patio, lawns, gardens, hammock, swing

RATES: $89–$209, including full breakfast and afternoon tea

CREDIT CARDS ACCEPTED: MasterCard, Visa, American Express, Discover

OPEN: Year-round

HOW TO GET THERE: From the Mid-Cape Highway (Route 6), take exit 11 to Route 137, and then turn left onto Route 28 south. At the rotary, continue left on Route 28, Old Harbor Road, toward Orleans. The inn is ½ mile farther, on the right.

What's Nearby: See What's Nearby on page 105.

ISAIAH HALL BED AND BREAKFAST INN

152 Whig Street, P.O. Box 1007
Dennis 02638
(508) 385–9928; (800) 736–0160
Fax: (508) 385–5879

▓ Warm and cozy and filled with fresh and fanciful American folk art, this delightful 1857 farmhouse was once home to Isaiah B. Hall, a barrel maker, whose brother Henry cultivated the first cranberry bogs in America not far from the inn. Seeing opportunity, the clever Isaiah designed and patented the first cranberry barrel to transport his brother's berries.

The shuttered, gray-shingled house and adjacent big white barn were turned into an inn in 1948. The sitting room welcomes with a fancy woodstove, a fireplace trimmed with ship tiles, and bird carvings on the mantel. A folksy painting of the inn hangs over the fireplace, a charming rendering of the town of Dennis hangs above the camel-back sofa, and a handsome red and blue Oriental rug sets off the room.

Up the steep stairs, the hall is just a bit tippy with age, and rooms are furnished with a mix of fishnet canopies, brass and iron beds, antique quilts, and nice old country pieces. Room 1 has a fireplace, a handsome highboy, and a pretty blue floral rug. Room 3 is done in pastel florals with a soft green painted dresser and a rocking chair at the window.

Stairs behind the kitchen lead to the carriage house, where an informal pine-paneled great room beckons for watching TV or socializing. A guest refrigerator, games, books, and high-speed Internet access are

WEB SITE: www.isaiahhallinn.com

INNKEEPERS: Jerry and Judy Neal

ROOMS: 10 rooms, 2 suites, all with private bath, canopy bed, air-conditioning, telephone, TV/VCR, clock, radio, robes, hair dryer; 4 with balcony; 1 with fireplace

ON THE GROUNDS: Gardens, lawn games

RATES: Rooms $85–$175, suites $150–$200, including full breakfast

CREDIT CARDS ACCEPTED: Master-Card, Visa, American Express, Discover

OPEN: Year-round

HOW TO GET THERE: From Route 6, the Mid-Cape Highway, take exit 8, turn left, and proceed about 1¼ miles to Route 6A. Turn right and continue for about 3½ miles to Hope Lane and make a left. At the end of Hope Lane, turn right on Whig Street; the inn is a short distance farther on the left.

among the amenities. Rooms here also have a rustic feel, with paneled walls, iron beds, comfortable sitting areas, and private decks. Larger rooms like the king suite can accommodate extra guests with a pull-out love seat as well as a king-size four-poster.

Everyone gathers for breakfast at a 12-foot cherry table beneath a stained-glass Tiffany-style chandelier adorned with fruits and greenery. The table is set with country crockery. The buffet menu includes juice, fruit, yogurt, cereal, breads, and muffins of all kinds, plus one hot dish, perhaps Belgian waffles, banana pancakes, or quiche. Tea and coffee are available for guests all day, along with homemade chocolate chip cookies.

Outside, the porch offers white rockers, and there are chairs and umbrella tables on the spacious lawn for enjoying the peaceful surroundings.

The inn is tucked away on a quiet street behind the Cape Playhouse, the oldest professional summer theater in the United States. If you come in season, you'll almost surely find some of the stars and directors in residence.

What's Nearby: The Cape Playhouse in Dennis has been a landmark summer theater since 1927; the complex includes the Cape Cinema, showing art films, and the Cape Museum of Fine Arts, with displays of work by Cape Cod artists. Also nearby are whale watching, antiquing, biking, and all the myriad pleasures of Cape Cod. And you can walk to the beach.

WHALEWALK INN

220 Bridge Road
Eastham 02642
(508) 255–0617; (800) 440–1281
Fax: (508) 255–0617

▨ Though it is an authentic 1830s Cape Cod whaling master's home, there's a pastel palette and a stylish feel to this airy, sophisticated inn. The original gray-shingled house with gingerbread white wooden trim has been added onto many times over the years, and the old barn is now connected to the main house. In the 1920s, the property belonged to the Kent family of the Lorillard tobacco fortune and functioned as a gentleman's farm. It was turned into an inn in 1953 and has really come into its own in the last decade, especially since Elaine and Kevin Conlin arrived in 2001, leaving business careers in Scottsdale, Arizona, to become New England innkeepers.

Elaine's touch can be seen in the main sitting room, done in warm peach tones, with swag curtains pulled away from the windows to allow plenty of light. Oriental

WEB SITE: www.whalewalkinn.com

INNKEEPERS: Elaine and Kevin Conlin

ROOMS: 11 rooms, 5 suites on the property (main house, barn, guest house, carriage house, spa pent-house, and saltbox cottage), all with private bath, air-conditioning, clock, radio; 14 with TV/VCR; most with fireplace; 4 suites with kitchen; 3 carriage house rooms with Jacuzzi; 2 rooms with soaking tub; 1 suite with deck; 5 carriage house rooms with patio

ON THE GROUNDS: 3¼ acres, lawn and patio, gardens, spa, bicycles free for guests' use

RATES: $175–$340, spa suite $450, including full breakfast, afternoon refreshments, evening hors d'oeuvres

CREDIT CARDS ACCEPTED: Master-Card, Visa, American Express, Discover

OPEN: January 1 to December 15

HOW TO GET THERE: Take the Mid-Cape Highway (Route 6) to the Orleans rotary; from there take the Rock Harbor exit left onto Rock Harbor Road and make the first right turn to Bridge Road.

rugs warm the inn's rooms and hallways, and her Waterford crystal collection sparkles in the sunlight.

The artwork throughout the inn features pastel seascapes and Cape Cod scenes, many of them done by local artists. One specially commissioned work shows the inn patio in full summer bloom.

Breakfast is served on that patio in warm weather, otherwise on the pleasant sun-porch, set with tables for two. A breakfast chef makes sure that mornings start beautifully, with dishes such as Captain Harding's Eggs, Cape Cod pancakes, pecan waffles with sugar-glazed bananas, or walnut waffles with pear and cranberry syrup. Fruit kuchen, banana bread, sour cream coffee cake, and pumpkin, pear, and corn breads are among the treats fresh from the oven.

The hospitable Conlins offer refreshments in the afternoon, and snacks at the end of the day when guests gather in the sitting room or the adjoining den for a BYOB (bring your own bottle) cocktail hour.

Each guest room is different in size and decor, but all feature soft color schemes, with many marbleized wall coverings and swirl pattern fabrics. The largest room, with a separate entrance, has walls the color of raspberry sherbet, a gas fireplace, a four-poster king-size bed, and a pine armoire. The five suites in various buildings on the property are all super-spacious, with fireplaces and full kitchens.

The newest facility at the inn is the spa building, offering fitness equipment, a sauna, and hot tubs. Massages and facials are available by appointment, a lovely way to add pampering to your visit.

What's Nearby: Eastham's Cape Cod National Seashore visitor center offers many nature programs and printed guides to hiking and biking. Orleans shops and restaurants are next door, and the 30-mile Cape Cod Rail Trail bike path is nearby. Indoor attractions include the Old Schoolhouse Museum, the Tool Museum, the Swift-Daley House, and the 1680 Old Eastham Windmill, the oldest working windmill on Cape Cod.

NAUSET HOUSE INN

Beach Road, P.O. Box 774
East Orleans 02643
(508) 255–2195

■ You can feel the warmth as soon as you walk in the door of this shingled 1810 farmhouse, a home that reflects the artistry and informal friendliness of the owners. With one of the most beautiful beaches on Cape Cod just ½ mile down the road, Nauset House is a special haven.

WEB SITE: www.nausethouseinn.com

INNKEEPERS: Diane Johnson; Cindy and John Vessella

ROOMS: 14 rooms; 8 with private bath; robes provided for guests with shared bath

ON THE GROUNDS: 1907 plant-filled conservatory; large yard with patio, tables, and chairs

RATES: $75–$170, including full breakfast and afternoon wine and refreshments

OPEN: April through October

CREDIT CARDS ACCEPTED: Master-Card, Visa, Discover

HOW TO GET THERE: Take the Mid-Cape Highway (Route 6) to exit 12, Orleans/Brewster, go right to the first stoplight, and then right again on Eldredge Park Way. Proceed through the next stoplight (Route 28) to the light on Main Street, turn right, and continue straight until you reach the fork in the road at the Barley Neck Inn. Bear left onto Beach Road; the inn is ⁹⁄₁₀ mile down Beach Road on the right.

The decor is comfortable country with a mix of art and antiques. It is easy to feel at home in the sociable living room, where a long white sofa and two chairs face the fire, and more seating and a game table are at the plant-filled back wall of windows. Shelves are stacked with books, and the coffee table and a side basket are piled high with a variety of magazines.

The plant-filled conservatory centered with a weeping cherry tree is a delightful hideaway for reading, cheerful even on the gloomiest day.

Diane, a former stained-glass artist from Connecticut, has honed her artistic talents on the Cape—she is now a painter, stitcher, and printmaker whose white line wood cuts have merited a one-woman show in Orleans. Her touches are everywhere—in the flower sprigs painted to match the name on guest-room doors, the hand stenciling, and the hand-painted furniture pieces.

Guest rooms vary in size, but even the smallest is filled with charm and individuality. The cozy Sea Lavender Room has a wooden floor painted a cheerful blue, a bird design on the headboard, and a crewel-embroidered chair. Sea Oats, one of the larger rooms in the adjacent guest house, is done with lace curtains, a dhurrie rug, and a faux chest painted on the wall. Iris, another larger room with a beamed ceiling, has quilts both on the bed and on the walls and an antique iron campaign bed serving as a sofa. Rosebud has a white iron bed and a balcony overlooking the backyard.

Cat lovers will enjoy Diane's faux cats leaning on the outside gatepost and reclining on the stair landing inside. The cloth cats adorning each bed are daughter Cindy's contribution. The dogs in residence, however, are real. Wiley, a little cairn terrier, and Ginger, a corgi, are very friendly.

Everyone in the family, including Cindy's husband, John, and son, Nicholas, pitches in for breakfast, served at long tables in the brick-floored dining room. The blackboard menu offers treats such as avocado, tomato, and cheese omelettes or ginger pancakes.

What's Nearby: Fabulous Nauset Beach is an East Orleans area attraction. The Cape Cod National Seashore also offers natural beauty nearby. Biking, boating, tennis, and golf are favorite local pastimes, along with whale-watching and sunset cruises. For more commercial pleasures, you can find a wide array of restaurants, galleries, and shops, especially antiques shops. Diane's hand-drawn map leads visitors to the best places.

WINGSCORTON FARM INN

11 Wing Boulevard
East Sandwich 02537
(508) 888–0534

◼ The first thing you see when you turn off the highway is a sign: FRESH EGGS AND CHICKENS FOR SALE. It tells you that this farm is for real. Up the hill is a working spread on thirteen acres, complete with chickens, sheep, cats, dogs, goats, horses, a llama, and a burro. In the midst of it all is a lovely white shingled farmhouse with dark green shutters, circa 1758, completely restored and filled with antiques and country charm.

The keeping room has a wood-paneled wall painted soft green, an enormous open-hearth fireplace, and an Oriental rug on the floor. A collection of pewter pieces is displayed on a double ledge across the mantel. Even more inviting is the library, paneled with dark wood and featuring wing chairs in front of the fire, a wall lined with well-stocked bookshelves, and magazines piled on a coffee table made from a ship's wheel. A fine ship model sits on the mantel, and old guns are displayed on the wall.

Guests gather around a long pine table with a mix of antique chairs for a big farm breakfast, served in a paneled dining room with a fireplace wall painted in a cheerful salmon color. The menu features meats, vegetables, eggs fresh from the farm, and often homemade pies and cakes.

Comfortable suites upstairs have wood-paneled walls, four-poster beds with fishnet canopies, woven rag rugs, and working fireplaces. One suite is done in Shaker style, just for variety.

The carriage house is a romantic retreat with beams, skylights, and a private deck and patio. Downstairs is a sitting area with a cozy woodstove and your own kitchen and table and chairs; a spiral staircase leads up to the sleeping area. Families will be pleased to note that the inn's cottage can accommodate up to six people and has a kitchen and a fireplace.

Innkeeper Sheila Weyers was working as a clinical psychologist when she purchased the farm in 1983 and began doing what she calls "accumulating animals." Pretty soon people who came to visit were so delighted with the place, they began asking to stay, and thus the farm evolved into a bed-and-breakfast where children and pets are welcome.

Children love seeing the many animals. The grounds and orchards make for a pleasant stroll, or you can take a short walk to a small beach.

What's Nearby: The historic town of Sandwich, the oldest on Cape Cod, is just down the road, with a working gristmill that has stood on the same spot since the seventeenth century. Sandwich offers a notable glass museum, plus magnificent gardens and more museums at Heritage Plantation. Come in June to see acres of rhododendrons in bloom.

INNKEEPER: Sheila M. Weyers

ROOMS: 3 suites, all with private bath, fireplace; 1 carriage house for two with full kitchen, woodstove; 1 cottage for up to six guests with kitchen, fireplace

ON THE GROUNDS: 13 acres, patio, walking trails, farm animals; small ocean beach nearby

RATES: $175–$200, including full breakfast

CREDIT CARDS ACCEPTED: MasterCard, Visa, American Express

OPEN: Year-round

HOW TO GET THERE: From Route 6, the Mid-Cape Highway, take exit 3 and turn left at the end of the ramp onto Quaker Meetinghouse Road. Go 1½ miles to the end, turn right onto Route 6A, and continue 2½ miles to Wingscorton Farm; watch for the sign on the left.

INN ON THE SOUND

313 Grand Avenue
Falmouth 02540
(508) 457–9666; (800) 564–9668
Fax: (508) 457–9631

■ The views are nothing short of dazzling—an unobstructed vista of blue Vineyard Sound and the island of Martha's Vineyard just across the water. You can gaze to your heart's content from the spacious outside decks as well as from the big living-room picture window and from most of the airy bedrooms. And when you want to get even closer to the water, the beach is just across the road and the summer ferry is a short stroll away.

This is an inn with a dream location—and finding it was a fifteen-year fantasy come true for innkeeper Renee Ross and her brother, David Ross. The pair had worked on several real estate projects together in New Jersey, while Renee pursued a career as a commercial interior designer and David worked in theatrical lighting. But all the time they were searching and searching for the perfect inn. Since they found it and moved to Falmouth in 1995, Renee has been putting her decorating talents to work to make the inside as bright and inviting as the location. They have also added a facade that provides private decks for four guest rooms.

The mood is beach casual, the look is contemporary, with country accents in mission oak. The white-paneled living room has two seating areas, one in front of a big stone fireplace, the other cozily tucked behind with a wall of books. Artistic touches such as the intriguing antique fish prints and pottery on the big square coffee table are by artist friends from a past time when Renee had an art gallery in Fort Lee, New Jersey.

WEB SITE: www.innonthesound.com

INNKEEPERS: Renee Ross and David Ross

ROOMS: 10 rooms, all with private bath, TV, clock, radio; 9 with ocean view; 4 with private deck

ON THE GROUNDS: Guest deck facing the water

RATES: $150–$295, including continental breakfast

CREDIT CARDS ACCEPTED: Master-Card, Visa, American Express, Discover

OPEN: Year-round

HOW TO GET THERE: Cross the Bourne Bridge to Cape Cod, and then go about a quarter of the way around the rotary and follow Route 28 south until the divided highway ends. Continue 1 mile to the first traffic light, turn left onto Jones Road, and continue through two sets of traffic lights; you will cross Route 28 and the road name will change to Worcester Court. At the blinking red light, Worcester Court becomes a divided road; make a right and quick left and continue on to the ocean. At Grand Avenue turn right and follow for ½ mile to the inn, which is on the right.

On the walls are black-and-white original pencil drawings of African animals, so richly detailed that they could easily be mistaken for photographs.

Bedroom color schemes carry out the hues of the sea and feature lots of summery wicker. Two front main-floor rooms with special views are Room 1, featuring deep coffee-color walls and brown and white plaid fabrics, and Room 2, paneled in pickled white beaded board and accented with gray and dark taupe bedding and accessories. Upstairs, beams add to the flavor of the rooms. Room 4D is done in crisp black and white and has a fine view from a bay window. Room 9J has a double shower in the bath and a private deck.

Breakfasts of fresh squeezed orange juice, seasonal fruits, fresh baked goodies, and a choice of beverages are available between 8:30 and 11:00 A.M. They can be enjoyed in your room, in the lounge, or out on the decks.

The Inn on the Sound stays open all year, offering romantic views of the winter-tossed sea and special themes such as a winter jazz weekend that features a sumptuous dessert buffet, a live performance, and dinner at some of Falmouth's best restaurants.

What's Nearby: A busy resort town centered around a historic village green, Falmouth offers notable beaches, lots of shops, waterside bike trails, hiking, and all kinds of water sports. Ferries to Martha's Vineyard leave from neighboring Woods Hole.

MOSTLY HALL

27 Main Street
Falmouth 02540
(508) 548–3786; (800) 682–0565
Fax: (508) 457–1572

■ How do you make a southern bride feel at home up north? Capt. Albert Nye had a bright idea. When he brought his sweetheart from New Orleans to Cape Cod, he surprised and no doubt delighted her with a plantation-style "raised cottage" house much like those she had left behind. The name was inspired by a visiting child more than a hundred years ago, who marveled at the dramatic central hallway, declaring of the house, "Mama, it's mostly hall."

More than a century and a half later, this spacious 1849 home, with its wraparound porch, 13-foot ceilings, and floor-to-ceiling windows, is still delighting guests. Its uniqueness has earned it a place on the National Register of Historic Places.

The formal parlor on the first floor is Victorian in feel, with a marble fireplace and a teardrop chandelier that is original to the house and was once lit with gas. A double

WEB SITE: www.mostlyhall.com

INNKEEPERS: Charlene and René Poirier

ROOMS: 6 rooms, all with private bath, air-conditioning, ceiling fan, clock, radio, TV, DVD player, robes, hair dryer, Wi-Fi

ON THE GROUNDS: Wraparound porch, 1½ acres of lawn, garden gazebo, bicycles free for guests' use, off-street parking

RATES: $135–$275, including full breakfast

CREDIT CARDS ACCEPTED: MasterCard, Visa, American Express, Discover

OPEN: Year-round

HOW TO GET THERE: Cross the Bourne Bridge to Cape Cod and follow Route 28 south for 14 miles to Falmouth. The inn is located across from the historic village green.

staircase leads to upstairs bedrooms. Each is different, but all are large and furnished with four-poster queen-size beds with draped or fishnet canopies, floral wallpapers, a pair of comfortable reading chairs, and Oriental rugs. The Poiriers have added many comforts, such as robes, TVs, DVD players, and hair dryers.

Up on the third floor is a delightful retreat, an enclosed widow's walk with a fireplace, the perfect place to settle in with a book or just daydream out one of the ten windows.

Breakfast is served at 9:00 A.M. in the dining room in front of the fireplace or on the porch when the weather is fine. House specialties such as cheese blintz muffins and puffy fruit pancakes are so popular, the innkeepers have collected them into a cookbook, *Breakfast at 9*. When you return in the afternoon in summer, you'll find lemonade and cookies; in the winter, warming cocoa and brownies.

The inn is very private, set back on more than an acre of lawns and gardens and with a secluded gazebo, yet it is right off the village green in the heart of the historic district and within easy walking distance of Falmouth's many shops, galleries, and restaurants.

What's Nearby: See What's Nearby on page 114.

THE KNOLL

230 North Main Street
Florence 01062
(413) 584–8164

■ Set behind a deep lawn and sweeping circular driveway, this expansive twelve-room English Tudor home built in 1910 is named for its location, a knoll overlooking seventeen acres of farmland and forest.

WEB SITE: www.crocker.com/~the knoll or www.bbonline.com/ma/the knoll

INNKEEPER: Leona (Lee) Lesko

ROOMS: 4 rooms sharing 2 baths

ON THE GROUNDS: Screened porch; 17 acres of farmland and forest with walking trails

RATES: $75, including breakfast

CREDIT CARDS ACCEPTED: None

OPEN: Year-round

HOW TO GET THERE: Take Interstate 91 exit 18 and follow Route 5 north into the center of Northampton. Turn left onto Route 9 west for 3 miles to the center of Florence. The Knoll is ½ mile farther on Route 9.

The grand living room, measuring 16 by 22 feet, beckons with two love seats facing a 5-foot fireplace, an organ, a TV, and a handsome antique grandfather clock. The library is a quiet nook for reading, and there is a handsome formal paneled dining room where generous full breakfasts are served. In season, the menu includes strawberries, raspberries, and rhubarb grown in the garden.

Homemade strawberry jam is one of host Lee Lesko's specialties; for eighteen years, the Leskos operated a strawberry farm on the property. They decided to open a bed-and-breakfast more than twenty years ago, after their children had grown up and the house seemed empty.

Up a graceful stairway are four good-size bedrooms sharing two baths, each decorated in pleasant, homelike fashion. Two rooms have queen beds, one offers twins, and the fourth room has a double bed. Throughout the house, the polished wood floors are covered with lovely Oriental rugs.

This is definitely a family home, comfortable and unpretentious, and it is a good value for anyone visiting the Pioneer Valley or its many colleges.

What's Nearby: Look Park, a short walk from the inn, offers tennis courts, picnic grounds, and a playground. The bed-and-breakfast is well located for visiting the craft shops in Northampton and nearby colleges. Smith College and Northampton are just 3 miles away, Amherst College and the University of Massachusetts in Amherst are 9 miles away, and Mt. Holyoke College in South Hadley is 15 miles away. Also nearby are the beautiful colonial villages of Deerfield and Old Deerfield, where a dozen house museums are filled with the finest Early American antiques.

HARBORVIEW INN

71 Western Avenue
Gloucester 01930
(978) 283–2277; (800) 299–6696

■ If the bright floral wallpapers and coordinated borders, ceilings, and curtain arrangements look like settings for a

magazine spread, that's no accident. The Harborview was selected by *Better Homes and Gardens* to be redone for a special home decorating issue a few years back. While owner John Orlando was delighted with the makeover, he saw to it that many of the original features of the house remained unchanged, carefully preserving treasures that hold special sentimental memories for him, such as the ship painting over the mantel, the brass-trimmed living-room lighting fixture, and the old-fashioned dining-room furniture.

John has lived on this block facing the water all his life and visited here often when he was growing up. When the tidy white clapboard house came on the market in 1993, he could not resist, even though he owns his own home nearby. John and his wife, Marie, who is a teacher, decided to turn the pleasant home into a bed-and-breakfast inn.

The big, cheerful living and dining room welcomes with comfortable furnishings grouped around the fireplace. Soft green walls and cheerful print curtains bordering the many windows add to the warmth.

Each cozy room is named for a nearby town, and each has its own decor. I'm partial to the Essex Room for its eaves and the windows and wing chair tucked in the dormers. The Rockport Room features plaid curtains and matching swag valances, with a ceiling papered to coordinate. The Magnolia Studio, done in bold blue flowery stripes, has the prize view; you can see fishing boats, a lighthouse and island, and, on a clear day, the Boston skyline across the water.

WEB SITE: www.harborviewinn.com

INNKEEPERS: John and Marie Orlando

ROOMS: 3 rooms, 3 suites, all with TV, private bath, phone, clock, radio; some with ocean view; 1 suite with fireplace

ON THE GROUNDS: Sunporch, patio

RATES: Rooms $99–$129, suites $139–$199, including continental breakfast

CREDIT CARDS ACCEPTED: Master-Card, Visa, American Express, Discover

OPEN: Year-round

HOW TO GET THERE: Take Route 128 north to exit 14, Route 133. Turn right off the ramp onto Route 133 and follow for about 3 miles to the very end, facing the ocean and intersecting with Route 127, also called Western Avenue. Turn left and cross the drawbridge. Just past the Fishermen Memorial statue, make a U-turn to reverse direction. The inn is just ahead on the right, with parking in the rear.

The suites are spacious, especially the Penthouse covering the entire third floor. The bedroom and convertible living room can sleep four to six, making it ideal for families. The downstairs suite has a charming bedroom with a lacy white bed and a particularly welcoming sitting room with hundred-year-old hunting murals on the walls.

Early each morning, John arrives to set up a continental breakfast on the buffet at the end of the room for guests to enjoy at their leisure. The offerings include juice, fresh fruit, cereals, bagels and English muffins, and an assortment of pastries and muffins.

The inn has conveniences such as phone, TV, and good reading lights in each room to accommodate its many business visitors. Gloucester is still a major fishing port, and the picturesque fleet is within easy walking distance of the inn. This is also the capital of Cape Ann's whale-watching excursions and the home of some of its best restaurants. As a native, John is just the person to steer you to them.

What's Nearby: New England's busiest fishing port and its whale-watching capital, Gloucester is also known for seafood restaurants and the art colony at Rocky Neck. The North Shore Art Association has its summer headquarters and spacious gallery here. A lovely ride beside the sea takes you to the Beauport Museum, a twenty-six-room mansion filled with prize decorative arts. Rockport's many attractions are minutes away.

DRAGONSFIELD

365 State Road (Route 23 East)
Great Barrington 01230
(413) 644–9338
Fax: (413) 644–0365

Here's an inn for escapists, nature lovers, and skiers. High on a hill and set far back from the road, Dragonsfield offers rooms with great light and wonderful views of the changing seasons. It's hard to say which vista is more appealing, the front lawn studded with apple trees or the expansive grounds in back rimmed by forest.

The house is fairly new, a reproduction saltbox, but you might think it was old by the wide floorboards and eighteenth-century brick around the fireplace. The cozy living-dining room done in blue and white has nice touches such as an Oriental rug and a brass chandelier. When Susanne Freeman traded a banking job in New York for the country life, she brought along her collection of antique porcelain, which is nicely displayed in a cabinet.

A downstairs bedroom is inviting with deep blue walls, a pristine white spread, and a handsome dresser. Upstairs is a room I like for its John Widdecomb furniture, a 1920s inlaid floral design, but the real second-floor showplace is the suite, with dramatic deep red walls, a huge bath, and a whole wall of windows with wide screen views.

Susanne serves a generous breakfast, always with fresh fruit of the season and often featuring her specialty, crustless quiche. When the weather is cooperative,

WEB SITE: www.dragonsfield.com

INNKEEPER: Susanne Freeman

ROOMS: 2 rooms, 1 suite, all with private bath, TV, air-conditioning, clock, radio

ON THE GROUNDS: 38 acres with panoramic views of the Berkshire Hills, century-old apple trees in front of inn, terrace

RATES: $95–$250, including full breakfast

CREDIT CARDS ACCEPTED: None

OPEN: Year-round, except last two weeks in December through New Year's weekend

HOW TO GET THERE: From Route 7 take Route 23 east just north of Great Barrington. The inn is 1⅗ miles farther on the left; watch for the numbers 365 painted on a rock and a small sign. Butternut Ski Area is ⅗ mile farther east on the right.

breakfast is moved to the expansive back terrace, where the morning entertainment is watching for deer, wild turkey, and all manner of songbirds.

The house offers grand views of Butternut Ski Bowl, which is only ⁴⁄₁₀ mile down the road, close enough to make you first on the lifts every morning.

What's Nearby: Great Barrington is the shopping center for the southern Berkshires and one of the region's dining hot spots. Monument Mountain, north of town, is favored by hikers; Benedict Pond, in Beartown State Forest, is nearby for summer swimming; and Butternut beckons skiers in winter. All the cultural attractions of the Berkshires are a short drive away.

BRANDT HOUSE

29 Highland Avenue
Greenfield 01301
(413) 774–3329; (800) 235–3329
Fax: (413) 772–2908

■ Light, airy, and spacious, this sixteen-room mansion set on three and a half acres is a very private retreat, yet it is convenient to many popular attractions. Built at the turn of the twentieth century in a quiet, hilltop neighborhood of fine Victorian homes, the colonial revival house was transformed during a two-year restoration into a showplace with handsome woodwork, polished wooden floors, and lots of big windows throughout.

There are many public spaces where guests can linger. Eclectic furnishings deftly combine modern art and design with Victorian antiques and lots of leafy green plants. In the expansive living room, a comfortable skirted white sofa piled with pillows sits in front of a stainless-steel-and-glass coffee table. The fireplace is a warming focal point on chilly days.

Beyond is the bay-windowed game room with a full-size billiards table. The dining room has a wall of windows looking out onto the garden; French doors lead outside. Fresh fruits, homemade granola, yogurt, cereals, and fresh baked pastries and breads are served at the big table every morning, and on weekends hot dishes such as pancakes or quiche are added, along with bacon or sausage. If you prefer, you can have a small private table, or even enjoy breakfast in bed.

The sunroom is also wrapped in windows. It is furnished with big, comfortable chairs and stocked with local menus to peruse for dinner possibilities. A refrigerator, microwave, and TV are provided for guests to share.

Upstairs bedrooms offer private TVs and phones to accommodate the many business travelers who use the inn during the week. The rooms are large and handsomely appointed, with big feather beds with embroidered white covers, lacy curtains, and Oriental scatter rugs. Accent pieces such as rockers and skirted dressing tables give a soft, welcoming feel. Rooms 1 and 9 have working fireplaces, while Room 6 boasts a bathroom with a stained-glass window and a whirlpool bath.

The real showplace is the third-floor loft suite, once the owner's private quarters, with a cathedral ceiling, a host of windows, lots of art on the walls, and a spiral staircase to the loft bedroom, where the bed is tucked beneath a peaked ceiling and skylights.

The grounds of the house are exceptional and include a private clay tennis court. Expansive porches and patios overlooking the lawns make for serene seating in pleasant weather, and in winter, guests can cross-country ski in the adjacent woods.

You could have a relaxing time just lolling around the inn, but there is much to see and do nearby. Greenfield is a classic old New England town, and interesting small shops are waiting to be explored.

WEB SITE: www.brandthouse.com

INNKEEPER: John Lavryssen and Steve Sears, owners; Kathy Ripold, innkeeper

ROOMS: 8 rooms, 1 penthouse suite, 7 with private bath; all with air-conditioning, phone, TV, robes; 2 with fireplace; 1 with whirlpool bath

ON THE GROUNDS: 3½ acres of lawn, large porches, flagstone terrace, red clay tennis court, adjacent woods for walking or cross-country skiing

RATES: $110–$325, including continental breakfast on weekdays, full breakfast on weekends

CREDIT CARDS ACCEPTED: MasterCard, Visa, American Express, Discover

OPEN: Year-round

HOW TO GET THERE: From Interstate 91, take exit 26, Route 2 and Route 5/Route 10, and follow the signs for Greenfield Center. Go east on Main Street to the end. Bear right at the blinking yellow light onto Crescent Street, go ⅒ mile, and at the intersection of Crescent Street and Highland Avenue, stay straight onto Highland. The inn is the fifth house on the left.

What's Nearby: Greenfield, the start of the famous Mohawk Trail scenic drive across the Berkshire Hills, provides its own spectacular valley views from the Poet's Seat Tower and hiking in Highland Park. The Yankee Candle flagship store to the south of Greenfield on Routes 5/10 is a tourist favorite. The house museums of Old Deerfield are just 4 miles away—and the college towns of the Pioneer Valley are nearby.

APPLEGATE

279 West Park Street
Lee 01238
(413) 243–4451; (800) 691–9012

Space and grace are the hallmarks of this white-pillared Georgian colonial home, set on six lush acres of apple trees, tall pines, and flower gardens. Built in 1920 as a summer home for a New York physician, the inn is elegant and pampering. Innkeepers Gloria and Len Friedman came to the Berkshires after raising a family and pursuing professional careers in New York. They are gracious hosts who enjoy pampering guests with many comforts and amenities.

Guests find a crystal decanter of brandy, chocolates, a vase of fresh flowers, and thick robes waiting in their rooms. Breakfast is served by candlelight on antique china. Wine and cheese are offered at 5:00 P.M. every day in the living room, a 35-foot space warmed by bookshelves and a window seat. Both living and dining rooms have fireplaces, and the living room offers a grand piano for musical guests. Handsome Oriental rugs are found throughout the house.

Among the oversize bedrooms upstairs, Room 1 is a favorite, measuring a spacious 35 by 18 feet, decorated with cabbage rose wallpaper and hunter green accents and boasting a king-size four-poster bed, a working fireplace, and a shower that can double as a steam bath. Room 2 is a change of mood, pale pink with a pine canopy bed hung with lace. Room 4 has fresh blue and white decor and an iron-and-brass bed. Room 5 is done in deep lavender, with sheer bed hangings and lots of lacy pillows. Room 3 is a bit smaller but has a sleigh bed, cozy chairs in front of the fireplace, and a nice view. In cooler months all the rooms have puffy down comforters on the beds. Two third-floor suites have king-size beds, minibars, and balconies. The most luxurious quarters are in the carriage house. Two suites offer a choice of a four-poster or antique bronze bed, both king size; whirlpools; fireplaces; TV/VCRs; CD players; minibars; and patios. The carriage house also has a separate cottage built above, once the chauffeur's quarters with a separate entrance, that has been reno-

WEB SITE: www.applegateinn.com

INNKEEPERS: Len and Gloria Fried-man

ROOMS: 8 rooms and suites in main house, 3 suites in carriage house, all with private bath, air-conditioning, fireplace, clock radio, robes; several with whirlpool tubs; suites and larger rooms with TV/VCR, CD player, balconies, wet bars; two-bedroom suite with kitchen facilities

ON THE GROUNDS: Outdoor heated swimming pool, patio, screened porch, lawns, gardens with private sitting areas, bicycles for guests' use

RATES: $120–$350, including full breakfast, evening wine and cheese

CREDIT CARDS ACCEPTED: Master-Card, Visa, American Express

OPEN: Year-round

HOW TO GET THERE: From Interstate 90, the Massachusetts Turnpike, take exit 2 and go right off the exit ramp and straight at the first stop sign onto Park Street. The inn is ½ mile farther on the left, across from the golf course.

vated into a very private two-bedroom, one-bath suite with a living room, kitchen facilities, dining area, whirlpool in the bath, and its own deck.

The dining room is set with four antique tables, each with its own silver candelabra. The morning selection includes a fresh fruit plate and freshly squeezed juice, along with yogurt, granola, cereals, and delicious home-baked treats such as sour cream–walnut muffins or cranberry scones. A changing menu of hot dishes follows, and Sunday brings a buffet featuring smoked fish and bagels.

A screened porch furnished with airy wicker runs all the way across the back of the house and overlooks a nicely land-scaped turquoise heated swimming pool. Golfers will find a course right across the street, and bikes are available for exploring Berkshire back roads. The inn is close to Stockbridge and to all the many attractions of the Berkshires, from dance, music, and theater in summer to skiing in the winter.

What's Nearby: Known as the "Gateway to the Berkshires" for its convenient location just off the Massachusetts Turnpike, Lee boasts a classic turn-of-the-twentieth-century downtown, several fine inns, and the Berkshire Outlet Village with designer brand names. Laurel Lake provides recreation. It is adjacent to the many attractions of Stockbridge and is a short drive from Lenox.

BIRCHWOOD INN

7 Hubbard Street, P.O. Box 2020
Lenox 01240
(413) 637–2600; (800) 524–1646
Fax: (413) 637–4604

■ This graceful, gabled white clapboard home has stood at the top of the hill overlooking the village since 1757. The first official town meeting was held in the library, part of the reason why this venerable inn is the only one in Lenox listed on the National Register of Historic Places. Since innkeeper Ellen Gutman Chenaux arrived, it has taken on country elegance.

The public rooms are inviting. The library is spacious, with floor-to-ceiling windows, French doors, window seats, and Oriental carpets, and the parlor is cozy, a nice spot for a quiet chat. Each has a fireplace.

Breakfast is served in a handsome dining room boasting nineteenth-century wainscoting and its own fireplace. Bountiful breakfast entrees may include peach upside-down French toast, Tuscany strata, or "Rise and Shine" soufflé, in addition to a buffet offering fruit dishes, cereals, and homemade muffins and breads.

Afternoon tea is another treat, featuring delectables such as rich, soft brownies; scones; fruit pies and tarts; and the inn's famous chocolate-chip cookies. It is served on the porch in summer, by the fireside in winter.

Guest rooms vary in shape, size, and personality. Ellen has named them after former owners of the house. The spacious Dana Room, done in bold florals and plaids, is special, with an antique love seat; a four-poster, queen-size canopy feather bed; and a fireplace. The romantic Egleston Room has a queen-size bed with a crocheted canopy, a fireplace, and a claw-foot tub. The newest room, the Wright-Smith Suite on the third floor, is in cheerful cherry red, with a gas fireplace and a day bed as well as a queen-size bed.

Guests love gathering on the big front porch, though more active types may wander over to adjacent Kennedy Park for hiking, biking, or cross-country skiing in season. Lenox shops and dining are conveniently right down the hill.

What's Nearby: Known as the "Inland Newport" for its many summer mansions, Lenox is the center of Berkshires culture and home to some of its best shopping and dining. In summer, the Boston Symphony is in residence at Tanglewood, and Shake-

WEB SITE: www.birchwood-inn.com

INNKEEPER: Ellen Gutman Chenaux

ROOMS: 11 rooms, all with private bath, phone, air-conditioning, clock radio, hair dryer; 6 with fireplace and TV; rooms in main inn have high-speed Internet access

ON THE GROUNDS: 2 acres of lawn, gardens, trees, stone fences

RATES: $120–$275, including full breakfast and afternoon tea

CREDIT CARDS ACCEPTED: Master-Card, Visa, American Express, Discover

OPEN: Year-round

HOW TO GET THERE: From the Massachusetts Turnpike (Interstate 90), take exit 2, Lee and the Berkshires. Proceed west on Route 20 for 5 miles. At the first traffic light past the village of Lee, turn left onto Route 183/Historic Lenox. At the Lenox monument, bear right onto Main Street (Route 7A) and continue nearly to the top of the hill. The inn is on the right.

speare and Company performs in handsome theaters in town. Lenox shares Laurel Lake with the town of Lee and offers many peaceful acres for hikers at Kennedy Park and the Pleasant Valley Wildlife Sanctuary.

BROOK FARM INN

15 Hawthorne Street
Lenox 01240
(413) 637–3013; (800) 285–7638

■ Here's an inn that seems just right for arts-conscious Lenox, with Mozart playing in the background, a library of 1,500 books, and poetry readings or storytelling frequently offered at tea time. Though it is just around the corner from the village, this 130-plus-year-old Victorian is a relaxing haven on a quiet block, with a very private pool and a hammock set among colorful flowers and lovely rock gardens. The home has hosted guests for more than fifty years; Leonard Bernstein stayed here when it was a rooming house known as Shadowood. The present name was given by a former owner, an English professor, in honor of the original Brook Farm, a literary commune of the mid-1800s whose members included Nathaniel Hawthorne.

With Linda and Phil Halpern as hosts, there's a warm country feel throughout the house. The large, high-ceilinged library invites you to linger—choose a book and curl up next to the fireplace, play a tune on the upright piano, or fit a few pieces into the jigsaw puzzle always in progress. Tea with homemade scones is served here at 4:00 P.M. every day. The porch is another nice place to settle in. There's a refrigerator for guests to store food and a guest pantry where tea, coffee, and hot chocolate are always available.

WEB SITE: www.brookfarm.com

INNKEEPERS: Linda and Phil Halpern

ROOMS: 15 rooms, all with private bath, phone, air-conditioning, clock, radio; 9 with fireplace

ON THE GROUNDS: Outdoor heated swimming pool, lawn with chairs and tables, rock gardens

RATES: $105–$395, including full breakfast and afternoon tea

CREDIT CARDS ACCEPTED: Master-Card, Visa, Discover

OPEN: Year-round

HOW TO GET THERE: From Interstate 90, the Massachusetts Turnpike, take exit 2, Lee. Turn right onto Route 20 west, then left onto Route 183. Proceed to the large monument in Lenox and bear left. Take a left onto Old Stockbridge Road and travel down the hill to Hawthorne Street on the right. The inn is on the left.

The dining room, brightened by a big bay window full of plants, has tables for two, four, six, or eight, so you can decide whether you want company or privacy at breakfast. Juice, fresh fruit, homemade granola, yogurt, egg strata, coffee cake, and muffins are the usual fare.

Each bedroom is unique; nine have fireplaces. The Bridal Suite is choice, with a softly white-draped canopy bed and French doors opening to a small balcony. Room 4 has pretty printed wallpaper, a fishnet canopy bed, and wing chairs in front of the fireplace; Room 1, done with pale blue prints, comes with fireplace, canopy, a love seat, and a wooden checkerboard with heart-shaped checkers. Even the smaller rooms have special features: Room A has cozy dormers, Room C has a stained-glass window.

The newest addition to the inn is the carriage house, named Shadowood for the original name of the inn. Rooms here are luxurious, with fireplaces, Jacuzzis, and private decks.

What's Nearby: See What's Nearby on page 124.

CLIFFWOOD INN

25 Cliffwood Street
Lenox 01240
(413) 637–3330;
(800) 789–3331
Fax: (413) 637–0221

At the turn of the previous century, Lenox was known as the "Inland Newport" for its many summer mansions belonging to prominent families. One of the most gracious was this 1889 mansion built in Stanford White belle epoque style for Edward Livingston, a diplomat to France.

Located on a street of fine homes just 2 blocks from the center of Lenox, this is a house with grand spaces, 12-foot ceilings, and polished inlaid floors. The enormous living room, with columns on either side of the marble fireplace and a full-length mirror, once served as a ballroom.

Joy and Scottie Farrelly were just the right people to move in, since they already had a sizable collection of fine furnishings, paintings, rugs, and antiques acquired in seventeen years of corporate life for Ralston-Purina, living in Europe and in Montreal. The furniture includes some fine pieces from France, Italy, and Belgium. The Farrellys are also dealers for Eldred Wheeler, makers of high-quality colonial reproduction furniture, and many of these pieces are used in the rooms.

WEB SITE: www.cliffwood.com

INNKEEPERS: Joy and Scottie Farrelly

ROOMS: 7 rooms, all with private bath, air-conditioning, ceiling fan; 6 with wood-burning fireplace; 5 with TV

ON THE GROUNDS: Spacious veranda overlooking outdoor pool, landscaped grounds, gazebo; five-hole putting green

RATES: $114–$254, including morning coffee and afternoon wine and cheese.

CREDIT CARDS ACCEPTED: None

OPEN: Year-round

HOW TO GET THERE: From Interstate 90, the Massachusetts Turnpike, take exit 2, Lee, and follow Route 20 onto Route 7A to Lenox village. Cliffwood Street is a short block, a right turn off Route 7A. The inn is on the left.

Up the graceful staircase are bedrooms named for family ancestors, each with a mix of decor and containing many sentimental family heirloom furnishings. The Jacob Gross Jr. Room, done in soft blues, has a king-size canopy bed, pineapple lamps, and a fireplace. The big, bright blue bathroom includes a bidet. The Walker/Linton two-room suite, which offers a fireplace and TV, has a dresser that belonged to Joy's grandmother, a rocker from her grandfather, and a convertible couch in the sitting room. The appealing Catherine White Room on the third floor has eaves and skylights, a king-size bed, a Victorian dresser, and a curved fireplace in the bathroom that can be seen from the bed. Joy, who does decorative painting, is responsible for the country scene on the fire screen.

What's Nearby: See What's Nearby on page 124.

GARDEN GABLES INN

141 Main Street, P.O. Box 52
Lenox 01240
(413) 637–0193

■ Though it is right off the main street of Lenox, this is a private, peaceful world apart. The original triple-gabled, rambling 1780 home maintains its Early American feel with cozy country decor and many eighteenth-century antiques. The secluded five-acre grounds are exceptional, and the 72-foot outdoor swimming pool is one of the biggest in the Berkshires.

Since the Mekinda family arrived from Toronto in 1988, the inn has gotten better every year. A former professional engineer, Mario Mekinda maintains grounds, gardens, and house with attention to every detail. He has added welcome amenities, such as private baths for every room, central air-conditioning, and in-room telephones.

The airy country decor throughout is Lynn Mekinda's bailiwick. The striking floral print in the entryway and running up the stairs gives a hint to what is in store. The bedrooms vary in size from quite small rooms to spacious suites, but all have fresh floral-print papers, comfortable furnishings, and attractive comforters on the beds. Suites in the house and a cottage on the grounds are choice, with sitting areas, canopy beds, cathedral ceilings, fireplaces, TV, and VCR. Some rooms have whirlpool baths and porches.

The downstairs sitting room beckons with a fireplace, grand piano, English antiques, comfortable seating in country upholstery patterns, and nineteenth-century Dutch watercolors on the walls.

The dining room is a bit more formal, with pale yellow walls, a brass chandelier, and three long tables. The generous breakfast buffet set out from 8:00 to 9:45 A.M. typically includes berries, melon, and other fresh fruits of the season; homemade blueberry and bran muffins; crumb cakes; yogurt; and cereals; plus extras such as hard-boiled eggs, French toast, or quiche.

One of the most inviting places in the house is the big wraparound porch, with hand-painted scenes of trees, birds, and flowers on the walls. Breakfast is served here in summer. Beyond are gardens, the pool, and acres of greenery, making this place feel like a true country escape, even though all the pleasures of the Berkshires are minutes away.

What's Nearby: See What's Nearby on page 124.

WEB SITE: www.lenoxinn.com

INNKEEPERS: Mario and Lynn Mekinda

ROOMS: 18 rooms, 2 suites, all with private bath, air-conditioning, phone, clock, radio; some with whirlpool, fireplace, TV

ON THE GROUNDS: 72-foot outdoor swimming pool, patio, walking trails

RATES: $95–$325, including full buffet breakfast

CREDIT CARDS ACCEPTED: MasterCard, Visa, American Express, Discover

OPEN: Year-round

HOW TO GET THERE: Take the Massachusetts Turnpike (Interstate 90) to exit 2, Lee. Follow Route 20 west to Route 183, turn left, and continue to the statue at the town center. Turn right onto Main Street (Route 7A), and Garden Gables is on your left, across from St. Ann's church.

ROOKWOOD INN

11 Old Stockbridge Road
Lenox 01240
(413) 637–9750; (800) 223–9750
Fax: (413) 637–1352

■ It's a Victorian vision—a painted lady in rosy hues with pointy rooflines and two round turrets. The center part of the building began life in 1825 as the Williams Tavern, located in the center of town. It was moved to the present site in 1880 and expanded, serving as lodging for the secretaries of the wealthy owners of the grand Berkshire "cottages" of that era. The location couldn't be better, still within walking distance of the village center but away from traffic.

WEB SITE: www.rookwoodinn.com

INNKEEPER: Amy Lindner-Lesser

ROOMS: 21 rooms, all with private bath, telephone with modem hookup, air-conditioning, robes, hair dryer

ON THE GROUNDS: Front porch furnished in wicker, large front lawn, Victorian flower garden, gazebo

RATES: $100–$375, including full buffet breakfast and afternoon refreshments

CREDIT CARDS ACCEPTED: MasterCard, Visa, American Express, Discover

OPEN: Year-round

HOW TO GET THERE: Take Route 20/7 north. At the traffic light at Route 183, make a left and proceed to the Lenox monument, about 2 miles. Bear left, keeping the monument on your right, and make an immediate left turn onto Old Stockbridge Road. The Rookwood is the second building on the left.

After a succession of owners, the present innkeepers, the Lesser family, arrived in 1996 and have accomplished a rare feat. They have retained the grand Victorian ambience of the past while creating a warm, unpretentious, family-friendly inn.

The sitting room is large and comfortable, with a Victorian fireplace, plenty of seating, and lots of antiques, including an old Victrola and a pump organ.

The dining room, papered in deep mauve, offers a choice of tables for two or larger tables where you can mingle with other guests. When I visited, the tables were attractively covered with lace over deep mauve tablecloths. Breakfast is served buffet style and always features a hot dish, treats such as challah French toast or frittatas.

Up the carpeted stairs are twenty-one rooms, each different in size and decor, but all attractively done and furnished with antiques. Many have attractive four-poster and canopy beds, spacious seating areas, and fireplaces. They have amenities such as robes, hair dryers, and a phone with a modem hookup.

Room 2, one of my favorites, has floral wallpaper, an attractive quilt on the bed, and a sitting area in the round alcove. It is one of several rooms with a private porch. I also liked Room 20, a large room with a big brass bed with a colorful quilt, walls in a pink ribbon design with a floral border at the ceiling, and nice pieces such as a platform rocker, a skirted vanity, an old trunk, and a floral couch facing the fireplace. Third-floor rooms under the eaves are cozy, and some offer skylights. In Room 10, two chairs are tucked into a dormer, forming a particularly snug sitting area.

The variety of sizes and shapes means there's something affordable for everyone. And a number of rooms can accommodate children, who are welcome here.

What's Nearby: See What's Nearby on page 124.

WALKER HOUSE

64 Walker Street
Lenox 01240
(413) 637–1271; (800) 235 3098

■ A little bit quirky, a little bit arty, and overflowing with warmth, this is an inn that definitely reflects the personalities of its owners. Peggy and Dick Houdek came to New England from California in 1980 following careers in the arts. Music brought them together— they met while Peggy was working for the San Francisco Opera—and then they moved to Los Angeles, where she became managing editor of *Performing Arts* magazine while Dick was director of public affairs at CalArts and a part-time music critic for the *Los Angeles Times*.

The Federal-style inn they bought when they headed east is one of the oldest homes in Lenox, dating from 1804, and they have filled its spacious rooms with their favorite things. Their love of music shows in rooms named for composers, the grand piano in the parlor ready for recitals or sing-alongs, and their big library of operas, concerts, and films on tape, which often provide the evening entertainment. Videotapes are shown on a 12-foot-wide screen in the room they call the Library Cinema.

Some of Peggy Houdek's other loves are in evidence as well, providing cozy clutter and something artistic, pretty, or fun to look at wherever you turn. Art and flowers are everywhere; paintings even line the walls going up the stairs.

WEB SITE: www.walkerhouse.com

INNKEEPERS: Peggy and Richard Houdek

ROOMS: 8 rooms, all with private bath; some with fireplace

ON THE GROUNDS: Spacious porch and veranda, 3 acres of lush grounds

RATES: $80–$220, including full breakfast and afternoon tea; 3-day minimum stay required for summer and holiday weekends, 2-night minimum for October weekends

CREDIT CARDS ACCEPTED: None

OPEN: Year-round

HOW TO GET THERE: Take the Massachusetts Turnpike (Interstate 90) to exit 2, Route 20 west. Travel through the town of Lee and about 6 miles of countryside to Route 183, and turn left toward Tanglewood and drive 1 mile. You will be on Walker Street, and Walker House is on the left.

Animals also come in for their fair share of space. The front hall features Peggy's collection of doorstops in the shape of cats, dogs, and a bird. The house is filled with cats, both a few of the live-in variety and in pictures and figurines. A monkey-shaped aquarium and a stuffed bear on a tricycle are on the sunporch, and when you come to breakfast, you may have to remove a fuzzy bear, lion, or tiger from your chair. In fact, this is one inn where you are welcome to bring your own pet (with prior approval only). All of this adds to the happy, homey feeling of a one-of-a-kind inn.

The breakfast chairs are gathered around several big round oak tables. The menu usually includes juice and fresh fruit; several kinds of breads, muffins, or croissants; and cold cereals. When the weather is cooperative, breakfast is served on the spacious back porch overlooking the grounds.

Guest rooms have distinct decors. Tchaikovsky is showy, featuring a big brass bed and a fireplace; Verdi is bold, with green leafy wallpaper, slim iron benches, and a wicker chest and chairs. Chopin is furnished with a soft canopy with ruffles and a purple chaise; Beethoven has a settee with wooden arms, crocheted bedcovers, and plants in the front window; and Handel sports a fishnet canopy, lace curtains, a small antique writing desk, and a claw-foot tub in the bath. Puccini is located downstairs off the porch, with its own separate small porch, and gives a warm feel with its rose-colored walls, lacy canopy bed, and fireplace. In all there are five working fireplaces.

Lenox village is right outside the front door, but you could just as easily be a million miles away when you're seated on the screened back porch, rimmed with flower boxes and hung with geraniums and begonias. The porch and the terrace beyond look out on three acres of dense, woody plantings that provide absolute peace and privacy.

What's Nearby: See What's Nearby on page 124.

HARBOR LIGHT INN

58 Washington Street
Marblehead 01945
(781) 631–2186

■ The narrow, hilly lanes of Marblehead were described 200 years ago by George Washington as having "the look of antiquity." The sheltered harbor of the historic seaport is occupied these days by the masts of sailboats rather than the clipper ships of Washington's day, but this is still one of the most picturesque spots on the Atlantic Coast, and the luxurious Harbor Light Inn puts you right in the midst of the quaint historic district. The rooftop walk offers a clear view of the landmark Marblehead Light.

The original early-eighteenth-century building and the "new" wing constructed in the nineteenth century were run down in 1986 when the Conways, who are also owners of Nantucket's Carlisle House Inn, bought and completely remodeled the structure. In 1992, the building next door was added. Now there are twenty-one fine lodgings featuring pencil-post or carved-mahogany canopy beds, antiques and good reproductions, and Oriental rugs.

WEB SITE: www.harborlightinn.com

INNKEEPERS: Peter and Suzanne Conway

ROOMS: 21 rooms, each with private bath, air-conditioning, TV; 10 with fireplace; some with skylight, double whirlpool bath

ON THE GROUNDS: Outdoor pool

RATES: $135–$295, including continental breakfast

CREDIT CARDS ACCEPTED: Master-Card, Visa, American Express

OPEN: Year-round

HOW TO GET THERE: Take Route 114 or 129 to Marblehead and proceed to Washington Street, paralleling the harbor. The inn is almost to the end of town, on the right at the intersection of Washington and Pearl Streets.

Original features such as arched doorways and wide floorboards remain. Prize rooms on the third floor have been remodeled with skylights, exposed beams, brick walls, and working fireplaces. One choice second-floor room has a private deck next to the pool, an English pine armoire, and a two-person whirlpool bath. All of the generous-size bathrooms have been completely modernized.

Guests have a choice of two formal parlors, each with handsome Oriental rugs. The larger and more inviting room has a fireplace, curve-back sofas, wing chairs, a traditional brass chandelier, and deep red walls.

The dining room also has a fireplace for chilly mornings. It is painted an attractive Wedgwood blue and decorated with maritime paintings. Needlepoint upholstery on the Chippendale chairs around the big table picks up the blue of the walls. Guests help themselves to the continental breakfast on the sideboard, a selection of fresh juice, fresh fruits, yogurt, and a variety of baked goods including breads, bagels, muffins, coffee cakes, and assorted quiches. On holidays there may be special treats such as smoked salmon or stuffed French toast.

The newest addition to the inn is an extra dining room/meeting room overlooking the pool and gardens.

The outdoor pool behind the inn is surrounded with tall hedges for privacy. Just outside the front door are Marblehead's upscale shops and galleries and a host of good restaurants that add to the pleasures of a visit.

What's Nearby: The merchants' mansions and gabled fishermen's cottages along Marblehead's hilly, twisting lanes mark a seaport with a more than 350-year-old history. The water views are magnificent, the harbor is a forest of sailboat masts, and there are ample shops and dining places to tempt visitors.

SEAGULL INN

106 Harbor Avenue
Marblehead 01945
(781) 631–1893
Fax: (981) 631–3535

■ Skip Sigler is a person who has found his calling. After twenty years and numerous moves as a corporate executive, he and his wife, Ruth, fell in love with Marblehead and the ocean views from their hilltop home on Marblehead Neck, the mansion-lined peninsula that shelters the harbor from the open sea. When yet another job transfer was announced, Skip refused to budge, and in 1994 he took on the role of innkeeper, one that he seems born to fill. His artistic talents were put to work building furniture and painting seagull murals for the inn, and his outgoing personality makes guests feel instantly at home. He was named "Host with the Most" in a "Best of Boston" feature in *Boston* magazine a few years ago.

Years before, the rambling, century-old shingled house had served as a summer hotel, so the transformation to a bed-and-breakfast inn was not difficult. A long hallway leads to three suites, which vary in size from the cozy, book-lined Library for two to the Seabreeze Suite sleeping five. The Lighthouse Suite, also with room for five, is actually a duplex apartment with a full kitchen, a private entrance, and a roof deck

WEB SITE: www.seagullinn.com

INNKEEPERS: Skip and Ruth Sigler

ROOMS: 3 suites, all with private bath, air-conditioning, phone, clock, radio, coffeemaker, TV, VCR; 1 with full kitchen, private entrance, roof deck. Bikes and kayaks available to guests.

ON THE GROUNDS: Decks with ocean views, gardens

RATES: $125–$300, including continental breakfast

CREDIT CARDS ACCEPTED: MasterCard, Visa

OPEN: Year-round

HOW TO GET THERE: Take Route 114 or 129 to Marblehead, turn right onto Ocean Avenue, and follow it over the causeway leading to Marblehead Neck. Follow Ocean Avenue for about 1½ miles. Just after you pass a large, castlelike home on the right, the road will curve around to meet Harbor Avenue. The inn is the long, blue house on the right after you make the curve; look for a flagpole with a seagull on it.

with spectacular ocean and harbor views. A hammock beckons on the lawn, and there is a barbecue grill for cookouts.

All the rooms offer nice touches, such as pretty quilts and throws, and amenities such as hair dryers, bottled water, nuts, and brandy. Skip crafted most of the inn's handsome Shaker-style cherry and walnut furniture himself, including the four-poster beds, and he laid the polished cherry floor in the sitting room. He also oversees the continental breakfast served at the kitchen counter or in the dining room each morning, featuring fresh fruit, homemade granola or oatmeal, bagels, and muffins warm from the oven.

Guests gather in the sitting room, where the fireplace is lit on chilly evenings. One wall holds an extensive free video lending library. An example of Skip's good humor can be found in his description of this room's decor: "a blend of handcrafted furniture and antiques, including the owner."

What's Nearby: See What's Nearby on page 132.

THORNCROFT INN

460 Main Street, P.O. Box 1022
Vineyard Haven
(Martha's Vineyard) 02568
(508) 693–3333; (800) 332–1236
Fax: (508) 693–5419

■ Just sailing away to the beautiful island of Martha's Vineyard is enough to put you in the mood for romance—and here's the perfect haven when you arrive. Thorncroft is an inn dedi-

WEB SITE: www.thorncroft.com

INNKEEPERS: Karl and Lynn Buder

ROOMS: 14 rooms in 3 buildings, all with private bath, air-conditioning, TV, phone, robes, hair dryer, iron and ironing board; most with refrigerator; 10 with wood-burning fireplace; some with whirlpool bath, private hot tub, private deck or porch

ON THE GROUNDS: 3½ acres of secluded grounds, with gardens, sitting areas

RATES: $210–$600, including full breakfast and afternoon tea, optional continental breakfast in bed

CREDIT CARDS ACCEPTED: Master-Card, Visa, American Express, Discover, Diners Club

OPEN: Year-round

HOW TO GET THERE: From the Vineyard Haven ferry dock, take a right at the first stop sign and then the next right onto Main Street. The inn is 1 mile farther on the left.

cated to romantic getaways for couples, especially those celebrating special occasions such as birthdays, anniversaries, or honeymoons.

The house, a Craftsman-style shingled cottage built in 1918, looks as though it would be right at home in the English countryside. Once the guest house for the Thorncroft estate, it is set behind a manicured lawn and neatly trimmed hedges.

A Victorian reading parlor, one of two sitting rooms, has elegant turn-of-the-twentieth-century furnishings, a fireplace, and antiques such as an old Victrola and vintage clothing to maximize the mood. The sunroom has a large game and work table, a guest refrigerator, and an ice machine.

Guests sign up the night before for their choice of two breakfast sittings, 8:15 or 9:30 A.M. Seating is in the larger dining room with a fireplace or a cheerful smaller room, both intimate spaces with individual oak tables seating from two to six, rimmed with high-back Victorian chairs. The menu changes daily, and there's always a tempting entree in store, such as almond French toast or breakfast burritos. If you're feeling lazy, you can have a tray delivered to your door at 9:00 or 10:00 A.M., laden with juice, fresh baked muffins, bagels, fruit, and yogurt.

Chances are good you'll be happy to linger in your room, since you'll likely have a fireplace and maybe a private deck and a whirlpool bath for two. Check into Room 1 and you'll be sleeping beneath a century-old, 8-foot, carved-walnut headboard. There's a matching marble-topped Victorian dresser in the room, not to mention a wood-burning fireplace and an enormous hot tub just for the two of you. Five rooms in the carriage house are extra spacious and done in colonial decor. Splurge for the Cottage, a private hideaway in the trees, and you can have your own big porch with a hammock, a king-size canopy bed, and a view of the fireplace from a whirlpool tub for two set in a mirrored alcove.

Karl and Lynn Buder, who have been here since 1981, each have master's degrees in administration, and I've never seen a more efficiently run operation, everything done with great care to make your stay perfect. Rooms are thickly carpeted and well lit; fireplaces are stacked with wood, ready for a match; and ice buckets and wineglasses and corkscrews are at hand when you need them. Each room has an iron and ironing board, and many have a refrigerator. You'll find a booklet describing the breakfast menus for the week, plus a notebook of information on what to see and do on the island, including maps and restaurant recommendations. The morning newspaper will be waiting at the door; at night, you'll find your bed turned down and a chocolate truffle waiting, the final touch to ensure sweet dreams.

What's Nearby: Martha's Vineyard is an island rimmed with glorious beaches and blessed with diverse scenery, from seaside cliffs at Gay Head to unspoiled wildlife preserves. Each town has a distinct personality. Edgartown is known for its handsome sea captains' homes, Oak Bluff is filled with gingerbread Victorian cottages, and Menemsha is the quintessential New England fishing village. The inn is 1 block from the ocean and within walking distance of the shops and restaurants of Vineyard Haven as well as the ocean views from West Chop Lighthouse.

CLIFF LODGE

9 Cliff Road
Nantucket 02554
(508) 228–9480
Fax: (508) 228–6305

■ Gaze out at the harbor from the widow's walk atop this 1771 inn, and you may be able to imagine how it felt to watch and wait for the clipper ships and whalers that once made this island outpost the third-largest town in Massachusetts—and one of the wealthiest. The mansions of old remain, adding to the attraction of the beaches that lure tourists by the thousands each summer. But you won't be bothered by crowds in this haven, a historic home on a quiet, cobbled residential street just a five-minute walk up the hill from town.

Walk up the curved stairway and past the columned portico of this gray-shingled historic home, and you'll enter a light, airy latter-day New England country world that the original sea captain owner would never have known. The house is done in soft blues and whites with Laura Ashley wallpapers and fabrics, light antique pine, and lots of wicker. Upstairs bedrooms feature pretty white eyelet bedding, more pine, rag rugs, art posters, and nautical scenes on the walls.

There are fine views from the second-floor balcony, but best of all are the spec-

WEB SITE: www.clifflodgenantucket
.com

INNKEEPER: Sally Beck

ROOMS: 11 rooms, all with private
bath, TV; 1 full apartment with private entrance

ON THE GROUNDS: Landscaped garden patio, off-street parking

RATES: Rooms $140–$280, apartment $450, including continental
breakfast and afternoon refreshments

CREDIT CARDS ACCEPTED: Master-
Card, Visa, American Express

OPEN: Year-round

HOW TO GET THERE: The inn is a 5-
minute drive from the Nantucket
ferry dock. Take a cab or ask the inn
for driving directions.

tacular island vistas from the lofty roof walk.
The views and the quiet led USA Today to
include Cliff Lodge in a feature a few years
ago that named the ten most romantic inns
in the country.

The buffet spread in the breakfast room
each morning includes juice, fresh fruit,
cereals, a variety of breads, and home-
baked muffins. It can be eaten on the patio
just out the door or in front of the fire on
chilly mornings. Trays are also available if
you prefer to have breakfast in your room. In
summer, iced tea is offered in the afternoon;
in winter, the beverage may be hot chocolate served in front of the parlor fireplace.

The personable host, Sally Beck, offers
lots of hospitable touches, such as providing
a refrigerator for guests in the butler's
pantry and offering beach towels.

What's Nearby: Incomparable beaches, historic cobbled lanes, and misty moors
make this island outpost a magnet for vacationers. Sea captains' mansions remain to
remind that Nantucket once supplied whale oil to the world, a tale nicely told at the
Whaling Museum. More island history can be learned at the Peter Foulger Museum,
and many historic homes are open for touring.

BLACKINTON MANOR

1391 Massachusetts Avenue
North Adams 01247
(413) 663–5795; (800) 795–8613
Fax: (413) 663–3121

■ This fine Italianate-style home was built in 1832, part of the lavish estate of Sanford Blackinton, a wealthy textile manufacturer so influential that this entire residential neighborhood is named for him. Floor-to-ceiling windows fill the house with light,
and the graceful curved staircase lends an elegant air.

Innkeepers Laura and Paul Macionus have brought warmth to offset the formal-
ity of the house. The living room, done in restful neutral shades, invites lingering
with two comfortable couches and a chaise around the fireplace. Musicians are wel-

come to sit down at the grand piano.

A full multicourse breakfast is served at a beautifully set table beneath a brass chandelier in the dining room. Fresh fruit, a variety of egg dishes or pancakes, and bacon may be on the menu. A breakfront and built-in shelves display fine china and silver.

Each of the bedrooms has different decor, but all offer a queen- or king-size bed. The Parlor Room on the first floor is one of the larger spaces, with striking dark red print wallpaper, a king-size four-poster, parlor stove in the fireplace, and a two-person Jacuzzi in the bath. The Carriage Room, offering views of the pool and garden, also has a parlor stove plus a private entrance.

The dramatic curving staircase leads to three rooms upstairs. Two of the three have balconies with mountain views. The most spacious is the English Suite, with an antique brass bed and parlor stove, and a second room with twin sofa beds. The Queen Anne Room has a lovely sleigh bed plus a daybed and an old-fashioned claw-foot bathtub.

The inn offers a peaceful setting, as well as a swimming pool that is a very welcome amenity in summer. And the location is ideal, just a few miles from the center of both North Adams and Williamstown, two towns filled with attractions.

WEB SITE: www.blackinton-manor.com

INNKEEPERS: Laura and Paul Macionus

ROOMS: 5 rooms, all with private bath, air-conditioning, TV, clock radio

ON THE GROUNDS: Lawns, garden, swimming pool

RATES: $110–$190, including full breakfast

CREDIT CARDS ACCEPTED: MasterCard, Visa

OPEN: Year-round

HOW TO GET THERE: From Route 7 follow Route 2 through Williamstown. Watch for the sign that reads ENTERING NORTH ADAMS. Proceed 3/10 mile to Ashton Avenue; go left on Ashton to the end. Turn right on Massachusetts Avenue (the street is not marked, but it is the street at the end of Ashton). Blackinton Manor is about 1/4 mile on the left at the corner of Church Hill Street. Coming from Boston and points east, follow Route 2 into North Adams, through the town and over the overpass bridge. Watch for the Super Stop and Shop on the left (about 2½ miles), and take the second right onto Ashton Avenue; from this point follow the directions above.

What's Nearby: North Adams is home to the striking MASS MoCA complex, the nation's largest contemporary art museum and an exciting showplace for avant garde work. It is 4 miles from Williamstown, where art lovers will find Impressionist masterpieces at the excellent Clark Art Institute and another fine collection at the Williams College Museum of Art. The Williamstown Theater Festival in summer often attracts top Broadway stars. North Adams is also the start of the Mohawk Trail, a 63-mile scenic route through the Berkshires. Notch Road in North Adams is a direct route uphill to the top of 3,941-foot Mount Greylock, the region's highest peak.

THE PORCHES

231 River Street
North Adams 01247
(413) 664–0400
Fax: (413) 664–0401

■ The most unusual inn in New England, the Porches opened its doors in July 2001 and is composed of seven Victorian-era row houses built a century ago as housing for factory workers. The name comes from two long front porches constructed to connect the buildings.

The rundown houses were an eyesore visible from the Massachusetts Museum of Contemporary Art (MASS MoCA), a museum across the road in a much-lauded renovation of a sprawling deserted factory complex. It was MASS MoCA board member and veteran innkeeper Nancy Fitzpatrick who saw the potential for an inn. Fitzpatrick, whose family owns the landmark Red Lion Inn in Stockbridge, has overseen the creation of a complex that personifies "industrial chic," with more than a little whimsy added by her own collection of 1950s kitsch.

The exterior has been restored without changing the feel of the original architecture, but skylights have been added to give interior light. Each house is painted a different color. Guests register in the main building, which also has a small living room with leather couches and chairs and a fireplace, a little gift shop, and the dining room, where continental breakfast is served, always featuring a coffee cake of the day. I liked the option of having my breakfast delivered to my room; it arrived in a silver metal lunchbox patterned after those that factory workers might have used.

Guest rooms in the various buildings feature four color schemes. Wooden floors have been painted olive green, red, pumpkin, and buttercup yellow, while beadboard walls are terra-cotta, pale blue, celery, and sage green, respectively. Much of the furniture was produced in New England, and the white-on-white patchwork bedspreads were

WEB SITE: www.porches.com

INNKEEPER: Olivier Glattfelder

ROOMS: 52 rooms and suites, all with private bath, cordless telephone, TV, DVD player, high-speed Internet access, minibar, iron, room safe; suites have whirlpool tub, living room with sofa bed; some with private porch

ON THE GROUNDS: Heated lap pool, hot tub, sauna, fitness room, walking trails

RATES: Rooms $125–$295, suites $175–$395, including continental breakfast; room-service breakfast on request

CREDIT CARDS ACCEPTED: MasterCard, Visa, American Express, Diners Club

OPEN: Year-round

HOW TO GET THERE: Take Route 7 north to Williamstown and turn right onto Route 2 east. In approximately 4 miles, in the center of North Adams, bear right to an off-ramp marked EXIT FOR DOWNTOWN BUSINESS DISTRICT, ROUTE 8. At the bottom of the exit ramp (at the traffic light), take a left onto Marshall Street. Drive under the overpass, passing the Massachusetts Museum of Contemporary Art on your left. Turn left onto River Street. The Porches is on the right. Coming from Boston, take Route 2 west into North Adams. At the set of lights just after the Super Big Y supermarket, take a right onto Holden Street and an immediate left onto St. Anthony's Drive (there is no street sign, but the church takes up the entire block). Turn right onto Marshall Street, then left onto River Street. The Porches is on the right. The yellow building is the Reception Building.

specially created for the inn. Natural linen window panels featuring grommets and wires in place of the usual rods were designed by Fitzpatrick and manufactured by Country Curtains, the catalog company started by her parents. Metal cabinets give a properly industrial touch.

The look may be spare, but the amenities are not. Beds are queen- or king-size, and the latest high-tech gadgets, from cordless phones to DVD players to high-speed Internet access, are available.

Bathrooms are big and well equipped, with slate floors and natural lighting, sometimes through interior frosted windows. Suites have whirlpool tubs, while other rooms feature claw-foot tubs and separate glass showers. Shaker-style wall pegs serve as holders for towels and robes, and the mirrors over the sink are framed by distressed metal salvaged from the exterior of the original building.

What really set the rooms apart are the humorous 1950s accessories that Fitzpatrick has collected for many years. These include vintage lamps and paint-by-number artwork, from country scenes to the Mona Lisa. The hallway walls are decorated with souvenir painted china plates typical of the period, including some for the Mohawk Trail, the scenic drive through the Berkshires that begins in North Adams.

For relaxation, the porches that run the length of the buildings are lined with high-back rocking chairs. Behind the inn, at the foot of a wooded slope, is a heated lap pool and a hot tub. A separate building, the last of the converted houses, offers meeting space and a sauna.

The Porches is the latest sign that North Adams, a town that was fading after its factories closed, has taken a decided turn up since the opening of MASS MoCA in 1999. Several new restaurants have come on the scene, and some of the best allow charging privileges to inn guests.

What's Nearby: See What's Nearby on page 137.

1782 WHITFIELD HOUSE

26 North Street
Plymouth 02360
(508) 747–6735
Fax: (508) 747–1497

■ Situated on Plymouth's second oldest street, a short stroll from the waterfront, this 1782 Federal-style redbrick colonial is among the town's most elegant small lodgings. It offers the chance to sample life as it might have been in the home of a wealthy trader in the town's early maritime heyday.

The house was the property of one family until 1987, when it was purchased by Dr. Brian Whitfield. He has meticulously restored the home and furnished it with antiques, Oriental rugs, and period accessories as if the home were still occupied by the original owners. Dr. Whitfield's sister, Barbara Marley, has come from California to serve as a gracious hostess.

The period living room is lovely, with an oak parquet floor and Italian marble fireplace. A large Oriental rug, Queen Anne chairs, a Chippendale sideboard, a seventeenth-century Oriental screen, and tiger maple side tables on either side of the sofa—one with an Imari lamp—are among the handsome furnishings. This room opens into a smaller sitting room with original artwork on the deep green walls and antique Oriental chests near French doors that offer a view of the garden.

The dining room, with faux-painted wallpaper and a cloud-covered ceiling, is furnished with a reproduction inlaid walnut and satinwood table, Chippendale chairs, and an antique crystal chandelier. A full breakfast is served on Blue Willow china and fine silver and glassware. Homemade quiche Lorraine is one of the house specialties. On fine days breakfast may move to the spacious mahogany deck, screened by tall rhododendrons that are more than a century old.

All of the bedrooms are authentically furnished and inviting, with canopy beds and fireplaces. Since I'm partial to blue, I like the

WEB SITE: www.whitfieldhouse.com

INNKEEPERS: Barbara Marley and Brian Whitfield

ROOMS: 4 rooms, 2 with private bath

ON THE GROUNDS: Located on a city block, deck, garden, off-street parking (a real boon in Plymouth)

RATES: $95, including full breakfast

CREDIT CARDS ACCEPTED: None

OPEN: Year-round

HOW TO GET THERE: Coming south on Route 3 toward Cape Cod, turn off at exit 6A, which merges with Route 44, Samoset Street. Travel to the second traffic light, turn right onto Court Street (also known as Route 3A), and proceed 5 blocks to North Street. The inn is on the left side of the street just after a yellow house. Turn into the cobblestone driveway.

Blue Room, with period printed wallpaper, soft blue painted wooden accents, and an antique carved fruitwood bed with a French lace canopy. The room still has its original wainscoting and working fireplace. It can open into the Stenciled Room, furnished with two antique cannonball beds, to form a suite. The willow and other traditional stencil patterns on the walls were done by a contemporary artist, Carolyn Hedge.

The Patriot's Room is located over the garage in a new section of the house added in 1993, so close to the style of the original that you would be hard pressed to tell the difference. It boasts hand-planed wide board floors, a reproduction eighteenth-century fireplace, and a carved eighteenth-century tall-post bed.

Cosseted in these lovely quarters, the real world seems far away, yet all the sights of Plymouth are just outside the door.

What's Nearby: Pilgrim history comes alive in Plymouth at sites such as Plymouth Rock, the *Mayflower II* replica, Plimoth Plantation (a living-history museum), and several Pilgrim-era museums. This is also the heart of cranberry country, with bogs in the countryside and the Cranberry World Visitors Center in town. A variety of cruises go out of the busy harbor, and beaches are also nearby.

CAPTAIN'S HOUSE

69 Marmion Way
Rockport 01966
(978) 546–3825; (877) 625–7678

When they talk about being on the rocks here, they aren't discussing cocktails. This comfortable white stucco home built in 1911 is directly on the rocky shoreline facing the Atlantic Ocean, and the seascapes are enough to keep you happily wave watching all day. The Parkers, who took over the inn in 2005, seem appropriate owners for an inn by the sea since they are descendants of Capt. Clayton Morrissey, Gloucester's most famous fisherman and the model for the landmark fisherman statue in that town. The Parkers have two children, Caitlin and Alex, and they welcome families at the inn.

This is an informal, simply furnished inn, focused on its setting. The living room has two sitting areas around fireplaces at either end of the room and wide water views. Bedrooms are fresh and sunny, with lots of

WEB SITE: www.captainshouse.com

INNKEEPERS: Gretchen and Tim Parker

ROOMS: 5 rooms, all with private bath; 4 with ocean views

ON THE GROUNDS: Porch overlooking the Atlantic Ocean

RATES: $100–$160, including continental breakfast

CREDIT CARDS ACCEPTED: MasterCard, Visa

OPEN: Late March through October

HOW TO GET THERE: Take Route 128 north to Gloucester, turn left onto Route 127, and continue to Route 127A (Broadway) in Rockport. Make a right onto Route 127A (Broadway) and continue to the harbor. Follow Route 127A by turning right again on Mt. Pleasant Street, which becomes South Street for about 1 mile. Turn left at Marmion Way.

wicker accents. Some have nonworking fireplaces; four offer a view.

Breakfast is served buffet-style on the enclosed sunporch, typically a coffee cake, muffins, cereal, and fruit, with the Atlantic view for dessert. Afterward, you can bring a chair out on the rocks and watch the waves in action. If you want to be closer to the water, you'll have to hire a boat.

What's Nearby: Rockport is an artists' enclave, a sailing mecca, and a town packed with picturesque shops and galleries. Besides sandy beaches, the rugged coastline offers scenic drives and walks in Halibut Point State Park overlooking the sea. Gloucester's restaurants, fishing, and whale-watching fleets are a five-minute drive away.

EDEN PINES

48 Eden Road
Rockport 01966
(978) 546–2505

■ The view from this inn perched on the rocks over the sea is enough to take your breath away. Water is the first thing you see through a big picture window when you walk into the living room. The adjoining sunroom and breakfast room has window walls on two sides to bring the scene into even better perspective. The view of the Atlantic and the twin lighthouses of Thacher's Island can be savored from every romantic guest room, and the plant-adorned terrace on the rocks puts you close-up with the lapping waves.

WEB SITE: www.edenpinesinn.com
INNKEEPERS: Mike and Nicky Kern
ROOMS: 6 rooms, all with private bath, air-conditioning, TV, clock, radio, ocean view; 5 with balcony
ON THE GROUNDS: Oceanfront patio
RATES: $140–$210, including generous continental breakfast and afternoon tea with snacks

Built in 1900 as a private summer cottage, the gracious gray-shingled house makes the most of the extraordinary location that was voted "Best View" by the *New England Travel Guide* a few years ago.

The living room has a cozy feel, with dark paneled walls and comfortable seating around a big fieldstone fireplace. Breakfast is served on the porch, a pleasing room done in wicker and filled with seasonal

CREDIT CARDS ACCEPTED: Master-Card, Visa

OPEN: April through December

HOW TO GET THERE: Take Route 128 north to Gloucester, and then turn left onto Route 127, continuing to Rockport center. Make a right at Route 127A (Mt. Pleasant Street, then South Street), continue for about 1 mile, and then turn left onto Eden Road.

flowers. The breakfast spread usually includes juice, fresh fruit, yogurt, cereal, English muffins, and an assortment of breads and coffee cakes. Tea and cookies are set out in the afternoon.

The oversize, well-appointed bedrooms on the second floor are eclectic in feel, though all have a fresh look, decorator fabrics, and their own lures. A sunny yellow and blue summery print sets the mood for Room 3, while Room 5 boasts a marble bath and a private balcony facing the ocean. Room 7, the Beacon Suite, has a secluded third-floor location, a king-size bed, an oversize balcony, and a sitting area with a prime view of the twin lighthouses. Wherever you are, you can hear the roar of the waves as you go to sleep. The most extraordinary views are from the terrace, now built of storm-proof brick after two wooden decks sailed off to sea.

What's Nearby: See What's Nearby on page 142.

OLD FARM INN

291 Granite Street
Rockport 01966
(978) 546–3237; (800) 233–6828
Fax: (978) 546–9308

The red-shingled farmhouse surrounded by old stone walls is the epitome of old New England. Walk inside to complete the picture with beams, a fireplace, rockers, country prints, a spinning wheel, and scores of early antiques and collectibles. All of this would be delightful anywhere, but Old Farm Inn is blessed with a bonus. It is directly across from Halibut Point State Park, an oceanfront nature preserve that is among the most picturesque settings along the rugged Cape Ann coastline. The combination is hard to beat.

Though the plaque out front says BUILT IN 1799 BY JAMES NORWOOD, former owner Bill Balzarini's research says the farmhouse is much older. This land has been farmed for more than 250 years, most recently by Antone Balzarini, Bill's grandfather, who was a dairy farmer in the early 1900s. Bill and his family renovated the old homestead and opened their home to travelers in 1964. He and his wife, Susan, still live in a house on the property, but the inn was sold in 1999 to the Vassallos, Rockport residents who had visited for many years and have maintained the warm, hospitable ambience.

WEB SITE: www.oldfarminn.com

INNKEEPERS: Rich and Shirley Vassallo

ROOMS: 4 rooms in Barn Guesthouse, all with private bath, coffeemaker, refrigerator, air-conditioning, TV, phone, clock radio. Also available in the town of Rockport for extended stays are Kiwi Cottage, a one-bedroom cottage, and Kiwi House, a three-bedroom home with fireplace and washer/dryer.

ON THE GROUNDS: Patio, 5 acres of fields, lawn, and woodland with walking trails

RATES: $75–$140; call for Kiwi House and Kiwi Cottage rates

CREDIT CARDS ACCEPTED: Master-Card, Visa, American Express

OPEN: Year-round

HOW TO GET THERE: Take Route 128 north to Cape Ann and follow the signs to Rockport, going halfway around two rotaries. At the first set of traffic lights, turn left onto Route 127 north. Continue for 4 miles to Rockport's Five Corners, where Route 127 north turns left toward Pigeon Cove and is also called Granite Street. The inn is 2½ miles farther, on the right.

There have been changes, of course, as is always the case with new innkeepers. All the guest rooms now are in the Barn Guesthouse, and the decor has been refurbished. The Wedgwood Room is done in soft shades of blue and cream, is furnished with an Oriental rug and king-size bed, and has a small kitchenette. It faces west for grand sunset views from nearby Folly Cove. The Pineapple Room has an elegant four-poster bed. These two rooms can be combined to form a suite. Sunshine lives up to its name with a sunny exposure, white cottage furniture, and cheerful print fabrics on the bed and at the windows.

The inn no longer serves breakfast, but it is available to guest at the nearby Emerson Inn for an additional charge.

The inn is far enough from town to offer tranquillity, yet close enough to provide easy access to all of Rockport's shops, galleries, and restaurants. And the beauty of the coastline awaits just outside the door.

What's Nearby: See What's Nearby on page 142.

SEACREST MANOR

99 Marmion Way
Rockport 01966
(978) 546–2211

■ Picture an English country house amid a garden setting, 300 yards from the sea. The pretty, shingled house, a blend of Georgian and Federal style, was built in 1911 as a summer home. Step down into the spacious living room, and if you

can take your eyes off the seascape framed by the picture window, you'll notice a fireplace, wing and side chairs arranged for conversation, a brass chandelier, big bouquets of fresh flowers, and a stunning full-length gold leaf mirror. It is a perfect setting for the formal English tea served each afternoon.

The inviting library has its own fireplace, leather upholstered seating, and walls lined with art as well as books. There are paintings everywhere in this inn, in every public room, even in the wide hall and up the stairway.

Breakfast is served on fine china at individual tables in a formal dining room overlooking the garden. The menu includes fresh fruit cup, Irish oatmeal, bacon and eggs, and daily specialties such as blueberry pancakes or corn fritters.

Upstairs rooms are simply decorated with floral papers, desks, and comfortable reading chairs. A unique touch is the flower holder shaped like a picture frame in each room.

Guests have all the amenities of a fine country inn. In the morning, the newspaper is waiting outside your door, and after dinner, you return to find the beds turned down and mints on the night table. If gentlemen leave their shoes outside the door, they will be back in the morning, neatly polished.

The two prize rooms, Rooms 7 and 8, have picture windows and private entrances to a big deck looking out at woods and the ocean beyond. The last third of the sundeck is open to all guests, a wonderful place to lie back on a chaise longue and contemplate the sea.

The grounds are also relaxing, with lovely gardens to admire, chairs and tables placed under shady umbrellas, and a hammock swaying gently under the trees. The bustle of Rockport is only a mile away, but you'd never know it from this serene retreat.

What's Nearby: See What's Nearby on page 142.

WEB SITE: www.seacrestmanor.com

INNKEEPERS: Dwight B. MacCormack Jr. and Kathleen O. Henderson

ROOMS: 8 rooms, all with TV, radio; 6 with private bath, 2 with shared bath (can be combined into a suite); 2 with deck; 3 with ocean view

ON THE GROUNDS: 2 acres of lawns and gardens, sundeck with ocean view

RATES: $98–$215, including full breakfast and afternoon tea

OPEN: April through October

CREDIT CARDS ACCEPTED: MasterCard, Visa, American Express

HOW TO GET THERE: Take Route 128 north to Gloucester, then turn left onto Route 127, and continue to Route 129A (Broadway) in Rockport. At the harbor, make a right and follow Route 127A (Mt. Pleasant Street, then South Street) for about 1 mile, and then turn left onto Marmion Way.

AMELIA PAYSON HOUSE

16 Winter Street
Salem 01970
(978) 744–8304

▓ Spiffily painted in light blue with formal white columns, this 1845 Greek Revival was restored in the mid-1980s by Ada and Don Roberts, who left past careers (as a personnel director and a mechanical engineer, respectively) to work together as innkeepers. Their inn manages to be formal without feeling stiff or stuffy.

The living room, papered in soft rose, has two quilted sofas around an octagonal glass-topped coffee table, long draperies, and a grand piano, but the effect is softened by bookshelves and family pictures all around the room. The dining room, with soft blue flowered wallpaper, has fresh flowers in the center of the formal table and rose-colored seats on the Chippendale-style chairs to match the ruffled drapes. The marble fireplace is topped with a gilt mirror and a collection of china teapots on the mantel. A continental breakfast of fresh fruits, cereals, and home-baked breads or scones is served family style to guests gathered around the table.

The four bedrooms all have polished wooden floors, Oriental-style rugs, and old-fashioned furnishings that include ruffled canopy beds, Victorian mirrored dressers, and pairs of Victorian chairs.

The inn is located in Salem's Historic District, just ½ block from the green and within walking distance of many sights.

Reserve early if you want to come to Salem in October for "Haunted Happenings," one of New England's biggest and spookiest Halloween celebrations.

WEB SITE: www.ameliapaysonhouse.com

INNKEEPERS: Ada and Don Roberts

ROOMS: 4 rooms, all with private bath, air-conditioning, TV, radio

RATES: $95–$150, including continental breakfast

CREDIT CARDS ACCEPTED: MasterCard, Visa, American Express, Discover—but cash or traveler's checks preferred

OPEN: April 1 to November 15

HOW TO GET THERE: Take Route 128 north to Route 114 east to Salem, cross the bridge into town, turn right onto Bridge Street, and then right onto Winter Street. The inn is in the middle of this short block, on the right.

What's Nearby: Salem is still best known for its infamous witch trials, and the Salem Witch Museum is one of its most popular sights, but there is much more to see and do. The Salem Maritime National Historic Site has restored the historic wharves of the once-thriving seaport; the home that inspired Nathaniel Hawthorne's *House* *of Seven Gables* is open for touring; and the two buildings of the Peabody Essex Museum are packed with treasures, many of them brought back from the Orient by Salem's early sea captains.

BERKSHIRE 1802 HOUSE

48 South Main Street (Route 7)
P.O. Box 395
Sheffield 01257
(413) 229–2612

■ Flowers, flowers everywhere—in lush gardens on the grounds, and planters on the porch, and arrangements around the house. In summer, there's no prettier spot than this old-fashioned inn. Whatever the season, the sweet sage green clapboard house with its generous porches and Victorian trim is the perfect place to be if you want to take advantage of the shops lining the main street of Sheffield, the antiquing capital of the Berkshires.

Nancy and Rick came from Boston to the Berkshires for Tanglewood concerts and fell in love with the area. They found an inn with nice features such as beams and arched doorways and have given it a pleasing homelike flavor. Soft leather sofas flank a glass coffee table near the living-room fireplace, and two tables welcome guests in the dining room, where the menu includes home-baked muffins and breads and daily specials such as frittatas, waffles with real maple syrup, ricotta pancakes, omelettes with vegetables fresh from the garden, and a guests' favorite, baked French toast with peaches, blueberries, and pecans.

WEB SITE: www.berkshire1802.com
INNKEEPERS: Nancy Hunter Young and Rick Kowarek
ROOMS: 7 rooms, all with air-conditioning; 5 with private bath
ON THE GROUNDS: Almost 2 acres of lawns and lovely gardens, screened porch
RATES: $95–$160, including full breakfast
CREDIT CARDS ACCEPTED: Master-Card, Visa, American Express, Discover
OPEN: Year-round
HOW TO GET THERE: The inn is on Route 7, 1 block south of the town center on the west side of the road.

Each guest room has its own personality. I like Room 5, with an antique mantel as the headboard and an inviting wicker rocker, as well as Room 1, with a queen-size iron-and-brass bed, a bright floral comforter, and an Oriental rug. Rooms 6 and 7, sharing a bath, are ideal for families or couples traveling together.

When the weather is mild, guests are welcome to take advantage of the picnic table under an umbrella on the side lawn. And Nancy's lovely gardens are not to be missed.

What's Nearby: Sheffield, the southern gateway to the Berkshires, is a town known for the many antiques shops that fill Route 7, the town's Main Street. It has its own summer culture with performances by the Barrington Stage Company and the Berkshire Choral Festival and is a short drive to the many pleasures of Lenox and Stockbridge (see pages 123 and 151).

FEDERAL HOUSE INN

1560 Pleasant Street (Route 102)
P.O. Box 248
South Lee 01260
(413) 243–1824; (800) 243–1824
Fax: (413) 243–1828

▓ The stately pillared house was and is the grandest in town. It was built in 1824 by Thomas Hurlbut, who founded the town's most important industry, the paper mill just across the road on the Housatonic River. The mill is still operating and still bears his name. The house remained in the Hurlbut family until the 1960s.

WEB SITE: www.federalhouseinn.com

INNKEEPERS: Jim Finnerty, Carole Murko, and Megan O'Conner

ROOMS: 10 rooms, all with private bath, air-conditioning; 3 with fireplace; 3 with TV

ON THE GROUNDS: Broad lawn and generous porches, umbrella table and chairs on side lawn

RATES: $105–$250, including full breakfast

CREDIT CARDS ACCEPTED: MasterCard, Visa, American Express, Discover

OPEN: Year-round

HOW TO GET THERE: From Route 7 follow Route 102 east through Stockbridge for 1 mile to South Lee. The inn is on the left.

The rooms are spacious and gracious. The living room has windows almost as tall as the lofty ceiling, a dark marble fireplace, and French doors that lead to a porch.

The cheerful breakfast room with filmy white curtains at the windows is furnished with ladder-back chairs set around tables for two and four, a china cabinet, and a handsome antique mirror over the fireplace. The menu begins with fresh fruit and what the innkeepers declare are the best pastries in the Berkshires. Among the special hot dishes served are berry French toast and ham nests.

Bedrooms are light and airy with lots of windows. Three rooms on the first floor have their original floors plus modern conveniences including TV sets and phones with dataports. Picking a favorite here is no easy task, but I am a bit partial to the Rose Room upstairs, with the original wide pine floors, stenciling, a Rutherford iron bed, and a cast-iron Franklin stove. The Thomas Hurlbut Suite is the largest of the rooms and offers a grand four-poster with a hand-tied canopy, a fireplace, and four large windows overlooking the grounds. The Crabtree Room upstairs is tucked away in a quiet spot, with two windows looking out at a flowering tree, and you can see some of the home's original wooden beams in the cozy Tack Room, done with an English fox-hunt theme.

Be sure to have a look at the beautiful Copper Beech tree on the lawn; the innkeepers think it is probably older than the house.

What's Nearby: South Lee is a tiny hamlet on the Housatonic River at the base of Beartown State Forest. The entire village is listed on the National Register of Historic Places. It is located just 1 mile from the many activities of Stockbridge; see What's Nearby, page 151.

HISTORIC MERRELL INN

1565 Pleasant Street
South Lee 01260
(413) 243–1794; (800) 243–1794

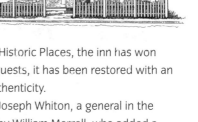

■ Many inns call themselves "historic," but none deserves the name more than this wonderful 1794 tavern, faithfully restored to reflect its past. The first Berkshire County property to be listed on the National Register of Historic Places, the inn has won numerous preservation awards, but happily for guests, it has been restored with an eye toward comfort and hospitality as well as authenticity.

The house was built originally as a home for Joseph Whiton, a general in the Massachusetts militia. In 1817 it was purchased by William Merrell, who added a third floor and operated it as a stagecoach inn for more than forty years. In recent times it had been used as a boardinghouse and was briefly considered for a stagecoach museum. Instead, the house was willed to the Society for the Preservation of New England Antiquities.

Previous owners bought the house from the society in 1980, signing a 500-year covenant guaranteeing the preservation of the building's significant historical features. These include the original facade, the eight Count Rumford fireplaces, and the false grain woodwork in the Tavern Room and on the stairs between the second and third floors. The original and very rare birdcage bar in the Tavern Room, with vertical posts to secure its contents, is believed to be the only complete unmodified circular bar in the United States.

Innkeeper Merrell would still recognize his bar, as well as the clapboard front of the inn, with its double-tier columned white balcony. Pieces such as the Boston bowfront chest of drawers in the front hall and the grandfather clock and the breakfront in the guest parlor date from the eighteenth century.

WEB SITE: www.merrell-inn.com

INNKEEPERS: George and Joanne Crockett

ROOMS: 10 rooms, all with private bath, air-conditioning, TV, Wi-Fi, phone, clock, radio; some with wood-burning fireplace

ON THE GROUNDS: 2 acres of park-like grounds leading to the Housatonic River; porches, tea-house, riverside gazebo

RATES: Rooms $99–$199, suite $155–$285, including full breakfast

CREDIT CARDS ACCEPTED: Master-Card, Visa, American Express

OPEN: Year-round

HOW TO GET THERE: The inn is 1 mile east of Stockbridge on Route 102. From Interstate 90, the Massachusetts Turnpike, take exit 2, Lee, and follow Route 102 west for 3 miles.

But it is doubtful that Merrell's lodgers knew anything like these elegant bedrooms. Some are country Early American and Victorian, but most are classic colonial, furnished with canopy beds, candlebeam lighting, elegant seating, and fine fabrics and rugs. Three large rooms have original wood-burning fireplaces; Room 1, with its dark paisley bedspread and white ruffled canopy, is particularly striking. Room 3, furnished with a country field bed with blue and white hangings, is one of the Crocketts' favorites. The back wing of the house is the Riverview Suite, elegant quarters with a private porch overlooking the river. A refrigerator, ice cubes, and an amenities basket for guests' use are in the fire escape room on the third floor.

Copies of portraits of John and William Merrell look on as guests gather in the Tavern Room, which is now the sitting room. In the keeping room, they can look over the breakfast menu, which includes juice and a choice of omelettes, scrambled eggs, blueberry pancakes, French toast, or cereals with bananas, walnuts, or raisins. Breakfast meats and a choice of breads for toast are also offered. The meal is served on dishes handmade at Bennington Pottery in Bennington, Vermont.

Afterward, the expansive grounds beckon, especially the chaise longue and chairs in the gazebo that was added several years ago down by the Housatonic River.

What's Nearby: South Lee is adjacent to Stockbridge; see What's Nearby on page 151.

BLUE WILLOW

2 Lincoln Lane, P.O. Box 843
Stockbridge 01262
Phone/Fax: (413) 298–3018

■ There is a fairy-tale look to this little gray clapboard cottage with flowery window boxes, a white picket fence, and a wooden folk-art guardian angel on the garage. Tucked away at the end of a secluded road opposite the Housatonic River, it seems far away from it all, yet the center of Stockbridge is less than ½ mile away.

The Ruggios moved here from Buffalo in 1983, when the 1825 cottage had been abandoned, and they have reclaimed its charm and filled the rooms with antiques. The name Blue Willow suggests the color scheme of the living room, where blue and white check sofas face the fireplace and blue and white plates adorn the mantel and the walls. A table and chairs are set in a bay window curtained in sheer white.

Two upstairs rooms are cozy. One has beams, an iron bed, and wicker chair, another a wooden poster bed and floral decor. The largest accommodation is in the carriage house, which offers two iron beds, a sleep sofa, and a convenient refrigerator. It is light and airy and has a pretty floral color scheme.

A candlelight breakfast is served each morning, with a Franklin stove nearby for extra warmth on chilly days. Apple French toast is one of the house specialties. Afterward, guests who like hiking will enjoy the inn's access to the Housatonic and the conservation land around it, and everyone will appreciate the proximity to the shops of Stockbridge and all the Berkshire attractions nearby.

What's Nearby: Norman Rockwell immortalized Stockbridge in his drawings, and the world's largest collection of his work can be seen at the Norman Rockwell Museum. Also in this charming town are Chesterwood, the home of sculptor Daniel Chester French; Naumkeag Museum and Gardens, designed by Stanford White; the Mission House, dating from 1739; and the Berkshire Botanical Garden. The Berkshire Theatre Festival is one of the oldest and most respected summer playhouses in the United States. As a bonus, Lenox and Tanglewood are within a ten-minute drive.

WEB SITE: www.bluewillowbb.com

INNKEEPERS: Lila and Joseph Ruggio

ROOMS: 2 rooms in the cottage, 1 in the carriage house, all with private bath, TV, air-conditioning, clock radio, hair dryer

ON THE GROUNDS: 1 acre, flower borders

RATES: $90–$200, including full breakfast

CREDIT CARDS ACCEPTED: None

OPEN: Year-round

HOW TO GET THERE: From Route 7 turn east toward Stockbridge on Route 102 (Main Street). Proceed ½ mile and look for Lincoln Lane on the right, a small gravel road. The inn is the last house on the right.

STOCKBRIDGE COUNTRY INN

Route 183, Box 525
Stockbridge 01262
(413) 298–4015
Fax: (413) 298–3413

■ There are some people who have a special knack for decorating, sure taste that can fill a room with fine antiques and still make it comfortable and welcoming. Diane Reuss is one of those people, and the tasteful rooms in her Stockbridge Country Inn are worthy of a magazine cover.

True, Diane has an advantage; her husband, Vernon, is an antiques dealer and collector, accounting for many of the exquisite American antiques and the original Audubon prints on the walls throughout the house. It's an ideal marriage, one that has produced one of the loveliest inns in the Berkshires.

WEB SITE: www.stockbridgecountry
inn.com
INNKEEPERS: Diane and Vernon Reuss
ROOMS: 8 rooms, all with private bath
ON THE GROUNDS: Inground heated swimming pool, lawns, patio
RATES: $179–$389, including full breakfast
CREDIT CARDS ACCEPTED: Master-Card, Visa, American Express, Discover
OPEN: Year-round
HOW TO GET THERE: From the Massachusetts Turnpike (Interstate 90), take exit 2, Lee, and follow Route 102 west through Stockbridge, continuing past the village to the intersection of Route 183. Turn south onto Route 183, where you will see the Norman Rockwell Museum just a little more than ½ mile ahead; the inn is another ½ mile past the museum on the right.

The 1856 Federal-style country home has been added to over the years without changing its period character. The big windows that have been installed add a cheery feel in every room. There are many places to mingle—a formal parlor and a casual family library and sitting room, both with fireplaces; a wicker-filled sunroom; and a big screened porch facing the outdoor swimming pool, where guests gather on warm summer days.

The parlor has a grand piano and Federal decor, with handsome chests, a camelback love seat, and Windsor chairs. The light-colored walls are accented with red chintz print fabrics, and there are many Audubons on the main walls.

The dining room is also formal, with an Oriental rug beneath the expansive table, a mix of Windsor and rush-seat chairs, a corner cupboard displaying fine china, a brass chandelier, and a Federal-era mirror on the wall. Light, cream-colored swag curtains match the walls; they cover only the tops of the wide wraparound windows, allowing light to come in. A collection of mainly blue glassware on the window ledge reflects the light.

The breakfast room is country cozy, with wide floorboards, dark blue floral wallpaper, cheerful red checked swags, and flower prints on the walls. The oval table is set with Windsor chairs and a wooden-back love seat. More red checks cover the wing chairs in the sitting area.

A big breakfast is served each day from 8:30 to 10:00 A.M., consisting of fresh juice and fruit, eggs in many varieties with bacon or sausage, special treats such as waffles, and coffee cakes or muffins. In summer, breakfast is often moved outdoors. Coffee and tea are available in the family room starting at 8:00 A.M.

Upstairs rooms vary in their wall coverings, but all have queen-size four-posters with canopies and many interesting antiques around the room. In winter, downy comforters are on each bed. Diane's favorite is Nell's Room, done in English chintz with pink cabbage roses and dark green accents, furnished with a four-poster rice bed made of cherry and two wing chairs in a linen rose print. Whatever room you have, you'll no doubt find much to admire in this tastefully appointed inn.

What's Nearby: See What's Nearby on page 151.

INN AT WEST FALMOUTH

66 Frazar Road, P.O. Box 1208
West Falmouth 02574
(508) 540–7696; (800) 397–7696

■ So you want to get away, just the two of you, to someplace beautiful and totally private, somewhere romantic, maybe with an ocean view? Look no further. This small, luxurious inn is perched on a hillside, two minutes from the highway but on a road so secluded you'll never find it without the innkeeper's directions. Sit on the terrace or your private balcony, gaze down at Buzzard's Bay in the distance, and the real world will quickly fade away.

The 1899 Victorian house was beautifully restored several years ago, winning an "Inn of the Year" award from *Country Inns* magazine for its exceptional decor.

Six lucky couples can occupy the tastefully decorated rooms. The decor of each room varies, from flowery chintz canopies to Oriental serenity in neutral shades of beige with grasscloth walls. Fabrics have been coordinated with a careful eye, blending a mix of solids, checks, florals, plaids, or prints in artful combinations. Antiques, embroidered coverlets, and colorful dhurrie rugs add to the picture. You can't go

WEB SITE: www.innatwestfalmouth.com

INNKEEPER: Sue Barry

ROOMS: 6 rooms, all with private bath with whirlpool, phone, air-conditioning; some with fireplace, private deck, ocean view

ON THE GROUNDS: Heated outdoor pool, clay tennis court, patio

RATES: $195–$375, including buffet breakfast

CREDIT CARDS ACCEPTED: MasterCard, Visa, American Express

OPEN: Year-round

HOW TO GET THERE: Directions given on confirmation of reservation.

wrong in any room, but Room 3 is a special choice, offering a big deck with an ocean view, a fireplace, and a king-size bed with a handsome carved headboard. Even the smallest room, all the way at the end of the house, has its own appeal, with a four-poster bed hung with taffeta, pouf paisley window shades, and a very private deck. All the rooms have sleek marble bathrooms equipped with whirlpool baths.

The paneled living room invites lingering, with comfortable sofas in front of an oversize marble fireplace, attractive English pine accents, and handsome floral draperies. Next door is a billiards room. An open bar and afternoon tea are available for guests.

A buffet breakfast of juice, fresh baked goodies, granola, crepes, quiche, blueberry pancakes, coffee, or a selection of teas can be enjoyed in the pastel dining room at tables for two. A wall of French doors and stained glass leads to a terrace with a small outdoor swimming pool. If you are feeling active, you can go below to work off those pastries with a game of tennis, and take the complimentary ride or a fifteen-minute walk downhill to the beach.

The busy town of Falmouth is only minutes away, but you'd never know it at this serene retreat.

What's Nearby: This peaceful enclave is minutes away from the beaches, shops, and restaurants of busy Falmouth. It is also convenient for ferries to Martha's Vineyard from Woods Hole, just beyond Falmouth.

FIELD FARM GUEST HOUSE

554 Sloan Road
Williamstown 01267
(413) 458–3135
Fax: (413) 458–3144

■ For lovers of contemporary art or unspoiled natural beauty, this home is a rare find. The curving modernistic cedar home designed by architect Edward Goodell was built in 1948 for Lawrence

WEB SITE: www.guesthouseatfield
farm.org

INNKEEPER: Bob Chok

ROOMS: 5 rooms, all with private
bath, scenic view; 3 with private
deck; 2 with fireplace

ON THE GROUNDS: 316 acres of
lawns, fields, ponds, and woodland
with magnificent mountain views;
outdoor swimming pool, terrace,
modern sculptures, picnic tables; 5
miles of hiking trails for cross-
country skiing

RATES: $150–$250, including full
breakfast

CREDIT CARDS ACCEPTED: Master-
Card, Visa, Discover

OPEN: Year-round

HOW TO GET THERE: Follow Route 7
north; at the intersection of Route 7
and Route 43, turn south onto
Route 43 and immediately turn right
onto Sloan Road. Field Farm Guest
House is slightly more than 1 mile
farther on the right.

Bloedel, a Williams graduate and well-known patron of the arts. It was designed to show off his priceless collection of modern art and to make the most of the setting on 316 acres, with peerless views of Mount Greylock in the distance.

In 1984, on Eleanore Bloedel's death, the house was willed to the Trustees of Reservations, an organization dedicated to preserving Massachusetts properties of exceptional scenic and historic value. Not sure what to do with it, the trustees consulted David and Judy Loomis, who had successfully restored River Bend Farm in Williamstown, and the couple helped set up the home as a unique bed-and-breakfast lodging.

Staying here feels like having your own country retreat. Guests are free to use the spacious living room, dining room, and terrace; to make use of the outdoor pool; and to roam the grounds. All the rooms have large picture windows looking over the grounds toward the mountains and interesting furnishings in spare modern design. Much of the sleek 1950s-era furniture of oak, cherry, and walnut was handmade by Mr. Bloedel. Both house and grounds are accented with modern sculptures. Some art remains, but much of the Bloedel art collection was donated to the Williams College Museum of Art and to the Whitney Museum of American Art in New York.

The bedrooms vary in size. The first-floor Gallery Room, which was used by Mr. Bloedel as a studio, is enormous and contains both a double bed and two twins; it has its own entrance. The two largest rooms upstairs are the North Room, which has its own balcony, and the Master Bedroom, with an even larger deck. Both have fireplaces bordered by custom tiles depicting trees, birds, and butterflies.

A resident innkeeper is always on hand to greet guests, give guidance, and provide a full breakfast of fruit; granola; a variety of baked goods that may include muffins, banana bread, or zucchini bread, and a hot dish. Among some of the tasty recent choices were Grand Marnier French toast, waffles with apple Calvados sauce, and an asparagus and Gruyère omelette.

The grounds are magnificent in every season, and they offer a rare opportunity to enjoy nature in complete serenity. There are picnic tables, too, if you'd care to eat while you commune with nature.

What's Nearby: Art lovers flock to Williamstown for the Clark Art Institute, renowned for its Impressionist art and silver collections, and for the Williams College Art Museum, one of the country's finest campus art collections. The surrounding countryside offers hiking, swimming, and antiquing, and the Williamstown Theatre Festival attracts major stars each summer.

RIVER BEND FARM

613 Simonds Road
Williamstown 01267
(413) 458–3121

This 1770 Georgian colonial home was built by one of Williamstown's original founders, Col. Benjamin Simonds, and a stay here is as close as you'll come to returning to Simonds's day. Owners Dave and Judy Loomis are history buffs who once spent their days sailing and restoring old wooden sailboats. During the late 1970s, they found and fell in love with this house, and they have restored it with absolute authenticity, earning a place on the National Register of Historic Places. Opening the house to guests six months of the year helped under-write the cost of the restoration.

The couple scraped down many layers of paper and paint to find the original wall colors for some of the rooms. Lighting fixtures are reproductions of candle chande-liers and wall sconces. In the kitchen, chairs hang on Shaker-style wall pegs, the ceiling is hung with herbs, and the room boasts all sorts of early domestic antiques, from wooden washtubs to butter tubs, jugs, iron pots, and cooking tools.

Wherever you look, there seems to be a fireplace. Breakfast is served in the keeping room, with a beehive oven in the fireplace and colonial furnishings. The offerings include granola, muffins, and honey, all homemade, plus fruits and juices. The tap-room, or sitting room, also has a welcoming fireplace. In all, the massive central chimney supports five fireplaces, two bake ovens, a smoking chamber in the attic, and a large ash pit in the cellar.

Bedrooms may have walls of whitewashed plaster or natural wood; simple muslin curtains hang at the windows. Beds are comfortable four-posters or rope beds. All the rooms hold many antiques, from chamber pots to spinning wheels. Judy's favorite is the Parlor, with a fireplace, an early rope bed, and Oriental rugs.

WEB SITE: www.riverbendfarmbb
.com

INNKEEPERS: Dave and Judy Loomis

ROOMS: 4 rooms sharing 2 baths

ON THE GROUNDS: Patio, gardens,
porch, horseshoes

RATES: $120, including continental
breakfast

CREDIT CARDS ACCEPTED: None

OPEN: May through October

HOW TO GET THERE: Follow Route 7;
the inn entrance is off Route 7, 1
mile from either Route 2 in
Williamstown to the south or the
Vermont border to the north.

There are no private baths, but the compensation is rates that are a pleasant surprise in the Berkshires. Many families or friends book the entire inn (up to ten people, $600). The location is a plus, in a country setting but just 1 mile from the many pleasures of Williamstown, a college town that boasts two outstanding art museums as well as a noted summer theater. The Clark Art Institute is renowned for its Impressionist art and silver collections.

The Loomises describe their house as "a sleep-in museum," and they enjoy sharing it with guests who appreciate the genuine Early American ambience.

What's Nearby: See What's Nearby on page 156.

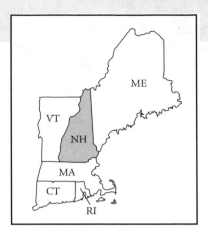

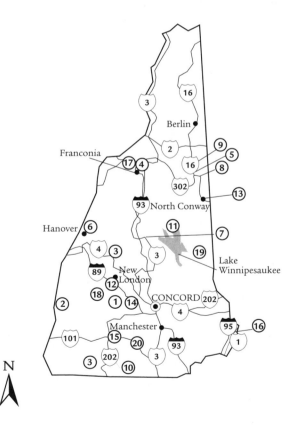

NEW HAMPSHIRE

Numbers on map refer to towns numbered below.

ROSEWOOD COUNTRY INN

67 Pleasant View Road
Bradford 03221
(603) 938–5253; (800) 938–5273

■ Away from town on a leafy country road, this rambling Victorian inn has been receiving guests since 1896. As a summer resort, it boasted a guest list of luminaries that included Jack London, Gloria Swanson, Mary Pickford, Douglas Fairbanks, and Mr. and Mrs. Charlie Chaplin.

WEB SITE: www.rosewoodcountryinn.com

INNKEEPERS: Lesley and Dick Marquis

ROOMS: 2 rooms, 9 suites with fireplace, whirlpool bath, and shower for two; all with private bath, clock, radio, air-conditioning; most with TV/VCR

ON THE GROUNDS: 12 acres with walking trails, gazebo, croquet, herb garden, 2 arched bridges over a stream

RATES: Rooms $119–$159, suites $169–$299, including full breakfast and Friday-evening wine and hors d'oeuvres

CREDIT CARDS ACCEPTED: MasterCard, Visa, American Express, Discover, Diners Club

OPEN: Year-round

HOW TO GET THERE: From Interstate 89 take exit 5 to Route 202/Route 9, heading west toward Henniker. Exit at Route 114 and turn right toward Bradford. At the traffic light at Routes 114 and 103, take a left onto Main Street. At the end of Main, curve left and go up the hill for about 1¾ miles to Pleasant View Road on your right. The inn is the third house on the right.

But it has never looked so elegant as since the Marquis family arrived several years ago to completely redo the interior and create a year-round haven. Both Lesley and Dick Marquis were in the medical field when they lived in Woonsocket, Rhode Island. They wanted a slower pace for bringing up their two daughters, and a country inn seemed the answer. Seeing the spiffy, better-than-new inn today, it is hard to believe that they started with an abandoned summer-only structure that needed heat, electricity, plumbing, a new septic system, a new roof, and some 126 new windows!

The inn has two formal living rooms with traditional camelback sofas, wing chairs, and fireplaces, but people tend to gravitate to the light, cheerful, country-style tavern room, where they find a woodstove, folk art and stenciling on the walls, and a jigsaw puzzle on the table.

An elaborate three-course "candlelight-and-crystal" breakfast is served from 8:00 to 9:30 A.M. in a spacious breakfast room done in pink and green with rose stenciling. A typical menu may offer "morning glory" muffins, poached pears in cranberry and orange compote, ham-and-asparagus quiche, and plum pudding. In summer, breakfast is often served on the porch. Beyond the dining room is a big open kitchen with more tables and chairs and a small gift shop.

From the center hall, the stairway leads upstairs to bedrooms with frilly curtains and valances, rose stenciling, and a romantic long-stemmed rose laid across each bed. The Abigail Adams Suite offers a bay window and roses twining over the canopy bed. For a change of pace, the Whispering Pines Room is more masculine, decorated with dark green accents, and the Sturbridge Room is more country in feel, with stencils, folk art, and a twig wreath on the wall. Williamsburg overlooks the garden. Suites, with fireplaces, whirlpool baths, and double-headed showers made for two, will please romantics.

The inn has a roster of special events, such as mother-daughter weekends, originally planned for the slower winter months but so well received that they are now held year-round. Another unique idea is a "his and hers" weekend when the guys go fishing and the gals go shopping. Special weekends for quilters, bird-watchers, and holidays are also on the busy schedule.

What's Nearby: The countryside around the inn offers lots of terrain for cross-country skiing in winter and for nature walks, birding, and swimming at a swimming hole in summer. Within a short drive are New London shops, summer theater, and Pats Peak skiing. It is just 8 miles to Lake Sunapee and Mount Sunapee Resort.

DUTCH TREAT INN

355 Main Street (Route 12), P.O. Box 1004
Charlestown 03603
(603) 826–5565; (877) 344–1944

Here's a historic and hospitable headquarters for exploring both New Hampshire and Vermont, just across the Connecticut River. The spacious house was built in two stages, 1754 and 1820. Dob and Eric Lutz arrived in 2003 to fill it with charm reflecting their many travels and their native land of Holland.

Everything has been refurbished, and a new six-person hot tub was added, much to the delight of skiers in winter. Antiques from Holland and Austria, where the couple lived for several years, are throughout the house. Public rooms have a soft blue color scheme reminiscent of fine Delft china.

The parlor is properly formal, with Victorian-style pieces upholstered in blue, tie-back curtains, and a handsome Oriental rug. The adjoining sitting room is for relaxing, with wingback chairs around the fireplace and shelves of books. The woodwork is painted that lovely shade of Delft blue.

WEB SITE: www.thedutchtreat.com

INNKEEPERS: Dob and Eric Lutz

ROOMS: 4 rooms, 1 suite, all with private bath, air-conditioning

ON THE GROUNDS: Lawns, gardens, porch with wicker furniture, six-person hot tub

RATES: Rooms $89–$109, suite $129–$149, including full breakfast, afternoon refreshments

CREDIT CARDS ACCEPTED: Master-Card, Visa

OPEN: Year-round

HOW TO GET THERE: From Interstate 91 take exit 7, Springfield, Vermont, and head east over the bridge into Charlestown. At Route 12, proceed south (right turn). The inn is 7⁄10 mile farther on the left.

Upstairs rooms have Dutch names, many antique pieces, and unique themes. The Delft Blue Room is cozy, with a blue and white print bedspread and pieces of Delft adorning the walls. The Lace Maker Room, a tribute to the painter Vermeer, has beams and exposed brick, a brass bed, and floral bedspread. The Tasman Room is named after the Dutch explorer Abel Tasman and is furnished with a pair of twin beds with wooden headboards and matching night-stands from Austria. The largest quarters, the Tulips Suite, has a four-poster bed, cheerful tulip-patterned curtains and bed-spread, and wicker seating. The bath features a claw-foot tub, double sink, and a bidet.

Guests come down each morning to a full breakfast in a lovely dining room with a fireplace and brass chandelier. The two round tables are often topped with colorful rugs, a Dutch tradition. The house specialty is known as the Dutch Treat, a recipe so special that the innkeepers keep it a secret.

There are many rewarding excursions within a short drive from the inn, and the friendly hosts are ready with suggestions. You can be sure of a warm welcome when you return, and the chance to discuss the day's events over a sociable hour featuring Dutch and New England cheeses and a choice of wine, beer, or soft drinks.

What's Nearby: Charlestown is a small New Hampshire town with some notable churches and many historic homes—sixty-three structures are part of the Main Street National Historic District. St. Catherine's Church has four signed Tiffany windows. The Fort at #4, a living-history museum, depicts the 1740s and holds many special events and reenactments. Several attractive farms are in the nearby countryside, including Putnam's Farm and Sugar House, one of the largest dairy farms in New Hampshire and a recommended stop for maple syrup. The Connecticut River is a short walk from the inn; boats may be rented at the Green Mountain Marina across the river. It is a short drive to the St. Gaudens National Historic Site and the Cornish-Windsor covered bridge leading to Windsor, Vermont.

Dartmouth College and the Mount Sunapee and Monadnock Mountain regions of New Hampshire are each about a half hour's drive from the inn.

HANNAH DAVIS HOUSE

106 Route 119 West
Fitzwilliam 03447
(603) 585–3344

■ Just off the town common of one of New Hampshire's prettiest towns stands this 1820 charmer, with pumpkin pine floors, six wood-burning fireplaces, nineteenth-century hardware on the original pine doors, and antique glass in most of the windows. Simple country furnishings, braided rugs, and antique quilts add to the period look.

The entry is through a big, inviting country kitchen with a fireplace; a cabinet divider with plants sets off the breakfast area. When the inn is full, a second dining room with antique pine is used. A small den provides a camelback sofa and two comfortable armchairs for watching the TV, which has a VCR.

One of the largest guest rooms in the house is the first-floor suite, with a private entrance and porch. It has fireplaces in both the bedroom, which has a king-size bed, and the sitting room, which has a camelback sofa that converts to a double bed.

Upstairs are three more bedrooms. Hannah is a snug room with an antique iron bed and a claw-foot tub with a brass shower. Canopy is large and bright, with a handsome cherry pencil-post bed with an antique crocheted canopy top, a wooden trunk at the foot, and another old-fashioned tub-shower. Chauncey is a standout, with a queen-size iron bed and convertible sofa, a fireplace, and a cheerful red color scheme that extends to the bathtub. All the bathrooms have period pedestal sinks.

Mike and Kaye Terpstra, the personable hosts, left careers as an engineer and social

WEB SITE: www.hannahdavishouse.com

INNKEEPERS: Mike and Kaye Terpstra

ROOMS: 3 rooms, 3 suites, all with private bath, clock, radio; some with fireplace, private entrance

ON THE GROUNDS: Large screened porch overlooking beaver pond

RATES: $80–$165, including full breakfast

CREDIT CARDS ACCEPTED: Master-Card, Visa, Discover

OPEN: Year-round

HOW TO GET THERE: From Interstate 91 take exit 28A (Bernardston, Massachusetts), and follow Massachusetts Route 10 north to Winchester, New Hampshire, and then New Hampshire Route 119 east to Fitzwilliam. The house is on the left. From the east take Massachusetts Route 2 west to Massachusetts Route 140 north to Massachusetts Route 12 north, and turn left onto NH 119; the house is less than ¼ mile farther, on the right.

worker, respectively, to make a first career change running a country grocery store for ten years. They moved on to became innkeepers in 1990, and they are still enthusiastic about their roles, constantly looking for ways to improve the house with new decks overlooking the pond and interesting new guest spaces.

Above the garage is my favorite addition, Popovers, with high ceilings, a big rounded window, an antique cannonball bed, a wood-burning fireplace, and a private deck. The Loft in the carriage barn is a total change, a two-story hideaway with its own entrance and a Southwestern decorative theme. Inside are beams, enormous barn board doors, a fireplace, and a loft bedroom with an angled antique cannonball bed. The bath has a footed tub and a big, five-sided glass shower.

Guests are given breakfast cards with the day's menu each morning. A typical list may include ruby-red grapefruit juice, homemade granola and applesauce, cinnamon-raisin bread, chilled peach soup, mushroom strudel, scrambled eggs, and Scarlet Runner beans.

What's Nearby: Fitzwilliam, a classic New England town with eighteenth-century homes surrounding the village green, is an antiquing center and is within easy reach of Peterborough's arts, Rhododendron State Park (a vision in July when the rhodys are in bloom), and all the outdoor pleasures of the Monadnock region.

BUNGAY JAR

791 Easton Valley Road
Franconia 03580
(603) 823–7775; (800) 421–0701

■ This is an inn of delights, an 1800s post-and-beam barn transformed into a haven of whimsy and charm, with decks and balconies perfectly placed to take in the mountain views and the glorious gardens. It isn't a surprise to learn that Bungay Jar has been featured in many magazines and on the cover of *Country Accents*.

Are you wondering about the inn's name? Bungay Jar refers to a quirky wind that blows across the valley, usually in spring, rattling the trees and ruffling the pond.

Jeffry Burr and Neil Blair took over this prize property in 2004 and have put their own stamp on things, retaining much of the inn's eclectic decor while upgrading and adding amenities.

The house rambles over four levels along the hillside. The former hayloft is now a two-story living room, with hand-hewn beams hung with quilts and weathered barn-board walls hung with antique farming tools. The sun lights up an antique glass bottle collection. A comfortable sitting area surrounds the big stone fireplace, and hundreds of books line the bookcases around a wingback reading chair. A guest lounge just off the living rooms is stocked with complimentary beverages and holds the guest phone and a computer with Internet access. Tea and treats are set out in the afternoon.

The dining area at the end of the room, furnished with round pub tables and Windsor chairs, is where a gourmet breakfast is served each morning, with house specialties such as perfect lemon pancakes or bacon-cheddar waffles. On fine days, breakfast is moved outdoors to the deck overlooking the garden and the mountains beyond.

Each guest room has a unique personality, Cinnamon boasts a cafe sitting area, private balcony, and a 6-foot soaking tub that once belonged to musician Benny Goodman. Sara's Room has a pencil-post canopy king bed and an interior private reading balcony overlooking the living room. I'd love the chance to stay in Stargazer, up on the top floor, with skylights, a king bed with mountain views, an antique Victorian gas stove, and a claw-foot tub perfect for bubble baths under the stars.

Three rooms are suites with Jacuzzi tubs, gas fireplaces, and private decks with garden and mountain views. Fiddlehead has a fern motif; Sunflower is in country blue and yellow. The Garden Suite, on the ground level, has garden lattice work on the ceiling, a white cottage-style bed, a small kitchenette, and a patio opening to the garden.

The garden is a highlight of the Bungay Jar, planted with a wildflower meadow that is filled with color in spring and perennial beds that span the seasons. Among its pleasures are fountains, a lily pond stocked with goldfish, and woodland paths leading to the river and a delightful surprise—a stacked stone "river people" sculpture garden.

WEB SITE: www.bungayjar.com

INNKEEPERS: Jeffry Burr and Neil Blair

ROOMS: 5 suites, all with private bath

ON THE GROUNDS: 8 acres, lawns with picnic tables, fabulous gardens, woodland paths leading to a lily pond and meandering river

RATES: $140–$245, including full breakfast

CREDIT CARDS ACCEPTED: Master-Card, Visa, American Express

OPEN: Closed April and November

HOW TO GET THERE: From Interstate 93 take exit 38, Franconia. Follow Route 116 (Easton Valley Road) south for about 6 miles, and look for the inn on the left.

What's Nearby: The magnificent mountain scenery of Franconia Notch State Park and skiing at Cannon Mountain are within easy reach of the inn. Easton Valley Road is relatively flat for this White Mountains area and is popular with bikers.

COVERED BRIDGE HOUSE

Route 302, P.O. Box 989
Glen 03838
(603) 383–9109; (800) 232–9109

It's not unusual to find photographers clustered in front of this inn. The little red-shuttered white colonial by the side of the road would be a find on its own, but this one comes with a bonus—the Bartlett Bridge, an 1850 trestled covered bridge that has been authentically restored.

Dan and Nancy Wanek were living in the Bronx in New York City when they read about an essay contest on "Why I Want to Be an Innkeeper," with this inn as the prize. The picturesque bridge was a special lure: It comes with a shop on the other side, an ideal setup for Nancy to sell her own creations, along with other local crafts and antiques.

The contest was canceled, but the Waneks won out anyway. The bank that took over from the past owners had the Waneks' names from their entry and contacted them to ask if they wanted to make a bid. They did, and in 1995, they moved to New Hampshire with their newborn son, Brian, who now has a sister, Allison.

They have furnished the inn in appropriate country style, with stenciling, braided rugs, pine furniture, pullback curtains, and a candle in each window. The homey living room is made pleasant with green plants, shelves of books and games, a rocking horse in a corner, and a TV set for guests.

Four tables for two and one larger table are set in a dining room decorated with leaf stenciling, ruffled valances over sheer lace curtains, and a polished hardwood floor that positively gleams. Fresh fruit, home-baked muffins and breads, and eggs any style are served every morning, along with a special dish, perhaps Belgian waffles with berry syrup or blueberry pancakes.

Bedrooms are named for the "notches,"

WEB SITE: www.coveredbridge house.com

INNKEEPERS: Dan and Nancy Wanek

ROOMS: 6 rooms, 4 with private bath

ON THE GROUNDS: 2 acres, with swimming hole on the Saco River, patio, outdoor hot tub; 1850 covered bridge leads to a gift shop

RATES: $64–$119, including full breakfast

CREDIT CARDS ACCEPTED: Master-Card, Visa, Discover

OPEN: Year-round

HOW TO GET THERE: From North Conway take Route 16/Route 302 north to Glen. At the Glen intersection, continue west on Route 302 for approximately 2 miles. The Covered Bridge House is on the right, just after the third bridge. Coming from the east, the inn is on the left just south of West Side Road.

passes in the nearby White Mountains. One downstairs bedroom, Carter Notch, is done in Victorian style, with a tall armoire, ornate sofa, and ribbon stenciling. Five more bedrooms upstairs are back in colonial mode, with colonial curtains and patch work quilts. Dixville Notch in the front corner has two twin beds, floral wallpaper, and a big rocker. It can be combined with Pinkham Notch, a pink and blue room with ruffled curtains, to form a suite.

Additions to the inn are a patio where breakfast is served in summer and an outdoor hot tub, a favorite with skiers.

The inn is an ideal location for family fun, with a swimming hole behind the inn on the Saco River. Since Dan and Nancy are young parents themselves, they welcome other families. The Waneks will provide a rollaway cot for the little ones.

What's Nearby: North Conway is just 7 miles to the south (see What's Nearby on page 178). Four major downhill ski areas are nearby, including Attitash, just down the road.

TRUMBULL HOUSE

40 Etna Road
Hanover 03755
(603) 643–2370; (800) 651–5141

■ Sunny and spacious, this gracious colonial home—with twin dormers, a columned front porch, and candles in the windows —was built in 1919 as a private residence. It has been nicely restored and refurbished as Hanover's first bed-and-breakfast inn, a welcome development for the many visitors to nearby Dartmouth College. The warmth of a home has been maintained, however, with fresh, livable decor that may inspire many guests with decorating ideas.

The living room is large, with a bay window and fireplace, shelves of books and puzzles, and a library of CDs that invite lingering. Furnishings include an oversize sofa, two comfortable armchairs with ottomans, and a handsome Oriental rug.

The elegant dining room is done with red walls that contrast nicely with the white wainscoting. The generous-size table is circled with comfortable oversize chairs. The breakfast menu includes a variety of interesting dishes such as scrambled eggs with smoked salmon, cream cheese, and chives; a mushroom-and-cheese omelette made with portobellos and Brie; and Dover toast, a version of French toast made with English muffins. Fresh fruits and fresh baked pastries are always part of the meal. Breakfast hours are flexible; guests can leave word the night before about what time they would like to come down.

WEB SITE: www.trumbullhouse.com

INNKEEPER: Hilary A. Pridgen

ROOMS: 4 rooms; 1 two-bedroom, two-bath suite; 1 guest cottage; all with private bath, TV/VCR, high-speed wireless Internet access, clock, radio

ON THE GROUNDS: Front and side porches, 16 acres with meadows, woods, brook; basketball half-court; hiking and cross-country-ski trails that traverse the property and link into the Appalachian Trail

RATES: Rooms $100–$235, suite or cottage $290, including full breakfast

CREDIT CARDS ACCEPTED: All

OPEN: Year-round

HOW TO GET THERE: From Interstate 89 take exit 18 toward Hanover and drive 7/10 mile. Turn right at the second light onto Etna Road for about 2¼ miles. Bear right at the T-junction; the Trumbull House is 3/10 mile on the right. From Interstate 91 take exit 13 and go just over 5 miles east, across the bridge and through Hanover to the T-junction; turn right onto Etna Road and look for the house 3/10 mile farther on the right.

Rooms are named for their color schemes. On the second floor are the Blue Room, with a queen-size sleigh bed, and the White Room, in the front corner, with rose-pattern wallpaper, a four-poster, and a sofa that converts to a queen-size bed. The two-bedroom Suite includes a dressing room with a window seat, a twin trundle bed, and plenty of room to accommodate a crib or cot. It comes with two full bathrooms, one with a whirlpool bath.

Third-floor rooms under the dormers have the cozy slanted walls that many people favor. I'd gladly curl up with a book on the window seat in the Green Room, an especially snug accommodation with dark green and pink wallpaper and a star quilt on the queen-size bed. The Yellow Room has its own window seat, plus a king-size bed tucked into a sleeping alcove and a trundle bed that can sleep two.

The guest cottage, with a king-size bed and convertible sofa, comes with a whirlpool tub, Jacuzzi, and a private deck.

Innkeeper Hilary Pridgen moved to Hanover after selling a business in Connecticut, renovating a separate wing of the house for her five children. She says she was attracted by the many outdoor activities in the Upper Connecticut River Valley, especially the hiking and cross-country trails on her own property, which she happily shares with guests.

What's Nearby: Hanover is one of America's most beautiful college towns, centered around the campus of Dartmouth College. It is the cultural center of the Upper Connecticut River Valley, with art at the Hood Museum and a range of top-notch performances and films at the Hopkins Center. The area also offers a wide range of year-round outdoor activities, from canoeing to skiing. The Montshire Museum of Science in neighboring Norwich, Vermont, is a fascinating stop for families. Woodstock and Quechee, Vermont, are also within easy driving distance.

SQUAM LAKE INN

Shepard Hill Road
Holderness 03245
(603) 968–4417; (800) 839–6205

■ Just steps from Squam Lake, the lovely lake featured in the movie *On Golden Pond,* this circa 1890 farmhouse with a wraparound porch beckons with warm vintage charm. Guests can relax in front of the fireplace on a Victorian settee in the sitting room or settle in with a book in the library, where they are also welcome to check the Internet. When the weather is warm, the porch and a spacious deck are favorite gathering places.

WEB SITE: www.squamlakeinn.com

INNKEEPERS: Rae Andrews and Cindy Foster

ROOMS: 8 rooms, all with private bath, robes, CD clock radio, air-conditioning, wireless Internet; 2 with gas fireplace

ON THE GROUNDS: Front porch, deck, 1880 barn

RATES: $140–$170, including full breakfast

CREDIT CARDS ACCEPTED: Master-Card, Visa, American Express, Discover

OPEN: Year-round

HOW TO GET THERE: From Interstate 93 take exit 24 and follow Route 3 south through Ashland, along the Squam River and Little Squam Lake, for approximately 5 miles. At a Citgo gas station, Route 3 forks left and Shepard Hill Road goes straight up the hill. Go straight for 150 yards; the inn is on the right.

Lots of big windows make the breakfast room a cheery place to start the day. Innkeepers Rae and Cindy use lots of seasonal ingredients for tasty specials that may include four-grain blueberry pancakes, Belgian waffles with strawberries and whipped cream, and French toast bake with a warm seasonal berry sauce. You can choose a table for two or meet other guests at the big table.

Guest rooms are newly decorated, with names that reflect the Lakes Region. Lake Winnipesaukee Room in cool greens and blues is decorated with a vintage oar and Winnipesaukee memorabilia. It features a king-size bed, as do Loon and the Chocorua Island Suite. All have at least a queen-size bed, and most rooms have a choice of ceiling fan or air-conditioning. I like the bright Bennett Cove Room downstairs for its many windows.

Rae and Cindy vacationed in the Lakes Region for a decade before they became innkeepers, and they love sharing their knowledge with you. Whether you want to hike, kayak, explore nature, go shopping, or have a special dinner, they know all the best places.

What's Nearby: Squam Lake, best known as the site of the movie *On Golden Pond*, is a short walk from the inn; boat tours are available. A private beach is a fifteen-minute walk away. Also nearby are the Science Center of New Hampshire, with trails and live animal displays, plus shops and all the attractions of New Hampshire's Lakes Region.

GLEN OAKS INN

Route 16A, P.O. Box 37
Intervale 03845
(603) 356–9772; (877) 854–6535
Fax: (603) 356–5652

■ This venerable, three-story Victorian with dark green awnings and a mansard roof has been receiving guests since 1890. Well situated on a quiet road just a few miles from North Conway, it offers unpretentious hospitality and spacious grounds with a swimming pool.

The entry opens into a long sitting area with a fireplace, floral wall-paper, Victorian furnishings, an upright piano against one wall, and shelves of books and games. A small room off the entryway is where guests can gather to watch TV.

An enclosed porch furnished with wicker runs across the front of the house. In summer it is screened to catch the breezes; in winter, with a gas fireplace going, it can be a cozy spot for relaxing.

A second, more formal parlor is actually older than the rest of the house. It was built around 1835 and was originally a general store on adjacent property until moved here to enlarge the home in the 1880s.

The attractive dining room is decorated with lace curtains at the windows, a muted-pattern floral wallpaper, and soft, striped wainscoting. Half a dozen double-skirted tables seat two or four.

Mitch has become an avid chef since he and Linda moved here in 2005 from California, swapping business careers for innkeeping. The breakfast menu changes daily, always with a choice of two entrees, from Belgian waffles with fresh strawberries and whipped cream to potato pancakes.

Guest rooms have an old-fashioned look, pleasantly decorated with carefully coordinated fabrics. Room 7, for example, has blue-printed wallpaper, a blue-striped coverlet, a blue valance over white lace curtains, and a white and blue flowered quilt at the foot of the bed. Room 6 is done in soft rose and lilac florals, with a white woven bedspread, a white and rose quilt at the foot, and a double-skirted table with a white cover over a rose floral design. Furnishings in this room include a high,

WEB SITE: www.glenoaksinn.com

INNKEEPERS: Mitch Scher and Linda Trask

ROOMS: 8 rooms in the inn, all with private bath, air-conditioning, phone, clock, TV/VCR; 3 with fireplace; 3 rooms in cottages, all with private bath, clock, phone, CD player/TV/VCR, refrigerator, 2 with gas fireplace; 1 with wood-burning fireplace and screened porch; 1 with whirlpool tub

ON THE GROUNDS: 24 wooded acres with stream, swimming pool; property adjoins Mount Washington Cross Country Ski Trail

RATES: $85–$195, including full breakfast and afternoon refreshments

CREDIT CARDS ACCEPTED: MasterCard, Visa, American Express, Discover

OPEN: Year-round

HOW TO GET THERE: Take Route 16/Route 302 north from North Conway and turn right at Route 16A, Intervale. The inn is 1½ miles ahead on the right.

carved wooden Victorian headboard, gas fireplace, wingback chair, and a vintage dresser.

Other room accommodations vary from brass beds to sleigh beds, but all have old-fashioned furnishings. Several rooms have ceiling fans, and Rooms 1, 5, and 6 have gas fireplaces.

The stone cottage on the grounds, dating from the early 1900s, was once the office of one of the first women lawyers in New Hampshire, Marion Weston Cottle. It now holds two guest rooms with four-poster beds and fireplaces, one of them wood-burning, and it offers a private screened porch. Another small cottage is a romantic retreat with a gas fireplace and whirlpool tub.

In winter, cross-country trails are waiting right outside the back door.

What's Nearby: Intervale is a quiet oasis midway between Jackson and North Conway, with easy access to the pleasures of both. It is also convenient to White Mountain ski areas.

NESTLENOOK FARM RESORT

Dinsmore Road, Box Q
Jackson 03846
(603) 383–9443; (800) 659–9443

It is a picturebook setting—a gingerbread Victorian house surrounded by gardens on a sixty-five-acre estate with a gazebo on the lawn and a graceful covered bridge over the pond. It isn't surprising to find that the grounds include a chapel to accommodate the many couples who want to be married here.

The inn lives up to its surroundings with lavish Victorian decor, including wood paneling imported from a mansion in Italy. In case you haven't gathered that this is a place dedicated to romance, a bay window in the dining room is home to an oversize Victorian birdcage populated with lovebirds.

The house is older than you might guess. The Dinsmore Room of the original farmhouse dates from 200 years ago and retains its original beams, fieldstone fireplace, and country look. But the rest is pure Victoriana, right down to many of the original tin ceilings.

The dining room has one of those tin ceilings, as well as hand-carved woodwork, an antique birdcage, and a Count Rumsford fireplace. A typical breakfast would offer squeezed orange juice, carrot or orange-cranberry muffins, and a main course that could be waffles with strawberries and whipped cream or an oven-baked omelette.

Even the rustic downstairs playroom, done with wood paneling and fieldstone, carries out the Victorian theme with an antique billiards table and Tiffany-style lamps. It offers a dart board, a TV, and a bar, along with a state-of-the art sound system and a CD laser disc library.

Each guest room is named for a Jackson artist, past or present, and features that artist's work. Window treatments are elaborate, and every guest room has a whirlpool bath built for two and either a fireplace or an elegant nineteenth-century parlor stove, collected from all over the world. The William Paskell Room boasts a hand-carved four-poster with an embroidered canopy, a Count Rumford fireplace, and French doors opening to a small balcony with views of the river. The Myke Morton Room, in the oldest part of the inn, has its original beamed ceiling and brick hearth, with access to the side porch.

Almost all the rooms have a view, of either the river or Emerald Lake, but none equals the C. C. Murdoch Suite, which occupies the entire third floor and gives a three-way view of the grounds, including vistas from a whirlpool bath beside a window.

WEB SITE: www.nestlenookfarm.com

INNKEEPER: Robert Cyr

ROOMS: 5 rooms, 2 suites, all with private bath, two-person whirlpool bath; 1 with fireplace; 6 with parlor stove

ON THE GROUNDS: 65 acres, outdoor swimming pool, gardens, arched bridge over lake, heated lakeside gazebo with fireplace, boating, fishing, ice skating, snowshoeing, hiking trails, chapel, farm animals

RATES: $125–$544, including full breakfast, wine and cheese, carriage or sleigh ride (weather permitting)

CREDIT CARDS ACCEPTED: MasterCard, Visa, Discover

OPEN: Year-round

HOW TO GET THERE: Proceed north from North Conway on Route 16 past the Route 302 intersection and watch for the Route 16A turnoff to Jackson on the right. Drive through the covered bridge and take the first right to the inn.

With an outdoor pool for swimming, a pond for boating, trails for hiking, a hammock for relaxing, and facilities for skating and snowshoeing in winter, there is good reason to call this a resort.

My favorite activity at Nestlenook is a ride in an Austrian sleigh (mounted on wheels in summer) to appreciate the exceptional setting. The handsome Percheron horses make a stop in the forest so that passengers can feed the deer, and they take a turn around the property to show off the horses, sheep, chickens, and other farm animals that add a final picturesque touch to the scene.

What's Nearby: Jackson is a picturesque White Mountains village reached via a covered bridge. It offers fine dining, a few choice shops, horseback riding, and prime hiking. Winter activities include ice skating, sleigh rides, downhill skiing at Black Mountain, and cross-country skiing on 167 kilometers of trails at the Jackson Ski Touring Foundation. The shops and outlets of North Conway are minutes away, and choice scenic drives and foliage watching are found throughout the White Mountain region.

BENJAMIN PRESCOTT INN

Route 124 East
Jaffrey 03452
(603) 532–6637; (888) 950–6637
Fax: (603) 532–6637

The handsome yellow Greek Revival farmhouse is a classic New England picture. Built in 1853 and surrounded by a century-old, 500-acre farm, this is a picturebook rambling roadside country inn, with mountain and pastoral views on all sides.

The sitting room is informal, with comfortable seating in front of a woodstove set into the fieldstone fireplace. A long buffet serves as a divider with a handsome dining room with a stencil border, antique clock, and an old-fashioned hearth oven.

Breakfast brings house specials such as Prescott three-cheese sausage and spinach pie or Benjamin baked eggs.

Guest rooms are named for members of the Prescott family, the original builders of the house. All offer fine views of the countryside.

Rachel, on the first floor, has handsome white wooden painted twin beds and cheerful flowered curtains. Up the stairs, the Colonel Prescott Room is a favorite, with cranberry walls and a handsome red and white quilt on the bed. I liked the Susannah Suite, which features an antique brass bed, and a small sitting room. For

WEB SITE: www.benjaminprescott
inn.com

INNKEEPERS: Sue and Charlie Lyle

ROOMS: 7 rooms, 3 suites, all with private bath, clock radio; suites with air-conditioning, TV

ON THE GROUNDS: Lawn with seating, hiking trails, surrounded by 500-acre farm

RATES: Rooms $90–$125, suites $110–$170, including full breakfast and afternoon refreshments

CREDIT CARDS ACCEPTED: Master-Card, Visa, American Express

OPEN: Year-round

HOW TO GET THERE: From Route 101 turn south onto Route 202 and east onto Route 124 in Jaffrey. Proceed on Route 124 for about 2¼ miles; the inn is on the left.

space you can't beat the John Adams Attic, which can sleep eight, with a king-size canopy bed in one room, a queen-size bed in the sitting room, and two additional beds tucked snugly under the eaves. This is a most inviting space, with a cathedral ceiling, a wet bar, and glass doors opening to a balcony with views of the fields.

Sue and Charlie, who took over the inn in June 2005, have instituted some welcome discounts for business travelers, seniors, and members of the military, as well as some interesting weekend packages. Be sure to ask about their special murder-mystery weekends.

What's Nearby: Jaffrey, a classic New England town with a green, is the home of Mount Monadnock State Park and one of the most popular climbing mountains in New England. It is within easy range of Peterborough and all the activities of the Monadnock region.

OLDE ORCHARD INN

108 Lee Road, R.R. 1, Box 256
Moultonborough 03254
(603) 476–5004; (800) 598–5845
Fax: (603) 476–5429

In spring the orchards are canopied with clouds of pink and white, and in fall the inn is scented with the delicious aroma of apples cooking in the kitchen. Whenever you arrive, you'll admire the house, which is, indeed, "olde." It was built by Bathchelder Brown for his bride, Abigail, in 1790, and one of their sons built the brick addition in 1812 for the growing family. The house and its orchards remained in the Brown family until the mid-1900s.

The Hills fell in love with the home, the property, and the historic barn and became owners in 2003. Both had interesting past careers, Clark in the high-tech/Internet industry, Jo as a librarian for the National Park Service and the John F. Kennedy Library in Boston. They owned a children's bookstore in southern New Hampshire for several years.

As innkeepers, they have created a warm, relaxing inn where it is easy to feel at home. Their black lab, Pepper, will greet you at the door, and the grandfather's clock in the entry will gently chime you into the inn. The living room, with white walls and colonial blue wood trim, has a fireplace and a library card-catalog end table. Guests are welcome to sample the hosts' collection of CDs.

Music is a big part of the inn. Musicians are invited to play the Steinway piano in the living room, the Hammond organ in the breakfast room, or to have a go at the didgeridoo. If you are lucky, the Hills's son Alex will be visiting from New York to offer a bit of jazz during breakfast.

The breakfast room features a beehive oven and a square table mounted on an old sewing machine treadle. The hosts will play the wind-up Victrola on request. A coffee bar is available for early risers, stocked with coffee and freshly baked muffins. A full breakfast is served by candlelight in the formal dining room, often featuring dishes made with fruit from the orchards.

On balmy days, the meal may be moved to the sunporch. This is one of the inn's most pleasant gathering places, with wicker chairs and rockers overlooking the pond. It is a fine place for watching sunsets.

The guest rooms ramble up and down stairs. They are named for apples, and each is unique, with handmade quilts, stenciled walls, Oriental rugs, and antiques. Baldwin on the first floor has a fireplace, and a nice view of the apple orchard. Maiden's Blush is a romantic choice, with a canopy queen bed, fireplace, and whirlpool tub. I also like Rome Beauty, tucked under the eaves and with an especially colorful quilt on the bed. Northern Spy, also under the eaves, is done in floral wallpaper with a bright red coverlet on the bed, and it comes with a whirlpool tub. Granny Smith, a smaller room tucked in a corner, is delightfully decorated to celebrate grandmas and includes a photo of Jo's mother on her first birthday.

The grounds of the inn are inviting, and Lake Winnipesaukee is a pleasant mile's walk from the inn. For a surprise, look in the barn, where a hot tub and sauna await.

WEB SITE: www.oldeorchardinn.com

INNKEEPERS: Jo and Clark Hills

ROOMS: 9 rooms, all with private bath, air-conditioning or fan, TV, clock, radio; some with wood-burning fireplace; some with whirlpool

ON THE GROUNDS: 12 acres, including 5 acres of apple orchards; berries; gardens; pond; sauna and hot tub in the barn

RATES: $85–$185, including full breakfast

CREDIT CARDS ACCEPTED: Master-Card, Visa

OPEN: Year-round

HOW TO GET THERE: The inn is 1 mile from Route 25. In the center of Moultonborough, turn east onto old Route 109. Take the first right onto Lee Road and continue ½ mile. The inn is on the right. From Wolfeboro turn left onto Lee Road and continue to the inn, on the left.

What's Nearby: The inn is in the heart of New Hampshire's Lakes Region, just 1 mile from Lake Winnipesaukee, the largest lake in the state. Cruise boats ply the lake in season. On the way is the Audubon Society's Loon Center, a game refuge with hiking trails, and a gift shop. Shopping is prime throughout the area, especially antiquing. The Old Country Store in Moultonborough is more than 200 years old, nearby Wolfeboro offers scores of shops, and Center Sandwich has a number of artisans' shops. Keepsake Quilting, the largest quilting store in the United States, is in Center Harbor, about a ten-minute drive away; the Annalee Doll Museum in Meredith is a fifteen-minute drive; and in winter, skiing at Gunstock is a half-hour trip. Many major New Hampshire ski areas are within an hour's drive. Tax-free factory-outlet shopping in either North Conway or Tilton is about a forty-minute trip.

MAPLE HILL FARM

11200 Newport Road
New London 03257
(603) 526–2248; (800) 231–8637

■ There's absolutely nothing fancy about this old-fashioned inn—which is exactly why many people fancy the place. The inn is as homey as a visit to Grandma's farm. The innkeepers have kids and love kids, and they welcome families to join them gathering eggs in the barn.

The house was built in 1824 and stayed in one family until 1976. It served as a summer boardinghouse from 1880 to 1950, charging $11 a week with three meals. Things cost a bit more now, but Dennis Aufranc, who took up innkeeping after twenty years at AT&T, has deliberately kept things simple and inexpensive.

The parlor has dark red tin walls with an embossed flower pattern, white wooden wainscoting, a woodstove, and an overstuffed sofa and chair for looking at the many books and magazines in the room. An adjoining small room provides a comfortable chair and ottoman for listening to an extensive collection of CDs and records. A second parlor, the old master bedroom, has a slightly more formal feel, with velvet upholstery and an Oriental rug, but painted wooden floors and a star quilt on the wall remind you that this is still a farmhouse. Hostess Roberta Aufranc made many of the quilts on the walls.

The dining area adjoins the big country kitchen. It has rough wooden wainscoting, beams, ruffled curtains, plants, and another woodstove. Out back is a deck where breakfast is served in summer. The rest of the year, guests gather at two long tables or one round table for two to enjoy Dennis's hearty fare. Guests are given a menu the night before with a choice of four breakfasts, from baked apple and toast

WEB SITE: www.maplehillfarm.com

INNKEEPERS: Dennis and Roberta Aufranc

ROOMS: 10 rooms, 6 with private bath; 1 lakefront three-bedroom house

ON THE GROUNDS: Chickens; deck with hot tub; barn with dance floor and basketball court; croquet, horseshoes; property has access to a beach on Little Lake Sunapee, with canoe, rowboats, picnic tables

RATES: Rooms $75–$135, house $450, including full breakfast

CREDIT CARDS ACCEPTED: Master-Card, Visa, American Express, Discover

OPEN: Year-round

HOW TO GET THERE: The inn is 1 block east of Interstate 89, exit 12.

for spartans to blueberry pancakes or Dennis's farm special—fresh baked biscuits, country bacon or sausage, eggs any way you like them, and delicious hash brown potatoes.

The rooms are simply furnished, but effort has gone into making them pleasant, such as the stenciling on many of the walls and the quilts on display. Room 1 on the first floor has a tin ceiling; Room 2 is done with twin beds, calico checked curtains, heart pattern quilts, and a comely quilt on display. The bed owned by the original farm family is in Room 4, made of dark pine with hand stenciling. Three rooms have sofas that pull out into twin beds. Four rooms on the third floor share two baths; they can work well for families since two rooms have double beds and two have twins.

The house has four porches, two open, two enclosed; one of the latter becomes a screened porch in summer. One deck holds a six-person hot tub. There's plenty to do on the grounds, and the property has access to a beach on Little Lake Sunapee, equipped with boats and picnic tables. If it rains, there's a basketball court in the barn.

The inn also specializes in reunions for families or groups of friends, with a reasonable package for ten couples that includes meals and a hayride.

What's Nearby: New London, home of Colby-Sawyer College, is a classy, unspoiled New England village with a long-established summer theater troupe and winter skiing at Mount Sunapee or Pat's Peak. Lake Sunapee is nearby for swimming and boating, and Mt. Sunapee State Park draws skiers in winter and thousands of browsers each August for the big annual fair of the League of New Hampshire Craftsmen. Dartmouth College is thirty minutes away.

BUTTONWOOD INN

Mt. Surprise Road, P.O. Box 1817
North Conway 03860
(603) 356–2625; (800) 258–2625
Fax: (603) 356–3140

■ High on a hilltop with mountain views, this expanded Cape-style 1820 farmhouse is a serene hideaway just 2 miles from the bustle of North Conway village. When Jeffrey and Elizabeth Richards arrived from Durham, Connecut, in 2002, they gave the inn a warm country flavor.

Guest rooms are warm and bright, each with its own decor. Some have floral wallpapers, others are in pristine white. Many have attractive quilts at the foot of the bed. I especially like the country mural on the wall in Room 2, and Room 10, which has a pencil-post bed and a roomy sitting area.

Elizabeth's breakfasts are highlights of a stay at the Buttonwood. There is always a freshly baked surprise such as white chocolate–apricot muffins or raspberry–sour cream coffee cake. Just be sure to save room for the main course, alternating savory and sweet, with treats such as turkey cheddar strata or peachy-keen pancake puffs. When the inn is filled, breakfast is served at two sittings, 8:00 to 9:00 A.M, and 9:00 to 10:00 A.M.

There are two sitting rooms, a traditional living room upstairs, and the Mt. Surprise Room downstairs, where guests can relax in a family room with a fieldstone fireplace, rustic furnishings, a braided rug, and New England village scene wallpaper on one wall. The room includes a bar, a guest refrigerator, and a TV and VCR with a collection of movies.

The grounds here are exceptional year-round. A 20-by-40-foot outdoor swimming pool beckons in summer, and there is access to 40 miles of trails for hiking in good weather or cross-country skiing in winter. The gardens are especially lovely in mid-June, when the lupines are in bloom.

What's Nearby: North Conway is the bustling center of the Mount Washington Valley, known equally for its scenic surroundings and for shopping, including more than one hundred manufacturers' outlets. The surrounding White Mountains are popular with skiers and hikers; hiking trail maps are available at the headquarters of the

---

WEB SITE: www.buttonwoodinn.com

INNKEEPERS: Jeffrey and Elizabeth Richards

ROOMS: 10 rooms, all with private bath; clock radio, hair dryer; 1 with gas fireplace; 1 family suite; 1 with fireplace and whirlpool bath

ON THE GROUNDS: 6 acres on the side of Mount Surprise, lawns, gardens, outdoor swimming pool, access to 40 miles of cross-country skiing and hiking trails

RATES: $120–$255, including full breakfast and afternoon refreshments

CREDIT CARDS ACCEPTED: MasterCard, Visa, American Express, Discover

OPEN: Year-round

HOW TO GET THERE: Coming from the south, take Route 16 to North Conway and turn right onto Kearsarge Street (traffic light in the village center just past the Scenic Railway Station on the left). Continue to the top of the hill, and at the T bear left and continue 1½ miles to the stop sign. Go straight across the intersection to Mt. Surprise Road, which bears to the left, and proceed to the inn.

Appalachian Club at Pinkham Notch, a short drive away. The top of Mount Washington, the highest peak in the Northeast, can be reached on foot, via auto, or aboard the steam-powered Cog Railway.

FARM BY THE RIVER

2555 West Side Road
North Conway 03860
(603) 356–2694; (888) 414–8353

◼ This white clapboard farmhouse with rocking chairs and flower boxes on the front porch not only looks like Grandmother's house, it actually belonged to owner Rick Davis's grandmother. Rick is the seventh generation to live in the house since King George III deeded it to one of his ancestors, John Thompson, in 1771. The post-and-beam barn dates from 1772, the house is circa 1785, and this was a working dairy farm until the 1960s.

Now it is an old-time, friendly inn, furnished with lots of family heirlooms and old photos. The living room is classic country, with cheerful wallpaper, sofas and armchairs in front of the fireplace, a bay window full of plants, and a picture window looking out at Cathedral Ledge, a site down the road that is famous among rock climbers.

Fireside breakfasts are served in winter in the dining room, where there is another sitting area with rockers and a TV. In summer, everything may move out on the deck, with garden and mountain views for dessert. The Davises made things even more scenic by adding a pond to the garden area. Breakfasts feature fresh fruits, muffins, and hot dishes such as blueberry pancakes, French toast amandine, an egg dish, or Belgian waffles with strawberries and cream.

Rick was a soil scientist, and his wife, Charlene, was an artist and college professor teaching landscape architecture until they married in 1993 and decided to turn the family homestead into a bed-and-breakfast inn the next year. The guest-room names have special meaning for Rick since they are for ancestors or former guests from the time when he helped his grandmother run the home as a boardinghouse.

All the rooms have high ceilings, at least two windows for cross ventilation, and views to the pastures, mountains, or gardens. All have air-conditioning as well. Flannel sheets keep guests cozy in cold weather, and in summer, fresh flowers from the perennial gardens are found everywhere.

Decor is a mix of colonial and Victorian. Uffer's Room is furnished with a rocker, hand-hooked rugs, walnut and maple furniture, and a king-size bed with a walnut headboard and a goose down comforter. It has a whirlpool bath in the bathroom. Mrs. Carroll's Room has been remodeled with a 5-foot picture window looking out at the mountains; the Thompson Room overlooks the garden. Both have a whirlpool

WEB SITE: www.farmbytheriver.com

INNKEEPERS: Rick and Charlene Davis

ROOMS: 10 rooms, all with air-conditioning, private bath; 1 with whirlpool bath; 2 with whirlpool bath, fireplace

ON THE GROUNDS: 70 acres, deck, gardens with pond, lawns with seating, sugar maple orchard; horseback riding year-round; foliage wagon rides in fall; sleigh rides, cross-country skiing, and snowshoeing available in winter (the inn will provide snowshoes); property extends to a sandy beach on the Saco River, an excellent spot for swimming, canoeing, or fly fishing

RATES: $100–$130 for basic rooms, $135–$195 for rooms with fireplace and/or whirlpool bath, $150–$200 for suites, including full breakfast and afternoon refreshments

CREDIT CARDS ACCEPTED: Master-Card, Visa

OPEN: Year-round

HOW TO GET THERE: From Interstate 95 north take the Spaulding Turnpike to Route 16 north to Conway. At the four-way lighted intersection, turn left onto Washington Street. Go 1 block and stay left where the road forks, onto West Side Road. The inn is 6 miles ahead on the right.

bath and a fireplace.

Father's and Ellen's Rooms form a two-room suite with a private bath or two separate guest rooms with a shared bath and private sinks. Father's Room, in a light and airy corner, belonged to the host's great-grandfather, Charlie Thompson.

The same kind of two-room arrangement applies to Delue's Suite on the first floor. The second room here, with a king-size bed and a fireplace, is called the Bride's Room since Charlene used this room to get ready to marry Rick. Her photos are on the wall.

The grounds of the inn offer enjoyment for all seasons, from strolls through the maple sugar grove to moonlit sleigh rides through the woods and pastures and along the Saco River. In fall, the color is fantastic. Horseback riding is available year-round.

On a back road paralleling Route 16/Route 302, the farm is also near Cathedral Ledge for rock climbing and convenient for North Conway shopping and all the activities of the White Mountains. Echo Lake State Park is just 1 mile, Diana's Bath 1½ miles, and a golf course ½ mile from the inn.

What's Nearby: See What's Nearby on page 178.

NERELEDGE

River Road, P.O. Box 547
North Conway 03860
(603) 356–2831; (888) 356–2831
Fax: (603) 356–7085

▥ It's easy to feel at home in this warm, comfortable, 1787 farmhouse inn, where you'll find families, hikers,

skiers, and bargain-hunting shoppers all happily sharing the premises. There's plenty of room for everyone.

Two adjoining living rooms, each good size, are decorated with country print wallpaper and curtains, Oriental rugs on the wide pine floors, ample seating, lots of plants, a woodstove, and a spinning wheel. The windows provide views of Cathedral Ledge and the Moat Mountain range beyond.

The "pub" room is another gathering place, with a wood-burning fireplace, game tables, a dart board, and a TV. As the name suggests, the room was once a pub and still has the old beamed ceiling, wooden booths, and the White Horse Pub sign over the fireplace. Both rooms offer TV and a VCR, and there's a small library of videos, including some for children. Since innkeepers Laura Glassover and Steven Hartman are parents of two young children, Lucas and Samantha, they are very welcoming to families.

WEB SITE: www.nereledgeinn.com

INNKEEPERS: Laura Glassover and Steven Hartman

ROOMS: 11 rooms, 6 with private full bath, 1 with private half bath, 4 with shared bath

ON THE GROUNDS: Porch

RATES: $69–$159, including full breakfast

CREDIT CARDS ACCEPTED: Master-Card, Visa, American Express, Discover

OPEN: Year-round

HOW TO GET THERE: From Route 16/ Route 302, turn west onto River Road; the inn is about 1 block ahead, on the right.

In summer, rockers on the wraparound porch are among the most popular seats in the house.

I really enjoyed having breakfast here in a particularly cheerful dining room with red print paper, white ruffled tieback curtains, red and white cloths, and fresh flowers on the table. Breakfasts are hearty, offering eggs any style, French toast or pancakes, and five kinds of juice. There is always an omelette of the day, in tasty combinations such as tomato, basil, and smoked mozzarella, or spinach, feta, and grilled fresh vegetables. All come with bacon or sausage. Steve's muffins are legendary; they come in flavors such as raspberry–white chocolate chip, black and white pecan chip, mixed berry, and carrot–brown sugar. Afternoon snacks quite often include apple pie or crumble, and the hosts will sometimes serve a piece for breakfast if you ask nicely.

Breakfast is served from 7:30 to 9:30 A.M. to suit various schedules, but the obliging innkeepers also do an early serving for mountain climbers or gung-ho skiers.

Rooms 9 and 11 are recommended for families with small children, as they are separate from the other rooms and have more space for cribs and cots. Room 9 has a single bed in an adjoining room and can be combined with Room 2 to form a family suite. As mentioned, children are most welcome, as evidenced by the high chair standing ready in the dining room. Kids sharing parents' rooms are charged a dollar for each year of their age per night.

Nereledge has an ideal location, within walking distance of many of North Conway's shops and dining. It is especially popular with lovers of the great outdoors because it is also a short walk from the Saco River and some prime hiking and mountain climbing. Climbing, hiking, and mountain biking maps are provided for guests.

What's Nearby: See What's Nearby on page 178.

FOLLANSBEE INN

P.O. Box 92
North Sutton 03260
(603) 927–4221; (800) 626–4221

This rambling 1840s inn is blessed with a sublime location, on the south shore of peaceful, pine-rimmed Kezar Lake, a wonderful source of recreation year-round.

The inn itself has old-fashioned appeal. Two comfortable sitting rooms offer a choice of moods. You can be cozy with a wood-burning stove and barn-wood walls or choose a plant-filled room facing the lake, where a service bar is stocked with beers and wines and a game table awaits with board games.

The dining room, also overlooking the lake, has a pleasant country look. Breakfast includes homemade granola, juices, and tasty hot dishes such as crème brûlée French toast with sausage or eggs Benedict. You can take your coffee out on the porch, facing the town green and a 1790s meetinghouse framed by the surrounding wooded hills.

Off the wide corridors upstairs are cozy bedrooms, named for ancestors of the town, such as Hannah and Abigail, and furnished country style, some with floral papers, others with pristine white walls and dark wood trim. The beds feature handsome patchwork quilts. Ichabod's Room, all in blue with ruffly white tieback curtains, has three windows facing the lake. Since the

WEB SITE: www.follansbeeinn.com

INNKEEPERS: Dave and Cathy Beard

ROOMS: 18 rooms, all with private bath

ON THE GROUNDS: Wraparound porch with lake views; adjacent lakefront with canoes, kayaks, boats for guests' use; weather permitting, the lake is used for skating; snowshoeing or cross-country skiing in winter; bicycles available to guests

RATES: $120–$190, including full breakfast

CREDIT CARDS ACCEPTED: MasterCard, Visa

OPEN: Year-round

HOW TO GET THERE: From Interstate 89 take exit 10. Turn left if coming from the south; turn right coming from the north. Proceed about 100 yards. Turn right onto North Road for about 1 mile. Turn right onto Route 114 for ¼ mile. Turn left just before the white church on the right, to the inn.

Beards arrived in 1999, two suites have been created on the third floor, and private baths have been added to all the rooms.

They've also upgraded the landscaping at the lakefront. Uncrowded Kezar Lake is ideal for boating, fishing, and swimming. The inn's lake frontage includes a pier with canoes, rowboats, kayaks, and a paddleboat, and lots of room for sunbathing and lounging. A short swim brings you to a floating raft, and if you want privacy, you can row to a secluded island for a picnic.

There's no more pleasant exercise than the 3-mile walk around the lake, with views of 2,914-foot Mount Kearsarge. The hardy can climb the mountain for panoramic views. Bikes are available for guests who want to explore the nearby countryside. In winter, when the weather cooperates, the lake becomes a playground for cross-country skiers and snowshoers, and the inn offers ski packages with nearby Mount Sunapee.

What's Nearby: North Sutton, part of the Sunapee region, is just 4 miles from New London, where the Barn Theater presents summer stock and Colby-Sawyer College has theater productions in winter. Skiing is nearby at Mount Sunapee and Ragged Mountain. Also nearby are historic sites such as the Musterfield Farm Museum, 1 mile up the road, and the John Hay Estate (also known as the Fells) on Lake Sunapee. The Saint-Gaudens National Historic Site and the Canterbury Shaker Village are each a short drive away.

APPLE GATE B & B

199 Upland Farm Road
Peterborough 03458
(603) 924–6543

Wooden red apples adorn the windows of this 1832 farmhouse next door to a picturesque apple orchard. The house has been charmingly furnished with antiques and country furnishings in keeping with its age.

The parlor has low ceilings and beams, a wing chair and sofa in front of the Rumford fireplace, an antique secretary, and a tic-tac-toe game with wooden apples and apple cores as pieces. Beyond is a music room and library with a woodstove, wing chairs and a rocker, bookshelves, an upright piano with a teddy bear pianist on the bench, and a TV/VCR in the cupboard.

In the dining room, another Rumford fireplace makes things cozy, and a built-in china cabinet displays cranberry- and apple-pattern dishes. Breakfast is served by the

WEB SITE: www.virtualcities.com/nh/applegate.htm

INNKEEPER: Dianne Legenhausen

ROOMS: 4 rooms, all with private bath, clock, radio

ON THE GROUNDS: Wraparound porch, 3 acres surrounded by woods and orchards, perennial garden along a stone wall in front

RATES: $75–$90, including full breakfast

CREDIT CARDS ACCEPTED: Master-Card, Visa

OPEN: Year-round

HOW TO GET THERE: From Route 101 turn south onto Route 123, and continue 1⁵⁄₁₀ miles. The inn is on the right, on the corner of Upland Farm Road.

light of the wrought iron chandelier over a handsome maple table. The menu features fresh fruit and dishes such as scrambled eggs, pancakes, waffles, or French toast topped with sautéed apples, and a homemade muffin of the day.

Rooms are appropriately named for apples; to complete the theme, guests find a package of apple chips for snacking waiting in their rooms. Granny Smith, a front corner room, is done in a soft green floral print with violets. It has ivy stenciling on solid green walls, a nonworking fireplace, and particularly fine views of the orchard. Cortland, another sunny front room, offers another nonworking fireplace, a pale yellow color scheme, a braided rug on wide floorboards, and a twig wreath over the queen-size bed. Crispin, in a back wing, is white and bright, with ruffled curtains, a painted headboard, and wildflower posters on the wall. McIntosh is the smallest room, with a three-quarter bed with a flowery bedcover, wicker accents, and an old-fashioned bathtub.

On the grounds, you can sit a spell on the wraparound porch or relax in the hammock in a backyard surrounded by many acres of unspoiled woodland. The road beside the orchard next door makes for a lovely walk.

What's Nearby: This is the closest inn (2 miles) to Peterborough, the picturesque hub of the Monadnock region, filled with shops and some of the area's best restaurants. The Peterborough Players are a long-established summer theater troupe, and Monadnock Music does many of its summer concerts here. It is a short drive to Jaffrey and hiking in Mount Monadnock State Park, and the Sharon Arts Center, with high-quality crafts and artwork, is just down the road.

THE GOVERNOR'S HOUSE

32 Miller Avenue
Portsmouth 03801
(603) 427–5145; (866) 427–5140

■ I was happy to see this handsome Georgian colonial open to guests once again, after several years as a private home. The house was built in 1917, but its most notable years were from 1930 to 1965, when New Hampshire governor Charles Dale lived here, offering hospitality to many visiting dignitaries. Owners Bob Chaffee and Barbara Trimble are still treating their guests like VIPs.

Besides the many amenities listed below, you'll find Frette bed linens and bathrobes, and a refrigerator with complimentary bottled water, sodas, and juice. All the rooms have access to the inn library upstairs, stocked with books and magazines; a free computer for checking e-mail; and extensive collections of CDs and DVDs to make use of the players in your room. There are two inviting leather chairs to settle in with a book, and if you are looking for an even cozier place to read, the wing chair and ottoman in the sunroom downstairs should fill the bill.

Everyone is invited to use the tennis court and ball machine outside, as well as the outdoor hot tub. And your hosts will serve your generous continental breakfast wherever you prefer, in front of the tile-rimmed fireplace in the formal dining room, on the terrace next to the tennis court, or in your own room. Wine and cheese are offered in the afternoon.

The guest rooms are nicely appointed. I admired the Governor's Room, with a sleigh bed, a fabric mock canopy at the head; deep red walls; and complementary fabrics. The Prescott Room has an actual canopy bed, attractive French print fabrics, and a whirlpool for two in the bath, while the Peacock Room has an art nouveau theme and a most interesting tall headboard. This is one of the two bathrooms with a surprise in the shower—a mural of *The Lady and the Peacock*. The Captain's Room has the second shower mural, this time a mermaid. The tile work is by a local artist.

The many attractions of Portsmouth are about a ten-minute walk from the inn, and if you don't feel like walking, your obliging hosts will loan you a bike.

WEB SITE: www.governors-house.com

INNKEEPERS: Bob Chaffee and Barbara Trimble

ROOMS: 4 rooms, all with private bath, air-conditioning and ceiling fan, TV/DVD player, Bose radio/CD player, phone, robes, hair dryer, iron and ironing board, coffeemaker

ON THE GROUNDS: Tennis court, outdoor hot tub

RATES: $165–$245, including continental breakfast and afternoon refreshments, use of tennis court and hot tub, complimentary bikes

CREDIT CARDS ACCEPTED: MasterCard, Visa, Discover

OPEN: Year-round

HOW TO GET THERE: Take Interstate 95 north to the Portsmouth exit (exit 3 from the north, exit 3B coming from the south), and go right at the end of the ramp onto Middle Road (Route 33) for 2-plus miles, turn left onto Middle Street (Route 1) for ⁹/₁₀ mile, then turn right at the light onto Miller Avenue (Route 1A). The house is on the right at the corner of Miller and Merrimac Street; the driveway is on Merrimac.

What's Nearby: The Strawbery Banke Museum, thirty-five buildings tracing three centuries of town history, is the main sightseeing draw in Portsmouth, along with several historic homes. Prescott Park on the Piscataqua River is known for its flower gardens and summer festival of theater and music on an outdoor stage. Cruises and whale-watching excursions embark from the riverfront. Market Square, the city's picturesque commercial center, is filled with interesting shops and dining places. The dozens of discount shops of Kittery, Maine, are a short drive from Portsmouth. Families also will want to visit the Children's Museum of Portsmouth.

INN AT STRAWBERY BANKE

314 Court Street
Portsmouth 03801
(603) 436–7242; (800) 428–3933

When Portsmouth was settled in 1630, it was known as Strawbery Banke. That's also the name of the town's biggest attraction, a living museum that chronicles 300-plus years of history. The Inn at Strawbery Banke isn't quite that old (early 1800s, to be exact), but it boasts an ideal location just around the corner from the museum and within walking distance of all of Portsmouth's considerable attractions.

The home was first known as Holbrook House, for the family that occupied it for one hundred years, until the early twentieth century. Since then it had been a residence, a rooming house, and apartments, and finally, in 1981, an inn. Since Sally O'Donnell arrived in 1990, it has expanded to seven guest rooms, three on the first floor, four on the second. Sitting rooms on each floor are outfitted with television, a telephone, and books and games.

The furnishings are simple, and the look is appropriately old New England, with stenciling and Early American decor. Some

WEB SITE: www.innatstrawbery banke.com

INNKEEPER: Sarah (Sally) Glover O'Donnell

ROOMS: 7 rooms, all with private bath, air-conditioning

ON THE GROUNDS: Small garden and strawberry patch

RATES: $100–$150, including full breakfast

CREDIT CARDS ACCEPTED: Master-Card, Visa, American Express, Discover

OPEN: Year-round

HOW TO GET THERE: From Interstate 95 heading north, take exit 7 and go right onto the Market Street Extension. Keeping to the left of the Sheraton, continue on Market Street into Market Square. Take an immediate left after North Church Street onto Church Street. Should you miss Church Street, take a left at the next stop light (Fleet Street). Go to the end of either street and take a left onto Court Street. Continue 2 to 3 blocks; the inn is on your right. Inn parking is in the lot adjacent to the inn. Going south on I–95, take exit 7, turn left onto Market Street, and proceed as above.

rooms retain their original wide pine flooring. Rooms 2, 3, 4, and 5 have ruffled canopy beds, Room 1 is furnished with an old-fashioned iron bed, Room 7 has a brass bed, and Room 6 has a wooden headboard and a particularly nice star quilt. Some have nonworking fireplaces as accents.

My favorite room in this inn is the breakfast room, with cheerful checked valances, ladder-back chairs at colonial-style tables, and a wall of windows decked with hanging plants and facing the garden and strawberry patch. Sally's breakfasts, served from 8:00 to 9:00 A.M., include fresh fruit, cereals, fresh breads, and muffins, breakfast meats, and main courses such as sourdough pancakes, quiche, and crepes.

Afterward, just step out the door and you are in the midst of old Portsmouth, one of New Hampshire's most delightful towns.

What's Nearby: See What's Nearby on page 186.

MARTIN HILL INN

404 Islington Street
Portsmouth 93801
(603) 436–2287

![] This long-established inn has a new owner, and the good news is that innkeeper Margot Doering has kept the elegant colonial decor that makes this such a special place. Calling herself a "corporate refugee," Margot left Boston and an eighteen-year career in banking in 2004, wanting a change. She took an innkeepers' course, and when this special inn became available, she was ready.

The inn is actually two houses, connected by a path through a little courtyard and water garden. The main building, a yellow clapboard colonial circa 1812, has the most elaborate guest rooms, formally furnished with four-poster beds and antiques and featuring spacious seating areas. The Master Bedroom is my favorite, done in blue and white, with a draped canopy bed, a mahogany mirrored English armoire, and Oriental-style lamps and rugs.

Rooms in the guest house across the garden, dating from 1850, have a less formal, more country feel with lots of florals. The Greenhouse on the ground floor has its own sunporch opening to the courtyard.

In winter, the downstairs library guest room in the main house becomes a living room where guests can gather. In summer, the garden beckons. The fact that both houses open onto the garden means that guests are hardly aware of the busy road outside.

WEB SITE: www.martinhillinn.com

INNKEEPER: Margot Doering

ROOMS: 4 rooms, 3 suites, in two historic houses, all with private bath

ON THE GROUNDS: Large perennial gardens

RATES: $115–$210, including full breakfast

CREDIT CARDS ACCEPTED: Master-Card, Visa

OPEN: Year-round

HOW TO GET THERE: From the south take Interstate 95, get off at exit 6, turn right onto Woodbury Avenue, proceed ½ mile to the stop sign at Bartlett Street, go right to the traffic light, and then turn left onto Islington Street. The inn is ⅗ mile farther. Coming from the north, take I-95, get off at exit 5, follow the Portsmouth sign to the traffic circle, go three-quarters of the way around to Woodbury Avenue, and follow the preceding directions from that point.

This inn's real showstopper is the dining room, straight out of *House Beautiful.* The mahogany Chippendale-style table and chairs are antiques, old silver gleams from the sideboard, the floor-to-ceiling corner cabinet displays fine china, and the room is softly lit by a chandelier of crystal and glass.

Margot's breakfasts do full justice to these elegant surroundings. The meal starts with seasonal fruits, maybe baked peaches with a touch of brandy, ripe melon, or broiled pineapple sprinkled with brown sugar and ginger. Entrees may be cornmeal pancakes with blueberries followed by a garden quiche of spinach and sweet pepper. Some other house specialties include Southwestern omelettes and apple-cinnamon waffles with homemade applesauce, garnished with toasted walnuts and sliced kiwis.

Margot has added a variety of events at the inn, centering on needlepoint, a fashion trunk show, or eating and shopping in Portsmouth, all the more reason to visit a delightful inn in a delightful town.

What's Nearby: See What's Nearby on page 186.

FOXGLOVE

1170 Route 117
Sugar Hill 03585
(603) 823–8840
Fax: (603) 823–5755

■ This handsome 1898 home at the very top of Sugar Hill was built by one of the founding families of the community, and it has had prestigious owners over the years.

The decor is elegant. The living room has cream wallpaper with the look of moiré silk, long draperies, and lots of antiques. Among them are an antique velvet Victorian couch, a Lincoln rocker beside the fireplace, an Italian writing desk, and a carved tiger oak sideboard housing games, puzzles, and an operating old-fashioned Victrola.

WEB SITE: www.foxgloveinnnh.com

INNKEEPER: Susann Atrat

ROOMS: 6 rooms, all with private bath

ON THE GROUNDS: 3 acres, porches, terraces, woodlands, fountain, hammocks

RATES: $85–$170, including full breakfast and afternoon refreshments

CREDIT CARDS ACCEPTED: MasterCard, Visa

OPEN: Year-round

HOW TO GET THERE: From Interstate 93 take exit 38, go right on Route 18 for ¼ mile, and turn left onto Route 117. The inn is about 2¼ miles up the hill on the right.

My favorite room at this inn is the solarium, a wonderful year-round room with windows all around to take in three acres of perennial gardens and the woods behind them. Innkeeper Susann Atrat takes special pride in the breakfasts she serves using elegant china, silver, and crystal. Among her many special dishes are poached pears filled with coffee-flavored mascarpone, sweet basil eggs, and lemon stuffed crepes.

The guest rooms have been named after some of Hollywood's most glamorous stars, films, and writers of the past and include photos and memorabilia. The house has hosted many stars and dignitaries thanks to a previous owner, Mrs. Frederica Walcott, wife of an ambassador to Japan. One of her good friends was Bette Davis, whose country retreat was around the corner. A note from Davis and her photos are in the front hallway.

The Bette Davis guest room is done in English country style and features an antique claw-foot bathtub. Other rooms salute Hepburn and Tracy, and the film *Casablanca*.

Two rooms I particularly like are the Ernest Hemingway library, with a fireplace, bookshelves, and an antique headboard, and the Judy Garland garden room in the carriage house, which has a fireplace and French doors to a private deck.

Dog lovers should note that Foxglove has a second innkeeper, Susann's two-pound Pomeranian *Liebchën*.

What's Nearby: Sugar Hill is a very special hamlet near Franconia, with a classic country church and magnificent views from the top of the hill. It is near the wonders of Franconia Notch State Park and the towns of the Upper Connecticut River Valley.

HILLTOP INN

9 Norton Lane
Sugar Hill 03586
(603) 823–5695; (800) 770–5695
Fax: (603) 823–5518

■ Tucked away in an idyllic village and graced with lovely informal gardens, this 1895 Victorian with a wide, welcoming front porch is loaded with country charm and warmth reflected from the friendly owners, Mike and Meri Hern.

Since the Herns arrived in 1984, the inn seems to get better every year, with former electrical engineer Mike overseeing renovations and Meri tending to the decorating and gardens. She wants guests to feel comfortable, so there's nothing formal here. One guest calls it like coming to Grandma's house—if Grandma has wonderful taste, that is.

In the sitting room, comfortable rockers beckon and a Victorian daybed serves as a sofa, draped with a handmade quilt and piled with floral pillows and some very lovable stuffed animals. Tiffany-style lamps are on the side table and hanging from the ceiling, and the lace and quilt-covered center table is usually laden with refreshments. Morning-glory-vine stencils adorn the cream walls, and draped lace curtains complete the picture.

Upstairs rooms are airy, each with an antique bed and a prize quilt. Most have floral-patterned wallpapers with carefully chosen coordinated borders. Much of the artwork on the walls is done by local artists. Suites have an extra daybed. Meri Hern uses crisp all-cotton sheets in summer, warm English flannel bed linens in winter.

Meri, who is also a successful caterer, shows off her culinary skills in the dining room, an attractive setting with dark wallpaper and light wood wainscoting. Each day brings a different treat; one of the favorites is French cinnamon toast with poached pears and the inn's own home-grown raspberries.

She has planted the backyard with Victorian-era perennials such as asters, bee balm, bleeding hearts, calendulas, foxgloves, peonies, tall phlox, and lots of herbs. Though the inn is cozy in winter, there's nothing nicer than sitting on the breezy porch or deck on a bright summer day, watching the birds flitting to the feeders and enjoying the scents and the serenity.

What's Nearby: See What's Nearby on page 189. The Hilltop Inn offers discount lift tickets for Cannon and Bretton Woods ski areas.

WEB SITE: www.hilltopinn.com

INNKEEPERS: Mike and Meri Hern

ROOMS: 6 rooms, all with private bath, ceiling fan

ON THE GROUNDS: Two porches with views of the hills or extensive perennial gardens; 20 acres of fields for strolling, bird and animal watching, and cross-country skiing in winter

RATES: $100–$195, including full breakfast, afternoon refreshments

CREDIT CARDS ACCEPTED: MasterCard, Visa

OPEN: Year-round

HOW TO GET THERE: From Interstate 93 take exit 38, go right on Route 18 for ½ mile, and turn left onto Route 117. The inn is 2½ miles up the hill on the right.

DEXTER'S INN

258 Stagecoach Road, P.O. Box 703
Sunapee 03782
(603) 763–5571; (800) 232–5571

■ Three tennis courts, a pool, lawn games galore, 20 acres for rambling, a hilltop location with mountain and lake views—few bed-and-breakfast inns can match the attractions at Dexter's, a virtual resort in the lovely Lake Sunapee region in New Hampshire. Indeed, it was a full-service resort specializing in tennis until a few years ago, when new owners decided to go the bed-and-breakfast route. Breakfast is comprised of a generous buffet, including egg dishes, pancakes, waffles, bacon, and sausage.

This is an informal Inn ideal for families. Besides the many outdoor activities, an indoor recreation room offers billiards, Ping-Pong, Foosball, and darts, and a special play room for kids has videos, games, puzzles, books for reading and for coloring, and stuffed animals. Another home-entertainment room features a big-screen TV.

Adults seeking a more peaceful spot can gather around the fireplace in the living room, stocked with a library of books, magazines, and newspapers, or in front of the fieldstone fireplace in the rustic pine-paneled tavern room.

WEB SITE: www.dextersnh.com

INNKEEPERS: John Augustine and Penny Berrier

ROOMS: 10 rooms in main house, 7 in annex, 1 two-bedroom cottage with kitchen, 1 two-bedroom condo efficiency

ON THE GROUNDS: 20 acres, swimming pool, 3 tennis courts, volleyball, badminton, basketball, horseshoes, shuffleboard and croquet, cross-country skiing, snowshoeing, and sledding in winter.

RATES: Rooms $125–$185, condo $200–$300, cottage $300–$400, including buffet breakfast

CREDIT CARDS ACCEPTED: MasterCard, Visa, American Express, Discover

OPEN: Year-round

The main house is a beauty, a colonial built in 1801. Rooms upstairs, no two alike, are simply furnished in colonial style, with pleasant country-pattern wallpapers, rockers, and oak dressers. Accommodations are larger in the annex across the road, with many rooms easily holding three or four people. Not only are children welcome, but you can bring the family dog, as well (with advance arrangements with the innkeepers).

Large families can choose the Holly House Cottage, which can sleep up to eight. You could easily settle in for a week here with so many amenities—two bedrooms, two baths, living and dining rooms, a screened porch, a fireplace, TV and VCR, phone, gas grill, washer-dryer,

HOW TO GET THERE: From Interstate 93 and Interstate 89, follow I–93 north to I–89 (near Concord, New Hampshire) and continue on I–89 north to exit 12, New London/Sunapee. At the end of the exit ramp, turn left onto Route 11 west and proceed 5⁷⁄₁₀ miles, past a gas station and information booth on your left. Just after the information booth, turn left onto Route 103B and proceed ⁹⁄₁₀ mile until you see a Dexter's Inn sign and Stagecoach Road on your right (Stagecoach Road is the street immediately after Chase Street). Turn right onto Stagecoach Road and proceed 1¼ miles to the inn. If coming north on Interstate 91, take exit 10, I–89, and proceed south to exit 12A (Georges Mills/Springfield). At the end of the exit ramp, turn right onto the access road and proceed for ⁹⁄₁₀ mile until the access road ends at Route 11 west. Turn right on Route 11 west, proceed 3⁷⁄₁₀ miles past the information booth to Route 103B, and then follow the preceding directions from that point.

and a full kitchen complete with dishes and cookware. Another larger accommodation is the two-bedroom, one-bath condo sleeping up to six, with its own screened porch and living room, TV, gas grill, and a fully equipped minikitchen.

With so much to do year-round at the inn, plus all the nearby attractions, Dexter's is a place many families make a tradition year after year.

What's Nearby: New Hampshire's Lake Sunapee, with both a lake and a ski area, offers year-round recreation, plus New England's largest and best craft show, the League of New Hampshire Craftsmen Fair, held in early August at Mount Sunapee State Park. The region also boasts three golf courses and the Norsk cross-country ski center.

WAKEFIELD INN

2723 Wakefield Road
Wakefield 03872
(603) 522–8272; (800) 245–0841

■ The first thing you notice at the Wakefield Inn is the beautiful freestanding spiral staircase, which curves its way up to the third floor with no visible means of support. It is one of the reasons why this inn is unique. Another is the history of the house. The southern ell of the building dates from the eighteenth century; the main block, three-and-a-half stories tall, was built in Federal style about 1804 for William Frost, a seaman who wanted a home bigger and more elaborate than any other in Wakefield. Unfortunately, Frost ran out of money, and his carpenters, Jacob and Isaac Chesley, were forced to take over the house, which was henceforth known as "Frost's Folly." It has been an inn since 1890, and both the house and its village are listed on the National Register of Historic Places.

WEB SITE: www.wakefieldinn.com

INNKEEPERS: Lin and John Koch

ROOMS: 7 rooms, all with private bath, ceiling fan

ON THE GROUNDS: Patio, 2 acres of lawn, and 4 wooded acres with trails

RATES: $90–$95, including full breakfast

CREDIT CARDS ACCEPTED: MasterCard, Visa, Discover

OPEN: Year-round

HOW TO GET THERE. Drive north on Route 16, continue past Route 109, and watch for the sign to Wakefield on the right. The inn is just off Route 16 on the right.

The inn retains many of its original features, such as the wide pine floorboards and Indian shutters. The welcoming parlor centers around a big three-way brick fireplace. The back side of the fireplace faces a particularly pleasant dining room, with baskets hanging from the beams and a floor-to-ceiling window looking out at the expansive lawn and gardens and the mountains beyond. The room has light blue wainscoting, a curio cabinet with a collection of cups and saucers, and a cabinet on one wall displaying blue and white china and cobalt blue glassware. Guests are seated at four tables to await a full breakfast with special dishes such as gourmet scrambled eggs cooked with mushrooms, pimentos, and cream cheese.

All the rooms upstairs are large and decorated in country style with ruffled curtains, stenciling, comfortable armchairs, and plants. Quilts are displayed both on the beds and on the walls. Rooms are named for early townspeople such as Chesley and Frost, with plaques telling something about each one. One room with an adjacent small sitting room honors the inn's most famous visitor, poet John Greenleaf Whittier. On the landing on each floor is a help-yourself basket of "most likely to be forgotten" items such as toothbrushes, shavers, and shampoo.

Wakefield is a town that has declared itself a "Bicycle Friendly Community," and there are many places to explore around nearby Lake Winnipesaukee and throughout New Hampshire's Lakes Region.

What's Nearby: One of the oldest settlements in New Hampshire, incorporated in 1774, the entire ridgetop village of Wakefield is a historic district ideal for strolling and bicycling. It is about 10 miles from Wolfeboro and the many attractions of Lake Winnipesaukee.

STEPPING STONES

6 Bennington Battle Trail
Wilton Center 03086
(603) 654–9048; (888) 654–904

■ If you love flowers or handicrafts, this small, lovely inn should not be missed. The first clue to what's ahead is the path to the front door, lined with flowering plants in handsome pottery containers. Cinder, the German shepherd mascot of the house, will likely greet you at the door. Inside, you'll hear classical music playing softly, and you may well find your host, Ann Carlsmith, in the room to the left that is devoted to her large loom, where she makes the handwoven throws, pillows, and rugs that adorn the house.

This artistic owner is also a landscape architect who has created a network of terraces and pathways leading to lush gardens that are in bloom from the first daffodils to autumn's last asters. Decks and porches provide vantage points for admiring the scene and enjoying the songs of the birds.

The living room is furnished with cherry and birch furniture, pale upholstery, a fireplace with an antique clock on the mantel, shelves of books, and plants filling the wide window. The top bookshelves show off Ann's collection of glazed stoneware.

The breakfast and garden room has a greenhouse window, a tile floor, and more fine pottery on display. Sofas and chairs and a woodstove at one end form a pleasant sitting area. The covered porch just outside gives another view of the gardens.

This part of the house was the original settlers' cabin built as part of a farmstead in the early 1700s. Ann has preserved one of the original beams at the top of the back stairs. The rest of the house was added in 1834, when Wilton Center enjoyed its heyday as a summer colony, and was little changed until Ann began her renovation in the late 1970s. She opened the house as a bed-and-breakfast in 1987.

Breakfast, served at the black walnut dining table, consists of juice, fruit of the season, fresh yogurt from a local farm, homemade muffins and breads, and a hot dish such as shirred eggs with fried tomatoes.

The largest upstairs bedroom has white painted Shaker-style furniture and walls done in a pale peach print with a garden basket border. Fern prints adorn the walls, and a whatnot shelf is filled with some of the host's collectibles, such as cornhusk dolls and folk art roosters. Her handwoven soft wool and mohair throw and pillow covers are in all the rooms.

I quite liked the second bedroom, which has big windows, twin maple beds, light green walls hung with garden prints, and

WEB SITE: www.steppingstonesbb.com

INNKEEPER: Ann Carlsmith

ROOMS: 3 rooms, all with private bath, clock

ON THE GROUNDS: Porches, terraces, lush gardens

RATES: $75–$85, including full breakfast

CREDIT CARDS ACCEPTED: None

OPEN: Year-round

HOW TO GET THERE: From Route 101 take Isaac Frye Highway north, up the hill, past the village to the junction of Bennington Battle Trail; look for the first house on the left.

fresh white curtains. A smaller room has a double bed, floral wallpaper, and more Shaker-style furniture. In season, every room in the house is brightened with bouquets of flowers from the exceptional gardens.

What's Nearby: The tiny, quiet hamlet of Wilton Center is picturebook New England, beautiful and unspoiled, with excellent hiking on the Wapack Trail and in Miller State Park nearby. Route 101 from Wilton east to Nashua is known as "Antique Alley" for its many shops, and all the pleasures of the Monadnock region are within a short drive.

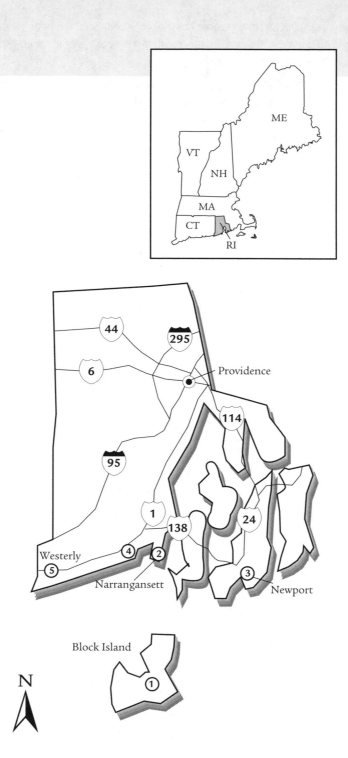

RHODE ISLAND

Numbers on map refer to towns numbered below.

1. Block Island, Blue Dory *198*, Rose Farm Inn *199*, The Sasafrash *200*, Sheffield House *201*, 1661 Inn *202*
2. Narragansett, The Richards *204*
3. Newport, Abigail Stoneman Inn *205*, Admiral Farragut Inn *207*, Cliffside Inn *209*, Francis Malbone House *210*, Ivy Lodge *212*, Old Beach Inn *214*
4. South Kingstown, Admiral Dewey Inn *215*
5. Westerly, Woody Hill *216*

BLUE DORY

Dodge Street, P.O. Box 488
Block Island 02807
(401) 466–5891; (800) 992–7290

■ Right around the corner from town is this neat little shingled cottage circa 1897, with a picket fence, blooming window boxes, and rockers on the porch. Since owner Ann Law took over several years ago, she has done more refurbishing and redecorating every season, turning the Blue Dory into one of the island's most attractive properties.

Enter the parlor and you find ruffled curtains and plants in the cheery bay window, high Victorian furnishings, and reasons to linger: a chess set and a TV with VCR. Guests stop by in the afternoon for freshly baked cookies and gather at 5:00 P.M. for wine and cheese.

A kitchen/dining room provides a pleasant spacious area for breakfast. The buffet, set out from 8:00 to 10:00 A.M., includes fresh fruits, juice, yogurt, cereals, fresh breads, rolls, pastries, and a hot dish. On sunny days, you can take your food to the outside deck. Guests are welcome anytime to go right into the kitchen to make coffee, tea, or hot chocolate.

The Burnell Dodge Suite on the first floor of the inn has its own Victorian sitting room with a daybed, as well as air-conditioning, TV, VCR, and refrigerator. Bedrooms on the second and third floor vary in size and decor, some quite small, but all have pretty floral fabrics, lacy curtains, lots of pillows, and a mix of antiques. The most desirable are the back rooms, which are away from street noise and facing the water.

The full inn consists of several adjacent buildings, from the Tea House, a hideaway for two with a porch looking out on the beach, to a cottage that can accommodate up to six people. The Waverly Suites, in a building next door to the inn, are the most

WEB SITE: www.blockislandinns.com

INNKEEPER: Ann Law

ROOMS: 11 rooms in main inn, 3 suites in 3 additional buildings and 4 cottages, all with private bath; some with water view; suites with air-conditioning, whirlpool, kitchen facilities

ON THE GROUNDS: Front porch with rockers, back porch

RATES: Rooms $65–$295, cottages $95–$625, suites $150–$525, including full breakfast, afternoon refreshments, and wine and cheese

CREDIT CARDS ACCEPTED: Master-Card, Visa, American Express

OPEN: Year-round

HOW TO GET TO BLOCK ISLAND: Block Island ferries leave from Point Judith, Rhode Island; Montauk, New York; and New London, Connecticut. Taxis and bike rentals are available at the ferry landing.

HOW TO GET TO THE INN: The inn is about 2 blocks from the ferry landing. Turn right on Water Street, then left onto Dodge Street. The inn is the third building on the right.

luxurious of the lodgings, with air-conditioning, cooking facilities, whirlpool baths, and decks with water views.

One of the most pleasant parts of the Blue Dory is the back deck of the main inn, furnished with wicker and white-painted wooden rockers and offering a view of the sea. Proximity to the water and the easy walk to town make the Blue Dory a prime location.

What's Nearby: Block Island enchants escapists with its miles of beaches, flower-splashed meadows, seaside cliffs, and pond-dotted moors. Old Harbor, where ferryboats arrive, retains its Victorian charm.

ROSE FARM INN

Roslyn Road, Box E
Block Island 02807
(401) 466–2034
Fax: (401) 466–2053

■ Off on a hilltop all to itself, bordered by stone walls and gardens, this inn has double appeal. For those who want authentic island flavor, the original shingle-and-stone farmhouse built in 1897 is the place. For something a little more posh, the newer Captain Rose House provides private entrances, canopy beds, and whirlpool baths.

WEB SITE: www.rosefarminn.com

INNKEEPER: Judith B. Rose

ROOMS: 19 rooms, 17 with private bath; beach towels provided; guest refrigerator available near the parlor

ON THE GROUNDS: Lawns, porches, sundeck, bicycle rental shop

RATES: $109–$289, including continental breakfast

CREDIT CARDS ACCEPTED: MasterCard, Visa, American Express, Discover

OPEN: May through October

HOW TO GET THERE: See HOW TO GET TO BLOCK ISLAND on page 198. From the ferry landing follow Water Street south, and when the road branches, take High Street up the hill. Rose Farm is on a little private road just past the Atlantic Inn.

Judy and Robert Rose, Block Island natives, restored a house that was built by Robert's grandfather to create the original inn. It offers rockers on the porch, a little Victorian parlor with a TV set, and a back sundeck looking out at the hillside.

The dining room, an enclosed circular porch, is particularly inviting, with windows all around and hanging plants to brighten the scene. The buffet breakfast here offers fresh fruits, cereals, pastries and muffins, and breads and bagels for toasting.

The rooms in the farmhouse have a variety of antiques, such as a century-old walnut bed and a Victorian ladies' bureau with a special compartment for hats and gloves.

Rooms 9 and 10 are choice, spacious rooms with print wallpaper, lace curtains, king-size canopy beds, and ocean views. All the rooms have pleasant vistas of either water or countryside. Eight rooms have private baths with walk-in tile showers; the two smallest rooms share a bath, a good setup for families.

The newer building offers more space and privacy. A porch surrounds the building, providing an outside sitting area for each room. The decor is Victorian country, with splashy flowered wallpaper and period antiques. Each first-floor room has a double whirlpool in the corner of the bedroom; each upstairs room has a single whirlpool, but these rooms also have the advantage of romantic dormers that create pleasant sitting nooks.

The inn has its own bicycle rental shop, Beach Rose Bicycles, very convenient if you want to explore the island. But many guests are happy just sitting on the porch, gazing at the meadows and dreaming.

What's Nearby: See What's Nearby on page 199.

THE SASAFRASH

Center Road, P.O. Box 1227
Block Island 02807
(401) 466–5486

■ The plain, gray-shingled exterior doesn't give a clue to the dazzling world inside this former church—walls filled with gilt-framed portraits and mirrors; tables and floors laden with antique candlesticks, oil lamps, and statues; antique furnishings of every period; and original stained glass that reminds of the building's origins.

This was the Primitive Methodist Church, built to house a small congregation in 1904 and active until 1975. When Shirley and her late husband, Sanford, took over, they used the soaring spaces as backdrop for an antiques shop. In 1987, with the help of architect Norman Latour, they transformed the structure into what started as a home for their retirement but wound up as a unique inn.

Shirley, a former school administrator and college professor, is a third-generation Block Island resident and an ardent preservationist. As much as possible from the church was saved, from windows to lighting fixtures to the oak floor. Throughout the house, light cream walls contrast with the deep brown original moldings and base-boards. The old church bell, deemed too heavy for its spot in the steeple, now decorates the front yard.

The use of space in the house is highly original, however, with new walls taking on odd shapes to complement the architecture. The living room is built on three

WEB SITE: www.blockisland.com/cosybandb/#sasafrash

INNKEEPER: Shirley Kessler

ROOMS: 3 rooms, all with private bath

ON THE GROUNDS: Large deck

RATES: Upon request

CREDIT CARDS ACCEPTED: None

OPEN: Memorial Day to Columbus Day

HOW TO GET THERE: See HOW TO GET TO BLOCK ISLAND on page 198. The location is about 1 mile from town, midway between Old and New Harbors. The innkeeper will help arrange transportation from the ferry.

tiers, with the former altar rail separating a semicircular elevated area. Eighteen-foot ceilings allow full height for some of the twelve Gothic stained-glass windows; other windows extend though open spaces to the second-floor bedrooms. A closed arch in the wall behind the altar has been opened up with French doors leading to a deck and a shady backyard. The room is filled with cozy nooks with velvet couches that invite a tête-à-tête. The adjoining Common Room furnished in wicker now serves as the TV room and offers a variety of reading materials.

The long dining room is furnished with country antiques, oak cabinets and chairs, a table seating eight, an antique chest of drawers as a sideboard, and a china cabinet displaying treasures. Here, as in the living room, the walls display early oil paintings, many by Rhode Island artists.

A corner staircase leads to the former choir loft and Sunday school rooms, now housing guest rooms. They are named for former pastors and members of the church and furnished with a mix of antiques, many from Block Island. The Rev. Melvin Lewis Room has a light oak bed decorated with burnt-in nature scenes; the Alice Haire Room has a half-circular spoked iron headboard and footboard. Bedspreads are brightened with appliquéd pillows.

Shirley serves a continental breakfast, always with a surprise dish.

This most unusual inn is still a showcase for antiques. The shop on the premises has been reopened and is, according to Shirley, "filled to the rafters."

What's Nearby: See What's Nearby on page 199.

SHEFFIELD HOUSE

High Street, P.O. Box 338
Block Island 01807
(401) 466–2494; (866) 466–2494

■ This picturebook 1888 Victorian, with a wraparound porch and towering turret, charms at first sight. The Crow's Nest in that turret offers spectacular views.

WEB SITE: www.thesheffieldhouse
.com

INNKEEPER: Diane Hayde

ROOMS: 6 rooms, 4 with private
bath

ON THE GROUNDS: porch with rockers, garden behind the inn

RATES: $55–$205, including full
breakfast

CREDIT CARDS ACCEPTED: Master-
Card, Visa

OPEN: Year-round

HOW TO GET THERE: See HOW TO GET
TO BLOCK ISLAND on page 198. When
you come off the ferry in Old Harbor,
walk to the left. At the end of the
street, beyond the statue, are two
streets going uphill. Take the one to
the right, High Street. The Sheffield
House is about halfway up the hill
on your right.

This is for inn lovers who like their bed-and-breakfasts to be small and cozy, with a hostess who makes you feel right at home. The common room downstairs is where guests gather for visiting, reading, games, puzzles, or watching TV. Breakfast is a nice start of the day with selections such as baked apple French toast, a variety of egg dishes, and home-baked treats that often include delicious scones. On fine days, you can take your breakfast out to the porch or to the pretty garden out back.

Guest rooms are simply and comfortably furnished with queen-size beds, reading lamps, and ceiling fans. They have printed wallpapers, lace curtains on the windows, and comforters on the bed. The bathrooms have walk-in showers.

The location is a big plus for Sheffield House, just a short walk from the ferry and convenient to all the beaches and beauty of Block Island. Innkeeper Diane Hayde loves Block Island (she chose it for her wedding in 1990), and she will do her best to see that you love it, too.

What's Nearby: See What's Nearby on page 199.

1661 INN

Spring Street
Block Island 02807
(401) 466–2421; (800) 626–4773

■ The name comes from the year Block Island was settled, but this is actually a classic white clapboard summer house circa 1870, built on a blufftop with breathtaking water views and expanded over the years. The Abrams family arrived a century later, avid sailors who had fallen in love with the island. They totally redid the house, turning seventeen small rooms into nine very large ones and adding modern plumbing. With this inn and their Hotel Manisses, offering fine dining just across the street, the family introduced a new level of style to this laid-back island.

Inside the inn are a big, wicker-filled living room and a dining room with cheerful

WEB SITE: www.blockislandresorts
.com

INNKEEPERS: The Abrams family:
Justin Abrams, Rita and Steve
Draper

ROOMS: 9 rooms in the main inn, all
with private bath and phone, 8 with
deck and ocean view, some with
whirlpool bath, refrigerator, and/or
kitchenette; 9 rooms in the 1661
Guest House, 5 with private bath; 3
rooms in the Nicholas Ball Cottage,
all with private bath, whirlpool bath
for two, fireplace, phone, TV

ON THE GROUNDS: Large deck with
stunning views of Block Island
Sound, guests offered complimentary island tours and a tour of the
Abrams farm, featuring llamas,
pygmy goats, camels, and kanga-
roos

RATES: $120–$410 for rooms in the
main inn, $50–$290 for rooms in the
1661 Guest House, $160–$330 for
rooms in the Nicholas Ball Cottage,
all including expansive full breakfast
buffet and afternoon hors d'oeuvres
in season; lower rates in winter

CREDIT CARDS ACCEPTED: Master-
Card, Visa

OPEN: Year round

HOW TO GET THERE: See HOW TO GET
TO BLOCK ISLAND on page 198. From
the ferry landing follow Water Street
south, and when the road forks,
take Spring Street up the hill to the
inn.

floral print wallpaper and marble-top tables adorned with flowers. Outside is a spacious covered deck with mesmerizing views of Block Island Sound.

Many guest rooms have private decks sharing that peerless view. The rooms are named for the island's original settlers, and each has its special attractions. The Edwards Room has a wraparound deck and a canopied bed beneath a loft that holds a double whirlpool bath. The Rathbun Room offers ship decor and an antique chair and lamp tucked into a small loft, while the Tosh Room boasts a full-length stained-glass window framed in antique wood. The Akurs Room, with two queen size beds, provides a kitchenette, a round oak table with chairs, and sliding glass doors to a deck.

Across the lawn is the more modest Guest House, an option for budget watchers, though you'll have to reserve far ahead to snag one of the economical shared-bath rooms. Adjacent is the top choice for romantics, the Nicholas Ball Cottage, a replica of the island's old Episcopalian Church that was destroyed in a hurricane in 1938. Three rooms here are all-weather havens, with whirlpool baths for two, fireplaces, and TV. Nicholas has a king-size bonnet-top canopy bed with a pastel paisley quilt, and white walls embellished with paintings inspired by the sea. You can have your pick of a whirlpool occupying a platformed alcove above, complete with a stained-glass window depicting a mermaid, or a floral-tiled shower built for two.

Breakfasts at the 1661 Inn, served on the large deck, are island legends. They include champagne, an omelette station, and a spread that may include fresh fruits, a whole baked bluefish, baked beans, corned beef hash, ham or sausage, fresh muffins, pancakes or French toast, and a variety of breads.

The afternoon "wine and nibbles" hour brings hot hors d'oeuvres such as egg rolls, cheese balls, smoked sausage in orange glaze, tortellini, or tiny quiches. Many of the herbs and vegetables used come from the Abramses' own farm and gardens, which inn guests are invited to tour.

What's Nearby: See What's Nearby on page 199.

THE RICHARDS

144 Gibson Avenue
Narragansett 02882
(401) 789–7746

This spacious stone house tucked away in the pines is a reminder of Narragansett's grander days; it was built of local granite in 1884 by a prominent family who had admired stone country manor houses in England. Graced with 10-foot ceilings, enormous windows, deep window seats, a working vintage elevator, and eleven fireplaces, the house is on the National Register of Historic Places.

E-MAIL: therichards144@ hotmail.com

INNKEEPERS: Nancy and Steven Richards

ROOMS: 2 rooms, 1 suite, 1 two-bedroom suite, all with private bath and working fireplace

ON THE GROUNDS: Garden with seating, water garden with fish, short walking trail

RATES: Rooms $125–$165, suites $165–$225, including full breakfast

CREDIT CARDS ACCEPTED: None

OPEN: Year-round

HOW TO GET THERE: From Route 1 take the Narragansett exit from the south or the Point Judith exit from the north, turn east (toward the water) on South Pier Road, and continue through two lights. At the stop sign, turn right onto Gibson Avenue. The Richards is the third drive on the left after the dead-end sign.

The Richards in question are Nancy and Steven, who moved here in 1987, only the third family to live in the house since its construction. They had owned another bed-and-breakfast home in town and knew just how to turn this one into a comfortable retreat for guests as well as their own (now grown) family.

Nancy's love of antiques and tasteful decorating in English country style can be seen in every room, and she sewed many of the handsome floral draperies at the windows. The paneled sitting room has the feel of a library, with books all around, a fireplace, and comfortable seating.

The dining room is more formal, with an Oriental rug, Schumacher documented prints on the wall, a crystal chandelier, an early English sideboard, swags and frills at the windows, and another of the many fireplaces. Guests gather around the table at 8:45 A.M. for a generous breakfast of fresh fruits and homemade breads and muffins and such specialties as soufflés, blintzes with blueberry sauce, quiche, eggs Florentine, and, occasionally, Steven's version of authentic Rhode Island johnnycakes.

French doors open to Nancy's beautiful garden; the flowers grace the dining table and many of the rooms. A shady garden bench invites you to linger outdoors.

The guest bedrooms are in an area set apart from the living quarters of the house. They have sitting areas and working fireplaces, handheld showers in the tubs, and distinctive color schemes. The soft Lavender Room has a canopy bed and a separate sitting room; the Yellow Room has a cheery country feeling and its own lacy canopy. The Rose Room has a new tiled shower. One large suite off its own hallway would be ideal for two couples, with two bedrooms, a sitting room, and a bath. All rooms offer a down comforter on the bed and a cut-glass decanter of sherry.

Though the house is totally private, it is only a mile from town and Narragansett's generous beaches. It's an ideal location.

What's Nearby: Once a posh enclave with a famous casino, Narragansett is enjoying a comeback, with some of the best dining on the Rhode Island shore. Scarborough State Beach provides ample room for sunning, and the South County Museum at Canonchet Farm attracts families for its demonstrations of old-time crafts and farming techniques. The Block Island ferry dock and lots of seafood restaurants are nearby in Galilee.

ABIGAIL STONEMAN INN

102 Touro Street
Newport 02840
(401) 847–8411; (800) 845–1811

■ Legendary Inns of Newport is a group of Newport's most luxurious inns, each quite extraordinary (also see Cliffside, page 209). Abigail Stoneman is the latest addition, opened in 2002, and there are few inns to match it anywhere.

Size is one of the things that make this inn a standout. The Renaissance-style Victorian built in 1866 for a prominent Newport banker has been reconfigured to turn fifteen rooms into just five expansive guest quarters, with an intimacy that allows for ultimate pampering.

The pampering starts with the pillow menu, twenty kinds of pillows, including cuddly body pillows and stress and neck-pain relievers, pillows designed for side, stomach, or back sleepers; all kinds of fillings—whatever assures you of ultimate comfort. Then there's the bath menu—thirty kinds of bath products to choose from, including soap, foam, salt, and skin-care and spa products. Whatever you choose, it

WEB SITE: www.abigailstonemaninn
.com

INNKEEPER: Winthrop Baker (owner),
Theodore Poloack (resident
innkeeper)

ROOMS: 2 rooms, 3 suites, all with
private marble bath, air-conditioning,
fireplace, two-person whirlpool, TV,
VCR, stereo, phone; some baths
with steam showers; high-speed
wireless Internet access in public
areas and most rooms

ON THE GROUNDS: On a city block

RATES: $295–$645, including breakfast and sumptuous afternoon tea

CREDIT CARDS ACCEPTED: Master-
Card, Visa, American Express, Discover, Diners Club

OPEN: Year-round

HOW TO GET THERE: To get into
town, see HOW TO GET TO NEWPORT on
page 208. Follow Memorial Boule-
vard uphill to the intersection with
Bellevue Avenue, make a left on
Bellevue, and continue past the
Hotel Viking and the Newport Fire
Station. Bellevue will turn into Touro
Street at the traffic light past the
Viking Hotel. The inn is on the cor-
ner of Touro Street and Mt. Vernon
Avenue. Parking is behind the inn on
Mt. Vernon.

will be delivered on a silver tray. The bottled
water menu offers more than twenty complimentary still and sparkling waters to be
enjoyed downstairs at the Water Bar or
delivered to your room.

The day starts with morning coffee, tea,
and juice delivered to your room, followed
by a multicourse breakfast, served downstairs at tables for two or in bed if you prefer. The "Duchess of Bedford" traditional
afternoon high tea includes finger sandwiches, sweets, scones with Devon cream,
and an amazing selection of forty-five black,
white, green, oolong, and botanical teas. If
you want absolute privacy, you can reserve
the Tea for Two room for breakfast or tea
time.

Guest quarters are named for significant
eras in Newport history and decorated with
antiques, art, and artifacts of each period.
All have high ceilings and tall windows, king-
size beds, elaborate wall and bed coverings
and draperies, marble baths, two-person
whirlpools, and at least one fireplace.
Guests receive maid service twice a day and
turndown service in the evening. And you
can arrange for massage and spa services in
your room. Again, there is a whole menu of
special services from which to choose.

The suites are the ultimate in space and style. Vanity Fair, a first-floor suite of
three rooms and two baths, has 11-foot ceilings, a cozy bay-window reading area,
and a whirlpool facing a two-sided fireplace that also serves the comfortable living
room. The decor saluting Newport's Gilded Age (1865–1900) includes a first-edition
cover of *Vanity Fair* magazine and works by William Makepeace Thackeray, who
wrote the book *Vanity Fair*.

Victoria, on the second floor, salutes the Victorian age (1819–1901) with a collection of authentic Queen Victoria memorabilia and features a handsome built-in Victorian mirror cabinet taken from a local estate. The marble bedroom fireplace is
surrounded by shelves of books, and the sitting room has its own fireplace. The suite
offers a whirlpool in the bedroom and a steam shower for two in the bath.

The Above and Beyond six-room suite is without doubt the most luxurious space in Newport. It occupies the entire third floor, some 1,500 square feet, including a kitchen/dining area and two bedrooms. A spiral staircase leads to a spectacular wood paneled library with a fireplace and walls lined with books. A hidden passageway in the library takes you to the marble-walled "bathing salon," with a whirlpool built into a wood-paneled deck, a unique chandelier and wall-sconce lighting system employing sixteen individual lights on dimmers, and a dormer window with distant harbor and bay views.

One of the guest rooms, the End of Innocence, salutes the inn's namesake, Abigail Stoneman, with memorabilia that recalls the attractive colonial widow who, in the 1760s, became Newport's first female innkeeper and an entrepreneur, opening a tearoom, coffee house, and provision shop. The inn's art collection, "Newport Women of a Certain Age," also celebrates women with some seventy-five paintings and prints featuring Newport's outstanding female residents, spanning more than 300 years. The art theme is a nice touch, one more unique feature that helps to set this unusual inn apart.

What's Nearby: Newport has something for everyone. Drive along magnificent Ocean Drive or take the Cliff Walk on the bluffs above the sea, visit mansions that are virtual palaces, and stroll along picturesque blocks lined with lovingly restored colonial row houses. You can also go beachcombing or boating, trace the history of the game and play on a grass court at the Tennis Hall of Fame, and shop for anything from antiques to imports, handcrafted jewelry to fudge, in hundreds of shops, many of them set among picturesque wharves dating from the eighteenth century.

ADMIRAL FARRAGUT INN

31 Clarke Street
Newport 02840
(401) 848–5300; (800) 524–1386
Fax: (401) 847–7630

■ This little charmer, one of Newport's oldest, dates from 1702, the era when Newport was one of the most important early American seaports. It stands on one of the narrow blocks of clapboard homes from that period that have undergone one of the most impressive restorations in the country. More then 200 of these eighteenth-century homes are on the National Register of Historic Places.

The home was remodeled in 1755 and had been almost unchanged since. Some of General Lafayette's aides de camp stayed here during the Revolutionary War. Spe-

WEB SITE: www.innsofnewport.com

INNKEEPER: Rick Farrick (owner)

ROOMS: 10 rooms, all with private bath, air-conditioning, phone, TV, clock, radio; 5 with fireplace; 1 with Jacuzzi

ON THE GROUNDS: Patio

RATES: $85–$295, including full breakfast and afternoon refreshments

CREDIT CARDS ACCEPTED: MasterCard, Visa, American Express, Discover

OPEN: Year-round; occasionally may close for one month in winter for maintenance

HOW TO GET THERE: To get into town, see HOW TO GET TO NEWPORT below. Pass the beach and go uphill on Memorial Boulevard, turn right onto Bellevue Avenue, and continue about 5 blocks. Bear left down Washington Square and stay left in order to reverse direction around Washington Square and turn right onto Clarke Street (it is a one-way street and must be entered from this direction). The inn is on the right.

cial care went into the restoration into an inn, using original paint colors such as the sea green color found on a 1702 doorjamb and the cobalt blue that was popular in early Newport. A British muralist, Rosemary Mahoney, was brought in to do the charming egret mural that covers the entry wall and goes up the stairway, as well as several other paintings upstairs. A local potter created the hand-painted sinks found in the bathrooms.

The original twelve-over-twelve paned windows and colonial cove moldings remain, and guests have breakfast in the old keeping room, seated near the fireplace at a long harvest table beneath a pewter chandelier or in high-backed wooden booths for two. The menu posted daily offers choices such as French toast, pancakes, or eggs with breakfast meats.

The guest rooms upstairs follow the contours of the house, varying in shape as well as decor. Rick Farrick, who owns neighboring inns on Clarke Street, has kept the colonial feel while upgrading the inn. Furnishings include many antiques, four-posters and feather beds, and Farrick has kept touches of whimsy from the old inn, such as a floor-to-ceiling tree painted by artist Mahoney, hidden in the closet of Room 4, and a chair that seats you between a pair of smiling painted wooden cats in Room 7.

Clarke Street is an ideal quiet location, a small one-way street removed from traffic yet only a short stroll from all the action down the hill on Thames Street.

What's Nearby: See What's Nearby on page 207.

How to Get to Newport

These directions will get you into town. At that point, consult the directions to your chosen inn.

To reach Newport from Interstate 95, take exit 3A in Rhode Island, Route 138 east, and follow it until you cross the Newport Bridge. Take the first exit off the bridge, Scenic Newport, and make the first right onto Farewell Street. Take a right turn at the second light on Farewell to America's Cup Avenue and follow it through town to the seventh set of lights, staying on the left. At the light, which marks the end of America's Cup Avenue, turn left toward Memorial Boulevard.

From Boston take Interstate 93 south to Route 138 south, and head south again on Route 24 through Fall River, following the signs. Exit at Route 138 south, Middletown/Newport Beaches. Go right at the bottom of the exit ramp (Turnpike Avenue) and proceed to the traffic light, and then turn right to continue on Route 138 south. Make a left at the light onto Route 138A south, Newport Beaches, which eventually becomes Memorial Boulevard.

CLIFFSIDE INN

2 Seaview Avenue
Newport 02840
(410) 847–1811; (800) 845–1811
Fax: (401) 848–5850

■ The outside is irresistible, a Victorian show-off with rows of bay windows, a mansard roof, and a turret, festooned with gingerbread trim. And the inside is even better. This flamboyant charmer is made to order for romantics, with some of the most elaborate decor in Newport, including lots of fireplaces, whirlpool baths, and showers for two.

The handsome parlor is done in pinks and corals, with teak floors, a fireplace, and one of the many bay windows that fill the house with light. The dining room is another period piece, and the place where guests discover the culinary talents of innkeeper Daniel Coggins and his staff. Along with a fruit-and-pastry buffet, they whip up dishes from stuffed French toast to Belgian waffles to eggs Newport. Breakfast is served from 8:00 to 10:00 A.M., but you can also have coffee service in your room from 7:00 to 9:00 A.M. Afternoon tea is worth coming home for; it comes with scones and shortbread and a changing array of cookies, tarts, meringues, eclairs, and chocolate cakes.

The bedrooms and suites are done with flowered papers, antique four-posters or tall Victorian headboards, carved armoires, and lots of Laura Ashley fabrics. Most have cozy sitting areas in a bay window or alcove, and some have window seats.

You can pick your own ambience. The Library Room on the first floor has built-in mahogany bookcases and a writing desk. The Attic on the third floor has a rustic feel, with pine cathedral ceilings and a skylight for stargazing right above the king-size

WEB SITE: www.cliffsideinn.com

INNKEEPER: Winthrop Baker (owner), Daniel Coggins (resident innkeeper)

ROOMS: 8 rooms, 8 suites, all with private bath, air-conditioning, TV/VCR, phone, Internet access, clock, radio, robes, whirlpool or steam bath, fireplace

ON THE GROUNDS: Free guest parking, outdoor tables, benches

RATES: Rooms $245–$375, suites $385–$575, including full breakfast, in-room coffee service, afternoon tea, beach chairs, and towels

CREDIT CARDS ACCEPTED: MasterCard, Visa, American Express

OPEN: Year-round

HOW TO GET THERE: To get into town, see HOW TO GET TO NEWPORT on page 208. From the north follow Memorial Boulevard (Route 138A) south past Easton's Beach, turn left onto Cliff Avenue, and then left again onto Seaview Avenue. The inn is on the left at the corner of Seaview. From town turn up the hill on Memorial Boulevard and continue to Cliff Avenue, just before the beach, and proceed as described earlier.

bed. The Atlantic Suite has its own entry, a sitting room with a fireplace, a plantation bed, and skylights above both bed and whirlpool bath.

Lovers will surely love the Governor's Suite, done in exuberant floral wallpaper and dominated by a massive four-poster bed. The fireplace is visible from the mahogany-paneled bathroom; you can sit in the whirlpool bath and watch the flames. This bathroom also has an authentic Victorian birdcage shower. If a sea view is your idea of romance, you can have it from the cupola tower of the three-story Tower Suite, which soars 25 feet to the octagonal ceiling.

Built in 1876 as a summer home for Governor Thomas Swann of Maryland, the house was later occupied by Beatrice Turner, a talented artist whose domineering father made her a recluse and who could still be seen wearing Victorian garb thirty years after it was out of style. After her death, more than 1,000 self-portraits were found in the house. Winthrop Baker, a former CBS executive who bought the house in 1989, honored Miss Turner by putting more than one hundred of her paintings on the walls and lining the stairway. No doubt she would be pleased if she could see them—but what would she think of the lovers in her old home making sparks fly in the whirlpool bath?

What's Nearby: See What's Nearby on page 207.

FRANCIS MALBONE HOUSE

392 Thames Street
Newport 02840
(401) 846–0392; (800) 846–0392
Fax: (401) 848–5956

■ In 1760, during Newport's heyday as a colonial port, wealthy shipping merchant Francis Malbone could afford the best. To design his Georgian colonial mansion, he hired Peter Harrison, the architect responsible for Newport's noted Touro Synagogue and Redwood Library. Harrison came through with a gracious home with spacious rooms and grand hallways, adorned with fine mantels, moldings, and cabinetry. In 1990, a group of local investors bought the house and turned it into an inn, retaining the best old features and wide plank floors but adding modern conveniences. Today that home is Newport's finest colonial-era inn.

The Malbone House is on Newport's busiest street, but you'd never know it once you step inside the door. Inside, all is serene elegance. Two formal parlors are in the front of the house, tastefully done with Oriental rugs to set off the polished floors and eighteenth-century reproduction furniture. The old dining room has an open-hearth fireplace with a beehive oven and maintains the period mood with a spinning wheel. The library is equally fine but a little less formal, stocked with newspapers and books and with two chairs beckoning in front of the fireplace.

WEB SITE: www.malbone.com

INNKEEPERS: Will Dewey and Anne Howard

ROOMS: 20 rooms, 4 suites, all with private bath, TV, phone, clock, CD/radio, robes; 18 with fireplace; 12 with whirlpool bath

ON THE GROUNDS: Inner courtyard with tables and chairs, private parking lot

RATES: Rooms $175–$305, suites $315–$475, including full breakfast and afternoon tea

CREDIT CARDS ACCEPTED: Master-Card, Visa, American Express

OPEN: Year-round

HOW TO GET THERE: To get into town, see HOW TO GET TO NEWPORT on page 208. At the end of America's Cup Avenue, don't turn left up Memorial Boulevard. Instead, bear right and continue straight ahead to lower Thames Street. The inn is 3 blocks farther on the left. From the north follow Memorial Boulevard to its end in town, turn left onto Thames Street, and follow the preceding directions.

Just beyond is the counting house, added in 1860, now a roomy suite with its own entrance and fine details such as a corner cupboard with a Newport shell motif. It has modern accoutrements that may have amazed Mr. Malbone—a shower for two and a double whirlpool bath.

Up the regal stairway are four big second-floor bedrooms with 12-foot ceilings. The walls are painted in deep colonial hues: dark green, slate blue, or cranberry red. Carved four-poster beds have white coverlets and piles of down pillows. Some are tall enough to require step stools to climb into bed. Mahogany and gilt mirrors, Oriental china, and handsome tiled fireplace hearths provide interesting accents. The "smaller" third-floor rooms are still 9 feet high and equally well furnished.

Behind the house is a landscaped courtyard, and beyond that is an addition of nine rooms opened in 1996, with rooms so perfectly matched to the house, it is hard to tell they are not original. All the new rooms have fireplaces and whirlpool baths.

An addition in 2001 was a neighboring

1750 home, renovated with guest parlors on the first floor and two luxury suites upstairs, and furnished with antiques and working fireplaces, and two-person marble showers and Jacuzzis in the bathrooms. The house is very popular with guests looking for a two-bedroom suite or for two couples traveling together.

The 1996 addition includes a larger dining room with a welcoming fireplace and four big round tables to better accommodate the added number of guests. General manager Will Dewey, a graduate of the Johnson and Wales culinary school, helps to oversee a delicious breakfast with treats such as peach or almond crepes, home-baked cranberry-nut muffins, raisin scones, eggs Benedict, French toast, or banana pancakes. There's always a big help-yourself bowl of fresh fruit and a pot of freshly brewed coffee. On warm days, guests can be served at the wrought iron tables in the courtyard. In the afternoon, tea and cookies and cakes are served in one of the living rooms or outside, depending on the weather.

Will has been with the inn ever since it reopened, and he has lots of history to share, including tidbits such as the fact that Francis Malbone had a tunnel dug from the cellar to the harbor, to smuggle rum or to avoid paying taxes to the king, depending on who tells the story. He'll also gladly tell you about restaurants and anything else you need to know make the most of Newport.

The owners have a new bed-and-breakfast inn, the Hilltop, which opened on Bellevue Avenue in April 2006.

What's Nearby: See What's Nearby on page 207.

IVY LODGE

12 Clay Street
Newport 02840
(401) 849–6865; (800) 834–6865
Fax: (401) 849–0704

■ The traditional Victorian exterior, with railed porch and pointed turret, doesn't give a clue of what awaits inside. I know of no inn with a more dazzling entry than this burnished oak 33-foot-high hallway wrapped with a graceful railed stairway leading to the second and third floors. Tucked at an angle in the entry is a brick fireplace, where a welcoming fire flickers on cooler days. Designed by the famous architect Stanford White in 1886 as a summer home for a New York City physician, Ivy Lodge is a fabulous reminder of Newport's glory days. However, while it is in the midst of the mansion area and the rooms are large, this was meant to be a comfortable home rather than a formal mansion, and it remains so as an inn.

WEB SITE: www.ivylodge.com

INNKEEPERS: Daryl and Darlene McKenzie

ROOMS: 8 with private bath, air-conditioning, TV, phone, dataport, hair dryer, iron and ironing board; 5 with working fireplace; 4 with whirlpool tub for two; most have VCR or DVD, clock radio, refrigerator, stereo/CD player

ON THE GROUNDS: Wraparound railed porch, ¾ acre of lawn, formal hedges, English garden, lawn games

RATES: $149–$399, including full breakfast, afternoon refreshments

CREDIT CARDS ACCEPTED: MasterCard, Visa, American Express, Discover

OPEN: Year-round

HOW TO GET THERE: To get into town, see HOW TO GET TO NEWPORT on page 208. From Memorial Boulevard turn right onto Bellevue Avenue, make a left turn onto Parker Avenue, and then a right onto Clay Street. The inn is on the left.

Daryl and Darlene McKenzie left careers as mortgage brokers in Dayton, Ohio, to take over this special house in 2000, and they have totally redone the rooms, creating authentic Victorian ambience with William Morris wallpapers and many antiques and good reproductions. Period lighting fixtures are throughout the house.

Inviting sofas flank the fireplace in the living room, and a second seating area is in front of the row of tall windows at the end of the room. A baby grand piano awaits musical guests.

Guests gather at a regal 21-foot dining-room table for a bountiful breakfast served each morning from 8:30 to 10:00 A.M. Windows framed by formal draperies stretch almost floor to ceiling at the end of the room.

A sideboard lavishly laden with fresh fruit, homemade granola, baked apples, bread pudding, and freshly baked muffins and breads complements the changing menu of hot dishes prepared by an in-house chef. Ginger pancakes with lemon sauce, breakfast burritos, and eggs Benedict with a special Grand Marnier and orange sauce are some of the special offerings. In the afternoon, the sideboard offers fruit, cookies, and hot and cold beverages.

All of the guest rooms are large, and many offer working fireplaces; the most luxurious have two-person whirlpool tubs. The first-floor Library with striking red accents is romantic, but without a doubt the prize room is the Turret, done in yellow and blue, with a carved wooden king-size bed, long draperies, antiques, and a fireplace. Along with the double whirlpool in the bath, there is a glass-and-marble stall shower and a double vanity. The Victoria, with its elaborately carved bedposts, pale walls, and striking armoire, is another favorite.

One of the nice features of the house is the wraparound porch furnished with overstuffed wicker furniture, a perfect place to relax and admire the tall trees, including a vintage Japanese maple. And if you feel like an old-fashioned game of croquet or bocce, they are waiting on the lawn.

What's Nearby: See What's Nearby on page 207.

OLD BEACH INN

19 Old Beach Road
Newport 02840
(401) 849–3479; (888) 303–5033

■ "I'm handy and she's artistic." It's an understatement, but that's the way Luke Murray explains how he and his wife, Cyndi, have transformed this 1879 Gothic Victorian so deftly into an inn filled with fresh personality and folksy charm. The couple has made many improvements to the house they bought soon after their marriage in 1989, and they continue to look for more.

Cyndi's decorating spans a variety of styles and is filled with unexpected touches to admire or to make you smile—an old doll dressed in lace or a handmade quilt, a carousel horse or a birdhouse, a folk painting or a stained-glass window. Sit down to breakfast, and your plate may have a rabbit design or roses—the dishes are different on every table.

The continental menu offers pastries, bagels or English muffins, homemade granola, fruit, yogurt, juice, and coffee. On Sunday, a hot entree is added. Depending on the weather, it may be served in the dining room in front of the fireplace or outside on the porch overlooking the grounds, beautifully landscaped with plantings, benches, a pond, and a pergola.

The public rooms show off the couple's collection of antiques. Upstairs, rooms are named for flowers and decorated accordingly, each with hand-painted pieces and small surprises. The Rose Room is pretty and feminine with pink and white striped paper, a canopy bed, and a fireplace. There's a rocking horse in the corner and rose stenciling around the bathroom sink.

The Ivy Room has a hunt theme, done in deep greens and reds with twig furniture and an antique cathedral stove. Ivy stenciling can be found in the bathroom—and inside the closet.

Morning Glory gives the feel of an indoor garden, with a picket fence headboard,

WEB SITE: www.oldbeachinn.com

INNKEEPERS: Luke and Cynthia Murray

ROOMS: 7 rooms, all with private bath, air-conditioning, clock, radio; 5 with fireplace; 4 with TV

ON THE GROUNDS: Patio, gazebo

RATES: Rooms $100–$195, 2 large suites $275–$350, including continental breakfast

CREDIT CARDS ACCEPTED: Master-Card, Visa, Discover

OPEN: Year-round

HOW TO GET THERE: To get into town, see HOW TO GET TO NEWPORT on page 208. Take Memorial Boulevard, turn left (or right if coming from the north) on Bellevue Avenue, proceed for about 3 blocks, and turn right onto Old Beach Road (at the Newport Art Museum). The inn is about 1 block farther on the right.

Adirondack chairs, and wicker furnishings. Cyndi's mother is responsible for the curtains, duvets, dolls, and cloth rabbits that decorate this and all of the rooms.

Magnolia and Sunflower, the two rooms in the remodeled carriage house across the lawn, offer extra privacy and TV.

You have to wonder how they find the time to do all this, since Cyndi has a full-time job as manager of the oceanographic information center at the University of Rhode Island and Luke is the manager of Newport's very popular Black Pearl restaurant. Whatever their secret, the Murrays have an obvious talent for innkeeping.

What's Nearby: See What's Nearby on page 207.

ADMIRAL DEWEY INN

668 Matunuck Beach Road
South Kingstown 02879
(401) 783–2090; (800) 457–2090

Just a shell's throw from a beautiful beach, this breezy Victorian lodging rates a listing on the National Register of Historic Places. The four-story shingled inn was built as a boardinghouse back in 1898 and named for Admiral Dewey, a great national hero that year for his role in the Spanish-American War. In spite of the ideal location, it had been empty and neglected for years until 1986, when a two-year restoration put things to rights. Joan, a warm and chatty host, will gladly fill you in on the trials and tribulations of those years, which have been recorded in a picture album. Now the inn is a page from the Victorian past, filled with period furnishings, lace curtains, and flowery wallpapers, but never so fussy as to spoil the free and easy air of the beach.

Settle in a rocker on the wraparound porch and breathe in the salt air, or come inside to the parlor, where you'll usually find some company lounging on the comfortable overstuffed furniture, looking through the piles of books and magazines or watching the 54-inch TV. The room is welcoming even in the winter and holds some interesting furnishings, such as the old library card catalog serving as a table.

Walk into the dining room to admire the grand Victorian tiled fireplace and the handsome blue and white plates and fine china on display. There's always a pot of coffee on the burner and a fruit basket on the table. Guests can gather around the expansive 1840 harvest table anytime from 8:30 to 11:00 A.M. to share a continental breakfast buffet of fruit juice, cereals, muffins, assorted breads, and a coffee cake of the day.

WEB SITE: www.admiraldeweyinn.com

INNKEEPER: Joan LeBel

ROOMS: 10 rooms, 8 with private bath, 2 with shared bath; many with ocean views

ON THE GROUNDS: Wraparound porch

RATES: $125–$175, including continental breakfast

CREDIT CARDS ACCEPTED: MasterCard, Visa

OPEN: Year-round

HOW TO GET THERE: From Route 1 follow the signs for Matunuck Beach Road and Theater by the Sea; the inn is on the corner of Matunuck Beach Road and Atlantic Avenue.

Head up the creaky railed stairway to the guest rooms. Many have sea views and seating to make the most of them, and all have interesting decor and antiques. Room 4, one of the front rooms, has a four-poster with twisted posts, dark striped paper, and a rose print comforter on the white chenille bedspread. Room 3 has a green lattice design on one wall, a rose print on the others, and a fine gilt mirror on the wall. Room 5 is done in paisleys and has a marble-top dresser, a velvet settee and chairs, and a fine inlaid Victorian headboard. The prize for headboards, however, goes to Room 6 for a tall Victorian beauty with a shell design on top.

You'll be provided with a beach towel when you want to walk across the road to Matunuck Beach, and there's an outdoor shower to wash off the sand when you get back. Don't miss an evening at Rhode Island's well-known Theater by the Sea just down the road, where productions are developed for summer theaters all over the country.

Joan, a longtime resident and owner of a local real estate brokerage office, can steer you to all the other best places on the shore, and if you are interested in shopping for antiques, ask her for tips—she's a connoisseur.

What's Nearby: Matunuck Beach is just across the road, Theater by the Sea a short drive away. Also nearby are the Trustrom Wildlife Refuge, the Block Island ferry, and the University of Rhode Island campus. The inn is just a thirty-minute drive to Mystic or Newport, an easy day trip in either direction.

WOODY HILL

149 South Woody Hill Road
Westerly 02891
(401) 322–0452

You'd swear this gray-shingled colonial with the gambrel roof had been here forever, but it was actually designed and built in 1972 by Ellen Madison, a retired high school English teacher with a Ph.D. Ellen's love for history comes naturally. She is the

fourth generation of her family to live on this property, and her ancestors have lived in Westerly since the 1660s.

This is her home, infused with her warm personality and furnished with exquisite taste, filled with authentic antiques she has collected or fine reproductions she has commissioned. The twenty-acre grounds and 40-foot outdoor swimming pool are big pluses, creating a totally private haven just minutes off the busy highway.

You won't find a finer colonial living room than this one, with six twelve-over-twelve paned windows and a fireplace, a colonial high-back settee in red and white plaid, Oriental rugs, and antique Windsor chairs. The clock on the mantel is an old family piece, and the portraits on the wall are of Abby and Joseph Saunders, Ellen's great-grandparents. Down a few steps is the book-lined library with a comfortably cushy sofa and wing chair for curling up with a book.

The big keeping room past the kitchen is warm and welcoming, with a walk-in fireplace filled with colonial iron cooking pots and utensils and a built-in bake oven. Breakfast is served at a big colonial table. Handsome furnishings include a tall case clock, crewel wingback chairs, a candle chandelier, and a spinning wheel. Ellen scours cookbooks for her recipes, especially sauces. A typical morning may bring waffles and bacon, and apple crisp with whipped cream. Ellen offers hearth cooking classes here in winter.

WEB SITE: www.woodyhill.com

INNKEEPER: Ellen L. Madison

ROOMS: 3 rooms, all with private bath, clock, radio, TV

ON THE GROUNDS: 20 acres, outdoor pool, porch swing

RATES: $110–$140, including full breakfast

CREDIT CARDS ACCEPTED: None

OPEN: Year-round

HOW TO GET THERE: From Route 1 turn up South Woody Hill Road at the McDonald's at Dunn's Corners. Continue on South Woody Hill Road for ¾ mile; the inn is on the right.

This inn can be a fine choice for families, since two rooms have more than one bed. The "family room" has two curtained queen-size tester beds and a trundle bed; Room 2 has Queen Anne cherry and mahogany furniture and a canopy bed. Both have nice old quilts and accent pieces such as old trunks and blanket chests. The cheerful garden room at the end of the house is surrounded by windows with garden views and has a private entrance.

Though it feels a million miles from anywhere, Woody Hill is very convenient for beaches, shopping, and sightseeing along the Rhode Island coast.

What's Nearby: Beautiful ocean beaches are just 2 miles away, the quaint town of Watch Hill is an easy drive, and the Rhode Island shore is rich in pristine nature preserves. Westerly can also be a convenient base for drives to Mystic Seaport, Foxwoods Casino, and the splendid Mashantucket Pequot Indian Museum.

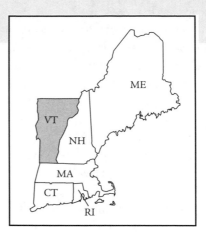

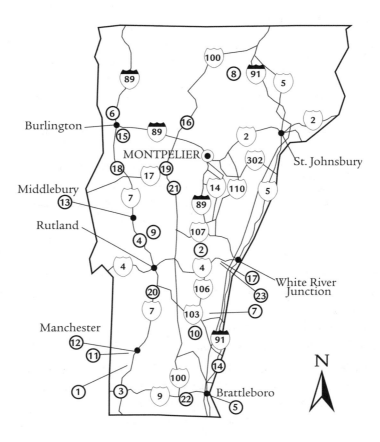

VERMONT

Numbers on map refer to towns numbered below.

1. Arlington, Country Willows *220*, Inn on Covered Bridge Green *221*
2. Barnard, Fan House *223*, Maple Leaf Inn *224*
3. Bennington, Molly Stark Inn *226*, South Shire Inn *227*
4. Brandon, The Gazebo Inn *228*, The Inn on Park Street *229*, Old Mill Inn *231*
5. Brattleboro, 1868 Crosby House *232*, Meadowlark Inn *233*
6. Burlington, Willard Street Inn *234*
7. Chester, Hugging Bear Inn *236*, Inn at Cranberry Farm *237*
8. Craftsbury Common, Craftsbury Bed and Breakfast on Wylie Hill *238*
9. Goshen, Judith's Garden B&B *239*
10. Grafton, Inn at Woodchuck Hill Farm *241*
11. Manchester Center, Inn at Ormsby Hill *243*, Manchester Highlands Inn *244*, Seth Warner Inn *246*
12. Manchester Village, 1811 House *247*
13. Middlebury, Cornwall Orchards Bed and Breakfast *248*
14. Putney, Hickory Ridge House *249*
15. Shelburne, Heart of the Village Inn *251*, Willow Pond Farm *252*
16. Stowe, Brass Lantern Inn *253*, Stone Hill Inn *255*, Timberholm Inn *256*
17. Taftsville, Applebutter Inn *257*
18. Vergennes, Strong House Inn *258*
19. Waitsfield, Inn at the Round Barn Farm *260*, Mad River Inn *262*
20. Wallingford, White Rocks Inn *263*
21. Warren, West Hill House *264*
22. Wilmington, The Inn at Quail Run *265*, Nutmeg Country Inn *267*
23. Woodstock, Ardmore Inn *268*, Canterbury House *270*, Charleston House *271*, Deer Brook Inn *272*, The Woodstocker *273*

COUNTRY WILLOWS

332 East Arlington Road
Arlington 05250
(802) 375–0019; (800)
796–2585
Fax: (802) 375–8054

■ An early Arlington entrepreneur named Fernando West built this village landmark in 1850, when East Arlington Road was a busy stagecoach route to and from Arlington village. You can still see the large marble stone at the front of the lawn, once used to step up into the stage.

WEB SITE: www.countrywillows.com

INNKEEPERS: Anne and Ron Weber

ROOMS: 4 rooms, 1 suite, all with private bath, air-conditioning, TV, robes, in-room coffee/tea service; 2 rooms with fireplace

ON THE GROUNDS: 1½ landscaped acres; lawns with picnic tables, benches and chairs; porch with hammock for two

RATES: $138–$200, including full breakfast and afternoon refreshments

CREDIT CARDS ACCEPTED: MasterCard, Visa, American Express

OPEN: Year-round

HOW TO GET THERE: Take Route 7 north to exit 3, Arlington and Route 313. Follow Route 313 for 1³⁄₁₀ miles to Warm Brook Road. Turn right and drive ⁷⁄₁₀ mile to the end of Warm Brook Road, and turn left onto East Arlington Road. Country Willows is ½ mile farther on the left, past the library and schools.

Now listed on the National Register of Historic Places, the home took on new life in the 1990s when it was restored by the Weber family as a cozy bed-and-breakfast inn. Anne and Ron Weber are veteran innkeepers who came to Vermont in 1987, purchasing the old Norman Rockwell home in West Arlington and converting it to an inn. In 1999, they sold their first inn and moved here to the historic district of the village, bringing with them the fine antiques they acquired during the years when they lived in Scotland, such as the 300-year-old sideboard in the dining room, with a plate rack that reaches to the ceiling. Photos on the wall of their Aberdeen years, which Anne dubs "life in the castle," always intrigue guests.

Castles are behind them, however. The atmosphere in their inn is all New England. The living room welcomes with chairs facing the brick fireplace, and a mix of Victorian and country antiques, including a tall grandfather clock. Arched doorways lead into the more formal dining room, where guests mingle around a long table lined with Chippendale-style chairs and lit with a crystal chandelier.

Both Webers share their culinary talents with bountiful breakfasts. Ron's apple compote recipe is always requested by guests, and Anne's baked walnut French toast recipe appeared in *Yankee* magazine. As members of the Vermont Fresh Network, they always offer foods grown and produced locally.

One special touch of Weber hospitality: Early coffee or tea can be served in your room.

The Arlington Room, the only guest room on the first floor, is a beauty, with a handsome cherrywood sleigh bed, wide board pine floors, high ceilings, and stenciled walls.

The Manchester Room upstairs is a favorite for its mahogany four-poster bed, fireplace, and a bathroom with both a stall shower and a Victorian claw-foot soaking tub with a mountain view. The Dorset Suite, with snug angled ceilings, has a satinwood inlaid mahogany queen-size bed in one room, and two antique four-poster single beds in the other.

My own choice would be the West Mountain Room, with a fireplace and a sitting area in front of two large windows with views of West Mountain. The king-size bed can be made into twins. Like many of the bedrooms, it boasts an attractive handmade quilt.

After years of living around the country and in Europe when Ron was a mechanical engineer and Anne a high school English teacher, the couple are now confirmed Vermonters. Their four children and six grandchildren live nearby, and they are very much part of their community, Ron serving on the town zoning board and Anne on the regional chamber of commerce. They truly enjoy sharing their knowledge of the area with visitors, and their enthusiasm for their adopted home is contagious.

What's Nearby: Arlington offers an exhibition of Norman Rockwell's work, as well as good dining and shopping. A cache of stores in picturesque East Arlington includes an antiques center and the popular East Arlington Cafe. The Battenkill River is renowned for fly fishing and is equally popular for canoeing. Manchester designer outlets are a short drive away, as is winter skiing at Bromley and Stratton Mountains.

INN ON COVERED BRIDGE GREEN

3587 River Road at Covered Bridge Road
Arlington 05250
(802) 375–9489; (800) 726–9480
Fax: (802) 375–1208

▦ The setting looks like a Norman Rockwell print, facing a covered bridge and a classic white-spired church. And, in fact, Norman Rockwell lived in this 200-plus-year-old farmhouse from 1943 to 1954. He did some of his best-known work in the studio he had built in back, with a two-story window facing north. You can rent the studio or sleep in his old bedroom in the main house if you like, sharing his onetime view of the covered bridge.

Since the Dickens family arrived in 1999, the inn has been completely renovated without losing its country charm. The living room, like all the rooms in the house, has acquired many antiques.

The dining room is elegant, with soft green wood accents, toile wallpaper, and a pewter chandelier. A full breakfast is served on fine china by candlelight, with soft music in the background and a cozy fire in the fireplace on cool mornings. Breakfast main courses change daily; a favorite, according to Julia Dickens, is baked French toast with caramel pecan topping.

Upstairs is Rockwell's own bedroom, now known as Spooners Room, furnished with a handsome carved cherry four-poster rice bed piled high with pillows. This room also includes a sitting room with a single sofa bed, to form a suite.

The view of the green with its little white church and the red covered bridge is shared by the Four Seasons Room, which has a country look, with floral paper, an iron bed, and an antique English armoire. All the rooms feature queen-size beds.

Dreaming in the Attic, tucked under the eaves, provides a different vista of pastures and mountainside. The two-sided fireplace can be enjoyed from the bed or the claw-foot spa tub in the bathroom.

Pondering on the Porch, another inviting choice, is done in soft celery greens and pinks with antique oak and wicker furniture. It has a two-person spa tub and its own private porch.

The only room not named for a Rockwell painting, the 1792 Room, honors the year the house was built. Once a woodshed, it has been turned into a spacious romantic lair with wainscoting and flowered wallpaper. The mahogany four-poster bed faces a corner fireplace, and the window offers a view of the covered bridge.

If it isn't rented, you can have a look inside the art studio, where Rockwell painted. If you go to the little Rockwell Museum in Arlington, you can see some of

WEB SITE: www.coveredbridge green.com

INNKEEPERS: Clint and Julia Dickens

ROOMS: 6 in the main inn, all with private bath, gas fireplace, air-conditioning; 4 with two-person spa tub; 2 bedrooms in Rockwell Studio; 1 loft bedroom in Honeymoon Cottage

ON THE GROUNDS: 5½ acres with expansive lawns, gardens, old apple orchard, walking path, mountain vistas. Battenkill River down the lane from inn.

RATES: $150–$250, including full breakfast

CREDIT CARDS ACCEPTED: Master-Card, Visa

OPEN: Year-round

HOW TO GET THERE: From Route 7A take Route 313 west for 5 miles to Covered Bridge Road; pass through the covered bridge to the inn.

the work he did here, using local residents as models. The large open room with the 10-foot-square north-light window where Mr. Rockwell painted is now comfortably furnished as a living room with a full kitchen and dining area where guests may gather around the fireplace, view the TV/VCR, or enjoy a meal. The upstairs bedroom has a balcony with prime views; the downstairs bedroom has its own deck. Both have private baths. Rooms are offered separately, sharing the sitting area and kitchen, or the entire studio can be rented.

I was taken with the more rustic Honeymoon Cottage, a grain storage shed that Rockwell turned into a small studio for his son, cutting a dormer into the roof to provide a large window with north light. The structure's wood pegs and handhewn post-and-beam construction is in full view, and the sleeping loft, reached via ladder, has panoramic views. The cottage offers a sitting room, a kitchenette, and a bathroom with a spacious two-person tiled shower.

The expansive grounds of the inn include a south-facing meadow, garden, an old apple orchard, and a grand view of the Battenkill Mountains. The Battenkill River is just down the lane at the covered bridge.

What's Nearby: See What's Nearby on page 221.

THE FAN HOUSE

Route 12 North, P.O. Box 294
Barnard 05031
(802) 234–9096

■ Innkeeper Sara Widness, a longtime friend from the travel business, has left Manhattan for Vermont, which is good news for bed-and-breakfast fans. Sara says she considers herself a "steward" of her new home, the Fan House, an expanded Cape Cod–style home with a history dating from 1840. She enjoys sharing some of the past—the bricks found in the attic said to have helped stave off an Indian attack, the fact that Vermont's first female lawyer lived here, the paintings on the walls done by William B. Hoyt, an artist who once lived in the house. But while she has kept the historic charm and features such as the original wide plank floors and weathered wood, she has filled the home with a touch of modern elegance and her own warmth, as well as the books and treasures she has gathered through many years of world travel.

The heart of the house is the Victorian kitchen, complete with 18-inch wooden floorboards and a turn-of-the-twentieth-century woodstove. Beyond is a living room where guests gather to get acquainted around the welcoming brick fireplace. A Gob-

WEB SITE: www.thefanhouse.com

INNKEEPER: Sara Widness

ROOMS: 2 suites with private bath, 1 room with private bath in hall, all with air-conditioning, clock radio, hair dryer, bathrobes

ON THE GROUNDS: 2 acres of lawn, stone sculptures, perennial and sunflower gardens

RATES: $120–$200, including full breakfast

CREDIT CARDS ACCEPTED: None

OPEN: Year-round

HOW TO GET THERE: Take Route 4 into Woodstock, and then continue on Route 12 north to Barnard. You'll see a country store on the right and a white church on the left; the Fan House is the third house on the left past the white church.

elin tapestry that once belonged to Sara's grandfather graces one wall, and her favorite painting, a scene of Tuscany, is over the fireplace. The adjacent library is well stocked with the books she has collected over a lifetime, including a collection of very old children's literature.

The three upstairs bedrooms are a mix of clean white walls and antique accent pieces. Amenities, such as air-conditioning, are strictly modern. The Fireplace Suite has a skylight above the four-poster king-size bed and a handsome tapestry on the wall. The Red Toile Suite is furnished with a handsome queen bed with lacy wrought iron head- and footboards and pillow and window accents to carry out the name. All the beds are made up with fine high-thread-count linens, and the bathrooms are stocked with oversize bath sheets and Bulgari amenities.

The day starts wonderfully with Sara's legendary cheese soufflé, made with the best Vermont cheese, or perhaps her special lemon pancakes. Afterward, take a stroll through the gardens and a walk through tiny Barnard, a hamlet dating from the 1700s. Sara will guide you to the special places only an insider would know, such as Silver Lake, a three-minute walk from the inn, a delightful place for a swim in summer, and the old-fashioned country store nearby. She'll also make a dinner reservation for you at the Barnard Inn, the exceptional restaurant in town.

What's Nearby: Barnard is a tiny, quaint New England village with a vintage country store. The many attractions of Woodstock are just 9 miles away.

MAPLE LEAF INN

Route 12, P.O. Box 273
Barnard 05031
(802) 234–5342; (800) 516–2753

▓ Gables and a gazebo, tall chimneys and a railed porch, and candles in each tall window make this Victorian-style inn

WEB SITE: www.mapleleafinn.com

INNKEEPERS: Gary and Janet Robison

ROOMS: 7 rooms, all with private bath, air-conditioning, TV/VCR, phone, clock, radio; many with fireplace, whirlpool bath, soaking tub

ON THE GROUNDS: 16 wooded acres, walking and cross-country-ski trails

RATES: $130–$260, including full breakfast

CREDIT CARDS ACCEPTED: All major cards

OPEN: Year-round

HOW TO GET THERE: Take Interstate 89 to Vermont exit 1 and follow Route 4 to Woodstock. Bear right onto Route 12, and continue 9 miles north to Barnard. The inn is ¼ mile south of the Barnard General Store.

look as though it has been here forever, but this is actually a new house built to look old—and planned with romance in mind.

Fate seemed to mean for Gary and Janet Robison to get together, for they met while each was on assignment in Saudi Arabia, he as an oil company executive, she as a teacher. When they returned to the United States, they wanted a cooler clime than Gary's Houston home, and a New England inn seemed the answer. The problem was finding an inn they liked. They looked and looked, but nothing seemed to fit their fan tastes, so they decided to start from scratch, taking advantage of the new while keeping the feeling of tradition.

Bathrooms have the octagonal tiles, wainscoting, and pedestal sinks found in older houses, but these tile floors are cozily heated, and the fixtures such as whirlpool baths, oversize showers, and soaking tubs for two are strictly contemporary. The rooms are big enough to accommodate king-size beds and sitting areas, and below the period mantels are efficient, working fireplaces.

When lovers arrive, they find logs set up ready for a match, and a keepsake cutout wooden maple leaf attached to a card welcoming them by name and noting the date. After dinner, the bed has been turned down, and there are chocolates on the night table.

Each room is distinctive, and most have a sample of Janet's artful stenciling. Winter Haven is in subdued colors and has a perfectly grand oak rolltop bed, while Summer Retreat is done in shades of blue to match a summer sky and furnished with a dreamy white iron bed with a fan quilt and two blue swivel rocking chairs. Sweet Dreams has a four-poster, while Morning Glory is all summery wicker. My favorite room, Country Garden, has a headboard reminiscent of a picket fence and a miniature garden on the mantel; in summer, blossoms from the real garden reach all the way up to the windowsill.

Downstairs is a comfortable living room with a bay window and a library with shelves showing treasures from the hosts' travels in the Middle East.

The dining room gleams with highly polished wooden floors, and tall lace-curtained windows look out into the trees. There is a table for each couple in residence, each with two pine ladder-back chairs. I particularly admired the cross-stitch replicas of U.S. "Love" postage stamps on the walls. They were done by Janet, each one an anniversary gift for her husband.

You'll need no lunch after one of Janet's lavish breakfasts. One feast began with cranberry upside-down breakfast bread, followed by a warm citrus compote with nutmeg and honey, and finally a savory Dijon egg puff with homemade olive bread. Afterward, you can walk it off with a stroll through the maple and birch forests that surround this very private inn.

What's Nearby: See What's Nearby on page 224.

MOLLY STARK INN

1067 East Main Street (Route 9)
Bennington 05201
(802) 442–9631; (800) 356–3076
Fax: (802) 442–5224

Fate seems to have meant Reed Fendler to be an innkeeper. Reed was wondering what to do after a family business closed in 1988 when an ad caught his eye. He hadn't ever thought about an inn, but here was a chance for a business of his own. Nearly two decades later, he couldn't be happier about his decision.

Though his outgoing friendliness sets the tone of the inn, Reed also has worked hard to make this modest 1890s Queen Anne Victorian a pleasant place to be by polishing the hardwood floors, adding features such as a woodstove in a brick alcove, and furnishing the inn with antiques, braided rugs, handmade quilts, and country cheer. The old-fashioned rooms also have gained new amenities such as ceiling fans, whirlpool baths, and gas-powered woodstoves. Reed's excellent photos adorn the walls.

Rooms vary in size, some being quite small; they have New England–inspired names. I could be very happy in Molly's Room, with its cozy sitting nook with a woodstove and a whirlpool bath in the bath-

WEB SITE: www.mollystarkinn.com

INNKEEPER: Reed Fendler

ROOMS: 6 in main house, 2 suites in Sugarhouse, 1 private cottage; suites, cottage, and some rooms with whirlpool and fireplace or woodstove

ON THE GROUNDS: 1 acre

RATES: Rooms $90–$125, Sugarhouse suites $150–$175; cottage $170–$195, including full breakfast

CREDIT CARDS ACCEPTED: MasterCard, Visa, American Express, Discover; cash preferred

OPEN: Year-round

HOW TO GET THERE: From Interstate 91 take exit 2, Route 9 west. The inn is on the south side of Route 9, 1 mile east of Bennington.

room. I like the lavender and white Connecticut Room, with a claw-foot tub and a sky-light in the bath. The Green Mountain Boys Room in the attic features snug eaves, stenciling, and a nice love seat in the sitting area. The General Stark Room is a two-room suite made sunny by six windows and cozy with a woodstove for nippy nights.

Romantics will want to head for the completely private cottage, which offers a whirlpool bath, woodstove, TV, stereo and phone, a cathedral-ceiling living room, and a king-size brass bed in the upstairs loft.

Another option is the Sugarhouse, an addition with two suites featuring vaulted ceilings, fireplaces, and oversize whirlpools. Each also has a small refrigerator.

Reed's big country breakfasts include special dishes such as cinnamon apple–cheddar cheese quiche or lemon–wheat germ pancakes.

The open kitchen is typical of the inn's friendly nature—you are welcome to come in anytime to have a home-baked cookie or make a cup of tea.

What's Nearby: Bennington is one of Vermont's most historic towns, with a classic green lined with magnificent eighteenth- and nineteenth-century homes. A 360-foot monument commemorates the Battle of Bennington, a turning point in the Revolutionary War; an elevator ride to the top yields a wonderful view of the countryside. The Bennington Museum should not be missed for its gallery of thirty-two original works by Grandma Moses, who lived not far away, and its displays of the well-known brown-glazed early Bennington pottery. The pottery works is still in operation in town, selling contemporary versions of the classic patterns.

SOUTH SHIRE INN

124 Elm Street
Bennington 05201
(802) 447–3839
Fax: (802) 442–3547

■ William C. Bull, the architect responsible for many of Bennington's finest Victorian-era homes, outdid himself with this Queen Anne mansion. No expense was spared to create a showplace for Louis Graves, whose residence was part of a family compound built in the late 1800s by a prominent Bennington clan.

Much care also went into a restoration preserving the rich woods and the fine craft work in the ornately carved fireplaces and elaborate plasterwork of the house. The library/sitting room has burnished mahogany paneling, a 10-foot ceiling, a lavish fireplace, and leaded glass doors. And the dining room is as frilly as a wedding cake,

WEB SITE: www.southshire.com

INNKEEPERS: George and Joyce Goeke

ROOMS: 9 rooms, 1 suite, all with private bath, phone, clock, radio; 7 with fireplace; some with whirlpool bath

ON THE GROUNDS: Located on a city block

RATES: $89–$200, including full breakfast

CREDIT CARDS ACCEPTED: Master-Card, Visa, American Express

OPEN: Year-round

HOW TO GET THERE: From Route 9 take Route 7 south for 1 block, and make a right turn onto Elm Street. The inn is 1 block farther on the left, at the corner of Elm and Jefferson Streets.

adorned with fancy carved plaster friezes. Breakfasts served here include juice, fruits, homemade muffins, and a generous entree such as quiche, stuffed French toast, or waffles.

All the guest rooms are good size, with thick carpeting, formal draperies, comfortable seating areas, and elaborate headboards that range from four-posters to tall Victorian beauties. My favorite room has a wing chair and reading lamp in front of a curved wall of windows and a tall carved mahogany headboard. The master bedrooms have king-size canopy beds and the original fireplaces. Four rooms in the more recently restored century-old carriage barn are even more luxurious, with fireplaces and whirlpool baths.

The inn is near the center of town, an ideal location for seeing the many historic sites of Old Bennington.

What's Nearby: See What's Nearby on page 227.

THE GAZEBO INN

25 Grove Street (Route 7)
Brandon 05733
(802) 247–3235; (888) 858–3235

◼ This small, venerable inn dating from 1865 is listed on the National Register of Historic Places. Since Donna and Lindsay Taylor took over, the mother-daughter team has made the decor more elegant without losing the inn's coziness. Names such as Satin Plum, Sheer Lilac, and Rose Velvet describe the decor of the four guest rooms, which feature feather beds, down comforters, and European bedding along with Victorian antiques from brass beds to wooden trunks. Air-conditioning keeps things comfortable in summer.

The Cinnamon Silk Suite has ample room for families, who are welcome here. Porta-cribs and high chairs are available for the asking, and the innkeepers are happy to help with babysitting arrangements.

Downstairs spaces include a sociable parlor where afternoon tea is served from

4:00 to 5:00 P.M. and an adjoining library with a TV and VCR. Another quiet reading nook is just off the dining room, fitted with two comfortable chairs, ottomans, and good lamps over each seat. A full breakfast is served in the pleasant dining room. The screened porch faces busy Route 7, but on summer days the gazebo on the lawn is a quieter haven away from traffic.

The inn is an easy walk from the center of town, and lakes and mountains are nearby. Donna and Lindsay will gladly map out your route for a perfect road or mountain-bike ride or for a refreshing hike, pointing out hidden treasures such as covered bridges along the way.

WEB SITE: www.brandon.org/
INNKEEPERS: Donna and Lindsay Taylor
ROOMS: 4 rooms, all with private bath, air-conditioning, robes, hair dryer
ON THE GROUNDS: Screened porch, 2 acres, back lawn with gazebo
RATES: $95–$120, including full breakfast and afternoon tea
CREDIT CARDS ACCEPTED: None
OPEN: Year-round
HOW TO GET THERE: The inn is just north of Brandon on Route 7.

What's Nearby: Located midway between Rutland and Middlebury, picturesque Brandon is a good base for exploring central Vermont and is an interesting village in itself. An important mid-nineteenth-century center for the manufacture of railroad cars, Brandon is filled with fine homes from this period. The entire village of 243 buildings is listed on the National Register of Historic Places.

The town has an unusual feature—two village greens—and a covered bridge built in the 1840s. Shopping includes several antiques stores in town, and the studio and shop of noted folk artist Warren Kimble is in the nearby countryside. The Neshobe Golf Course is a public course open to visitors.

The surrounding area offers ample opportunity for hiking and biking; swimming at Lake Dunmore in Branbury State Park is fifteen minutes away. The New England Maple Museum in Pittsford and the Marble Exhibit in Proctor are popular attractions nearby. Killington Ski Area is about 30 miles away.

THE INN ON PARK STREET

69 Park Street (Route 73)
Brandon 05733
(802) 247–3843; (800) 394–7239

This handsome French Second Empire home built in 1856 on one of Brandon's historic maple-lined main streets has a special innkeeper. Judy Bunde came to Vermont after thirty-five years in the Boston area, where she owned and operated a

WEB SITE: www.theinnonpark
street.com

INNKEEPER: Judy Bunde

ROOMS: 5 rooms, 3 with private
bath; all with clock radio, ceiling fan;
some with TV

ON THE GROUNDS: Rockers on the
porch, nice back lawn with white
wicker furniture and hammock

RATES: $115–$240, including full
breakfast

CREDIT CARDS ACCEPTED: Master-
Card, Visa

OPEN: Year-round

HOW TO GET THERE: Park Street is
Route 73, near the center of Brandon.

dessert business, Sweet Endings, serving restaurants, hotels, and shops. Needless to say, her breakfast pastries and evening desserts are a good reason to visit. Another good reason: Judy has called on the many friends she made during her bakery years to institute a series of Cooking with Chefs weekends, a special time to meet and work with professionals in the inn's big country kitchen.

This is a comfortable home with a big welcoming living room with a fireplace, bookshelves, and a grand piano, and a handsome dining room painted deep red with white wainscoting and woodwork and built-in shelves showing off fine china. Guests are seated in Windsor chairs around the big table, where delicious breakfasts are served. My special favorite space at this inn is the big side porch furnished with wicker, the perfect place to relax on a fine afternoon.

The bedrooms have been beautifully redecorated since Judy arrived. One of the most spacious rooms is Teresa, located on the first floor. It has 10-foot ceilings, tall windows, a four-poster bed, TV/VCR, bookshelves in the corner, and a bath with twin pedestal sinks and a Jacuzzi tub.

On the second floor, the Calder is another large room with high ceilings, a four-poster, a crisp white matelasse bedspread, down pillows and duvet, and a love seat and wing chair overlooking the maples on Park Street. It is most often combined with the Andrea Room to form a suite; Andrea's antique iron double bed is just right for children. I also like Nancy, a room with deep red walls and king-size bed with a fresh white bedspread and floral pillow accents.

If you come for one of the Cooking with Chefs weekends, you have a welcome reception and a light supper on Friday night, and on Saturday you will work directly with the chef for three or four hours preparing dinner for the group. You can be an active participant or just sit back and watch. Either way, you'll have a delicious dinner to look forward to.

What's Nearby: See What's Nearby on page 229.

OLD MILL INN

79 Stone Mill Dam Road
Brandon 05733
(802) 247–8002; (800) 599–0341

■ Secluded but not isolated—that's the location of this New England charmer, a rambling 1786 farmhouse just outside Brandon. It is on five acres of woods, meadows, and farmland, with a big red barn housing innkeeper Pat's art studio/workshop. Besides the property, which offers a rippling brook and an old-fashioned swimming hole, the inn adjoins a public golf course, so guests can enjoy the open vistas and can tee off in summer or glide away when snow is on the ground. Lovely gardens surrounding the farmhouse provide flowers and vegetables for the inn.

Much of the charm of the inn is due to the original folk art, painted chests and lamps, and handmade quilts that keep the farmhouse flavor. A wonderful country mural covers the whole wall of the breakfast area, a long glassed-in gallery that is the first thing you see when you enter the house. A library with antique furnishings and a sitting room with a woodstove are nice places to relax. The owners' personal art collection is found throughout the inn.

Upstairs guest rooms, named for native Vermont wildflowers, have lace curtains at the windows, quilts on the beds, and folk art on the walls. The Violet Room offers a queen-size four-poster; the Winterberry Room has an antique single bed plus a double. Trillium is prime, with both a queen bed and a single, and with a deck overlooking the farms and distant landscape.

Roger, the inn chef, specializes in fresh and organic breakfasts. Egg dishes alternate with choices such as pancakes and French toast. Forget about your diet. The muffins, biscuits, and breads are homemade and irresistible.

What's Nearby: See What's Nearby on page 229.

WEB SITE. www.oldmillbb.com

INNKEEPERS: Pat Cavanagh Kowalsky and Roger Kowalsky

ROOMS: 4 rooms, all with private bath; 3 with air-conditioning

ON THE GROUNDS: Porch, 5 acres of lawn and woodland, rope swing, hammock, brook for fishing, swimming hole, barn with stalls for miniature horses, chicken coop; property adjoins a golf course for cross-country skiing and snowshoeing

RATES: $99–$125, including full breakfast

CREDIT CARDS ACCEPTED: Master-Card, Visa

OPEN: Year-round

HOW TO GET THERE: Take Route 7 into Brandon, and pick up Route 73 east; Stone Mill Dam Road is about ¾ mile east of Brandon village. Make a left turn just beyond the white farmhouse.

1868 CROSBY HOUSE

175 Western Avenue (Route 9)
Brattleboro 05301
(802) 257–4914; (800) 528–1868

■ If you are looking for a cozy, luxurious little inn easy to reach off Interstate 91, this is definitely the place. Since the pretty yellow and white Victorian house seems modest from the outside, I was pleasantly surprised to discover three positively sumptuous guest rooms within—along with a hostess who likes to pamper guests. She'll even leave an early-morning cup of coffee outside the door or bring a continental breakfast to your room, if you like.

Lynn Kuralt has lived here for more than thirty years and raised six children in the house. When the kids left home, she was "rattling around," according to Lynn, and after extensive renovations, the house opened as an inn in 1996. It is easy to believe this enthusiastic hostess when she says she loves what she is doing.

The 1868 Victorian home has a pleasant parlor with a marble fireplace and a baby grand piano, and an oak-paneled dining room with a woodstove where Lynn serves full breakfasts using her best china, silver, and crystal. Vermont cheddar frittatas is one of her specialties.

A little sitting room at the top of the stairs is stocked with books and videos and a refrigerator with refreshments for guests.

Each of the guest rooms has different features but equally fine amenities. Deborah's Winter Solace is furnished with a four-poster mahogany bed, a black marbleized slate fireplace, and a double shower with twin heads in the bath. Marjorie's Autumn is in soothing rose tones, with a paneled queen-size bed, antique rocker, an unusual green slate fireplace, and its own double shower. Those who enjoy whirlpools should opt for Winifred's Summer Retreat, a sunny

WEB SITE: www.crosbyhouse.com

INNKEEPER: Lynn Kuralt

ROOMS: 3 with private bath, phone, TV, VCR, CD player, whirlpool bath or double shower; 2 suites with separate entrance

ON THE GROUNDS: Summer porch for breakfast, lawn with gazebo, stone walls, pond, perennial gardens; trails behind the house available for walking, jogging, or cross-country skiing

RATES: $120–$150, including full breakfast

CREDIT CARDS ACCEPTED: MasterCard, Visa, American Express, Discover

OPEN: Year-round

HOW TO GET THERE: Take Interstate 91 exit 2; turn left, drive ½ mile on Route 9 toward Brattleboro. The house is on the left.

room in blue and white with a canopied bed, paneled fireplace, and a whirlpool bath built for two with a waterfall faucet.

All the rooms have comfortable sitting areas, phones, TV, and CD players, conveniences planned to please the many business guests who stay here but equally appreciated by visitors on a holiday.

What's Nearby: Brattleboro is a southern gateway to Vermont, with a number of companies nearby and many good restaurants. Book lovers will find a number of shops in town. It is convenient to the annual summer Marlboro Music Festival, to canoeing and kayaking on the Connecticut and West Rivers as well as to exploring the unspoiled villages of New Hampshire's neighboring Monadnock area. Downhill skiing at Mount Snow is about thirty minutes away.

MEADOWLARK INN

Orchard Street, P.O. Box 2048
Brattleboro 05303
(802) 257–4582; (800) 616–6359

It's less than 2 miles to busy Interstate 91, and downtown Brattleboro is minutes away, yet this 1870 farmhouse with the wraparound porch and pink shutters is a world apart, set on a hillside with grand views of the hills of Vermont and New Hampshire.

The feeling here is comfortable, informal country. The big living room has a welcoming fireplace and a few overflow breakfast tables at the rear. The dining room offers mesmerizing views from a bay window. The innkeepers are both graduates of the Cambridge School of Culinary Arts, so you know you can expect an excellent breakfast.

In the main house I liked a second-floor guest room, with a sleigh bed, Victorian dresser, and wicker accents, along with the Pine Room, which has paneling, a whole wall of windows, and a working fireplace.

But the rustic carriage house is hard to resist. The beamed center

WEB SITE: www.meadowlarkinnvt.com

INNKEEPERS: Deborah Jones and Lucia Osiecki

ROOMS: 8 rooms with private bath, phone, clock radio, CD player; some with fireplace, two-person Jacuzzi, views, TV, refrigerator

ON THE GROUNDS: 3 acres, open lawn, horseshoes, flower beds; screened wraparound porch, two walking loops; guests have golf privileges at the Brattleboro Country Club

RATES: $120–$180, including full breakfast

CREDIT CARDS ACCEPTED: MasterCard, Visa, American Express

OPEN: Year-round

HOW TO GET THERE: From Interstate 91 take exit 2 and turn west; turn right at the second street (Orchard Street) and proceed 1½ miles to the inn, on the right.

has been turned into a sitting area with rustic furniture, a winning country scene mural on one wall, and a gas fireplace. Guest rooms here also have beams, along with ceiling fans, attractive wallpapers, and simple country furnishings. Rooms in the rear have whirlpool tubs.

The grounds here are exceptional—cows in the pasture, frogs in the pond, views all around. It's no wonder the guests are frequently found relaxing outdoors.

What's Nearby: See What's Nearby on page 233.

WILLARD STREET INN

349 South Willard Street (Route 7)
Burlington 05401
(802) 651–8710; (800) 577–8712
Fax: (802) 651–8714

Until recently, Burlington, Vermont, was a city with everything going for it—except a special inn. Happily, that problem has been remedied with the conversion of a residence worthy of its hometown. The location is ideal, on a residential block adjoining Champlain College, near Burlington's vibrant downtown and on a hill high enough to look out at Lake Champlain.

The grand, gabled, redbrick house with fancy white trim was built in 1881 by Charles Woodhouse, president of the Merchants Bank and a prominent Vermont state senator. It remained a private home for one hundred years and then was converted into a retirement home for twelve years, until Beverly and Gordon Watson, owners of a popular restaurant in town, came along. The Watsons had to battle the local zoning laws for two years, but they prevailed, renovated the home, and opened for business in 1996.

The fine features of the home remain. The lovely cherrywood used for paneling in the entry hall and for the front stairway has been burnished to a soft luster. The parlor is a Victorian vision, with a marble fireplace and crystal chandelier, furnished with a period rose-colored sofa and coordinating print chairs, a grand piano, and an antique grandfather clock.

The standout room is the solarium and breakfast room, a big, sunny, plant-filled space with a green and white checkerboard marble floor and three walls of windows. A comfortable arrangement of sofa, love seat, armchairs, and rocker beckon on one side, while individual tables are set for breakfast on the other. A generous breakfast is

WEB SITE: www.willardstreetinn.com

INNKEEPERS: Beverly and Gordon Watson

ROOMS: 14 rooms, all with private bath, TV, air-conditioning, phone, clock radio, wireless Internet access; some with nonworking fireplace and lake views

ON THE GROUNDS: Handsome back lawn and garden

RATES: $125–$225, including full breakfast and afternoon tea

CREDIT CARDS ACCEPTED: Master-Card, Visa, American Express, Discover

OPEN: Year-round

HOW TO GET THERE: South Willard Street is actually Route 7, the main road through Burlington; the inn is at the corner of South Willard and Cliff Streets.

served from 7:30 to 10:00 A.M. and offers dishes such as eggs Benedict or waffles with fruit. Freshly made coffee and tea are available for guests all day, and when you check in, you find a welcoming home-baked cookie in your room.

The prize rooms in the house are the four original bedrooms at the top of the stairs, each with a nonworking fireplace and private bath. The former servants' quarters in the south wing are now occupied largely with the Woodhouse Suite, boasting a dramatic black iron canopy bed, a working gas fireplace, two-person shower, and a view of the lake and gardens.

All the rooms have been carefully decorated with coordinating fabrics. Room 5, done in a blue and white small print with striped shades and a floral striped coverlet, has a king-size four-poster, twin daybed, and nice Victorian chest. Room 4, with a soft peach overall print on the walls and green leafy tile around the fireplace, provides a bonus: a bay window with a view of Lake Champlain. But I'd happily settle for the smaller space of Room 12 on the third floor, a summery room with ribbon-trellis patterned wallpaper, wicker furniture, and an enclosed widow's walk with an even more sensational lake view.

Less of the lake is visible from the inn in summer, when the trees fill in, but for compensation, you have a lovely back lawn and a garden, reached via a double marble stair from the solarium.

What's Nearby: Burlington is an inviting city on the shores of Lake Champlain, and with a pedestrians-only downtown, it is always lively. There's excellent shopping along Route 7, the main road through town, from discount outlets to the Vermont Teddy Bear Company. Just to the south in Shelburne are two major Vermont sites: the Shelburne Museum, one of America's finest showcases for folk art, and Shelburne Farms, a model of progressive cattle and dairy farming for a century. Shelburne Farms is one of the many outdoor sites in and around Burlington for the Vermont Mozart Festival, a popular annual summer event. Burlington is also nicely situated for skiers in winter, less than an hour from Stowe or Sugarbush.

HUGGING BEAR INN

244 Main Street (Route 11)
Chester 05143
(802) 875–2339; (800) 325–0519

■ This friendly Victorian house opposite the pretty village green in Chester just may be the happiest inn in New England. How can anyone resist smiling at a place overflowing with teddy bears?

For starters, there's a lovable, life-size teddy waving from the porch and crowds of little guys peeking out of the turret windows. Step inside and bears are everywhere—sitting in an armchair, peeking through the banisters, posing on the bookshelves, perched on the piano bench, sitting in a high chair, cuddling up in a doll cradle, even hanging from the antlers on the landing. Some are soft and fuzzy au naturel, others come clad in an array of outfits, including a firefighter, Santa, and movie-star garb. The round front turret room, filled with greenery and musical instruments, is home to the owner's own collector bears in all manner of dress, from Victorian night clothes to formal bride and groom attire. It isn't just the kids who love this cuddly menagerie; adults with a smidgen of child left inside are equally enchanted.

WEB SITE: www.huggingbear.com

INNKEEPER: Georgette Poehland Thomas

ROOMS: 6 rooms, all with private bath, air-conditioning

ON THE GROUNDS: Hugging Bear Shoppe with thousands of teddy bears; big front porch

RATES: $70–$165, including full breakfast and afternoon refreshments—and discounts at the Hugging Bear Shoppe

CREDIT CARDS ACCEPTED: MasterCard, Visa, American Express, Discover

OPEN: Year-round

HOW TO GET THERE: Take Interstate 91 to Vermont exit 6, Rockingham, then Route 103 for 10 miles to Chester. Stay on Main Street (Route 11); the inn is on the right opposite the green.

It was all the idea of owner Georgette Thomas, a former social worker who saw an article about the healing power of teddy bears and agreed that "Everyone needs a hug." That was in the early 1980s, and the inn idea has expanded into a shop in back that is one of the largest in New England.

Even without the bears, this is an appealing house, circa 1850, with fine woodwork and lots of windows. The rooms in the front round turrets look out on the green. I loved the Pooh Room, where the bedspread, pillows, curtains, and shades are adorned with my childhood favorite characters from A. A. Milne's classic, *Winnie-the-Pooh*. Many rooms have extra beds for the kids, and every bed comes with a bear, though you can also "borrow" a bear from the collection downstairs.

Guests can gather in the Victorian parlor and the adjoining library, with a fireplace, piano, TV, and shelves laden with books, games, and puzzles. In warm weather, the front porch rockers provide the perfect spot for people-watching.

Mix-and-match chairs surround the trestle table in the bay-windowed dining room, where the day starts with a hearty, all-you-can-eat breakfast of fruits and juice, cereals, eggs, and a treat of the day, which may be blueberry pancakes or French toast. In the afternoon, crackers and cheese are served. The words *Hugging Bear Inn* are spelled out in a string of alphabet blocks on the wall.

Many inns aren't comfortable for small children, but here's one where you can be sure they will feel right at home.

What's Nearby: Chester's village green is lined with shops and dining. Nearby villages of Grafton and Londonderry make for pleasant exploring, and Okemo skiing is only 8 miles away in Ludlow.

INN AT CRANBERRY FARM

61 Williams River Road
Chester 05143
(802) 463–1339;
(800) 854–2208
Fax: (802) 463–8169

■ You follow a dirt road and cross over a covered bridge to find this secluded inn, a sprawling modern post-and-beam clapboard building designed to look like an old Vermont house and barn. Step inside and prepare to be dazzled.

WEB SITE: www.cranberryfarminn.com

INNKEEPERS: Pam and Carl Follo

ROOMS: 11 rooms, including 3 suites, all with private bath, individual thermostat; 3 with fireplace; some with whirlpool, private deck

ON THE GROUNDS: 60 acres of meadow and forest, 3 miles of cross-country-skiing and walking trails, swimming pond

RATES: Rooms $133–$149, suites $219, including full breakfast and afternoon refreshments

Here's a living room that really deserves the name "great room." With a 30-foot cathedral ceiling, beams and tall arched windows reaching almost the entire height, it is one of the most striking rooms I've seen. Comfortable seating is arranged in clusters to make for cozier settings, all on Oriental rugs and with views of the double fireplace.

The dining room behind has barn-board paneling and beams and faces the other

CREDIT CARDS ACCEPTED: Master-Card, Visa, American Express, Discover

OPEN: Year-round

HOW TO GET THERE: The inn is 4 miles from Interstate 91. Take exit 6, follow Route 103 west, turn right at Brockways Mills Road, and continue for ⁷⁄₁₀ mile, crossing the Williams River Bridge. Turn left and stay on the dirt road along the river for ³⁄₁₀ mile to the inn. From Chester take Route 103 east toward Rockingham, turn left at Williams River Road, cross the covered bridge, and follow the dirt road ½ mile to the inn driveway.

side of the brick fireplace. Breakfasts, served from 8:00 to 9:00 A.M., are generous, with fruits, yogurts, cereals, homemade pastries, and hot entrees. Cranberry-orange-nut pancakes is a signature dish.

Upstairs is another inviting space, the Library Loft, with another fireplace, book-lined walls, and a stock of games and puzzles as well as reading material.

Guest rooms are on all three levels of the house, nicely furnished with four-poster and canopy beds, ruffled curtains, and colorful quilts. Each is slightly different, and some feature woodstoves or fireplaces and soaking tubs.

The largest rooms are at the corners. Those on the ground level have nice views of the grounds, and one provides extra privacy with its own entrance and deck.

What's Nearby: See What's Nearby on page 237.

CRAFTSBURY BED AND BREAKFAST ON WYLIE HILL

Wylie Hill
Craftsbury Common 05827
(802) 586–2206

■ The number of guests who come back year after year attests to the appeal of this homey, unpretentious 1860s farmhouse on a hilltop. Some come to bike or hike or canoe. Me, I'd be happy just to settle into one of the lawn chairs and take in the 360-degree views of sheep grazing on the hillside and mountains in the distance. As a bonus, the inn is located in the prettiest town in the tranquil area of Vermont known as the Northeast Kingdom.

The living room offers comfortable seating, a gas stove, lots of reading material, fresh flowers, watercolors on the walls, and a view worth painting from the windows. The breakfast room adjoining an open kitchen has a built-in cupboard original to the house and more nice art on the walls. Here's where hostess Margaret Ramsdell serves a generous morning meal at a table set with pottery, sterling silver, and fresh flowers. Cinnamon apple pancakes is one of her signature dishes.

Lots of guests sit themselves down in the two easy chairs by the woodstove in

WEB SITE: www.scenesofvermont
.com/craftsburybb

INNKEEPER: Margaret Ramsdell

ROOMS: 6 rooms, sharing 3 baths

ON THE GROUNDS: Expansive hilltop
setting with views, cross-country-ski
trails on property that connect to a
Nordic center

RATES: $65–$90, including full breakfast

CREDIT CARDS ACCEPTED: Master-
Card, Visa

OPEN: Year-round

HOW TO GET THERE: Take Interstate
91 or Interstate 89 north. Go north on
Route 14 to Craftsbury Common. Follow signs to the bed-and-breakfast,
1¼ miles north of the common.

this room to watch the action at the bird feeders outside the window. Margaret can tell you the name of every winged visitor.

This is an old-fashioned bed-and-breakfast with comfortable bedrooms that share baths, much like staying with a friend. The setup works especially well for families or groups of friends. Asked to pick a favorite room, the hostess chooses one papered in a nice soft green print for its views to the south and west.

An innkeeper since 1984, Margaret has lived in Craftsbury Common since 1962 and raised her family here. She can tell you all you want to know about local history or what's going on in the village or guide you to the most scenic bike rides in the area. And she knows when to leave you to enjoy the blessed peace and quiet and to savor hilltop vistas of sunrise, sunset, or "Moonlight in Vermont."

What's Nearby: Craftsbury Common is a hamlet of white clapboard buildings and a village green, located in the quiet, scenic area known as the Northeast Kingdom, an ideal region for back-road drives and exploring unspoiled villages. The Craftsbury Outdoor Center offers hiking, canoeing, and cross-county skiing; the inn trails connect to their Nordic center.

JUDITH'S GARDEN B&B

423 Goshen-Ripton Road
Goshen 05733
(802) 247–4707

What a treat on a dreary winter day to drive into the snow-bordered driveway and find myself facing a greenhouse filled with greenery and flowers. Inside, a skylit balcony is another cheerful haven that is wall-to-wall with plants.

Judith Irven has become a master gardener and professional landscape designer since she moved to Vermont full time in 1994. She honed her skills with courses at

WEB SITE: www.judithsgarden.com

INNKEEPERS: Judith Irven and Dick Conrad

ROOMS: 3 rooms, all with private bath, clock

ON THE GROUNDS: 30 acres, extensive gardens, forest, trails, ponds, shady benches, Adirondack views

RATES: $100–$115, including full breakfast

CREDIT CARDS ACCEPTED: None

OPEN: Year-round

HOW TO GET THERE: Take Route 7 to Brandon; in the center of town, pick up Route 73 heading east; travel for 4½ miles, passing through Forest Dale, and turn left at the sign for Goshen. Take the first left after crossing over the bridge into town. Bear right, passing the Goshen Town Office. The inn is 2⁹⁄₁₀ miles up the hill on the right.

the Vermont Technical College and in summer her abundant perennial gardens are showplaces, brimming with blooms. Her landscape gardening talent has become so well known, in fact, that several other innkeepers have hired her services.

Judith discovered this secluded 1830s home in the woods while staying at the neighboring Blueberry Hill Inn on an inn-to-inn hiking tour many years ago and already owned it when she met her husband, Dick Conrad. Since Dick went to college in nearby Middlebury, Vermont seemed a logical destination when the couple decided it was time to leave the corporate world in New Jersey. Two years of renovations were necessary before they opened for business as a bed-and-breakfast inn in 1994, changes that included a new wing with big windows, skylights, a cathedral ceiling, and a sunny dining area leading to the greenhouse.

A charming small piano and a clock on the wall are among the antiques in the living room, some of them heirlooms from Judith's family in England. The room is inviting, with wide floorboards and a Victorian sofa facing the woodstove installed in the native stone fireplace. Bare windows accent the clean, airy look found here and throughout the house.

There are three simply but attractively furnished bedrooms, one downstairs facing the gardens, two more on the second floor with slanted eaves walls and beams. Among many nice small touches are the handmade quilts on the beds, spoked Tubbs headboards made in Vermont, and local pottery pieces in the bathrooms. In summer, vases of fresh flowers from the garden are in every room.

Breakfast is served at a spacious table in front of a second woodstove, with the plant-filled balcony in view. The menu includes lemon-blueberry muffins and dishes such as ricotta cheese puff pancakes with gooseberry sauce, with fresh-picked flowers and herbs adorning the plates in summer. Judith will sometimes prepare an informal dinner for guests, with tasty menus that may include home-baked bread, fresh tomato soup, and baked salmon with balsamic onions, garden vegetables, and rosemary-roasted potatoes.

The expansive property offers pleasures year-round. In summer there's plenty of room for walks, and chairs are set out in the front of the house for mountain gazing, and in back a screened gazebo surrounded by flower beds overlooks a meadow pond. The 1,700-foot elevation ensures cool breezes. In winter, snowshoeing and cross-country skiing are available right outside the door. And in fall, the forest foliage is nothing less than breathtaking.

What's Nearby: Goshen is a tiny hamlet, a fifteen-minute drive from Brandon and a half hour from Middlebury. The Moosalamoo region of the Green Mountain National Forest has extensive mountain trails for hiking, blueberry picking at Hogback Mountain, and swimming at Sugar Hill Reservoir or Branbury State Park. The inn has direct access to the 40-mile cross-country-ski trail system at Blueberry Hill.

INN AT WOODCHUCK HILL FARM

Middletown Road
Grafton 05146
(802) 843–2398

■ Here's a hilltop hideaway on 200 very private acres that manages to remain comfortable and friendly, even though there are wonderful antiques and collectibles everywhere you look. Add a porch with a soaring 75-mile view, and the combination is hard to beat.

Mark Gabriel grew up in this house at the end of a country road, originally built in 1790 for the town's first minister. His boyhood books are still in a secretary in an upstairs room. His parents used to run an antiques shop in the barn, and the house is filled with their beautiful finds, everything from Early American antiques to Mexican tiles. The warmth of the family home remains, even though Mark, his wife, Marilyn, and their two children now occupy a separate house nearby. Both Gabriels are practicing psychotherapists.

Antiques begin as soon as you come into the front hall, where there is a fine German antique clock and an ornate carved sideboard. The wood-paneled living room is one of the most inviting I've seen, still with the original beamed, low ceiling and wide floorboards. A wide picture window beckons with a window seat, and you'll also find seating in front of the fireplace and a whole wall of books.

The dining room, done in a cheerful print and with its own fireplace, boasts a handsome, tall grandfather clock and a reverse painted mirror done by Mark's mother. Guests gather at one of the three tables for a full breakfast served from 8:00

WEB SITE: www.woodchuckhill.com

INNKEEPERS: Mark and Marilyn Gabriel

ROOMS: 6 rooms in main house, 4 with private bath, 2 with shared bath, some with phone, nonworking fireplace; barn with double room and suite with baths; residence with kitchen and bath; studio with kitchen, bath, private deck; all suites have refrigerators, microwaves, coffeemakers, and telephones

ON THE GROUNDS: Large, open porch with 75-mile view; 200 hilltop acres; gazebo; barn; stone walls; woodlands; 2 swimming ponds with docks; wood-fired sauna

RATES: $99–$145 for rooms in the main house; $165 for studio with kitchen; $165 for barn suites; $270 for barn residence with kitchen; $220 for two-bedroom suite; $400 for Spruce Cottage (sleeps seven); all including full breakfast (accommodations with kitchens receive the makings for breakfast in their quarters) and afternoon cheese and crackers

CREDIT CARDS ACCEPTED: Master-Card, Visa, American Express

OPEN: Mid-May through December, plus some winter holiday weekends

HOW TO GET THERE: Stay on Grafton's main street, Route 121, and proceed west out of town; bear left onto Middletown Road and continue 2 miles up the hill. Go left onto Woodchuck Hill Road. The inn is on the right at the top of the hill.

to 9:00 A.M. that includes fresh baked goods and a changing menu of specials, from egg dishes to favorites such as French toast.

The second floor offers four airy corner rooms, each with two walls of windows. One is done in blue and white, with a small crystal chandelier, a big fireplace, a sitting room with a beckoning rocking chair, and a bath with a skylight and a Mexican tile mirror. Another has a four-poster canopy bed, sunny yellow and red prints, and an Oriental rug. The blue and white room with twin beds, a rag rug, and a fireplace is where Mark Gabriel grew up.

Two third-floor rooms couldn't be cozier, each with eaves and beams. One has an extra bed for a child. Since the Gabriels have children, they welcome kids, who can share the play equipment outside.

The studio adjoining the main house comes with a kitchen and tile-adorned bath, along with a 10-foot glass door opening to a private deck.

The restored barn has its own entrance and parking area. It retains the rustic barn-wood paneling, high ceilings, and beams and has its own share of antique furnishings. Inside are a two-bedroom suite with bath, kitchen, fireplace, and skylight, and a bedroom–sitting room with another fireplace and a private bath. Behind is a large apartment called the residence, which can accommodate two to four people. The whole barn can be rented for a large family or group of friends.

Beautiful Grafton is just down the hill, but you may find it hard to leave if the weather is fine. Behind the barn is the pond, where you can sun on the dock, take a swim, and try out that wood-fired sauna hidden in the trees. And if you sit on the breezy porch, you can be away from it all and still hear the band concert going on in town.

What's Nearby: The picture-perfect town of Grafton has a classic inn with an excellent dining room, a few shops and galleries, a cheese factory, and a cider mill. Stratton and Magic Mountains are nearby for skiers, and Grafton has its own cross-country-ski center, along with trails for hiking or mountain biking. Nearby Newfane has a wonderful country store and more fine dining.

INN AT ORMSBY HILL

Route 7A
Manchester Center 05255
(802) 362–1163; (800) 670–2841
Fax: (802) 362–5176

■ You say you are searching for a sumptuous room with a fireplace and a whirlpool bath big enough for two, plus a gourmet breakfast lavish enough to last all day? Look no further. This 1764 Federal manor house has been transformed into a lair of luxury, with model-perfect bedrooms and endless amenities. The dining room and conservatory, with a wall of windows facing the mountains, is one of the most spectacular rooms I've seen anywhere.

WEB SITE: www.ormsbyhill.com

INNKEEPERS: Chris and Ted Sprague

ROOMS: 10 rooms, all with private bath, air-conditioning, clock, radio, velour terry robes, fireplace, whirlpool bath for two; 5 with flat-screen TV

ON THE GROUNDS: 2½ acres of lawns, croquet

RATES: $170–$305, including full breakfast and afternoon tea

CREDIT CARDS ACCEPTED: Master-Card, Visa

OPEN: Year-round

HOW TO GET THERE: From Interstate 91 take Route 30 west and turn south at Manchester on Route 7A, continuing for 10 miles. The inn is on the right.

The house, which is on the National Register of Historic Places, has an intriguing past. The original portion still contains Manchester's first jail cell in the basement, complete with marble floor. It was also part of the Underground Railroad used by runaway slaves. The home was purchased in the late 1800s and expanded by Edward Isham, a law partner of Robert Todd Lincoln, son of Abraham Lincoln. It later was used as a boys' school, until it became a five-room bed-and-breakfast in 1987. When Ted and Chris Sprague arrived in 1995, they converted a wing of old dormitory rooms into five additional guest rooms with pampering baths.

The rooms are exceptional, most with lavishly carved canopy beds, some meticulously decorated with coordinated Waverly fabrics. The Ethan Allen Room, with bold striped wallpaper and a paisley print canopy with matching scalloped valance, drapes, duvet, and pillows, was in the past named a Waverly Room of the Year in *Country Inns* magazine.

I'm partial to the Library Room on the first floor, the library in the old house, which still has its shelves of books, original beams, and molding. The bath has both a double whirlpool and a separate two-person shower.

The largest room, the Taft Room, comes with a vaulted ceiling, a king-size canopy bed, and a bath with a corner whirlpool tub and a large shower for two that doubles as a steam sauna. Ethan Allen has a whirlpool tub that gives views of both fireplace and mountains, plus its own private entrance and deck. A comfortable TV room is at the end of the second-floor hall, where the sound won't disturb anyone.

The sitting room, part of the original house, still has its beams, wooden ceiling, and big fireplace. Beyond is the gathering room, with comfortable wing chairs before the fire and shelves stocked with games and books. Then comes the showstopping conservatory, with its breathtaking wall-to-wall views. In warm weather you can step outside to the porch, furnished with white wicker and plants.

Chris Sprague gained a top reputation as chef of an inn in Maine, and her breakfasts showcase her talent. After juice and fresh fruit starters, you may enjoy lemon-almond bread, fresh raspberries and blueberries in cream, and unusual main courses such as leek, bacon, and Gorgonzola polenta with roasted tomato sauce or individual ricotta cheese pies in phyllo with sliced ham. Better save room, because after breakfast comes dessert, which may be warm peach crisp with white chocolate sauce or warm gingerbread with vanilla ice cream. When the inn is full, breakfast is offered buffet style from 8:00 to 10:00 A.M., with the hot entree served at 9:00 A.M.

What's Nearby: Looking for bargains? Manchester Center has dozens of upscale outlet stores at the intersection of Routes 30, 11, and 7A, with many shops just down the hill from the inn. For more sports-minded guests, bikes can be rented at Battenkill Sports in Manchester Center, hikers will find both Vermont's Long Trail and the Appalachian Trail nearby, and Bromley and Stratton Mountain ski areas are both nearby. For history and culture, Manchester Village is just a few miles to the south on Route 7A (see page 248). In summer, the area offers three theaters, and concerts by the Vermont Symphony Orchestra under the stars at Hunter Park.

MANCHESTER HIGHLANDS INN

216 Highland Avenue, Box 1754
Manchester Center 05255
(802) 362–4565; (800) 743–4565
Fax: (802) 362–4028

■ Comfortable and spacious, this turreted 1898 Victorian "painted lady" couldn't have a better location, on a quiet hilltop with mountain views, but just up the hill from the popular outlet stores of Manchester Center. Few inns offer so many hospitable public spaces. The parlor beckons with Victorian furnishings, a sunny bay window, and a  piano. The sunroom offers a light, bright setting of plants and wicker, plus TV and a chess set. Downstairs, you can relax in either of two big, wood-paneled recreation rooms. One includes a large stone fireplace and a TV/VCR with a library of videotapes. The game room has Ping-Pong, pool tables, and a wood-burning stove.

The dining room is inviting, with rose-red walls, a fireplace, and the original pressed tin ceiling. A second room with warm wooden wainscoting provides additional seating. Hearty breakfasts include house specialties such as lemon soufflé pancakes and morning glory muffins. Some favorite dishes, including amaretto French toast and apple Brie omelette, have been collected into the inn cookbook.

Rooms are named for Vermont sites and specialties, from Morgan Horse to Green Mountain. All have filmy curtains and down comforters. My favorites are the rooms in the round turret, such as the one called Turret, with a four-poster bed and a Victorian sofa in front of the big bay window, and another called Tower, with an iron bed tucked under the eaves.

A tunnel to the carriage house means you can get back and forth without a worry about weather. Suites, such as Ethan Allen, have connecting rooms and are ideal for families.

The grounds are a big plus for this inn. In summer, the 18-by-45-foot outdoor swimming pool is a refreshing break after a hard day of hiking or shopping. Or you can forget about the rest of the world and

WEB SITE: www.highlandsinn.com

INNKEEPERS: Diane and Didier Cazaudumec

ROOMS: 9 rooms in main Victorian inn, 6 rooms in attached carriage house, all with private bath, clock, radio, Wi-Fi; some with fireplace

ON THE GROUNDS: Wraparound porch, outdoor swimming pool, lawns with mountain views, hammock, croquet

RATES: $125–$184, including full breakfast and afternoon refreshments

CREDIT CARDS ACCEPTED: MasterCard, Visa, American Express

OPEN: Year-round

HOW TO GET THERE: Take Interstate 91, Route 7A, or Route 7 to Routes 11/30; Highland Avenue is between Route 7 and Route 7A in Manchester, about a block to the north, up the hill on the right.

just gaze at the mountains from the wraparound porch, a wooden chair, or a hammock on the lawn.

What's Nearby: See What's Nearby on page 244.

SETH WARNER INN

Route 7A
Manchester Center 05255
(802) 362–3830
Fax: (802) 362–1268

■ There are dozens of inns around New England with Early American decor, but only a few done with the taste and care of this small, moderately priced, eighteenth-century home nestled between two mountain ranges. Candles in each window give a clue to the welcome within. Exposed beams, fireplaces, and hand stenciling are found throughout, along with authentic colonial colors and carefully coordinated quilts and curtains.

Downstairs are a sitting room with seating around the fireplace and an inviting library. In the dining room, a country breakfast is served by candlelight each morning. Stasia Tetreault's specialties include baked apples and pears, feather eggs with turkey ham, baked French toast, and apple cranberry muffins. She serves tea or cider in the afternoon and wine or brandy in the evening after dinner.

Seth Warner was a Revolutionary War hero, and the rooms are named for him and his family members. I think he would be pleased to see the Seth Warner Room, with its net canopy bed with a handmade quilt at the foot, crisp white ruffled curtains, antique chest and chair, beams, folk art, and stenciling. Other rooms have brass and pencil-post beds and equal care in the decoration.

In winter, many guests come to ski at nearby Bromley or Stratton Mountains or to look for bargains in Manchester's many outlet stores. In summer, hiking and fishing are nearby, or you can relax on the lawn, feed the ducks in the pond, and admire the mountains. Whenever you arrive, you'll find the inn a delight.

What's Nearby: See What's Nearby on page 244.

WEB SITE: www.sethwarnerinn.com

INNKEEPERS: Stasia Tetreault and Richard Carter

ROOMS: 5 rooms, all with private bath, clock

ON THE GROUNDS: 5 acres, with a duck pond, gardens, brook

RATES: $125–$135, including full breakfast, afternoon tea, and after-dinner refreshments

CREDIT CARDS ACCEPTED: MasterCard, Visa, American Express, Discover

OPEN: Year-round

HOW TO GET THERE: The inn is on Route 7A, 2½ miles from the Route 11/30 intersection in Manchester Center.

1811 HOUSE

Route 7A
Manchester Village 05254
(802) 362–1811; (800) 432–1811

■ You'll search hard to find a more
authentic or beautiful showcase of Early American furnishings than this elegant inn,
where every room is filled with distinguished English and American antiques, Oriental
rugs, and a mix of antique fine and folk art. The original home actually dates from
1770; the name is for the year when the top floor was added and the residence first
became an inn. For thirty-five years the house was owned by Mary Lincoln Isham,
Abraham Lincoln's granddaughter, and two of the most popular rooms are named for
her and for her father, Robert Todd Lincoln, both spacious quarters with canopy beds
and fine traditional wallpaper

Like most old houses, this one rambles, and some of the rooms down the hall are
a bit smaller. Rooms at the back of the house have a bonus: a view of the extensive
gardens, the golf course of the neighboring Equinox Hotel, and the Green Mountains
beyond.

The Mark Skinner Room has beams and a nice pencil-post canopy bed, but my
top choice would be the Robinson Room, which provides a deck to enjoy the views.
Done in appealing shades of deep blue, it is
one of many rooms in the main house with
an old-fashioned claw-foot tub, this one also
boasting an enormous old showerhead.
Three rooms in the cottage next to the main
house have more modern baths and working fireplaces.

Despite the exceptional furnishings, this
is a comfortable inn, with several places for
guests to gather. Both living room and
library have fireplaces, and the library also
offers television and a ready decanter of
sherry. Guests are welcome to come into
the kitchen to help themselves to tea and
cookies during the day. Downstairs is a
recreation room with billiards and Ping-Pong
tables and another TV set.

The dining room, with its own fireplace,
is furnished in Chippendale style and is an

WEB SITE: www.1811house.com

INNKEEPERS: Marnie and Bruce Duff,
Cathy and Jorge Veleta

ROOMS: 11 rooms in main house, 3
rooms in adjacent cottage, all with
private bath, air-conditioning; many
with fireplace

ON THE GROUNDS: 7 acres of lawns,
flower and rose gardens, pond,
views of Equinox golf course, and
the Green Mountains beyond

RATES: $140–$280, including full
breakfast

CREDIT CARDS ACCEPTED: Master-
Card, Visa, American Express, Discover

OPEN: Year-round

HOW TO GET THERE: From Interstate
91 take Route 30 to Manchester,
turn south onto Route 7A, and proceed 1 mile farther to the inn.

appropriate setting for breakfasts served on fine china and sterling silver. Host Marnie Duff's repasts are served from 8:00 to 9:30 A.M., featuring fresh juice and fruit with a variety of pancakes, omelettes, or traditional English fried eggs with grilled mushrooms, ham, bacon, and scones. The Sunday special is eggs Benedict. Guests may dine at one of three large tables or go into the pub room, an unusual find in a small inn, done in tartan plaids with dark wood tables, Windsor chairs, and a typical English pub dartboard. Bruce Duff is an avid bartender; his offerings include sixty-five kinds of single malt whiskey and a selection of fine wines.

The Duffs have been here since 1990, leaving a home near Chicago where Bruce was in financial planning and Marnie raised a family and taught cooking. They have done lovely things outside as well as within the house, creating terraced flower and rose gardens, an added attraction for a very special inn.

What's Nearby: Manchester Village was a posh resort during pre–Civil War days, when the venerable Equinox House was a well-known summer hotel, and it retains the marble sidewalks and handsome homes from those days. Two main sights here are Hildene, the Georgian mansion built by Robert Todd Lincoln, son of Abraham Lincoln, and the Southern Vermont Art Center, both offering hilltop views and walking trails. Manchester Center shopping and attractions are just a mile to the north; see What's Nearby on page 244.

CORNWALL ORCHARDS BED AND BREAKFAST

1364 Route 30, RD 4, Box 428
Middlebury (mailing address is Cornwall 05753)
(802) 462–2272

It was a happy day for visitors to Middlebury College when this comfortable eighteenth-century farmhouse on fourteen acres opened for business in 1995 just 2 miles from the campus. The look is clean and uncluttered, the views are vast, and the sunsets over the Adirondacks are unbeatable.

Two of the Gerlin children had gone to Middlebury, and parents Bob and Juliet fell in love with the town. "We found it harder and harder to leave," explains Juliet. After a three-year search, this 1783 home (with an 1816 addition) seemed just right, though it took a year of renovation to make it suitable for a bed-and-breakfast, adding bedrooms by raising the roof to create a dormer.

The rooms have a fresh look, with lots of Vermont pine and a mix of old and new. The living room offers two seating areas, one clustered around the fireplace; shelves of books; and nice accents such as an Oriental rug and an antique rocking chair. On the mantel are an antique clock and folk carvings by an elderly Vermont artisan.

WEB SITE: www.cornwallorchards
.com

INNKEEPERS: Juliet and Bob Gerlin

ROOMS: 5, all with private bath

ON THE GROUNDS: 14 acres with
mountain views, garden, deck

RATES: $100–$125, including full
breakfast

CREDIT CARDS ACCEPTED: None

OPEN: Year-round

HOW TO GET THERE: Coming from
the south on Route 7, just past the
Middlebury Inn, go left onto Route
125/30 (Main Street). Take Route 30
past Middlebury College. Cornwall
Orchards is exactly 2 miles on the
right from Middlebury College Golf
Course.

Bedrooms are comfortable with little fuss. One offers two spool beds; others have modern hardwood headboards. Simple curtains are fresh white with tailored lace trim. Bathrooms include nice touches such as Mexican tiles and hand-painted mirrors.

The dining room is the brightest room in the house, with a modern table, an old pine cupboard, and wide views of the Adirondacks to the west, the same view that can be enjoyed from the deck outside. The breakfast menu rotates egg dishes one day, choices such as blueberry pancakes the next.

All of this is quite a change from their former lives in Connecticut, where Bob was an attorney and Juliet was assistant to a prominent musician. But they are relishing their life in the country, especially English-born Juliet, who makes her own jams and applesauce, has planted raspberries, and is raising chickens.

The Gerlins, who have nine grandchildren, make a point of welcoming children to the inn.

What's Nearby: Middlebury is both college town and classic Vermont village with a central green and many handsome old buildings. The Vermont State Art Center at Frog Hollow, a converted mill by a waterfall, displays the work of the state's top craftspeople, while the Vermont Folklife Center preserves the traditions of the past. The Sheldon Museum depicts nineteenth-century life in the state, and University of Vermont Morgan Horse Farm breeds horses for competition and sport on an 1870s farm with a splendid Victorian barn. At the college, the Center for the Arts offers theater, dance, and music, and the uncrowded Middlebury Snow Bowl and Cross-Country Center are available for skiers. There are two eighteen-hole golf courses in the area.

HICKORY RIDGE HOUSE

53 Hickory Ridge Road South
Putney 05346
(802) 387–5709; (800) 380–9218
Fax: (802) 387–5387

This is a gem, a mellowed brick home circa 1808, on the National Register of Historic Places, tucked away on a hillside in a country village. The house, with its five

WEB SITE: www.hickoryridgehouse
.com

INNKEEPERS: Miriam and Cory
Greenspan

ROOMS: 6 rooms in main house, 1
room and 1 suite in a separate cottage, all with private bath, phone, TV,
clock radio, VCR, air-conditioning; 5
with working fireplace

ON THE GROUNDS: 8 acres; lawns,
woods, gardens, groomed trails,
woodland, stream, hammock, terrace with umbrella-shaded tables

RATES: Rooms $125–$175, suite
$185, two-bedroom cottage $305,
including full breakfast

CREDIT CARDS ACCEPTED: Master-
Card, Visa, American Express

OPEN: Year-round

HOW TO GET THERE: From Interstate
91 take exit 4 and follow signs to
Putney center. Turn left at the Putney General Store, proceed 1⁷⁄₁₀
miles, and turn left onto Hickory
Ridge Road. The inn is the fourth
driveway on the left, opposite a big
red barn.

brick chimneys, fanlight, and curved Palla-
dian window, would do credit to a Christmas
card. The red barns and rolling hills across
the road are such a classic Vermont scene,
they made me wish I could paint.

Miriam and Cory Greenspan have owned
Hickory Ridge House since 2001. Their furnishings seem just right, in keeping with the
age of the house but comfortable. The
paints are all authentic Federal colors.

The living room has creamy walls with
blue trim on the wainscoting, moldings, and
the tall windows. An antique rocker and a
comfortable armchair frame the fireplace,
and an old disc phonograph sits against one
wall. The morning room furnished with
wicker has an upright piano.

The dining room trim and wainscoting
are barn red. Stenciling and a woodstove
add to the country look.

One guest room with a cherry four-
poster bed is downstairs; the rest are
upstairs in the original house and down the
hall over the attached carriage house. I
stayed in one of the large front rooms on the
second floor, with walls in a deep robin's-egg blue, a mahogany four-poster, and a
fireplace stacked with logs ready for a match. A comfortable chair and ottoman with
a good reading light, a TV hidden in a cabinet, and a phone by the bed were amenities I always appreciate.

The second front room is sunny yellow with white curtains, a Victorian bed, a
wicker rocker, a Pennsylvania Dutch chest, and another working fireplace. Another
prime room at the far end of the hall has a sleigh bed, a slanted ceiling, beams, a gas
fireplace, and a double row of windows facing the grounds.

The property here is exceptional. In winter, cross-country trails connect with
those of a neighboring school, making for miles of groomed skiing. In summer the
deck overlooks gardens and a meadow. Just 3 miles from Interstate 91 and less than
a mile from the village, it is a fine base for exploring and returning to a peaceful
retreat.

What's Nearby: Putney is an attractive village, home to two private boarding schools, a small college, a classic inn, a few crafts and antiques shops, and a country store dating from 1843. The Yellow Barn chamber music festival takes place each summer. Canoeing on the Connecticut River is a popular pastime. The attractions of Brattleboro are only a few miles away (see page 233).

HEART OF THE VILLAGE INN

5347 Shelburne Road (Route 7)
Shelburne 05482
(802) 985–2800; (877) 808–1834
Fax: (802) 985–2870

■ This Queen Anne Victorian has a prime location in the heart of Shelburne Village. Built in 1886 as the home of a well-to-do merchant, Cyrus Van Vleit, it was best known more recently as the home of the Gadhue family, who lived here for fifty years and ran an antiques business in the carriage barn. It had been transformed into a cozy and welcoming inn.

The gracious old house has two Victorian parlors for reading and relaxing, each with a lace-curtained bay window, one with a fireplace. The cheerful dining room holds four small tables and more lace curtains. Baked puff pancakes with fresh fruit and creative egg dishes are among the tasty courses; lots of Vermont products are featured. When I arrived, the wonderful smell of cookies baking perfumed the house: It was almost time for tea.

Rooms are named for former residents who played important roles in Shelburne's history. Five upstairs rooms with varying color schemes are furnished with antiques; some of the baths have claw-foot tubs and pedestal sinks. Harrington, with yellow walls and navy curtains and lots of windows, is spacious and appealing, and is one of several rooms that feature European rain showerheads.

The largest rooms are in the converted carriage barn. Bostwick still has

WEB SITE: www.heartofthevillage.com
INNKEEPER: Pat Button
ROOMS: 8 rooms, 1 suite, all with private bath, air-conditioning, clock radio with CD player, phone, hair dryer, TV; 1 room with whirlpool bath
ON THE GROUNDS: Wraparound porch, lawn, garden
RATES: $95–$225, including full breakfast and afternoon tea
CREDIT CARDS ACCEPTED: MasterCard, Visa, American Express
OPEN: Year-round
HOW TO GET THERE: Follow Route 7 to Shelburne Village; the inn is on the east side of the road across from the Town Hall, just south of the traffic light for Shelburne Village.

the original slatted wood barn walls, adding a rustic touch. The king bed, done in a black and brown paisley print, can be converted to two twins. The most luxurious of the rooms is the two-room Webb Suite, with beams, skylights, and a whirlpool tub.

Since innkeeper Pat Button arrived in 2003, she has added special weekends to the inn's agenda, such as a knitting workshop that features instruction, plus treats such as yoga and massage.

The inn's location near the village green puts you within a walk of shops and the enticing Shelburne Country Store, an advantage that was really welcome. As I arrived during a snowstorm, I could forget about the car and walk to my choice of three restaurants for dinner.

What's Nearby: The Shelburne Museum, one of the nation's best collections of folk art and Americana, is five minutes from the inn, as is Shelburne Farms, an 1800s agricultural estate that remains a model working farm. The farm grounds are one of the main sites of the Vermont Mozart Festival held each year in summer. Shelburne borders Burlington, with its many activities (see page 235) and is close to the Vermont Wildflower Farm in Vergennes.

WILLOW POND FARM

133 Cheesefactory Lane
Shelburne 05482
(802) 985–8505

▧ Out here in the country on 200 wide-open acres, you feel as though you could be miles from town, but in fact both Shelburne Village and Burlington are just minutes from this attractive, reasonably priced retreat.

Sawyer and Zia Lee built this contemporary house in 1990 as their retirement home, with lots of large windows to make the most of the view. Vermont residents for more than fifty years, they know the area well and enjoy sharing their home and their knowledge with guests; they can steer you to the best of the back-road scenic drives.

Their combination living and dining room is light, spacious, and inviting, with seating around the woodstove set into a carved wooden mantel, several nice Oriental rugs, bookshelves, blue and white china on display, and floral plates, flower paintings, and prints on the walls.

The dining area has a bay window full of plants. Here you'll also find my favorite piece, an upright piano hand-painted with original folk art. Breakfast is served around 8:30 A.M. at an oval table for eight. Breakfasts vary from waffles and eggs Benedict to

WEB SITE: www.bbonline.com/vt/willowpond

INNKEEPERS: Sawyer and Zia Lee

ROOMS: 3 rooms, all with private bath

ON THE GROUNDS: Wraparound deck, gardens, 200 acres of pastures, woods, ponds, meadows with walking trail

RATES: $100–$135, including full breakfast

CREDIT CARDS ACCEPTED: MasterCard, Visa, Discover

OPEN: Year-round

HOW TO GET THERE: From Interstate 89 take exit 14E onto Route 2 east and turn right at Dorset Street. Continue south about 4¼ miles to the flashing light, and turn left onto Cheesefactory Road. Drive east, and at the fourth driveway on the right (⁹⁄₁₀ mile), turn onto Cheesefactory Lane. The house is at the end of the lane on the left. Coming north from Shelburne on Route 7, turn right onto Webster Road. Stay right, drive east up the hill to the golf course, and turn left onto Spear Street. Drive north ¼ mile and turn right onto Barstow, which will become Cheesefactory Road. Past the flashing light, watch for the fourth driveway on the right and follow the preceding directions from that point.

Sawyer's special cornmeal blueberry pancakes. Irish oatmeal and homemade popovers are among guests' favorites. All main dishes are served with locally made sausage or super-crisp bacon and Vermont maple syrup.

The main bedroom upstairs, Room 3, is quite large, with a big arched window offering views of the Adirondacks. There's a sitting area with a rocker, a TV, and two skylights, one in the modern bath. Room 1 has ring quilts, a rocker, and a nice birch desk-bureau; Room 2 offers pond views from a love seat in the window and its own patchwork quilts.

The grounds are exceptional. There are some twenty birdhouses in view, usually populated with nesting tree swallows. A rose garden and beautiful perennial gardens bloom in summer, and yellow clematis vines climb on the pergola at the end of the wraparound porch. With a landscape so serene, it's hard to believe that busy Route 7 is just minutes up the road.

What's Nearby: The inn is about 6 miles from the Shelburne Museum, 8 miles from downtown Burlington (see page 235). Boating, biking, swimming, hiking, antiquing, and ferry rides across Lake Champlain are also offered nearby.

BRASS LANTERN INN

717 Maple Street (Route 100)
Stowe 05672
(802) 253–2229; (800) 729–2930
Fax: (802) 253–7425

WEB SITE: www.brasslanterninn.com

INNKEEPER: Andy Aldrich

ROOMS: 9 rooms, all with private bath, air-conditioning; 6 with fireplace and whirlpool

ON THE GROUNDS: Patio with Mount Mansfield views

RATES: $80–$225, including full breakfast, afternoon refreshments, and guest privileges at Stowe Gym

CREDIT CARDS ACCEPTED: Master-Card, Visa, American Express

OPEN: Year-round

HOW TO GET THERE: Take Interstate 89 to exit 10, Waterbury, which puts you on Route 100, and follow Route 100 north about 10 miles to Stowe Village. Continue past the village center on Route 100, which is also Maple Street, for approximately ½ mile; the inn is on the left.

The views couldn't be better. From the wall of windows across the living room and dining room and the terrace outside, Mount Mansfield, Vermont's highest peak, is clearly in sight.

Andy Aldrich, a Vermont native and custom-home builder, was just the right person to see the possibilities in this early-1880s farmhouse north of the village. He has kept the wide planked floors, fireplaces, and exposed beams of the original home and barn and added comforts such as individual heat/AC zoning in each guest room, modern baths, and soundproofing that muffles any noise from the road just outside. The restoration won an award from the Vermont Builders Association. The inn is included in the National Trust for Historic Preservation's *Guide to Historic Bed and Breakfast Inns*.

The comfortable public rooms include an L-shaped living room with seating around the fireplace and at the windows along the long back wall, where books and games, an upright piano, stereo, CD, VCR, and a TV in an old oak armoire provide entertainment. Stenciling and ruffled curtains make things homey. Here and throughout the inn are candlesticks, wreaths, and other accessories made by Vermont artisans.

The dining room, with more stenciling and baskets hanging from the beams, has an oak table for each room. I love the views from the big picture windows. Andy takes pride in his big breakfasts, featuring local products such as good Vermont ham, Cabot cheese, and maple syrup. The breakfasts won him an award a few years ago from the Gourmet Dinners Society of America. The menu always includes fresh fruits and breakfast meats, fresh baked muffins and rolls, and a hot dish such as vegetable quiche or Andy's "world-famous" apple crepes.

Guest rooms are country comfortable, with wide floorboards, stenciling, and handcrafted quilts. Eclectic decor includes canopy, brass, and wooden Victorian beds. The biggest rooms are in the converted barn, where there are dormer walls, fireplaces, and whirlpool tubs. Many rooms have mountain views.

Guests can enjoy gym privileges and aerobics classes at the Stowe Gym, and outdoors-enthusiast Andy has drawn up his own tours of the area for bicyclers and hikers. An added touch of hospitality is the downstairs bathroom and shower available for use after checkout, so you can enjoy the full day of skiing or whatever and still be able to change for the trip home.

What's Nearby: The beautiful village in the shadow of Mount Mansfield is legendary for skiing, hiking, and biking, but it offers more sophisticated pleasures as well—scores of shops and a choice of some forty-five restaurants. Ben and Jerry's Ice Cream Factory can be toured in Waterbury, 10 miles to the south.

STONE HILL INN

88 Houston Farm Road
Stowe 05672
(802) 542–6991
Fax: (802) 253–7415

■ Tasteful, comfortable, and pampering, Stowe's most luxurious small inn was a dream come true for the owners—and should be as well for couples seeking a near-perfect getaway. Amy Jordan was a hotel concierge and Hap a chef when he came to work at a Virginia Beach restaurant owned by Amy's family. When they fell in love, they found each had the same fantasy: owning a small, elegant, romantic inn.

That dream came to life when Stone Hill was built in Stowe in 1998. Romance is guaranteed in lavish guest rooms, each with a king-size bed and a two-way gas fireplace, designed so that you can watch the glow from your bed or the double whirlpool in the bathroom. Each room has a distinctive color scheme and decor, and making a choice is difficult. Moss Glen has a white iron headboard and a dramatic red wall and matching armchair, while West Bank has a sleigh bed and fabrics in autumnal shades of rust and green. I like Cotton Brook for its cheerful yellow walls and a modern steel four-poster with soft draping on the wall behind the bed. Every room has ample seating and sliding glass doors leading to the beautiful grounds.

Public rooms are equally inviting. A comfortable cushioned sofa and armchairs are gathered around the big stone fireplace in the sitting room. On the other side of the fireplace, the game room offers billiards,

WEB SITE: www.stonehillinn.com

INNKEEPERS: Amy and Hap Jordan

ROOMS: 9 rooms, all with private bath, two-way fireplaces, fireside whirlpools for two, separate showers, two sinks, sliding glass doors to grounds and garden, air-conditioning, TV/VCR, CD/clock radio, robes, hair dryer

ON THE GROUNDS: 10 acres with gardens, pond, waterfall, walking trails, hill for sledding in winter, outdoor hot tub

RATES: $265–$390, including full breakfast and evening hors d'oeuvres; snowshoes provided in winter

CREDIT CARDS ACCEPTED: Master-Card, Visa, American Express, Discover, Diners Club

OPEN: Closed in April and in November from Veterans Day until the first weekend in December

HOW TO GET THERE: From Interstate 89 take exit 10 (Waterbury/Stowe) and then follow Route 100 north for 11 miles. At the three-way stop in the village of Stowe, turn left onto Route 108 (also known as Mountain Road). Proceed 3 miles, and turn right onto Houston Farm Road (you will also see the inn sign at the intersection). Turn left into the first driveway.

board games, and puzzles and a video library for the VCR in your room.

In the breakfast room, individual tables for two are set at the tall windows that line three walls, offering views of the lavish garden in summer and a fanciful snowscape in winter. As you might expect with an ex-chef in charge, the meal is fine. Fresh fruit and homemade baked goods start things off, and a choice of three entrees includes dishes such as gingerbread pancakes or a bacon and onion quiche. Eggs any style are always an option.

At the end of the day, delicious hors d'oeuvres are served, including treats such as vegetable quesadillas with fresh salsa or shrimp with remoulade sauce. The guest pantry is open all day, stocked with hot and cold beverages.

This is truly an inn for all seasons. In summer, the lavish garden, walking trails, and a backyard hammock beckon. In winter, the inn offers snowshoes to guests, and skiers enjoy the ski boot and glove-drying service and keyed storage lockers. The outdoor hot tub under the stars is romantic whatever the season.

What's Nearby: See What's Nearby on page 255.

TIMBERHOLM INN

452 Cottage Club Road
Stowe 05672
(802) 253–7603; (800) 753–7603
Fax: (802) 253–8559

Though it is equally appealing in summer, Timberholm is my idea of ideal ski lodging—a rustic lodge easy to reach but away from the busy mountain road, with wall-to-wall mountain views from the long living room/dining area.

The lodge was built in 1949 and has been remodeled many times since. The living room has two seating areas, one focused on the window, another around the big fieldstone fireplace. Hearty breakfasts are served at the long table by the window. Oven omelettes with a variety of fillings are often on the menu, served with ham or sausage.

WEB SITE: www.timberholm.com

INNKEEPER: Darrick Pitstick

ROOMS: 8 rooms, 2 suites with TV, all with private baths

ON THE GROUNDS: Deck with mountain views, hot tub, 4 acres of lawn with gazebo, flowers, vegetable garden

RATES: $79–$149, including full breakfast and afternoon tea

CREDIT CARDS ACCEPTED: MasterCard, Visa, Discover

OPEN: Year-round

HOW TO GET THERE: Take Interstate 89 to exit 10. Follow Route 100 north to Stowe Village and turn left onto Route 108, Mountain Road. Proceed about 2¼ miles to Cottage Club Road and turn right. Timberholm Inn is a short distance ahead on the right.

Guests come home each winter afternoon to help-yourself hot soup. There's also a big outdoor hot tub to ease weary muscles.

The wood-paneled guest rooms are furnished simply. Two-room suites here are fine family accommodations and provide TV for the kids. Some can accommodate six. Room 7 and Suite 2 have the warm-weather advantage of balconies.

There's also a downstairs playroom with a TV and VCR, books and games, a skittles board, a piano, and a second cozy fireplace. Skiers have their own entrance on this level.

The view is romantic, whether in white or in lush green. In summer, the deck sports hanging plants, greenery, and lots of outdoor furniture, and the gazebo on the lawn is frequently used for weddings.

What's Nearby: See What's Nearby on page 255.

APPLEBUTTER INN

Happy Valley Road
Taftsville 05073
Phone/Fax: (802) 457–4158;
(800) 486–1734

■ This twin-gabled clapboard charmer, circa 1854, is hidden just off the main road just outside Woodstock, in the tiny hamlet of Taftsville. Tastefully decorated with the original wide pine floorboards, stenciling, Oriental rugs, and antiques, the inn offers cozy gathering places and spacious guest rooms. Guests are welcome to play the Mason & Hamlin grand piano in the music room, to chat or watch TV in the sitting room known as the Yellow Room, or to enjoy the country quiet on the porch overlooking the grounds.

A sunny breakfast room with views of the barn and gardens is the setting for treats such as crepes, French toast, or berry and apple bread pudding, plus fresh

WEB SITE: www.applebutterinn.com

INNKEEPERS: Barbara Barry and Michael Pacht

ROOMS: 6 rooms, all with private bath, air-conditioning

ON THE GROUNDS: 13 acres, barn, apple trees, great views of river and hills

RATES: $95–$215, including full breakfast and afternoon tea

CREDIT CARDS ACCEPTED: Only to hold reservations; payment by cash or check

OPEN: Year-round

HOW TO GET THERE: From Interstate 89 take exit 1 in Vermont, Route 4 west, toward Woodstock for about 8 miles. Turn left onto Happy Valley Road just past the Taftsville Country Store. The inn is on the left.

baked muffins, scones, or biscuits. The inn's trademark homemade apple butter is always available. On fine days, guests like to take their coffee out to the porch. Gracious hosts Barbara and Michael offer tea and treats in the afternoon, as well.

Guest rooms vary in decor, but all offer antiques, down comforters and pillows, and fine linens. Many have cushy pillowtop mattresses. Among several rooms named for apples, my favorite is Granny Smith, a large room with a four-poster king-size bed, skylights, and a fireplace. Cameo on the first floor is also choice, with a big brass bed, cathedral ceiling, skylights, and a private entrance.

The inn's lawns make a fine setting for picnicking or reading in the summer, sledding and cross-country skiing in winter. And all the attractions of Woodstock are just down the road.

What's Nearby: Tiny Taftsville is only 3 miles from either Woodstock or Quechee and their many shops and restaurants, and it is also an easy drive to Hanover, New Hampshire. Sugarbush Farm is just up the road from the inn for maple syrup. The whole region abounds with hiking trails and back-road bicycling possibilities.

STRONG HOUSE INN

94 West Main Street
Vergennes 05491
(802) 877–3337
Fax: (802) 877–2599

The creamy yellow 1834 clapboard house with dark green shutters is just what many people picture when they think of old New England. On the National Register of Historic Places, it was built by Samuel Paddock Strong, president of the Bank of Vergennes and a director of the Rutland and Burlington Railroad. It is full of elegant details, from the Greek Revival exterior molding to the freestanding main stairway inside.

It is easy to see why Mary Bargiel fell in love with the home in 1992, so much so that she moved from Miami to Vermont and a new life as an innkeeper. She has furnished the inn in a style worthy of its heritage and introduced many nice features, such as formal English teas and quilting workshop weekends.

Mr. Strong's portrait still presides over the living room, restored to its original splendor, with hand-painted leaf accents on the walls.

The dining room is nicely done, with Chippendale chairs of mahogany and cherry, and an antique buffet holding a silver tea service. Mary has her own special breakfast recipes for dishes such as French toast, made with French bread soaked in Grand Marnier and orange juice, and apple dumplings, a winter favorite. Her teas, held periodically from November through May, are lavish three-course affairs open to the public.

Guests are welcome to come into the kitchen to make coffee, tea, or hot chocolate. Part of Mary's collection of teapots is displayed over the stove; she sells them in a little boutique in the hall, along with tea, quilts, and the same fleecy slippers guests are asked to don at the front door in snowy or muddy weather.

Each bedroom is distinctive. Sheraton has an antique German bed, a mirrored armoire, and a flowered green and white quilt, while the English Hunt Room is in deeper tones with hunter green walls and a paisley coverlet. The Country French Room under the eaves is ideal for families, with an iron-and-brass queen-size bed plus a trundle bed. The Empire Room, the former master bedroom, comes with a fishnet canopy bed and two wing chairs in front of a working fireplace. The Vermont Room has a country pine bed and prime mountain views.

The Rabbit Ridge Country House has six lavish rooms, four with private porches or decks, three with fireplaces, and all with wonderful views of the Otter Creek Valley to the east and the Adirondacks to the west. Rabbit Ridge guests have the option of a continental breakfast delivered to their rooms or a full breakfast in the main house.

WEB SITE: www.stronghouseinn .com

INNKEEPERS: Mary and Hugh Bargiel

ROOMS: 12 rooms and suites in the main house and Rabbit Ridge Country House, all with private bath, air-conditioning, phone with dataport, high-speed wireless Internet, some with fireplace, TV

ON THE GROUNDS: 6 acres with gazebo, pond, walking trails, and herb, perennial, and vegetable gardens; pumpkin patch in fall; ice skating, cross-country skiing, sledding, and snowshoeing in winter

RATES: Rooms $95–$135, suites $149, country house rooms $180–$280, including full breakfast and afternoon refreshments

CREDIT CARDS ACCEPTED: Master-Card, Visa, American Express

OPEN: Year round

HOW TO GET THERE: From Route 7 turn west at Vergennes, and proceed for about 2 miles on Main Street; the inn is ahead on the right.

The most recent addition to the inn is the Ticonderoga Room, accommodating meetings of up to thirty people. Food service can be arranged, and the inn has a full liquor license.

The six-acre property offers gardens and walking trails in summer and a host of winter activities.

What's Nearby: Vergennes is a quiet and convenient location in the Champlain Valley, 22 miles from Burlington, 12 miles from Middlebury, 7 miles from Lake Champlain, and 30 miles from the Sugarbush and Mad River Valley ski areas. It is well situated for visiting the Shelburne Museum, Shelburne Farms, and the Vermont Wildflower Farm.

INN AT THE ROUND BARN FARM

1661 East Warren Road; RR 1, Box 247
Waitsfield 05673
(802) 496–2276

This may just be the ultimate bed-and-breakfast inn, a perfect blend of rustic charm and elegance. Until the 1960s, the rambling nineteenth-century farmhouse and attached horse barn were part of a working dairy farm, and the 245-acre property remains surrounded by pastures and farmland.

But no farmer ever enjoyed such luxury as awaits today in a beautiful inn where rooms vary from traditional formal colonial, complete with canopy beds and high-boys, to dreamy rooms in the converted horse barn, with peaked ceilings, rustic beams, fireplaces, and sumptuous decor.

The landmark twelve-sided dairy barn built in 1910 is one of only a handful of round barns remaining in Vermont. Jack and Doreen Simko, who had a ski house nearby, had always admired the barn. Jack was ready to retire from the family floral business when the farm came on the market in 1986, and they jumped at the chance to own it. A photo album in the house details the progress of the eighteen-month renovation.

The Simkos retired from active innkeeping in 1996, leaving daughter AnneMarie DeFreest in charge. Her husband, Tim Piper, is sharing the helm.

Step into the first-floor library and sitting room and you'll find formal draperies and furnishings, a large Oriental rug, a wall of books, and a plate of fresh baked cookies. Most likely classical music will be playing and, in winter, a fire blazing in the fireplace. This is where everyone gathers in the late afternoon for the day's treat, perhaps a fresh baked apple pie with cheddar cheese and cold apple cider.

INNKEEPERS: AnneMarie DeFreest and Tim Piper

ROOMS: 12 rooms, all with private bath, individual thermostat, clock, robes; luxury rooms have fireplace, whirlpool bath, and/or steam shower

ON THE GROUNDS: 245 acres, terrace, indoor lap pool, lawns with seating areas, gardens, 5 ponds, ducks, Tubbs Snowshoe center with free 30 kilometers of winter trails

RATES: $160–$315, including full breakfast, afternoon refreshments, and evening hors d'oeuvres

CREDIT CARDS ACCEPTED. Master-Card, Visa, American Express

OPEN: Year-round

HOW TO GET THERE: From Route 100 turn east onto Bridge Street, go through the covered bridge, and bear right at the fork onto East Warren Road. The inn is 1 mile ahead on the left.

The spacious beamed dining room is country in feel and rimmed with wide windows. On display are some of the whimsical pigs that are found throughout the inn. Guests are seated at tables for two, four, or six between 8:30 and 9:30 A.M. A bountiful menu offers a choice of hot entrees. Among the most popular are egg strata, blueberry waffles, and French toast with sautéed apples, pears, and blueberries. In summer, breakfast may move outside to the stone terrace.

Downstairs is a recreation room with an antique pool table, piano, TV/VCR, a stock of books and games, and a refrigerator filled with complimentary soft drinks and a microwave for guests' use.

Rooms in the attached barn, reached via a second-floor hallway, all have exposed rafters and barn-board ceilings, fireplaces, whirlpools, ceiling fans, and air-conditioning. The Richardson Room offers skylights for stargazing, windows with mountain views, and a bath with oversize whirlpool and a glass-enclosed shower. The romantic Dana Room has a black iron canopy bed with a white coverlet and white chiffon canopy draped from the ceiling.

If you favor traditional decor, Joslin is a beauty, with raspberry walls, a king-size canopy bed and coverlet in a deep red and white toile pattern, a fireplace, and a bathroom with both oversize whirlpool tub and a separate steam shower. Sherman has a mahogany sleigh bed, coordinated Waverly fabrics wallpaper, and three windows looking out at the fields.

My favorite room, Sterling, is a somewhat smaller room, on the main floor. It used to be the dining room, accounting for two whole walls of windows taking in the countryside. The walls are stenciled, the headboard is hand-painted, there's a peaked ceiling with a skylight over the bed, and you can be warmed by the fire while you gaze at the view.

What's Nearby: The Mad River Valley offers great skiing at Sugarbush and Mad River Glen, as well as golf, indoor and outdoor tennis, swimming, horseback riding, and hiking in summer. The inn offers free cross-country skiing at nearby Ole's Touring Center. The towns of Warren and Waitsfield are filled with boutique shopping for crafts and clothing.

MAD RIVER INN

Tremblay Road, P.O. Box 75
Waitsfield 05673
(802) 496–7900; (800) 832–8278

■ Many country inns with Victoriana, ruffles, feather beds, and antiques are not compatible with small children; this one is the exception. Along with its frills, Luc has converted this 1860s farmhouse into an inn that includes a spacious family room with TV, stereo, VCR, and a billiards table, as well as a guest refrigerator and BYOB bar. Those under age twelve pay only $13 per night in their parents' rooms.

Of course, couples are also happy here, enjoying the parlor with fancy floral swag curtains and Victorian furnishings, attractive bedrooms, lavish breakfasts, and a delightful afternoon tea. And skiers appreciate the hot tub on the porch.

Rooms are carefully done with coordinated fabrics and a mix of styles. Colleen Marie has romantic Victorian roses, lace accents, and a king-size white wicker bed. The Hayden Breeze Room, done in pastel paisleys with a brass bed, is my favorite for its many windows. The George Martin Room has a big brass bed and relics from Grandpa's railroad career in the early 1900s. The Abner Doubleday and Hector Felix Rooms combine into a suite that is ideal for families. Rooms are modest and some of the baths created from closets are small, but the overall effect is charming.

Breakfast is served family style at a long table with Chippendale-style chairs and always includes home-baked muffins and a hot dish of the day. The inn's vegetable, fruit, and herb gardens supply many of the ingredients, and flower gardens provide a pretty garnish. The afternoon tea is a standout here, with treats such as ginger tarts and pecan–chocolate chip tarts. The inn's tea recipes have appeared in cookbooks.

The paneled downstairs playroom has a pool table, TV/VCR, and a rack to accommodate skiers.

Grounds that border the Mad River are a big bonus in summer, as is the recreation path along the river.

What's Nearby: See What's Nearby on page 261.

WEB SITE: www.madriverinn.com

INNKEEPER: Luc Maranda

ROOMS: 9 rooms, all with private bath; some with TV, air-conditioning

ON THE GROUNDS: 7 acres on Mad River, porch, hot tub, gardens, on Mad River Recreation Path

RATES: $105–$175, including full breakfast, afternoon tea

CREDIT CARDS ACCEPTED: Master-Card, Visa, American Express; cash or personal check preferred for final payment

OPEN: Year-round

HOW TO GET THERE: Take Interstate 89 to exit 9, Route 100B, or exit 10, Route 100, and proceed south on Route 100 to Tremblay Road, 1 mile north of Waitsfield. Turn right onto Tremblay; the inn is on the right.

WHITE ROCKS INN

1774 Route 7 South
Wallingford 05773
(802) 446–2077; (866) 446–2077

■ This columned Greek Revival farmhouse has stood by the roadside since the 1840s; even the Gothic red barn is on the National Register of Historic Places. Rooms are large and elegantly furnished, making this a very desirable home base for exploring the area.

The original features of the house—the wide-board floors, wainscoting, and ornate moldings— have been carefully preserved. The small sitting room is formal, with Victorian decor, a nice place for quiet conversation. The paneled library is furnished for comfort, with leather couches facing the fireplace and lots of books.

Breakfast is served by candlelight at a long table in the dining room, a handsome setting with red walls and white wainscoting and woodwork. The inn's signature dish is baked eggs Dijon. Other favorites are the stuffed French toast and baked treats such as flaky biscuits or goat cheese popovers. On fine days, breakfast may be moved to the porch, also a favorite spot to enjoy lemonade or iced tea in the afternoon. In winter, refreshments are served in front of the fire.

Bedrooms are well furnished with canopy beds and antiques. Three rooms have fireplaces. The front rooms are particularly large and sunny. One that I especially admired is the Arthur Davison Room, with dark blue printed wallpaper and a pink and white canopy bed. The Gilbert Douglas Room has a handsome canopy bed and its original 1800s wallpaper. Two cottages on the grounds offer kitchen facilities, and the Milkhouse Cottage has a fireplace and a whirlpool bath.

The many-acred grounds of the inn are a plus, with panoramic views all around. A hiking trail behind the barn leads to a picnic table at the top of the hill. In winter, the hills are great for sledding.

The barn behind the house is a classic that has been featured on calendars. The romantic, rustic ambience makes it a popular place for country weddings, and the private cottages on the grounds are perfect for honeymoons.

WEB SITE: www.whiterocksinn.com

INNKEEPERS: Malcolm and Rita Swogger

ROOMS: 5 rooms with private bath, 3 with fireplace; 2 cottages with kitchenette, 1 with fireplace and whirlpool bath

ON THE GROUNDS: 20 acres, porch, landmark red barn often used for weddings; cross-country skiing or snowshoeing on property

RATES: Rooms $120–$200, cottages $200–$270, including full breakfast

CREDIT CARDS ACCEPTED: Master-Card, Visa, American Express

OPEN: Year-round

HOW TO GET THERE: The inn is located on the west side of Route 7, 1¾ miles south of Wallingford.

What's Nearby: Wallingford is 10 miles from Rutland, where attractions include the Chaffee Art Center, featuring the work of more than 200 Vermont artists and artisans, and the Norman Rockwell Museum. Manchester outlet shopping is 18 miles to the south. The Long Trail and Appalachian Trail are nearby for hikers; for skiers, both Okemo and Killington are less than a half-hour drive.

WEST HILL HOUSE

West Hill Road, RR 1, Box 292
Warren 05674
(802) 496–7162; (800) 898–1427

■ This 1850s farmhouse on a quiet country lane is deceptive. From the outside it looks small, but since Dotty Kyle and her husband, Eric Brattstrom, arrived in the early 1990s, Eric's skills from his former career in the construction business have been put to good use expanding the inn and adding all kinds of amenities, from whirlpool baths to a wood-fired brick bake oven.

Guests still enter into the old part of the house, to a comfortable low-ceilinged library with two seating areas, one around the fireplace at the far end of the room. There are shelves of books to be read and games to play.

You can watch the action on the golf course through the plant-adorned picture window in the dining room. It's especially picturesque in winter when cross-country skiers glide by. Breakfast is served at the long oval table at 8:30 A.M., a bit earlier for skiers in winter. A big bowl of fresh fruit, yogurt, and homemade granola are staples. Each day brings a different treat, such as sticky buns or fruit muffins, and a main course that may be waffles, strata, or a frittata.

Beyond the kitchen is Eric's most notable addition, the Great Room, so named, says Dotty, because people walking in inevitably say just what I did, "What a great room!" The large room features a soaring beamed ceiling, barn-board siding, and walls of windows. An adjoining sunroom has a home theater set up with a big flat-panel TV, and there's an honor bar and a refrigerator stocked with wine, beer, and soft drinks. (The inn is fully licensed.)

The sunroom opens to an outside deck. Up a spiral staircase is the Four-Poster Suite, with beams and a slanted roof, a queen-size canopy bed, a study/second bedroom, a bathroom with shower, and a spa room with a double Jacuzzi and a fire stove. A private deck leads to its own parking area.

Beds have two sets of pillows, down and synthetic, so guests can have their choice. This is one of many amenities that are unexpected in a small country inn, things such as magnifying mirrors, hair dryers, and French milled soap in the bath. Every room has good reading lights, and, in winter, down comforters on the bed.

WEB SITE: www.westhillhouse.com

INNKEEPERS: Dotty Kyle and Eric Brattstrom

ROOMS: 8 rooms and suites, all with private bath, phone, air-conditioning, high-speed Internet access, clock radio, hair dryer, fireplace, whirlpool bath or steam shower, TV/VCR

ON THE GROUNDS: 9 acres, wide front porch, back terrace, perennial gardens, meadows, red barn with game room and party space, beaver pond, mountain views

RATES: $135–$200, including full breakfast and afternoon tea

CREDIT CARDS ACCEPTED: MasterCard, Visa, American Express, Discover

OPEN: Year-round

HOW TO GET THERE: From Route 100 take the Sugarbush access road 3 miles to the top, turn left onto Inferno Road for 1 mile, and then turn right onto West Hill Road. The inn is the first house on the right.

Many rooms are made distinctive by Dotty's artwork. The Wildflower Room, with a fireplace and a double whirlpool bath, has sponged walls and a hand-painted border matching the wildflower quilt. The attractive Blue Room, with an Oriental rug on the old wide floorboards and a hand-sewn quilt, features a hand-painted floral spray on one wall. Dotty tells me more murals have been added since my last visit.

The Pony Room will please those who like things rustic, with its barn siding walls and exposed beams. The Stetson Suite on the main floor offers a sitting room with a TV/VCR, and whirlpool bath as well as a two-person steam shower. The Garden Room has a steam bath and its own entrance.

Mirroring the personalities of the hosts, this is a lively, sociable inn. The brick oven is often used to bake flat breads such as focaccia or pizza that make the kitchen a lively gathering place at cocktail hour. Hospitable Dotty will also prepare a candlelight dinner on Saturday night if as many as six guests want to dine in, and she is, by her own description, "a demon birthday cake baker" who loves to surprise guests. It's no surprise that guests tend to come back again and again.

What's Nearby: Sugarbush golf course is across the road, and the ski mountain is less than a mile away. The Mad River Valley has many opportunities for hiking, biking, tennis, swimming, and horseback riding. The villages of Waitsfield and Warren are filled with boutique shopping for crafts and clothing. The Vermont Festival of the Arts is a major draw in August.

THE INN AT QUAIL RUN

106 Smith Road
Mount Snow Valley
Wilmington 05363
(802) 464–3362; (800) 343–7227
Fax: (802) 464–7784

WEB SITE: www.theinnatquailrun
.com

INNKEEPERS: Victoria and Ray
Lawthorne

ROOMS: 11 rooms, most with fireplace, a 2-room suite with fireplace,
all with private bath, TV with HBO; a
three-bedroom cottage with
kitchen, living room, washer/dryer,
and gas fireplace (can sleep eight)

ON THE GROUNDS: Eight-person outdoor hot tub, heated pool, 15 acres
with access to hiking trails, toboggan
runs, and a 25 mile cross-country-ski
and snowmobile trail system

RATES: $100–$210, including full
breakfast; full cottage for eight people $550, including breakfast

CREDIT CARDS ACCEPTED: Master-
Card, Visa, American Express, Discover

OPEN: Mid-May through March;
closed April to mid-May

HOW TO GET THERE: From Interstate
91 take exit 2 to Route 9 west to
Wilmington. At the stoplight in
Wilmington, go north on Route 100
for approximately 4 miles to a right
fork in the road. Take the fork and
make the first right turn just after
the bridge to Smith Road. Follow
Smith Road, bearing left, up the hill
for ¼ mile. The inn is on the left.

Nestled in the woods on fifteen acres in ski country, this is a delightful retreat in any season. The living room has nonstop views of the mountains through the picture win- dow and has a fireplace. An informal bar offers refreshments (the inn has a full liquor license) and a TV.

Wrought iron tables and chairs in the long dining gallery are set against a wall of windows that are open in summer. This room also faces the mountains, as does the free-form pool outside, a wonderful spot on a warm summer day. When the expansive grounds turn to winter white, there is ample opportunity for cross-country skiing, snow- shoeing, and tobogganing right on the prop- erty.

Main-floor rooms are on the small side but have been nicely freshened with airy print fabrics and wallpapers. Room 4 is a corner room with a fireplace and is done in a blue floral print, and Room 5 has a deep red Ralph Lauren print and a country pine bed.

Downstairs lodgings are a bit more spa- cious. Room 8, a large corner room, is strik- ing with dark blue walls and blue floral Ralph Lauren fabrics. It offers a fireplace and a striking view of Haystack Mountain. Room 10, with a twin bed plus a queen-size bed, is ideal for families. The inn welcomes "well- behaved children" as well as "well-behaved dogs." Rooms in the cottage on the grounds are also available to families if the entire unit has not been rented. The cot- tage includes a kitchen, a sitting room, and a washer/dryer.

The downstairs lounge keeps all ages happy with a Ping-Pong table, puzzles, games, a big-screen TV, VCR, and a library of more than seventy videos. Outside the door is a big outdoor hot tub that is a special favorite with skiers.

This inn is known for its scrumptious breakfasts, which are available to the public. A typical menu may offer choices of raspberry stuffed French toast, crème brûlée French toast, spinach and mushroom quiche, lobster and boursin omelette, eggs

Benedict, pumpkin pancakes with ginger butter, mushroom and cheddar omelette, blueberry or banana-walnut pancakes, or eggs to order. The public pays $12.95 for this feast, but breakfast is included in the room rate for guests.

What's Nearby: Mount Snow and Haystack mountains are just 3½ miles away, with downhill skiing in winter and golf in summer. Wilmington is 5 miles to the south (see page 268).

NUTMEG COUNTRY INN

153 Molly Stark Trail (Route 9)
P.O. Box 1899
Wilmington 05363
(802) 464–3351; (800) 277–5402
Fax: (802) 464–7331

The history of this red clapboard farmhouse dates from 1777, and it still has its exposed handhewn beams, iron door fixtures, dormers, and tin ceiling. But it's doubtful that the original owners ever dreamed of the comforts that have been added, from central air-conditioning to jetted whirlpool bathtubs for two.

This is a larger inn than most, with fourteen guest rooms and suites rambling throughout the original house and the attached barn and carriage house. They feature brass, iron, and four-poster beds; antique dressers; and quilts. This being a very old house, some rooms are small, but all are stylishly decorated with elaborate floral fabrics and coordinating wallpapers. Some have traditional fireplaces or cast-iron woodstoves, with a stack of logs and kindling ready to light. The largest quarters are the suites, offering sitting rooms, modern windows in the eaves, fireplaces, TVs with VCRs, and whirlpool baths.

The guest parlor has its own fireplace and comfortable seating. Fresh baked cookies and other treats are available in the afternoon. Billiards, darts, and board and card games are available. The dining room has lots of windows bringing in views of the countryside, and colonial-style tables with ladder-back chairs. It is large enough to accommodate individual tables for guests.

Susan Goodman spent many years as a chef and later in the catering and event-planning business. You can enjoy her skills in her excellent breakfasts, with delectable pastries plus main dishes that may include caramelized pear French toast, spinach and feta omelette with a roasted tomato salsa, or buttermilk pancakes topped with seasonal fresh fruit. Take-home samples can be had at the in-house bakery shop, stocked with pastries, cakes, pies, and cookies. Susan's specialty is wedding cakes, in case you are in the market. Recently the Goodmans also began offering dinners on

WEB SITE: www.nutmeginn.com

INNKEEPERS: Gerry and Susan Goodman

ROOMS: 10 rooms and 4 suites, all with private bath, air-conditioning, phone, TV; 11 with wood-burning fireplace; suites have whirlpool, VCR

ON THE GROUNDS: 2 acres of meadows, brook stocked with trout, access to hiking and cross-country trails, croquet, bocce, horseshoes

RATES: Rooms $99–$219, suites $184–$299, including full breakfast

CREDIT CARDS ACCEPTED: Master-Card, Visa, American Express, Discover

OPEN: Year-round

HOW TO GET THERE: Take Interstate 91 to exit 2, Route 9, and proceed west for about 20 miles to Wilmington. The inn is ¾ mile past the village traffic light, on the right.

Friday and Saturday nights, which are open to the public. Desserts, as you can imagine, are a highlight.

The inn provides many outdoor pleasures. In summer, the brook is stocked with trout, and miles of hiking trails begin right outside the back door. In winter, there is access to cross-country-ski trails, and the inn provides snowshoes for guests. Ask about their romantic winter packages that include sleigh rides.

What's Nearby: Route 9, known as the Molly Stark Trail, runs between Bennington and Brattleboro and is one of the most scenic drives in the state. Wilmington is a midway point, a pleasant village offering interesting shops for browsing and access to the Mount Snow Valley, with skiing and golf at Mount Snow/Haystack; these areas are from 5 to 7 miles from the inn. Hiking trails can be found in the wooded acres next to the inn and in the nearby Green Mountain National Forest. In summer, it is a short drive to the Marlboro Music Festival, which draws some of the finest chamber musicians in the world.

ARDMORE INN

23 Pleasant Street, P.O. Box 466
Woodstock 05091
(802) 457–3887; (800) 497–9652

■ This gracious Greek Revival home has stood on Woodstock's Pleasant Street, the main shopping street of the village, since 1850. It was restored in 1994, and refurbished once again when the Hollingsworths arrived from California in 2003. They have given a more welcoming, comfortable feel to a home that was somewhat formal.

The living room is now a library, with bookcases across one wall, a fireplace, overstuffed leather chairs, and a soft mocha color scheme. The dining room has a carved

WEB SITE: www.ardmoreinn.com

INNKEEPERS: Charlotte and Cary Hollingsworth

ROOMS: 5 rooms, all with private bath, clock, radio

ON THE GROUNDS: Screened porch, garden

RATES: $135–$215, including full breakfast and afternoon refreshments

CREDIT CARDS ACCEPTED: Master-Card, Visa, American Express, Discover

OPEN: Year-round

HOW TO GET THERE: Take Interstate 89 to Vermont exit 1, Route 4, and continue west for 10 miles into Woodstock. The inn is at the edge of the village center on the left.

plaster ceiling, the home's original brass lighting fixture, and an antique Nantucket plank table with ladder-back chairs.

You won't have to worry about lunch after the lavish breakfasts served here. The meal begins with seasonal fresh fruits, followed by entrees that may include pumpkin pecan waffles with cranberry maple butter, Grand Marnier French toast, or a California omelette, served with bacon or sausage. And then comes dessert, anything from Ben and Jerry's ice cream to homemade pumpkin pie.

Upstairs, Tully is one of my favorite rooms for its curved "eyebrow" windows, and Tarma has special appeal with its dormer ceilings and a quiet location in the back of the house. The innkeepers plan to redecorate all the guest rooms. One that is complete is the first-floor Sheridan room, a large room with a fireplace and Jacuzzi tub, done with Ralph Lauren fabrics in shades of butterscotch and sage green. All the rooms now have Lauren linens and towels.

One of the nicest changes they have made is to enclose the porch, revealing the exposed beams. It is lit by electrified Coleman lanterns and furnished with comfortable Adirondack rockers. Screened in summer, cozy year-round, this is a wonderful spot for breakfasting on summer mornings or a relaxing after a day of antiquing or biking around Woodstock.

What's Nearby: Woodstock is one of Vermont's most beautiful towns, with a classic village green, streams and bridges meandering through town, and Paul Revere bells in its church steeples. The town is filled with appealing shops and galleries, and you can also enjoy antiquing and fine dining, all within a short stroll of the inn. Billings Farm and Museum is the prime sightseeing in town, a working dairy farm with a series of handsomely restored barns re-creating life on a Vermont farm in the 1890s. Biking and hiking in the area are prime. In winter, there is a cross-country-skiing center on the Woodstock Country Club's fine public golf course, and the Suicide Six ski area offers downhill slopes.

CANTERBURY HOUSE

43 Pleasant Street (Route 4)
Woodstock 05091
(802) 457–3077

■ The Vermont mystique is strong. Sue and Bob Frost had never even visited the state, but when they decided it was time for a change from corporate life in New Jersey in 1998, this is where they headed to make their longtime dream of innkeeping come true. They wanted to live in a village, and they picked one of the prettiest in this or any other state.

Their 1880s home has many attractive features. The focus of the living room is the double-ledge Victorian mantel above the gas fireplace. Furnished with antiques of the period, the room has two seating areas, one for conversations, the other a cozy nook in the corner with a chaise that is perfect for curling up with a book. Ruffled curtains give a warm feel to the room. A TV and VCR are available for guests.

The cheerful dining room is brightened by six windows. Guests are seated at one of two big tables for a full breakfast; French toast is a favorite on the menu.

Carrying out the inn name, rooms are named for *The Canterbury Tales*. All are nicely done, with a mix of furnishings, antiques, color schemes, and brass, iron, wicker, and canopy beds. I was taken with Friar's Tale, with a pair of canopy beds, pastel star quilts, and pretty blue and green floral wallpaper, or Knight's Tale, with a white iron queen-size bed and flowery appliqué bedspread. Monk's Tale is the prize room, with its own entrance, TV, stereo, fireplace, and a claw-foot tub in the bath. Chaucer's Garrett, the third-floor suite, has a king-size bed, private sitting area, and a TV, as does the Squire's Tale.

This is one of three inns especially recommended for their prime locations on Pleasant Street, within walking distance of Woodstock's many shops and dining places.

What's Nearby: See What's Nearby on page 269.

WEB SITE: www.thecanterbury house.com

INNKEEPERS: Sue and Bob Frost

ROOMS: 7 rooms, 1 suite, all with private bath, air-conditioning, clock; 1 with fireplace; 3 with TV

ON THE GROUNDS: Patio with lawn furniture

RATES: $115–$185, including full breakfast

CREDIT CARDS ACCEPTED: Master-Card, Visa, American Express

OPEN: Year-round

HOW TO GET THERE: Take Interstate 89 to Vermont exit 1, Route 4, and continue west for 10 miles into Woodstock. The inn is at the edge of the village on the left.

CHARLESTON HOUSE

21 Pleasant Street (Route 4)
Woodstock 05091
(802) 457–3843; (888) 475–3800

■ This narrow, 1835 brick-and-frame Greek Revival town house is listed on the National Register of Historic Places, and it has been carefully restored and furnished to preserve its period grace while adding lots of comforts for today's visitors. The location is ideal, with everything in the center of town within walking distance.

The attractive living room has swag curtains, Federal-style sofas, and an Oriental rug on dark, wide floorboards, all carrying out a restful rose and blue color scheme.

The formal dining room has a big table where everyone gathers to enjoy one of the inn's vaunted candlelight breakfasts. The full menu begins with fruits and breads, followed by "Good Company" eggs or a Swiss soufflé.

Each room is quite different, but all are tastefully done with attractive wallpapers and coordinated fabrics. You may have a traditional motif with an antique carved four-poster, wing chair, and long, formal draperies; a country look with a patchwork quilt; or a room furnished in summery wicker. Summer Kitchen, B and B, and Mount Peg have four-posters, fireplaces, whirlpool baths, and TVs.

Dixi and Willa Nohl took over this elegant little inn in February 1998. They have lived in Vermont for more than thirty years, so they are well equipped to guide guests to the area's best attractions.

What's Nearby: See What's Nearby on page 269.

WEB SITE: www.charlestonhouse.com

INNKEEPERS: Dieter (Dixi) and Willa Nohl

ROOMS: 9 rooms, all with private bath, air-conditioning, clock radio; 3 with fireplace, whirlpool bath; 5 with TV

ON THE GROUNDS: In-town location

RATES: $135–$220, including full breakfast

CREDIT CARDS ACCEPTED: Master-Card, Visa, American Express

OPEN: Year-round

HOW TO GET THERE: Take Interstate 89 to Vermont exit 1, Route 4, and continue west for 10 miles into Woodstock. The inn is on the left as you approach the center of the village.

DEER BROOK INN

535 Woodstock Road (Route 4 West)
Woodstock 05091
(802) 672–3713

Travelers who want to be close to both Woodstock and the Killington ski area will find this colonial-era farmhouse a warm haven. Built in 1820, it was once the main house of a dairy farm.

It has been nicely modernized without losing features such as the original beams and wide board floors. Innkeepers David Kanal, a former Manhattanite, and George DeFina, who taught school in Woodstock, took over in 2003, and they have given the inn a homey, comfortable feel, with lots of cheerful print wallpapers and ruffled curtains at the windows. The living room has a cozy fireplace; the dining room offers a lovely view of the surrounding hills from a wall of windows. A sumptuous three-course breakfast is served every morning.

Some of the upstairs rooms have slanted walls and beams, plus skylights added during the renovation. Each is different, a mix of brass, iron, and sleigh beds, and a canopy bed in the suite. I like Room 1, with a skylight and a view of the river. All have nice quilts, antique accents, and original watercolors on the wall.

The hosts are enjoying their new roles as innkeepers and take pleasure in helping guests make the most of the area. They are happy to make arrangements for horseback riding, canoeing, or sleigh rides, and they'll make recommendations as well as reservations for dinner.

What's Nearby: Killington ski area is 8 miles away, and Woodstock is 5 miles away. See What's Nearby on page 269.

WEB SITE: www.deerbrookinn.com

INNKEEPERS: David Kanal and George DeFina

ROOMS: 4 rooms, 1 suite with TV, all with private bath, air-conditioning, individual thermostats, clocks

ON THE GROUNDS: 5 acres of lawn, wooded areas, perennial gardens, lovely views

RATES: Rooms $105–$140, suite $125–$165, including full breakfast

CREDIT CARDS ACCEPTED: Master-Card, Visa, American Express

OPEN: Year-round

HOW TO GET THERE: Take Vermont exit 1 off Interstate 89 north, and go 10 miles west on Route 4, continuing through Woodstock. The inn is 5 miles west of Woodstock, on the right.

THE WOODSTOCKER

61 River Street (Route 4)
Woodstock 05091
(802) 457–3896; (866) 662–1439
Fax: (802) 457–3897

■ This comfortable informal inn is an ideal place for anyone looking for spacious, well-decorated rooms within an easy walk of Woodstock village. The inn consists of an 1830s farmhouse and barn, attached by a long hallway. Two of the barn rooms under the eaves are spacious suites with living rooms; one has a little balcony. In the front of the house, Room 4, the former master bedroom, has a handsome big brass bed and an antique pine armoire. Upstairs I like Room 6, decorated in a cheerful yellow sunflower print and with wicker accents, and Room 5, a change of pace with Southwestern decor.

The heart of the inn is the combination living and dining room, with rustic beams, leather couches, lots of books, and several tables where guests enjoy a bountiful breakfast each morning. Dora Foschi and David Livesley, who purchased the inn in the summer of 2005, hail from London, England, and have brought some of their favorite English dishes with them, such as boiled eggs and "soldiers," scrambled eggs with European breakfast meats, and a selection of breads served with organic marmalade. One of their specialties is a fresh berry soufflé using locally grown organic fruits whenever possible. Along with fresh ground coffee, they offer "proper" leaf teas.

The couple spent many holidays in Vermont before deciding to make it their home, and they enjoy sharing their favorite places with guests. They've brought warm British hospitality with them to New England.

What's Nearby: See What's Nearby on page 269.

WEB SITE: www.woodstockervt.com

INNKEEPERS: Dora Foschi and David Livesley

ROOMS: 7 rooms and 2 suites, all with private bath, clock; 1 room with balcony; suites with TV; most with air-conditioning

ON THE GROUNDS: Backyard with seating

RATES: $95–$225, including full breakfast

CREDIT CARDS ACCEPTED: MasterCard, Visa, American Express

OPEN: Year-round

HOW TO GET THERE: From Interstate 89 take Vermont exit 1, Route 4, and proceed west for 10 miles into Woodstock. The inn is on Route 4, also called River Street, just beyond the village, on the right.

INDEXES

Alphabetical Index

B&Bs Serving Afternoon Tea

Abigail Stoneman Inn, 205

Applebutter Inn, 257

Birchwood Inn, 122

Brook Farm Inn, 124

Captain Lindsey House Inn, 89

Captain's House Inn of Chatham, 103

Chester Bulkley House, 49

Cliffside Inn, 209

Eden Pines, 142

Five Gables Inn, 71

Francis Malbone House, 210

Friendship Valley Inn, 2

Gazebo Inn, The, 228

Hartwell House, 84

Heart of the Village Inn, 251

Inn at Ormsby Hill, 243

Mad River Inn, 262

Manor House Inn, 57

Moses Nickerson House, 105

Red Brook Inn, 28

Seacrest Manor, 144

Seth Warner Inn, 246

Starbuck Inn, 11

Stonecroft, 12

Strong House Inn, 258

Thorncroft Inn, 133

Timberholm Inn, 256

Walker House, 129

West Hill House, 264

Willard Street Inn, 234

B&Bs Serving Dinner
for Guests Only

Judith's Garden B&B, 239

Norumbega, 67

Nutmeg Country Inn, 267

Stonecroft, 12

West Hill House, 264

B&Bs with Mountain Views

Admiral Peary House, 73

Applebutter Inn, 257

Brass Lantern Inn, 253

Bungay Jar, 164

Buttonwood Inn, 177

Cornwall Orchards Bed and Breakfast,
248

Craftsbury Bed and Breakfast on Wylie
Hill, 238

Deer Brook Inn, 272

Dexter's Inn, 191

Dragonsfield, 118

1811 House, 247

Farm by the River, 179

B&Bs with Outdoor Hot Tubs

B&Bs with Separate Cottage Accommodations

B&Bs with Swimming Pools

B&Bs with Tennis Courts

B&Bs with Water Views

Family-Friendly B&Bs

Romantic B&Bs

ABOUT THE AUTHOR

Eleanor Berman has been writing about New England and staying in New England bed-and-breakfasts since the early 1980s. She is the author of *New York Neighborhoods* and the award-winning *Traveling Solo,* both published by The Globe Pequot Press, and other travel books. Her travel and feature articles have appeared in many major magazines and newspapers.